Delictual Liability

In Memoriam
W A W

Delictual Liability

Joe Thomson LLB, FRSE
Regius Professor of Law, University of Glasgow

Second Edition

Butterworths
Edinburgh
1999

United Kingdom	Butterworths, a Division of Reed Elsevier (UK) Ltd, 4 Hill Street, EDINBURGH EH2 3JZ and Halsbury House, 35 Chancery Lane, LONDON WC2A 1EL
Australia	Butterworths, a Division of Reed International Books Australia Pty Ltd, CHATSWOOD, New South Wales
Canada	Butterworths Canada Ltd, MARKHAM, Ontario
Hong Kong	Butterworths Asia (Hong Kong), HONG KONG
India	Butterworths India, NEW DELHI
Ireland	Butterworth (Ireland) Ltd, DUBLIN
Malaysia	Malayan Law Journal Sdn Bhd, KUALA LUMPUR
New Zealand	Butterworths of New Zealand Ltd, WELLINGTON
Singapore	Butterworths Asia, SINGAPORE
South Africa	Butterworths Publishers (Pty) Ltd, DURBAN
USA	Lexis Law Publishing, Charlottesville, VIRGINIA

A CIP Catalogue record for this book is available from the British Library.

First published 1994

ISBN 0 406 92321 3

Typeset by Phoenix Photosetting, Chatham, Kent
Printed by William Clowes Ltd, Beccles, Suffolk

Visit us at our website: http://www.butterworthsscotland.com

Preface

In this second edition, I have attempted to analyse the important developments in the law of delict over the last five years. These have been substantial. I have endeavoured to incorporate the major cases up until 1 November 1999. However, the decision of the House of Lords in *McFarlane v Tayside Health Board* was still pending at the time of writing: my treatment of wrongful birth actions must therefore be read in the light of the speeches in that case.

I am pleased to thank Ewan McIntyre for continuing to advise me on road traffic law. Lloyd Embleton was an exemplary research assistant whose work was invaluable in the preparation of this edition. My wife, Annie, showed immense understanding when I was perplexed and shared my delight on the days things went well.

This edition remains dedicated to the memory of my teacher, the late Bill Wilson. As the years pass, his loss to the study of law in Scotland does not diminish.

Joe Thomson
School of Law
University of Glasgow
17 November 1999

Contents

Preface v
Table of statutes ix
Table of cases xiii
List of abbreviations xxix

Introduction 1

PART I. INTENTIONAL DELICTS

1. Intentional delicts in respect of persons and property 11
2. The economic delicts and fraud 35

PART II. UNINTENTIONAL DELICT – GENERAL PRINCIPLES OF LIABILITY

3. The duty of care 57
4. Duty of care as a threshold device 69
5. Breach of a duty of care 111
6. Causation and related issues 129

PART III. DELICTUAL LIABILITY IN SPECIFIC SOCIAL AND ECONOMIC CONTEXTS

7. Professional liability 149
8. Product liability 157
9. Delictual liability for animals 169
10. Delictual liability arising from ownership or occupation of property 177

11.   Breach of statutory duty and public law issues   193

12.   Employers' liability and vicarious liability   205

13.   Delict and the family   221

14.   Delict and road traffic   235

15.   Defamation and verbal injury   243

PART IV. DAMAGES

16.   Damages   265

APPENDIX

Damages (Scotland) Act 1976   287

Index   297

Table of statutes

PAGE

Abolition of Feudal Tenure etc (Scotland) Bill 1999 99

Administration of Justice Act 1982 227
s 8 .... 224, 225, 274
  (1)–(3) 225
  9(1) 225, 233, 274
  (2) 226, 289
  (3) 225
  10 277
  11 278
  12(1)(a),(b) 280
  (2) 282, 289
  13 .... 224, 225
  14(1) 289
  (2)(a) 291
  (b)(i),(ii) 292
  (4) 294, 296
Sch 9, Pt I 291

Age of Legal Capacity (Scotland) Act 1991
s 1(1)(a) 222
  (3)(c) 222
  2(4) 12
  (4A), (5A) 222

Animals (Scotland) Act 1987: 193, 198
s 1(1) 171
  (b) 172, 173
  (c) 173
  (2)(a) 173
  (b) 175
  (3)(a), (b) 172, 173
  (4), (5) 174
  (6) 176
  (8) 170, 171
  2(1)(a), (b) 174
  (c) 175, 176
  (2) 175
  3 171
  5(1)(a), (b) 171
  5(2)(a)–(c) 171
  7 173

PAGE

Carriage of Goods Act 1992 .. 103

Children (Scotland) Act 1995
s 1(1)(d) 222

Civil Aviation Act 1982
s 76 20

Consumer Protection Act 1987: 193, 198, 227, 284
s 1(1) 158
  (2) 160
  (a)–(c) 161
  2(1) 159, 163, 164, 284
  (2)(b), (c) 161
  (3) 162
  (4) 161
  (f) 166
  (6) 158
  3(1) 163
  (2)(a), (b) 163
  (c) 164
  4(1)(a), (b) 165, 166
  (c) 165, 166
  (i), (ii) 162
  (d), (e) 165, 166
  5(1)–(3) 159
  (4) 160
  6(4) 166
  7 166
  45(1) 159, 160

Criminal Procedure (Scotland) Act 1995
s 170(1) 18

Damages Act 1996
s 1 274

Damages (Scotland) Act 1976 . 226, 287–296
s 1 287–289
  (1) 228, 229, 232
  (4) 233
  (5) 231

PAGE

Damages (Scotland) Act 1976 –
    contd
  s 1(7) 233
    1A 232, 233,
                        289, 290
      (5A) 231
    2 290
      (1) 227
      (2) 227, 228
      (3) 227
      (4) 244
    2A 227, 290, 291
      (1)(a), (b), (2) 228
    4 291
    6 .... 291, 292
    7 292
    8 .... 4, 292
    9 293
      (1), (2) 228, 275
    9A 293, 294
      (1) 228, 273
    10 294
      (2) 230
    12 .... 294, 295
  Sch 1 .... 230, 295, 296
Damages (Scotland) Act 1993 .   227
  s 1(1) 232, 289
      (2), (3) 289
    2 290
    3 .... 244, 290
    4 291
    5 .... 273, 294
    7(2) 291,
                        292, 294
      (3) 291,
                        294–296
    Schedule, para 1 291
                3 .... 292, 294
Dangerous Wild Animals Act
    1976
  s 7(4) 172
  Sch 3 172
Defamation Act 1952
  s 4(5) 251, 252
    5 253
    6 254
    12 259
Defamation Act 1996
  s 1 258
    2 252
      (4) 252
    3 252
      (2), (3), (5) 252

PAGE

Defamation Act 1996 – *contd*
  s 4 252
      (2), (3) 252
    13 255
    14 256
    15 257
  Sch 1 257
Divorce (Scotland) Act 1976
  s 10 16
Dogs Acts 1906–1928 170
Dramatic and Musical
    Performers' Protection
    Act 1958 195

Employers' Liability
    (Compulsory Insurance)
    Act 1969 210
Employers' Liability (Defective
    Equipment) Act 1969
  s 1(1) 206

Factories Act 1961 .... 196, 209

Guard Dogs Act 1975
  s 1 .... 175, 176

Health and Safety at Work etc
    Act 1974 209
  s 47 193
Hire Purchase Act 1964
  Pt III 24, 26
Human Rights Act 1998 2

Interest on Damages (Scotland)
    Act 1958 276
Interest on Damages (Scotland)
    Act 1971 276
International Transport
    Conventions Act 1983 ...   289
  s 1 233
  Sch 1, para 4(a) 289

Lawburrows Acts 1429 and
    1581 5
Law Reform (Contributory
    Negligence) Act 1945 136,
                        145, 176
  s 1(1) 143
    5(a) 144
Law Reform (Husband and
    Wife) Act 1962
  s 2(1), (2) 221

PAGE

Law Reform (Husband and
  Wife) (Scotland) Act 1984
  s 1(1)   16
    2(2)   16
Law Reform (Miscellaneous
  Provisions) Act 1971
  s 4   231
Law Reform (Miscellaneous
  Provisions) (Scotland)
  Act 1940
  s 3   139,
                                                146
Law Reform (Miscellaneous
  Provisions) (Scotland)
  Act 1985
  s 10   85
Law Reform (Miscellaneous
  Provisions) (Scotland)
  Act 1990
  s 68   84
    69 . . . . 224, 225
Law Reform (Parent and Child)
  (Scotland) Act 1986   227
  s 1(1)   295
  Sch 1, para 15   296
Law Reform (Personal Injuries)
  Act 1948
  s 2(1)   277

Mental Health (Scotland) Act
  1984
  s 18   18
    53–55   18
Merchant Shipping Act 1988
  s 31(1)   195

Occupiers' Liability (Scotland)
  Act 1960   193,
                                        198, 209
  s 1(1), (2)   187
    (3)(a)   188
    2(1)   188,
                                              189, 191
    (3) 191, 198
    3   191

Parliamentary Papers Act 1840:   256
Prescription and Limitation
  (Scotland) Act 1973
  s 6   283
    (2)   284
    7   283
    (1), (2)   284

PAGE

Prescription and Limitation
  (Scotland) Act 1973 – *contd*
  s 11(3)   283
    17(1), (2)   284
    (3)   285
    18(3)   285
    18A(1) 824, 285
    (2)   285
    19A   285
    22A   284
    22B   284
    (4)   285
    22C   284
    (3)   285
  Sch 1, para 1(d)   283
    2(g)–(ggg)   284
Protection from Harassment
  Act 1997   227
  s 8(1)–(5)   19
    (8)   294
    9   19

Rehabilitation of Offenders Act
  1974   207
  s 4   248
Road Traffic Act 1988 . . . . . 239, 240
  s 1–3   236
    3A   236
    38(7)   235
    143(a), (b)   237
    149   142
Road Traffic Act 1991   236

Scotland Act 1998
  s 41   256
Social Security Act 1975   289
Social Security Act 1989   278
Social Security Administration
  Act 1992
  Part IV (ss 81–104)   278
Social Security (Northern
  Ireland) Act 1975   289
Social Security (Recovery of
  Benefits) Act 1997   278
  s 3, 6, 7   279
  Sch 1   280
  Sch 2   279
Southern Rhodesia Act 1965 . .   48

Trade Union and Labour
  Relations (Consolidation)
  Act 1992   50
  s 10(1)   244

PAGE

Trespass (Scotland) Act 1865   21

Unfair Contract Terms Act
    1977 . . . . 84, 86, 87

PAGE

Unfair Contract Terms Act –
    contd
    s 16   84, 191

Winter Herding Act 1686   170

Table of cases

PAGE

A v United Kingdom [1998] 2 FLR 959, (1998) Times, 1 October, ECHR: 15
AB v CD (1904) 7 F 72 248
AB v Tameside and Glossop Health Authority [1997] 8 Med LR 91, CA: 151
AB v XY 1917 SC 15, 1916 2 SLT 210 247
Adam v Jackson [1917] AC 309 258
Admiralty Comrs v SS Susquehanna (Owners) [1926] AC 655, HL 271
Admiralty Comrs v SS Volute [1922] AC 129, HL 136
Advocate (Lord) v Scotsman Publications Ltd 1988 SLT 490, affd 1989
    SLT 705, HL 30, 31, 33
Alcock v Chief Constable of South Yorkshire Police [1992] 1 AC 310,
    [1991] 4 All ER 907, HL............................... 74
Allan v Barclay (1864) 2 M 873 266
Allan v Greater Glasgow Health Board 1998 SLT 580, OH 77
Allen v Flood [1898] AC 1, HL 35, 36,
                                                          42, 45
Allied Arab Bank Ltd v Hajjar (No 2) [1988] QB 944, [1988] 3 All ER
    103 49
Anderson v Dundee City Council 1999 GWD 1-52 183
Anderson v Forth Valley Health Board 1998 SLT 588, OH 77
Anderson v Marshall (1835) 13 S 1130 14
Anderson v St Andrew's Ambulance Association 1943 SC 248, 1943 SLT
    258 146
Anns v Merton London Borough Council [1978] AC 728, [1977] 2 All ER
    492, HL 97, 98
Ansbacher, Henry & Co Ltd v Binks Stern (1998) Lloyd's Rep Bank 1,
    (1997) Times 26 June, CA 53
Argyll and Clyde Health Board v Strathclyde Regional Council 1988
    SCLR 120, 1988 SLT 381, OH 185
Argyllshire Weavers Ltd v A Macaulay (Tweeds) Ltd 1965 SLT 21, OH: 261
Attorney-General v Guardian Newspapers Ltd (No 2) [1990] 1 AC 109,
    [1988] 3 All ER 545, HL............................... 32, 33
Auld v Shairp (1874) 2 R 191 244
Auld v Shairp (1875) 2 R 940 248

B v Burns 1994 SLT 250 255
B v Harris 1989 SCLR 644, 1990 SLT 208 15
BOC v Groves 1993 SLT 360, OH 146
Baigent v British Broadcasting Corpn 1999 GWD 10-474 .... 252, 259
Baigent v McCulloch 1998 SLT 780, OH 257
Bank of Credit and Commerce International (Overseas) Ltd (in Liquida-
    tion) v Price Waterhouse (No 2) [1998] Lloyd's Rep Bank 85, (1998)
    Times, 4 March, CA 88

PAGE
Barnett v Chelsea and Kensington Hospital Management Committee
 [1969] 1 QB 428, [1968] 1 All ER 1068 130
Barrett v Enfield London Borough Council [1999] 3 WLR 79 .... 200, 201
Barrett v Ministry of Defence [1995] 3 All ER 87, CA 69, 145
Barrymore v News Group Newspapers Ltd [1997] FSR 600, Ch D 31
Beggs v Motherwell Bridge Fabricators Ltd 1997 SCLR 1019, 1998 SLT
 1215 .... 189, 226,
 229, 231
Behrens v Bertram Mills Circus Ltd [1957] 2 QB 1, [1957] 1 All ER 583: 170
Bell v Blackwood, Morton & Sons Ltd 1960 SC 11, 1959 SLT (Notes) 54,
 OH 217
Bennet (H & J M) (Potatoes) Ltd v Secretary of State for Scotland 1986
 SLT 665, OH 53, 54
Berkoff v Burchill [1996] 4 All ER 1008, [1997] EMLR 139, CA 249
Blackhall v MacInnes 1997 SLT 649, OH 144
Blake v Lothian Health Board 1993 SLT 1248, OH 284
Bolam v Friern Hospital Management Committee [1957] 2 All ER 118,
 [1957] 1 WLR 582 150
Bolitho v City and Hackney Health Authority [1998] AC 232, [1997] 4 All
 ER 771, HL 130, 150,
 151
Bolton v Stone [1951] AC 850, [1951] 1 All ER 1078, HL 120
Bonar v Trafalgar House Offshore Fabrication Ltd 1996 SLT 548 281
Bourhill v Young 1942 SC (HL) 78, 1943 SLT 105 .... 72, 73,
 115, 127
Bradford v Pickles [1895] AC 587, HL 22
Brannan v Airtours (18 January 1999, unreported), CA 145
Brimelow v Casson [1924] 1 Ch 302 37
Brisco v Secretary of State for Scotland 1997 SC 14 206
Bristol and West Building Society v Aitken Nairn 1999 SLT 43, OH 153
Bristol and West Building Society v Rollo Steven and Bond 1998 SLT 9,
 OH 270
British Motor Trade Association v Gray 1951 SC 586, 1951 SLT 247 ... 36, 37
British Steel Corpn v Granada Television Ltd [1981] AC 1096, [1981] 1
 All ER 417, HL 33
British Telecommunications plc v James Thomson & Sons (Engineers) Ltd
 1999 SC (HL) 9 65
British Transport Commission v Gourlay [1956] AC 185, [1955] 3 All ER
 796, HL 274
Brooks v Lind 1997 Rep LR 83, 1997 GWD 13-570 248
Broom v Ritchie & Co (1905) 6 F 942 261
Brown v Lee Constructions Ltd 1977 SLT (Notes) 61, OH 20
Brown v Rolls Royce Ltd 1960 SC (HL) 22, 1960 SLT 119 126
Brownlie v Thomson (1859) 21 D 480 253
Bryan v Maloney (1995) 11 Const LJ 274, HC (Aus) 98
Buckley v Farrow [1997] PIQR Q78, CA 224
Burke v Burke 1983 SLT 331, OH 16
Burns v Diamond (1896) 23 R 507, (1896) 3 SLT 274 260

C v M 1923 SC 1, 1922 SLT 634 259
Caledonian Rly Co v Greenock Corpn 1917 SC (HL) 56, 1917 2 SLT 67: 185
Cambridge Water Co v Eastern Counties Leather plc [1994] 2 AC 264,
 [1994] 1 All ER 53, HL 178

PAGE

Cameron v Hamilton's Auction Marts Ltd 1955 SLT (Sh Ct) 71, 71 Sh Ct
  Rep 285 169
Campbell v Cochrane (1905) 8 F 205 257
Campbell v F and F Moffat (Transport) Ltd 1992 SCLR 551, 1992 SLT
  962, OH 268
Campbell v Gillespie 1996 SLT 503, OH 231
Campbell v Muir 1908 SC 387, 15 SLT 737 22
Candlewood Navigation Corpn Ltd v Mitsui OSK Lines Ltd, The Mineral
  Transporter [1986] AC 1, [1985] 2 All ER 935, PC 102, 105
Canterbury v Spence (1972) 464 F 2d 772 13
Caparo Industries plc v Dickman [1990] 2 AC 605, [1990] 1 All ER 568,
  HL 64, 81–83,
                                                              149, 200, 203
Capital and Counties plc v Hampshire County Council [1997] QB 1004,
  [1997] 2 All ER 865, CA 202
Carr-Glynn v Frearsons [1998] 4 All ER 225, [1998] 3 FCR 487, CA ... 155
Carrick Jewellery Ltd v Ortak 1989 GWD 35-1624, OH 27
Carroll v British Broadcasting Corpn 1997 SLT (Sh Ct) 23 .... 245, 247,
                                                              253, 254, 257
Carroll v Fearon [1998] PIQR P416, CA 157
Carson v Howard Doris Ltd 1981 SC 278, 1981 SLT 273 285
Cavanagh v Ulster Weaving Co Ltd [1960] AC 145, [1959] 2 All ER 745,
  HL 125, 126
Cavin v Kinnaird 1993 SCLR 618, 1994 SLT 111 236
Century Insurance Co Ltd v Northern Ireland Road Transport Board
  [1942] AC 509, [1942] 1 All ER 491, HL 216
Chadwick v British Transport Commission [1967] 2 All ER 945, [1967] 1
  WLR 912 71
Charleston v News Group Newspapers Ltd [1995] 2 AC 65, [1995] 2 All
  ER 313, HL 246
Charlton v Forrest Printing Ink Co Ltd [1980] IRLR 331, CA 124
Christie v Robertson (1899) 1 F 115 253
Clark v McLean 1994 SCLR 564, 1995 SLT 235 285
Clark v Scottish Power plc 1994 SCLR 202, 1994 SLT 924 273
Clarke v Kato [1998] 4 All ER 417, [1998] 1 WLR 1697, HL 240
Clay v A J Crump & Sons Ltd [1964] 1 QB 533, [1963] 3 All ER 687, CA: 60
Cleland v Campbell 1998 SLT 642, OH 283
Clelland v Morton Fraser Milligan 1997 SLT (Sh Ct) 57 85
Clippens Oil Co Ltd v Edinburgh and District Water Trustees 1907 SC
  (HL) 9, 15 SLT 92 274
Cloy v Adams & Sons 1999 GWD 19-908 182
Cohen v Shaw 1992 SCLR 182, 1992 SLT 1022, OH 223, 230
Colborne v Wallace 1993 GWD 17-1121 236
Coleridge v Miller Construction Ltd 1997 SLT 485, OH 65, 101
Comex Houlder Diving Ltd v Colne Fishing Co Ltd (No 2) 1992 SLT 89,
  OH 91
Commission of the European Communities v United Kingdom (C300/95)
  [1997] All ER (EC) 481, ECJ (Fifth Chamber) 166
Commissioner of Police for the Metropolis v Reeves (15 July 1999,
  unreported), HL 142, 144
Cowan v National Coal Board 1958 SLT (Notes) 19, OH 268
Cowie v Atlantic Drilling Co Ltd 1995 SC 288, 1995 SCLR 335, 1995
  SLT 1151 283

PAGE

Cowie v Tudhope 1987 GWD 12-395 15
Craig v Inveresk Paper Merchant Ltd 1970 SLT (Notes) 50, OH 261
Credit Lyonnais Bank Nederland NV v Export Credits Guarantee
    Department [1999] 1 All ER 929, HL 212
Crofter Hand Woven Harris Tweed Co Ltd v Veitch 1942 SC (HL) 1,
    1943 SLT 2 45–47
Crombie v McDermott Scotland Ltd 1996 SLT 1238, 1996 Rep LR 122,
    OH 208
Cullen v North Lanarkshire Council 1998 SC 451, 1998 SLT 897 209
Cullin v London Fire and Civil Defence Authority (31 March 1999,
    unreported), QB 71
Cunningham v Scotsman Publications Ltd 1987 SC 107, 1987 SCLR 314,
    OH 257
Cuthbert v Linklater 1935 SLT 94 .... 247, 249
Cutler v Wandsworth Stadium Ltd (in liquidation) [1949] AC 398, [1949]
    1 All ER 544, HL 196

D & F Estates Ltd v Church Commissioners for England [1989] AC 177,
    [1988] 2 All ER 992, HL 92, 94, 96
Daborn v Bath Tramways Motor Co Ltd and Smithey [1946] 2 All ER
    333, CA 122
Dahl v Chief Constable, Central Scotland Police 1983 SLT 420, OH 17
Davidson v City of Glasgow District Council 1993 SLT 479, OH 139
Davidson v Kerr 1997 Hous LR 11, 1996 GWD 40-2296, Sh Ct 183
Davie v New Merton Board Mills Ltd [1959] AC 604 206
Dawson v Bingley Urban District Council [1941] 2 KB 199, CA 194
Defreitas v O'Brien [1995] 6 Med LR 108 151
De Maudsley v Palumbo [1996] FSR 447, (1995) Times, 19 December,
    Ch D 32
Denheen v British Railways Board 1988 SLT 320, 1986 SLT 249, OH ... 225
Derbyshire County Council v Times Newspapers Ltd [1993] AC 534,
    [1993] 1 All ER 1011, HL 244
Derry v Peek (1889) 14 App Cas 337, HL 53
Devlin v Strathclyde Regional Council 1993 SLT 699, OH 141, 190, 191
Dingley v Chief Constable of Strathclyde Police (No 1) 1998 SC 58, OH: 130
Donaghy v National Coal Board 1957 SLT (Notes) 35 138
Donald v Rutherford 1983 SLT 253, 1984 SLT 70 285
Donlon v Colonial Mutual Group (UK Holdings) Ltd 1998 SC 244, 1997
    SCLR 1088 87
Donoghue v Stevenson 1932 SC (HL) 31, 1932 SLT 317 .... 58–63, 66,
                                                          78, 79, 86,
                                                          89, 90, 93,
                                                          95, 98, 107,
                                                          149, 157, 158,
                                                          169, 177,
                                                          204–206,
                                                          223, 246
Dorset Yacht Co Ltd v Home Office [1970] AC 1004, [1970] 2 All ER
    294, HL 66, 118, 140
Doughty v Turner Manufacturing Co Ltd [1964] 1 QB 518, [1964] 1 All
    ER 98, CA 117
Downie v Chief Constable of Strathclyde Police 1997 SCLR 603 12
Duff v Highland and Islands Fire Board 1995 SLT 1362 202

PAGE

Duffy v Lanarkshire Health Boad 1998 SCLR 1142, 1998 Rep LR 119, OH: 225
Duke of Argyll v Duchess of Argyll [1967] Ch 302, [1965] 1 All ER 611: 30, 31
Dulieu v White & Sons [1901] 2 KB 669 70
Dumbreck v Robert Addie & Sons (Colleries) Ltd 1928 SC 547, 1928
    SLT 341 20
Dumbreck v Robert Addie & Sons 1929 SC (HL) 51, 1929 SLT 242 187
Duncan v Associated Scottish Newspapers Ltd 1929 SC 14 250
Duncan v Glacier Metal Co Ltd 1988 SCLR 320, 1988 SLT 479, OH ... 277
Duncan v Ross Harper & Murphy 1993 SLT 579, OH 145
Dundee (City of) District Council v Cook 1995 SCLR 559 186
Dunlop v McGowans 1979 SC 22, 1979 SLT 34 280
Dunlop v McGowans 1980 SC (HL) 73, 1980 SLT 129 283
Dunlop Pneumatic Tyre Co v Dunlop Motor Co 1907 SC (HL) 15, 15
    SLT 362 28
Dynamco Ltd v Holland and Hannen and Cubitts (Scotland) Ltd 1971 SC
    257, 1972 SLT 38 .... 101, 103

Eastern Marine Services (and Supplies) Ltd v Dickson Motors Ltd 1981
    SC 355, OH 82
Edgar v Lord Advocate 1965 SC 67, 1965 SLT 158 224
Edwards v Butlins Ltd 1998 SLT 500, 1997 GWD 21-1052 207
Eisten v North British Railway Co (1870) 8 M 980 4
Electrical, Electronic, Telecommunication and Plumbing Union v Times
    Newspapers Ltd [1980] QB 585, [1980] 1 All ER 1097 244
Elguzouli-Daf v Commissioner of Police of the Metropolis; McBrearty v
    Ministry of Defence [1995] QB 335, [1995] 1 All ER 833, CA 109
Emerald Construction Co Ltd v Lowthian [1966] 1 All ER 1013, [1966] 1
    WLR 691, CA 37
Empress Car Co (Abertillery) Ltd v National Rivers Authority [1998] 1 All
    ER 481, HL 140
Erven Warnink BV v J Townend & Sons (Hull) Ltd [1979] AC 731 .... 28, 29
Evans v Motor Insurers Bureau [1999] Lloyd's Rep IR 30 239
Evans v Triplex Safety Glass Co Ltd [1936] 1 All ER 283 .... 157, 160
Exchange Telegraph Co Ltd v Giulianotti 1959 SC 19, 1959 SLT 293,
    OH 32

FC Finance Ltd v Brown & Son 1969 SLT (Sh Ct) 41 .... 5, 24–26
FC Finance Ltd v Langtry Investment Co Ltd 1973 SLT (Sh Ct) 11 24
Faccenda Chicken Ltd v Fowler [1987] Ch 117, [1986] 1 All ER 617, CA: 30
Fairbairn v Scottish National Party 1979 SC 393, 1980 SLT 149 253
Fairlie v Carruthers 1996 SLT (Sh Ct) 56 172
Farquhar v Neish (1890) 17 R 716 257
Faulds v Townsend (1861) 23 D 436, 33 SJ 224 .... 24, 25
Feely v Co-operative Wholesale Society 1990 SCLR 356, 1990 SLT 547,
    OH 188
Ferrelly v Yarrow Shipbuilders Ltd 1994 SCLR 407, 1994 SLT 1349 226
Fleming v McGillivray 1946 SC 1, 1945 SLT 301 146
Fletcher v Wilsons (1885) 12 R 683 252
Forbes v City of Dundee District Council 1997 SLT 1330, 1997 SCLR
    682, OH 200
Ford Motor Co Ltd v HLM Design Ltd 1997 SLT 837, OH 269
Forsyth's Curator Bonis v Govan Shipbuilders 1989 SCLR 78, 1989 SLT
    91 225

PAGE

Foskett v McClymont 1998 SC 96, 1998 SLT 892 .... 172, 173
Fraser v D M Hall & Son 1997 SLT 808, OH 273
Fraser v Mirza 1993 SC (HL) 27, 1993 SLT 527 .... 256, 258
Fry's Metals Ltd v Durastic Ltd 1991 SLT 689, OH 180

GA Estates Ltd v Caviapen Trustees Ltd (No 1) 1993 SLT 1037, OH: 178, 186
Galbraith's Curator ad Litem v Stewart (No 2) 1998 SLT 1305 ...... 117, 222
Galoo Ltd (in liquidation) v Bright Grahame Murray [1994] 1 WLR 1360,
    [1995] 1 All ER 16, CA 82, 136
Gaughan v Bedfordshire Health Authority [1997] 8 Med LR 182, QBD: 152
Gibson v British Rail Maintenance 1995 SC 7, 1995 SLT 953   207
Gibson v National Cash Register Co Ltd 1925 SC 500, 1925, SLT 377 ..   52
Gibson v Orr 1999 SC 420, OH 65, 66, 201
Gilbert v Yorston 1996 SCLR 1122, 1997 SLT 879, OH 247, 259
Gillon v Chief Constable of Strathclyde Police 1997 SLT 1218, (1996)
    Times, 22 November, OH   121
Girvan v Inverness Farmers Dairy (No 2) 1998 SC (HL) 1, 1998 SCLR
    72, 1998 SLT 21   276
Gold v Haringey Health Authority [1987] QB 481, [1987] 2 All ER 888,
    CA 77, 151
Gold Coin Joailliers SA v United Bank of Kuwait [1997] 6 Bank LR 60,
    (1996) Times 4 November, CA   88
Goldsmith v Bhoyrul [1998] QB 459, [1997] 4 All ER 268, QBD   244
Goodwill v British Pregnancy Advisory Service [1996] 2 All ER 161, CA ..   77
Gordon v Wilson 1992 SLT 849, [1992] 3 Med LR 401, OH   151
Gorris v Scott (1874) LR 9 Exch 125   197
Graham (Thomas) & Co Ltd v Church of Scotland General Trustees 1982
    SLT (Sh Ct) 26   179
Grant v Allan 1987 JC 71, 1988 SLT 11   30
Grant v Australian Knitting Mills Ltd [1936] AC 85, PC   60
Grant v Sun Shipping Co Ltd 1948 SC (HL) 73, 1949 SLT 25   139
Grant (William) & Sons Ltd v William Cadenhead Ltd 1985 SC 121, 1985
    SLT 291   27
Gray v Dunlop 1954 SLT (Sh Ct) 75, 70 Sh Ct Rep 270   181
Gray v Scottish Society for the Prevention of Cruelty to Animals (1890) 17
    R 1185   254
Groves v Lord Wimborne [1898] 2 QB 402, CA   194
Grunwald v Hughes 1964 SLT 94, 1965 SLT 209, OH   60
Guy v Strathkelvin District Council 1997 SCLR 405, OH   191

Haggart's Trustees v Lord President Hope (1824) 2 Sh App 125   255
Hague v Deputy Governor of Parkhurst Prison [1992] 1 AC 58, [1991] 3
    All ER 733, HL   195
Haig (John) & Co Ltd v Forth Blending Co Ltd 1954 SC 35, 1954 SLT 2,
    OH 27, 29
Hambrook v Stokes Bros [1925] 1 KB 141, CA   73
Hamilton v Fife Health Board 1992 SCLR 288, 1992 SLT 1026, OH ...   229
Hamilton v Fife Health Board 1993 SC 369, 1993 SLT 624   223
Hanlon v Cuthbertson 1981 SLT (Notes) 57, OH   145
Hardie v Sneddon 1917 SC 1, 1916 2 SLT 197   222
Harris v Abbey National plc 1997 SCLR 359   5
Harrison v Michelin Tyre Co Ltd [1985] 1 All ER 918, [1985] ICR 696 ..   217
Harrods Ltd v Harrodian School [1996] RPC 697, (1996) Times 3 April, CA: 28

PAGE
Harvie v Robertson (1903) 5 F 338, 10 SLT 581 186
Hedley Byrne & Co Ltd v Heller & Partners Ltd [1964] AC 465, [1963] 2
    All ER 575, HL 79–85, 152
Heenan v Dillon 1999 Fam LR 62 19
Henderson v John Stuart (Farms) Ltd 1963 SC 245, 1963 SLT 22 .... 169, 170
Henderson v Merrett Syndicates Ltd [1995] 2 AC 145, [1994] 3 All ER
    506, HL 86–88,
                92, 96,
             100, 103,
             149, 152,
             153, 155
Henderson v Merrett Syndicates Ltd (No 2) [1997] LRLR 265, QBD
    (Comm Ct) 152
Henderson v Moodie 1988 SCLR 77, sub nom Henderson v Chief
    Constable, Fife Police 1988 SLT 361, OH 17
Hicks v Chief Constable of South Yorkshire Police [1992] 2 All ER 65,
    HL 227, 273
Hill v Chief Constable of West Yorkshire [1989] AC 53, [1988] 2 All ER
    238, HL 108, 109,
             119, 200, 203
Hill v Lovett 1992 SLT 994, OH 169, 170,
             189, 209
Hill v Wilson 1998 SC 81, 1998 SLT 69, OH 275, 277
Hislop v Durham (1842) 4 D 1168 205
Hodgson v Trapp [1989] AC 807, [1988] 3 All ER 870, HL 278, 279
Horrocks v Lowe [1975] AC 15, [1974] 1 All ER 662, HL 258
Hotson v East Berkshire Area Health Authority [1987] 2 All ER 909, HL: 131
Hudson v Ridge Manufacturing Co Ltd [1957] 2 QB 348, [1957] 2 All ER
    348 207
Hughes v Lord Advocate 1963 SC (HL) 31, 1963 SLT 150 .... 116, 117,
             127, 267
Hulton (E) & Co v Jones [1910] AC 20 250
Hunter v British Coal Corpn [1999] QB 140, [1998] 2 All ER 97, CA ... 71
Hunter v British Steel Corpn 1980 SLT 31 209
Hunter v Canary Wharf Ltd [1997] AC 655, [1997] 2 All ER 426, HL .. 182, 186
Hunter v Hanley 1955 SC 200, 1955 SLT 213 150
Hutcheson v Ascosmit Co 1992 SLT 1115 282

ICI v Shatwell [1965] AC 656, [1964] 2 All ER 999 .... 142, 145
Incorporation of Fleshers of Dumfries v Rankine Dec 10 1816 FC 244
Ingham v John G Russell (Transport) Ltd 1991 SC 201, 1991 SLT 739,
    1991 SCLR 596 .... 225, 226, 233
Initial Services Ltd v Putterill [1968] 1 QB 396, [1967] 3 All ER 145, CA: 33
Invercargill City Council v Hamlin [1996] AC 624, [1996] 1 All ER 756,
    PC 98
Island Records Ltd, ex parte [1978] Ch 122, [1978] 3 All ER 824, CA ... 195

Jobling v Associated Dairies Ltd [1982] AC 794, [1981] 2 All ER 752, HL: 131
Jolley v Sutton London Borough Council [1998] 3 All ER 559, CA 117
Junior Books Ltd v Veitchi Co Ltd 1982 SC (HL) 244, 1982 SLT 492: 89, 91–94,
             96, 100,
           103, 104,
           107, 149

PAGE

Kay's Tutor v Ayrshire and Arran Health Board 1987 SC (HL) 145, 1987
    SLT 577, HL, affirming 1986 SLT 435 . . . . 130, 134
Keane v Walker Contracts (Scotland) Ltd 1999 GWD 9-410 . . . . 188, 189
Keicher v National Coal Board 1988 SLT 318   277
Kelvin Shipping Co, The Baron Vernon v Canadian Pacific Railway Co,
    The Metagama 1928 SC (HL) 21, 1928 SLT 117   267
Kennedy v Glenbelle Ltd 1996 SC 95   184
Kennedy v Lees of Scotland 1997 SLT 510   224
Kenyon v Bell 1953 SC 125, 1952 SLT (Notes) 79, OH   131
Kenway (John) Ltd v Orcantic Ltd 1979 SC 422, 1980 SLT 46, OH   82
Kerr v Earl of Orkney (1857) 20 D 298, 30 SJ 158 . . . . 6, 177
Kerr v Kennedy [1942] 1 KB 409, [1942] 1 All ER 412   247
Kirby v National Coal Board 1958 SC 514, 1959 SLT 7 . . . . 212, 216
Kirk Care Housing Association Ltd v Crerar and Partners 1996 SLT 150,
    OH   284
Knowles v Liverpool City Council [1993] 4 All ER 321, [1993] LR 1428,
    HL   207
Kozikowska v Kozikowski 1996 SLT 386   225
Kubach v Hollands [1937] 3 All ER 907, KB   157
Kyle v P & J Stormonth Darling WS 1993 SC 57, 1994 SLT 191, affirming
    1992 SLT 264, OH   155

Landcatch Ltd v The Braer Corpn; Landcatch Ltd v International Oil
    Pollution Compensation Fund 1999 GWD 20-962   102
Lang Bros Ltd v Goldwell Ltd 1980 SC 237, 1982 SLT 309 . . . . 28, 29
Lappin v Britannia Airways Ltd 1989 SLT 181, OH   282
Latimer v AEC Ltd [1953] AC 643, [1953] 2 All ER 449, HL 124, 206
Lawson v Scotdem Ltd 1999 GWD 8-393   273
Lees v Tod (1882) 9 R 807   53
Lego System A/S v Lego M Lemelstrich Ltd [1983] FSR 155   28
Leigh and Sillavan Ltd v Aliakmon Shipping Co Ltd, The Aliakmon [1986]
    AC 785, [1986] 2 All ER 145, HL, affirming [1985] 2 All ER 44,
    CA 103–105, 107
Leitch v Leydon 1931 SC (HL) 1 . . . . 22, 23
Lewicki v Brown & Root Wimpey Highland Fabricators Ltd 1996 SC 200,
    1996 SCLR 680, 1996 SLT 1283   277
Lewis v Buckpool Golf Club 1993 SLT (Sh Ct) 43 . . . . 14, 143
Liddle v Morton 1996 SLT 1143   5
Lim Poh Choo v Camden and Islington Area Health Authority [1980] AC
    174, [1979] 2 All ER 910, HL 272, 273
Lister v Romford Ice and Cold Storage Co Ltd [1957] AC 555, [1957] 1
    All ER 125, HL   21
Littlejohn v Wood & Davidson Ltd 1997 SLT 1353   195
Lonrho Ltd v Shell Petroleum Co Ltd (No 2) [1981] 2 All ER 456, [1982]
    AC 173, HL 45, 48–50,
                                                                      195, 197
Lonrho plc v Fayed [1990] 2 QB 479, [1989] 2 All ER 65, CA   42
Lonrho plc v Fayed [1992] 1 AC 448, [1991] 3 All ER 303, HL 49, 50
Lonrho plc v Fayed (No 5) [1994] 1 All ER 188, [1993] 1 WLR 1489, CA: 47

McAllister v Imperial Chemical Industries plc 1997 SLT 351, 1996 Rep
    LR 136, OH   230
McCabe v News Group Newspapers Ltd 1992 SLT 707, OH   247

PAGE

McCann v Scottish Media Newspapers Ltd 1999 GWD 10-473 246
McClelland v Greater Glasgow Health Board 1999 SC 305 269
McCluskey v Wallace 1998 SC 711 222
MacColl v Hoo 1983 SLT (Sh Ct) 23 .... 177, 181
McColl v Barns 1992 SCLR 907, 1992 SLT 1188, OH 282
McCullagh v Lane Fox and Partners [1996] 1 EGLR 35, (1995) Times,
22 December, CA 85
McCullough v Norwest Socea Ltd 1981 SLT 201, OH 285
Macdonald v Fédération International des Football Associations 1999
SCLR 59, OH 78
MacDougall v Clydesdale Bank Trustees 1993 SCLR 832 154
MacDougall v MacDougall's Executors 1994 SLT 1178, OH 154
McDougall v Strathclyde Regional Council 1999 SLT 1124 114
McDyer v Celtic Football and Athletic Co Ltd 1999 SLT 2 188
McErlean v J & B Scotland Ltd 1997 SLT 1326, 1997 GWD 6-253, OH: 206
McFarlane v EE Caledonia Ltd [1994] 2 All ER 1 .... 71, 75
McFarlane v Tayside Health Board 1997 SLT 211, OH 77
McGhee v National Coal Board 1973 SC (HL) 37, 1973 SLT 14 133–135
McGlone v British Railways Board 1966 SC (HL) 1, 1966 SLT 2 190
McGregor v AAH Pharmaceuticals Ltd 1996 SLT 1161, OH 205
McGuffie v Forth Valley Health Board 1991 SLT 231 188
Mackay v Borthwick 1982 SLT 265, OH 144
McKay v Essex Area Health Authority [1982] QB 1166, [1982] 2 All ER
771, CA 76
McKeen v Chief Constable, Lothian and Borders Police 1994 SLT 93, OH: 16
McKendrick v Sinclair 1972 SC (HL) 25, 1972 SLT 110 4
Mackenzie v Cluny Hill Hydropathic Co 1908 SC 200, 15 SLT 518 17
McKew v Holland and Hannon and Cubitts (Scotland) Ltd 1970 SC (HL)
20, 1970 SLT 68 137
McKillen v Barclay Curle & Co Ltd 1967 SLT 41 269
McKinnell v White 1971 SLT (Notes) 61, OH 222
McKnight v Clydesdale Buses Ltd 1999 GWD 4-213 203
McLaughlan v Craig 1948 SC 599, 1948 SLT 483 177
McLaughlan v Orr Pollock & Co (1894) 22 R 38 248
Maclean v Lothian and Borders Fire Brigade 1998 SCLR 1004, OH 273
McLelland v Greater Glasgow Health Board 1999 SC 305 77
McLeod v Aberdeen City Council 1999 GWD 23-1115 206
MacLeod v Kerr 1965 SC 253, 1965 SLT 358 51
McLoughlin v O'Brian [1983] 1 AC 410, [1982] 2 All ER 298, HL 73, 74
McManus' Executrix v Babcock Energy Ltd 1999 SC 569 225–227,
231–233, 275
McMillan v McDowall 1993 SLT 311, OH 272
McNulty v Marshalls Food Group Ltd 1999 SC 195 275
McPhee v Macfarlane's Exr 1933 SC 163, 1933 SLT 148 18
Macrae v Reed & Mallik Ltd 1961 SC 68, 1961 SLT 96 277
McRostie v Ironside (1849) 12 D 74 248
McWilliams v Lord Advocate 1992 SCLR 954, 1992 SLT 1045, OH 229
McWilliams v Sir William Arrol & Co and Lithgows Ltd 1962 SC (HL)
70, 1962 SLT 121 131
MTM Construction Ltd v William Reid Engineering Ltd 1998 SLT 778,
1997 SCLR 778, OH 220
Malcolm v Dickson 1951 SC 542, 1951 SLT 357 114
Malcolm v Fair 1993 SLT 342, OH 145

PAGE

Maloco v Littlewoods Organisation Ltd 1987 SC (HL) 37, 1987 SCLR
  489, 1987 SLT 425 .... 118, 178, 179
Manners v Whitehead (1898) 1 F 171   85
Marshall v William Sharp & Sons Ltd 1991 SCLR 104, 1991 SLT 114 ...   219
Martin v Bell-Ingram 1986 SC 208, 1986 SLT 575 .... 83, 84
Massey v Crown Life Insurance Co [1978] ICR 590, [1978] 2 All E4 576,
  CA   211
Maynard v West Midlands Regional Health Authority [1985] 1 All ER
  635, [1984] 1 WLR 634, HL   151
Mazure v Stubbs Ltd 1919 SC (HL) 112, 1919 2 SLT 160   248
Meek v Burton's Gold Medal Biscuits Ltd 1989 SLT 338, OH   281
Melrose v Davidson and Robertson 1993 SC 288, 1993 SLT 611   84
Merivale v Carson (1887) 20 QBD 275, CA   254
Merkur Island Shipping Corpn v Laughton [1983] 2 AC 570, [1983] ICR
  490, HL 39, 42
Mersey Docks and Harbour Board v Coggins and Griffith (Liverpool) Ltd
  [1947] AC 1, [1946] 2 All ER 345, HL   218
Metall und Rohstoff AG v Donaldson Lufkin and Jenrette Inc [1990] 1 QB
  391, [1989] 3 All ER 14, CA   49
Middlebrook Mushrooms Ltd v Transport and General Workers Union
  [1993] ICR 612, (1993) Times, 18 January, CA   37
Midland Bank plc v Cameron, Thom, Peterkins & Duncans 1988 SCLR
  209, 1988 SLT 11, OH 152, 153
Millar v Bassey [1994] EMLR 44   37
Mitchell v Glenrothes Development Corpn 1991 SLT 284, OH   275
Mitchell v Laing 1998 SC 342, 1998 SCLR 266, 1998 SLT 203   279
Mogul Steamship Co Ltd v McGregor, Gow & Co (1889) 23 QBD 598,
  CA 45, 47
Monson v Tussauds Ltd [1894] 1 QB 671, CA 245, 249
Monteith v Cape Insulation Ltd 1998 SC 903   230
More v Boyle 1967 SLT (Sh Ct) 38   22
Morgans v Launchbury [1973] AC 127, [1972] 2 All ER 606, HL   220
Morrison v Ritchie & Co (1902) 4 F 645 .... 249, 251, 259
Morrisson v Robertson 1908 SC 332, 15 SLT 697   51
Morrow v Neil 1975 SLT (Sh Ct) 65   5
Mortgage Corpn Ltd v Mitchells Roberton 1997 SLT 1305, OH 152, 153
Morton v Wm Dixon Ltd 1909 SC 807, 1909 1 SLT 346 .... 125, 126
Moyes v Lothian Health Board 1990 SLT 444   14
Muir v Glasgow Corpn 1943 SC (HL) 3, 1944 SLT 60 .... 112, 114, 119
Mullin v Richards [1998] 1 All ER 920, CA   114
Murdoch v Glacier Metal Co Ltd [1998] Env LR 732, [1998] EHLR 198:   183
Murphy v Brentwood District Council [1991] 1 AC 398, [1990] 2 All ER
  908, HL 90, 98, 99
Murray v Fraser 1916 SC 623   16
Murray v Reilly 1963 SLT (Notes) 49, OH   156
Mustad (O) & Son v S Allcock & Co Ltd and Dosen [1963] 3 All ER 416,
  [1964] 1 WLR 109, HL   32
Mutch v Robertson 1981 SLT 217   248

Nacap Ltd v Moffat Plant Ltd 1987 SLT 221, rev 1986 SLT 326 102,
                                                              105, 107
Neill v Docherty and Akram (23 May 1996, unreported), HC 145
Neilson v Rodger (1853) 16 D 325   244

PAGE
Neville v C & A Modes Ltd 1945 SC 175, 1945 SLT 189   213
Nolan v Iceland Frozen Foods (3 December 1997, unreported)   118
Nordic Oil Services Ltd v Berman 1993 SLT 1164, OH 82, 98
Norman v Future Publishing Ltd [1999] EMLR 325   246
North of Scotland Banking Co v Duncan (1857) 19 D 881   261
North Scottish Helicopters Ltd v United Technologies Corpn Inc (No 2)
    1988 SLT 778, OH   106

O'Brien's Curator Bonis v British Steel plc 1991 SC 315, 1991 SCLR 831,
    1991 SLT 477 . . . . 269, 275
O'Connor v Mathews 1996 SLT 408, OH   276
Omega Trust Co Ltd v Wright Son & Pepper (No 1) [1997] 1 EGLR 120,
    CA   85
Onifade v Secretary of State for Social Security 1999 GWD 17-819   200
O'Rourke v Camden London Borough Council [1998] AC 188, [1997] 3
    All ER 23, HL   197
Osborne & Hunter Ltd v Hardie Caldwell 1999 SLT 153   283
Osman v United Kingdom 5 BHRC 293, (1998) Times, 5 November,
    ECHR 109, 203
Outram v Reid (1852) 14 D 577 . . . . 248, 250, 251
Overseas Tankship (UK) Ltd v Morts Dock and Engineering Co, The
    Wagon Mound [1961] AC 388, [1961] 1 All ER 404, PC   267

Pace v Culley 1992 SLT 1073, OH   144
Page v Smith [1996] AC 155, [1995] 2 All ER 736, HL 71, 116, 269
Palmer v Beck 1993 SLT 485, OH   85
Palmer v Tees Health Authority (1999) Times, 6 July   200
Paris v Stepney Borough Council [1949] 2 All ER 843, CA, [1951] AC
    367, [1951] 1 All ER 42, HL   121
Paris v Stepney Borough Council [1951] AC 367, [1951] 1 All ER 42, HL: 208
Park v Tractor Shovels Ltd 1980 SLT 94, OH   218
Parker-Knoll Ltd v Knoll International [1962] RPC 265, HL   29
Patel v Hooper & Jackson [1999] 1 All ER 992, CA   270
Paterson v Costain Mining Ltd 1988 SCLR 71, 1988 SLT 13, OH   282
Paterson v Welch (1893) 20 R 744   260
Paton v Loffland Bros North Sea 1994 SLT 784   285
Patterson v H Landsberg & Son (1905) 7 F 675, 13 SLT 62   52
Paul v Jackson (1884) 11 R 460   259
Peach Publishing Ltd v Slater & Co; Slater 7 Co v Sheil Land Associates
    Ltd [1998] BCC 139, CA   88
Pearce v United Bristol NHS Trust [1999] PIQR 53   14
Pearson v Educational Institute of Scotland 1997 SC 245, 1998 SLT 189:   257
Perrett v Collins [1998] 2 Lloyd's Rep 255, (1998) Times, 23 June, CA . .   65
Phestos Shipping Co Ltd v Kurmiawan 1983 SC 165, 1983 SLT 388   23
Phillips v Grampian Health Board 1991 SCLR 817, 1992 SLT 659   231
Philp v Morton (1816) Hume 865   261
Pickford v ICI plc [1996] ICR 566, [1996] IRLR 622, CA   206
Pickford v ICI plc [1998] ICR 673, [1998] 3 All ER 462, HL   130
Platform Home Loans Ltd v Oyston Shipways Ltd [1999] 1 All ER 833,
    HL   271
Platt v Liverpool City Council CCRTF 97/0072/C, CA   190
Polemis and Furness, Withy & Co Ltd, Re [1921] 3 KB 560, CA 266–268
Porter v Strathclyde Regional Council 1991 SLT 446 . . . . 129, 188

PAGE

Potter v McCulloch 1987 SLT 308, OH 281
Powell v Boladz [1998] Lloyd's Rep Med 116, CA 51
Prentice v William Thyne Ltd 1989 SLT 336, OH 281
Preston v Grampian Health Board 1988 SLT 435 277
Primrose v Waterston (1902) 4 F 783, 10 SLT 37 255
Pringle v Bremner and Stirling (1867) 5 M (HL) 55 17
Prophit v British Broadcasting Corpn 1997 SLT 745, OH 247, 253
Pullar v Window Clean Ltd 1956 SC 13, 1956 SLT 17 196

Quilty v Windsor 1999 SLT 346 .... 30, 247, 257
Quinn v Cameron and Roberton Ltd 1956 SC 224, 1957 SLT 2 123
Quinn v Leathem [1901] AC 495, HL 45
Quinn v McGinty 1999 SLT (Sh Ct) 27 210

RCA Corpn v Pollard [1983] Ch 135, [1982] 3 All ER 771, CA 48, 195
RHM Bakeries (Scotland) Ltd v Strathclyde Regional Council 1985 SLT
    214, HL 178, 184, 185
RSP Architects Planners and Engineers v Ocean Front Pte Ltd (1998) 14
    Const LJ 139, CA (Sing) 94
Rae v Strathclyde Joint Police Board 1999 GWD 12-571 208
Ramsay v Mackay (1890) 18 R 130 245
Ready Mixed Concrete (South East) Ltd v Minister of Pensions and
    National Insurance [1968] 2 QB 497, [1968] 1 All ER 433 211
Reavis v Clan Line Steamers Ltd 1925 SC 725, 1925 SLT 386, OH 100,
                                                              104, 126
Reckitt and Colman Products Ltd v Borden Inc [1990] 1 All ER 873, HL: 27
Reeman v Department of Transport [1997] 2 Lloyd's Rep 648, CA 82
Reid v Edinburgh Acoustics Ltd (No 2) 1995 SCLR 791n, 1995 SLT 982,
    OH 156
Reid v Mitchell (1885) 12 R 1129 12
Renfrew Golf Club v Ravenstone Securities Ltd 1984 SLT 170, OH 283
Revill v Newberry [1996] QB 567, [1996] 1 All ER 291 20
Rich (Marc) & Co AG v Bishop Rock Marine Co Ltd, The Nicholas H
    [1994] 3 All ER 686, [1994] 1 WLR 1071, CA 83
Rich (Marc) & Co AG v Bishop Rock Marine Co Ltd, The Nicholas H
    [1996] AC 211, [1995] 3 All ER 307, HL 64, 65
Richardson v Pitt-Stanley [1995] QB 123, [1995] 1 All ER 460, CA 210
Richardson v Wilson (1879) 7 R 237, 17 SLR 122 257
Robbie v Graham and Sibbald 1989 SCLR 578, 1989 SLT 870, OH 84
Robertson v British Bakeries Ltd 1991 SLT 434, 1991 SCLR 450 281
Robertson v Fleming (1861) 23 D (HL) 8, 4 Macq 167 .... 153, 154
Robertson v Forth Road Bridge Joint Board 1995 SC 364, 1996 SLT 263: 71, 74
Robertson v J Sidney Smith 1999 GWD 4-214 236
Robertson v Turnbull 1982 SC (HL) 1, 1982 SLT 96 224
Robertson v Watt & Co (4 July 1995, unreported) 155
Roe v Minister of Health [1954] 2 QB 66, [1954] 2 All ER 131, CA ... 115, 165
Rome v Watson (1898) 25 R 733, 5 SLT 377 255
Rondel v Worsley [1969] 1 AC 191, [1967] 3 All ER 993, HL 155
Rookes v Barnard [1964] AC 1129, [1964] 1 All ER 367, HL 43, 44, 48
Rorrison v West Lothian College (1999, unreported), OH 208
Rose v Plenty [1975] ICR 430, [1976] 1 All ER 97, CA 214, 215
Ross v Bryce 1972 SLT (Sh Ct) 76 15
Rossleigh Ltd v Leader Cars Ltd 1987 SLT 355, OH 37

PAGE

Roxburgh v Seven Seas Engineering Ltd 1980 SLT (Notes) 49, OH 31
Rylands v Fletcher (1868) LR 3 HL 330 178

S v Newham London Borough Council [1998] 1 FLR 1061, [1998] 3
   FCR 277, CA 257
Sabri-Tabrizi v Lothian Health Board 1998 SC 373, 1998 SLT 607 ... 138, 141
Saeed v Waheed 1996 SLT (Sh Ct) 39, 1995 SCLR 504 .... 21, 78
Saif Ali v Sydney Mitchell & Co [1980] AC 198, [1978] 3 All ER 1033,
   HL 155, 156
Sayers v Harlow Urban District Council [1958] 2 All ER 342, [1958] 1
   WLR 623, CA 137
Scala Ballroom (Wolverhampton) Ltd v Ratcliffe [1958] 3 All ER 220,
   [1958] 1 WLR 1057, CA 47
Scott v Glasgow City Council 1997 Hous LR 107, Sh Ct 191
Scott v Lothian Regional Council 1999 Rep LR 15 152
Scott Lithgow Ltd v GEC Electrical Products Ltd 1989 SC 412, 1992
   SLT 244, OH 91, 92
Scottish Milk Marketing Board v Dryborough & Co Ltd 1985 SLT 253,
   OH 28
Seager v Copydex Ltd [1967] 2 All ER 415, [1967] 1 WLR 923, CA 32
Shell UK Ltd v McGillivray 1991 SLT 667 23
Short v J & W Henderson Ltd 1946 SC (HL) 24, 1946 SLT 230 212
Sidaway v Bethlem Royal Hospital Board of Governors [1985] AC 871,
   [1985] 1 All ER 643, HL 13, 151
Sim v Stretch [1936] 2 All ER 1237, HL 246
Simaan General Contracting Co v Pilkington Glass Ltd (No 2) [1988] QB
   758, [1988] 1 All ER 791, CA 94
Simmers v Morton (1900) 8 SLT 285, OH 248
Skerries Salmon Ltd v The Braer Corpn 1999 GWD 1-63 102
Smart v HM Advocate 1975 JC 30, 1975 SLT 65 12
Smith v Carter 1994 SCLR 539, 1995 SLT 295, OH 83
Smith v Crossley Bros Ltd (1971) 95 So Jo 655, CA 217
Smith v Duncan Stewart & Co Ltd (No 2) 1961 SC 91, 1961 SLT 67 ... 244
Smith v Eric S Bush and Harris v Wyre Forest District Council [1990] 1
   AC 831, [1989] 2 WLR 790, [1989] 2 All ER 514, HL 83–85
Smith v P & Co Bulk Shipping Ltd [1998] 2 Lloyd's Rep 81, QBD 123
Smith New Court Securities Ltd v Scrimgeour Vickers (Asset Management)
   Ltd [1997] AC 254, [1996] 4 All ER 769, HL 54, 269, 270
Smoldon v Whitworth [1997] PIQR P133, (1996) Times, 18 December, CA: 143
Sneesby v Goldings [1995] 2 EGLR 102, CA 152
South Australia Asset Management Corpn v York Montague Ltd [1997]
   AC 191, [1996] 3 All ER 365, HL 270
Spence v Crawford 1939 SC (HL) 52, 1939 SLT 305 51
Spring v Guardian Assurance plc [1995] 2 AC 296, [1994] 3 All ER 129,
   HL 87, 88, 257
Squires v Perth and Kinross District Council 1986 SLT 30 180
St George's Healthcare NHS Trust v S; R v Collins, ex parte S [1998] 3
   WLR 936, [1998] 3 All ER 673, CA 13
Standard Chartered Bank v Pakistan National Shipping Corpn [1995] 2
   Lloyd's Rep 365 271
Steel v Glasgow Iron and Steel Co Ltd 1944 SC 237, 1945 SLT 70 115
Steele v Scottish Daily Record and Sunday Mail Ltd 1970 SLT 53 260
Stein v Beaverbrook Newspapers Ltd 1968 SC 272, 1968 SLT 401 ... 247, 259

PAGE

Stephens v Avry [1988] Ch 449, [1988] 2 All ER 477   31
Stevenson v A & J Stephen (Builders) Ltd 1996 SLT 140, OH   99
Stevenson v British Coal Corpn 1989 SLT 136   276
Stevenson v Pontifex and Wood (1887) 15 R 125   280
Stevenson, Jordan and Harrison Ltd v MacDonald and Evans (1952) 69
    RPC 10, [1952] 1 TLR 101, CA   211
Stewart v Thain 1981 JC 13, 1981 SLT (Notes) 2   15
Stovin v Wise and Norfolk County Council [1996] AC 923, [1996] 3 All
    ER 801, HL   202
Stratford (JT) & Son Ltd v Lindley [1965] AC 269, [1964] 3 All ER 102,
    HL   38
Strathclyde Regional Council v Border Engineering Contractors Ltd 1997
    SCLR 100, 1998 SLT 175, OH   283
Sutherland v British Telecommunications plc 1989 SLT 531   247
Sutherland v North British Steel Group Ltd 1986 SLT (Sh Ct) 29   131
Sutherland v Stopes [1925] AC 47, HL........................   253
Swan v Andrew Minto & Son 1998 Rep LR 42   169
Swinney v Chief Constable of Northumbria Police [1997] QB 464, [1996]
    3 All ER 449, CA   109

Tait v Brown & McRae 1997 SLT (Sh Ct) 63   152
Taylor v Glasgow Corpn 1922 SC (HL) 1, 1921 2 SLT 254   189
Taylor v Glasgow District Council 1997 SC 183, 1997 SLT 537 ..... 213, 220
Taylor v Leslie 1998 SLT 1248, 1998 Rep LR 110, OH   145
Telnikoff v Matusevitch [1992] 2 AC 343, [1991] 4 All ER 817, HL   254
Thake v Maurice [1986] QB 644, [1984] 2 All ER 513   77
Thomson v British Steel Corpn 1977 SLT 26, OH   217
Titchener v British Railways Board 1984 SC (HL) 34, 1984 SLT 192 ...   141,
                                                                    190, 191
Torquay Hotel Co Ltd v Cousins [1969] 2 Ch 106, [1969] 1 All ER 522,
    CA   39-41
Turner v Metro-Goldwyn-Mayer Pictures Ltd [1950] 1 All ER 449, [1950]
    WN 83, HL.......................................   254
Twomax Ltd v Dickson, McFarlane and Robinson 1982 SC 113, 1983
    SLT 98, OH   82

Uddin v Associated Portland Cement Manufacturers Ltd [1965] 2 QB 582,
    [1965] 2 All ER 213, CA   145
Ultramares Corpn v Touche (1931) 255 NY 170 .... 57, 81
United Wholesale Grocers Ltd v Sher 1993 SLT 284, OH   212

Vasey v Surrey Free Inns plc [1996] PIQR P373, CA   217
Verity v Lloyds Bank plc [1996] Fam Law 213   88
Vernon v Bosley (No 1 [1997] 1 All ER 577   75
Videan v British Transport Commission [1963] 2 QB 650, [1963] 3 WLR
    374, CA   115

Waddell v British Broadcasting Corpn 1973 SLT 246   247
Walker v Northumberland County Council [1995] 1 All ER 737, [1995]
    IRLR 35, CA   208
Walker (John) & Sons Ltd v Douglas Laing & Co 1993 SLT 156, OH ...   29
Walker (John) & Sons Ltd v Douglas McGibbon & Co Ltd 1972 SLT 128,
    OH   29

PAGE

Walker (John) & Sons Ltd v Henry Ost & Co Ltd [1970] 2 All ER 106,
[1971] 1 WLR 917 29

Wallace v City of Glasgow District Council 1985 SLT 23 188

Ward v Scotrail Railways Ltd 1999 SC 255 .... 19, 208

Wardlaw v Bonnington Castings Ltd 1956 SC (HL) 266, 1956 SLT
135 132–134

Waste Systems International Inc v Eurocare Environmental Services Ltd
1999 SLT 198, OH 33

Watson v Duncan (1890) 17 R 404 247

Watson v Fram Reinforced Concrete Co (Scotland) Ltd and Winget Ltd
1960 SC (HL) 92, 1960 SLT 321 128

Watson v McEwan (1905) 7 F (HL) 109 255

Watt v Hertfordshire County Council [1954] 2 All ER 368, [1954] 1 WLR
208, CA 122

Watt v Jamieson 1954 SC 56 182

Watt v Thomson (1870) 8 M (HL) 77 255

Waugh v James K Allan Ltd 1964 SC (HL) 102, 1964 SLT 269 112

Webster v Lord Advocate 1985 SC 173, 1985 SLT 361 183

Weir v J M Hodge & Son 1990 SLT 266 154

Weir v National Westminster Bank plc 1993 SC 515, 1994 SLT 1251 .. 88, 149

Weir v Wyper 1992 SCLR 483, 1992 SLT 579, OH 145

Wells v Wells [1998] 3 All ER 481, [1998] 3 WLR 329, HL 274, 275

Western Bank of Scotland v Addie [1867] 5 M (HL) 80 52

Wheeler v J J Saunders Ltd [1995] 2 All ER 697, [1995] 3 WLR 466, CA: 183

Wheeler v New Merton Board Mills Ltd [1933] 2 KB 669, CA 198

White v Chief Constable of the South Yorkshire Police [1999] 1 All ER 1: 71, 75

White v Inveresk Paper Co Ltd 1987 SC 143, 1988 SLT 2, OH 281

White v Jones [1995] 2 AC 207, [1995] 1 All ER 691, HL 154, 155, 270

Whitefield v Barton 1987 SCLR 259, Sh Ct 120

Whitehouse v Jordan [1981] 1 All ER 267, [1981] 1 WLR 246, HL 151

Whyte v Walker 1983 SLT 441, OH 285

Wilkinson v Downtown [1897] 2 QB 57 51

Will v Sneddon, Campbell and Munro 1931 SC 164, 1931 SLT 125 245

Williams v Hemphill (A & W) Ltd 1966 SC (HL) 31, 1966 SLT 33 215

Williams v Natural Health Foods Ltd [1998] 2 All ER 577, HL 87, 88

Williamson v Umphray and Robertson (1890) 17 R 905, 27 SLR 742 257

Wilsher v Essex Area Health Authority [1988] AC 1074, [1988] All ER
871, HL 135

Wilson v National Coal Board 1981 SC (HL) 9, 1981 SLT 67 277

Winans v Macrae (1885) 12 R 1051 21

Winnick v Dick 1984 SC 48, 1984 SLT 185 141

Winter v News Scotland Ltd 1991 SLT 828 248

Wooldridge v Sumner [1963] 2 QB 43, [1962] 2 All ER 978, CA 143

Wotherspoon v Strathclyde Regional Council 1992 SCLR 806, 1992 SLT
1090 231

Wragg v D C Thomson & Co Ltd 1909 2 SLT 315 .... 249, 251

Wright v British Railways Board [1983] 2 AC 733, [1983] 2 All ER 698,
HL 272

X (minors) v Bedfordshire County Council [1995] 2 AC 633, [1995] 3 All
ER 353, HL 197,
199–201

X v Y [1988] 2 All ER 648, [1988] RPC 379 33

PAGE

Yewans v Nokes (1880) 6 QBD 530   210
Young v Rankin 1934 SC 499, 1934 SLT 445   223
Youssoupoff v Metro-Goldwyn-Mayer Pictures Ltd (1934) 50 TLR 581,
    CA   246
Yukong Line Ltd of Korea v Rendsburg Investments Corpn of Liberia (No
    2) [1998] 1 WLR 294, [1998] 4 All ER 82, QBD   50

List of abbreviations

AC	Law Reports, Appeal Cases (House of Lords and Privy Council) 1890–
All ER	All England Law Reports 1936–
App Cas	Law Reports, Appeal Cases (House of Lords) 1875–90
CA	Court of Appeal
Ch	Law Reports, Chancery Division 1890–
D	Dunlop's Session Cases 1838–62
ECHR	European Court of Human Rights
ECJ	European Court of Justice
Exch	Exchequer Reports 1847–56
F	Fraser's Session Cases 1898–1906
FC	Faculty Collection (Court of Session) 1752–1825
FSR	Fleet Street Reports 1963–
GWD	Green's Weekly Digest 1986–
HL	House of Lords
Hous LR	Housing Law Reports
Hume	Hume's Decisions (Court of Session) 1781–1822
ICR	Industrial Cases Reports 1972–
IRLR	Industrial Relations Law Reports 1972–
JC	Justiciary Cases 1917–
KB	Law Reports, King's Bench Division 1901–52
LR	Law Reports
M	Macpherson's Session Cases 1862–73
M & W	Meeson & Welsby 1836–47
Macq	Macqueen's House of Lords Reports 1851–65
Med LR	Medical Law Reports
NY	New York Court of Appeals Reports 1847–1955
OH	Outer House
PC	Judicial Committee of the Privy Council
QB	Law Reports, Queen's Bench Division 1891–1901, 1952–
QBD	Law Reports, Queen's Bench Division 1875–90
R	Rettie's Session Cases 1873–98
RPC	Reports of Patents, Designs and Trade Marks Cases 1884–

S	P Shaw's Session Cases 1821–38
SC	Session Cases 1907–
SC (HL)	House of Lords Cases in Session Cases 1907–
SCLR	Scottish Civil Law Reports 1987–
SJ	Scottish Jurist 1829–73
SLR	Scottish Law Reporter 1865–1925
SLT	Scots Law Times 1893–1908, and 1909–
SLT (Notes)	Notes of Recent Decisions in Scots Law Times 1946–81
SLT (Sh Ct)	Sheriff Court Reports in Scots Law Times 1893–
Sh	P Shaw's Scotch Appeals (House of Lords) 1821–26
Sh Ct Rep	Sheriff Court Reports in Scottish Law Review
So Jo	Solicitor's Journal 1856–
TLR	Times Law Reports 1884–
WLR	Weekly Law Reports 1953–
WN	Law Reports, Weekly Notes 1866–1952

Introduction

The essence of the modern Scots law of delict is the obligation of a person to compensate another who has suffered loss as a result of the wrongful actions of that person. This obligation to pay compensation is called reparation. The obligation to make reparation when loss has been suffered as a result of a person's wrongful actions is obediential; it arises *ex lege* regardless of the will of the wrongdoer. In this respect, delictual obligations differ from contractual obligations which arise as a result of the agreement of the parties to a contract. However, the delictual obligation is similar to the obligation to make restitution when a person has been unjustifiably enriched by another, since the latter obligation also arises *ex lege*.

But unlike the obligation to make restitution, the delictual obligation to make reparation arises only when the loss has arisen as a result of the wrongful act of the person who caused the harm. It is only when a person has been at fault that the obligation to make reparation arises. In Scots law we use the term '*culpa*' to describe fault. *Culpa* covers both intentional and unintentional conduct which causes loss to another, but before there is liability the law must regard the conduct as wrongous. This is encapsulated in the brocard *damnum injuria datum*, ie loss caused by wrongous conduct.

Some examples will make the point clearer. If A intentionally assaults B causing him harm, A is under a delictual obligation to compensate B for his injuries: A is guilty of *culpa* because he deliberately intended to harm B by assaulting him, which the law regards as a wrongous act. If A drives his car carelessly on a public highway, and as a result injures B, a pedestrian, then A is under a delictual obligation to compensate B for his injuries: A is guilty of *culpa* because of his careless driving, which the law regards as a wrongous act. Thus we can say that modern Scots law begins from the premise that there is an obediential obligation on a person to make reparation to another who has sustained harm or loss as a result of the *culpa* or fault of the wrongdoer, ie the wrongdoer's intentional or unintentional, but careless, conduct, which caused the harm or loss.

1

It is, however, not the case that a person who suffers loss as a result of another's intentional or unintentional, but careless, conduct will always be entitled to reparation. The act which causes the harm or loss must be regarded by the law as wrongful (*injuria*). For policy reasons, certain acts are not regarded as wrongful in this sense. So for example, as we shall see,[1] A is free to undercut the prices of his competitor, B, even if B suffers economically; nor does it matter if A deliberately undercuts B's prices with the intention of putting B out of business. The reason for this is that in our society competition is to be encouraged even if persons suffer economically as a result. This is an example of *damnum absque injuria*, ie loss without wrongful conduct.

Before there is an obligation to make reparation, the victim must suffer harm or loss. But, in addition, this harm or loss must arise from an intrusion by the wrongdoer on a right or interest of the victim which is recognised by the law as reparable. One of the fascinating aspects of the law of delict is to see when the courts are prepared to recognise interests as reparable and when they are not.

So, for example, the law has long recognised as reparable a person's right to physical integrity so that if there is an intrusion on that right as a result of culpable conduct, the wrongdoer must make compensation for pain and suffering (solatium) and any economic loss arising from the injuries sustained, for example, loss of earning capacity. But the Scots law of delict has, hitherto, not recognised as a reparable interest a person's privacy and protection of that interest is likely to be achieved only by legislation.[2]

An area which has caused controversy is whether the law should recognise as a reparable interest economic loss sustained by a person where the economic loss does not derive from injury to that person's body or damage to his property.[3] So, for example, if A carelessly damages an electric cable owned by B with the result that there is a loss of power to C's factory, should C be able to obtain compensation for his loss of production (pure economic loss) if the power cut did not cause any physical damage to the machinery in his factory? B, of course, can seek reparation from A in respect of the physical damage to B's cable.

Scottish lawyers maintain that Scots law is based on principle rather than remedies. It is probably true to argue that the modern

1 Page 35 below.
2 See 'Infringment of Liberty' (Lord Chancellor's Dept, Scottish Office, July 1993). It remains to be seen whether the courts will recognise a need to protect privacy as a consequence of the Human Rights Act 1998.
3 This matter is discussed at length in Chapter 4.

Scots law of delict is based on the general principle of an obediential, *ex lege* obligation to make reparation for loss sustained as a result of conduct which constitutes *culpa*. This, however, was not always the case and is, indeed, a comparatively recent development. In medieval times, before there was a centralised system for the prosecution of criminal offences, there was a close relationship between what would now be considered delictual actions and the enforcement of the criminal law. What we discover is that there were specific remedies to deal with particular situations which were common in those turbulent times. Stair lists the following:[1]

'besides those of a special name and nature, which are chiefly these, assythment, extortion, circumvention, spuilzie, intrusion, ejection, molestation, breach of arrestment, deforcement, contravention, forgery, which comes in more properly in the process of improbation'.

Three of these deserve further consideration to illustrate the close relationship which existed at that time between delictual or quasi-delictual liability and the enforcement of the criminal law.

Assythment was concerned with the regulation of acts which caused death and was an attempt to avoid blood feuds. The remedy of assythment was an action for a sum of money

'to be payit be the committaris of slaughter, to the kin, bairnis and friends of any person that is slane . . . gevin to thame in contentatioun of the hurt, damnage and skcith sustenit be thane throw the wanting of the person who is slane, and for the skaith incurrit be thame thairthrow, and for the pacifying of their rancor'.[2]

Several features of the action should be noted. There had to be a crime which caused death or physical injury to the victim. The action could be brought by any person, however remote, who was a relative of the deceased or injured person. The damages depended on the wrongdoer's means, ie they were not simply compensatory, and, finally, no assythment was due if the wrongdoer was executed. Assythment arose *either* if the wrongdoer was convicted and because of his position received a lesser penalty than was due *or* if there was no conviction and the family of the deceased issued a document known as a letter of slains acknowledging receipt of assythment and petitioning the Crown not to proceed with a prosecution. The latter situation was more important because it short circuited the need for a criminal trial. With the establishment of a centralised system of public prosecution it became contrary to public policy that the victim or his

1 *Institutions* IX, 5, 6.
2 Balfour *Practicks* p 516.

family should be able to circumvent the normal prosecution process by issuing letters of slains. In practice, actions for assythment died out though they were still theoretically possible if the wrongdoer had been prosecuted but had not suffered the due pains of the law. At the same time, the common law developed an action under which the spouse and ascendants and descendants of a person who had been killed as a result of the defender's *culpa* could obtain reparation in respect of the death, ie they could bring an action in delict.

An attempt to revive an action of assythment was made in *McKendrick v Sinclair*.[1] A workman was killed by an electric shock allegedly due to the negligence of his employer. He had financially supported his sister and two brothers. They could not bring an action in delict because at common law brothers and sisters of the deceased had no title to sue.[2] However, the Lord Advocate was not prepared to prosecute the defender or to concur if the relatives had sought a private prosecution. The old practice of letters of slains was inappropriate as the employer denied liability for culpable homicide. Accordingly, assythment would only have been available on the old authorities if there had been a conviction. As this was not the case, the action failed since it did not fall within the recognised parameters of the remedy.[3] Lord Simon of Glaisdale was, however, prepared to dismiss the action on a more radical ground: that in spite of being a common law remedy assythment had fallen into desuetude, ie had become absolescent:

'This Brunnhilde [assythment] would awake in our uncongenial modern Niebelheim. This Rip van Winkle would find *Eisten*'s case firmly embodied in the law, that private prosecutions are extinct, that capital punishment for homicide has been abolished, and that damages are related to loss to the pursuer and not to the means of the defender. Even if this Sleeping Beauty were so attractive as to tempt your Lordships to favour her with your kisses she could not live happily ever after'.[4]

Assythment was finally laid to rest when it was abolished by section 8 of the Damages (Scotland) Act 1976 which extended title to sue in respect of the death of a relative to include the deceased's brothers and sisters[5] thus closing the lacuna revealed in the *McKendrick* case.

1 1972 SC (HL) 25, 1972 SLT 110.
2 *Eisten v North British Railway Co* (1870) 8 M 980.
3 *McKendrick v Sinclair* 1972 SLT 110 at 113 per Lord Reid and at 120 per Lord Kilbrandon, 1972 SC (HL) 25.
4 1972 SLT 110 at 117.
5 For discussion of the right to sue in respect of the death of a relative, see Chapter 13.

The second old remedy we should consider is contravention of lawburrows. This was a method of primitive law enforcement in the absence of an effective police force and system of public prosecution of criminal offences. If a person had reasonable grounds to believe that he or his family or their property was in danger from another person, he could apply to a court to have that person find caution (ie to lodge a sum of money in court) not to harm him or his family or their property. This was known as lawburrows. In other words, the defender was ordered not to molest the pursuer or the family or their property on pain of losing caution ie the money lodged in court. If the defender contravened the non-molestation order, he could be sued in an action of contravention of lawburrows for forfeiture of the caution.[1] With the advent of effective law enforcement agencies, the use of lawburrows declined, though there is no doubt that the action is still technically competent.[2]

Finally there was the action of spuilzie. This action arose when the defender interfered with the possession of another's moveable property, for example, stole cattle or sheep. The pursuer was the owner of the property.[3] The action was to have the property returned, or its value. But the quasi-criminal nature of the action is illustrated by the fact that the pursuer was entitled to violent profits, ie all the profits which the pursuer might have made from the property while in possession of the defender. In many situations, spuilzie has been overtaken by the general principle of liability for *culpa*.[4]

We have seen, then, how these specific remedies had important quasi-criminal aspects. While it is clear that lawburrows and spuilzie remain, theoretically at least, part of Scots law, in practice they have largely been overtaken by the development of effective law enforcement agencies and the general principle of liability to make reparation for loss caused as a result of the defender's *culpa*. Stair laid the basis for the general principle of delictual liability when he recognised that to cause damage by delinquence gave rise to an obediential obligation to make reparation for the damage caused: *damnum injuria datum*. This was a general innominate remedy, based on the defender's *culpa*, which included deliberate

1 Lawburrows Acts 1429 and 1581.
2 On lawburrows generally see 13 *Stair Memorial Encyclopaedia* paras 901–926; *Morrow v Neil* 1975 SLT (Sh Ct) 65; *Liddle v Morton* 1996 SLT 1143.
3 Though there is a dictum of the sheriff in *FC Finance Ltd v Brown & Son* 1969 SLT (Sh Ct) 41 that lawful *possession* of property was sufficient.
4 See, for example, *Harris v Abbey National plc* 1997 SCLR 359 (liability based on gratuitous deposit of property rather than spuilzie).

as well as careless conduct. Stair treated the nominate Scottish remedies as simply aspects of the general obligation to make reparation for loss caused by *culpa*.[1] This general obligation was accepted by the later institutional writers.[2] In attempting this synthesis, reliance was, of course, placed on Roman law and in particular liability under the Lex Aquilia which included liability for unintentional, but careless, conduct.

Although the modern Scots law of delict can be traced back to the institutional writers, their treatment is not extensive. Instead, the principles of the law of delict are largely the creation of the courts. The judges have had to develop the law to take account of the increase of potential injury to persons and damage to property created by industrialisation, mass production and distribution of goods, easier access to information, and the motor car. At the same time, they have also appreciated that there must be limits on a person's liability, particularly for unintentional conduct, if that person is to continue to engage in conduct which is socially and economically desirable, even if it is potentially harmful. The traditional Scots law solution has been to restrict liability by insisting that it is only triggered by the defender's fault and by refusing to recognise certain kinds of harm as reparable interests. This book is largely concerned with the rules of common law and statute which have developed to achieve this balance. However, in some areas it has been considered socially and economically desirable that persons should recover compensation for physical injury or damage to property without the need to establish fault on the part of the defender. While the concept of *culpa* has proved flexible enough to create liability where the degree of *moral* blame on the part of the defender is small,[3] nevertheless, some degree of fault is required.[4] Accordingly, legislation has been necessary to introduce into Scots law what is known as strict liability, ie where a person can be liable in delict for breach of duties imposed by a statute without the need for the person who suffers the injury or damage to establish fault. In a modern context, it is therefore important to discuss the principles of strict liability in relation to the breach of

1 *Stair* I, 9, 2.
2 See, for example, Erskine *Institute* III, 1.
3 Particularly as the criterion for fault in the context of unintentional conduct is the failure to reach the standards of the reasonable person, as opposed to the standards which the particular defender could morally be expected to reach: see Chapter 3 below.
4 But, for example, where a person has used his property in a potentially very dangerous way, the degree of fault is small: *Kerr v Earl of Orkney* (1857) 20 D 298, 30 SJ 158: see pp 177 ff below.

statutory duties imposed by some, at least, of the most important statutes.

Nevertheless, it is the author's primary intention to concentrate on the common law principles which underlie delictual liability for *culpa*, ie intentional and unintentional wrongdoing. The book begins with a study of delictual liability for intentionally harmful conduct; the second part contains an analysis of the general principles of liability for unintentional, but careless, conduct; the third part considers delictual liability in the context of some important social and economic relationships. Included in this part is a chapter on defamation and verbal injury where different principles apply. The book ends with a short chapter on damages.

Part I

INTENTIONAL DELICTS

Chapter 1. Intentional delicts in respect of persons and
          property   11

Chapter 2. The economic delicts and fraud   35

CHAPTER 1

Intentional delicts in respect of persons and property

INTRODUCTION

As we have seen,[1] *culpa* includes (a) deliberate conduct intended to harm the victim or the victim's property and (b) unintentional, but careless, conduct, which has harmed the victim or the victim's property. In the case of unintentional conduct, the range of victims is prima facie indeterminate, ie it could potentially include any person who has been harmed by the conduct. Because of this, the law has had to invent devices for limiting the number of persons who are entitled to sue in delict if they suffer loss or harm as a result of another's careless conduct. The most important of these devices is the concept of a duty of care:[2] it is only a person to whom the defender owes a duty of care who can sue in delict for loss arising from the defender's careless conduct.[3]

However, where an act is done deliberately to harm a particular person, there is not the same degree of difficulty, since the potential pursuer is normally determinate:[4] the pursuer is the person whom the defender *intended* to harm by his conduct and there is no need to invoke the concept of a duty of care. Intentional delicts in relation to persons and property are discussed in this chapter.

---

1 Page 1 above.
2 There are other devices such as remoteness of injury and causation: see pp 126 ff and Chapter 6 below.
3 The duty of care is discussed at Chapter 3 below.
4 There can be cases where this might not be so: A may intend to harm B by blowing up B's house but injure C instead; while it is thought that A will be liable to C, such cases are rare in practice.

B. INTENTIONAL DELICTS RELATING TO PERSONS

(1) Assault

'Everyone who lives under the protection of the law has an absolute right to the safety of his person; and wherever this right is invaded there is in Civil law a provision for redress of injury, as well as in penal law a punishment for the crime.'[1] A physical assault is a common law crime provided there is the necessary evil intent on the part of the perpetrator (*dolus*).[2] Assault also constitutes a delict. But even though an assault is not criminal because of the absence of *evil* intent, it is still an actionable delict, provided the defender intended to invade the physical integrity of the pursuer. So where A playfully attacked B in order to make B engage in sport, it nevertheless constituted an actionable wrong even although it was done 'for a lark'.[3] If the assault does not result in serious physical injuries, the damages awarded will not be substantial, in spite of the insult caused to the victim.[4]

If, however, the 'victim' consents to the act, it does not amount to an assault for the purposes of delict,[5] since the essence of the delict is *non-consensual* invasion of bodily integrity. Where this principle is important is in respect of medical procedures. If a doctor or dentist carries out a medical procedure on an adult[6] without the patient's consent, then the doctor or dentist is liable to make reparation.[7] Although this will usually not be a crime because of the absence of evil intent on the part of the doctor or dentist, it is still a delict. The patient can obtain reparation not only for any resulting patrimonial loss but also for *contumelia*, ie the insult suffered as a result of the non-consensual invasion of bodily

1 Bell *Principles* para 2028.
2 See R A A McCall Smith and D Sheldon *Scots Criminal Law* (2nd edn, 1997) p 36.
3 *Reid v Mitchell* (1885) 12 R 1129.
4 See, for example, *Downie v Chief Constable of Strathclyde Police* 1997 SCLR 603 (the pursuer was awarded £1,500 in respect of an assault by two policemen; the victim had recovered without the need of medical treatment).
5 In criminal law, if there is evil intent on the part of the accused, the consent of the 'victim' is irrelevant: a person cannot consent to a crime: *Smart v HM Advocate* 1975 JC 30, 1975 SLT 65.
6 A person under the age of 16 will have legal capacity to consent if the doctor or dentist is of the view that the young person is capable of understanding the nature and probable consequences of the medical treatment or procedure: Age of Legal Capacity (Scotland) Act 1991, s 2(4).
7 However, in an emergency, if the patient is, for example, unconscious, a doctor may proceed without the patient's consent if it is *necessary* for the patient's well-being to do so.

integrity. The fact that the procedure was carried out for the patient's benefit is irrelevant.[1]

The question then arises as to when the patient's consent is valid in order that the doctor or dentist concerned can avoid potential delictual liability. It is clear that a patient must be given sufficient information upon which to give consent. All medical and dental procedures involve a risk to the patient even if *properly* carried out. This could be, for example, side effects of a drug or an operation or other medical procedure. In the United States,[2] there has evolved a doctrine known as 'informed consent'. Under this doctrine, if the patient is not informed of all the risks inherent in the proposed medical procedure which a reasonable *patient* should know, then the patient's apparent consent is vitiated and the doctor or dentist can be sued for assault.

An attempt to introduce this doctrine into English law was rejected by a majority of the House of Lords in *Sidaway v Board of Governors of the Bethlem Royal Hospital*.[3] Instead, it was held that a doctor need only disclose to a patient the risks inherent in a medical procedure which are regarded by *a responsible body of medical opinion* as proper to disclose. Two important points follow. First, provided the doctor or dentist has disclosed those risks which a responsible body of medical or dental opinion would disclose, the patient's consent is valid and the patient cannot sue in assault where an injury is sustained, the risk of which it was *not* necessary to disclose. The injury must, of course, be inherent in the medical procedure when properly carried out; if the injury arose as a result of careless treatment, the patient can sue the doctor or dentist for breach of a duty of care since the patient has *not* consented to the risk of injury as a result of professional incompetence.[4] Second, if the doctor or dentist has not disclosed those risks which a responsible body of medical or dental opinion would disclose, then if the patient sustains *any* injury which is inherent in the medical procedure when properly carried out, the patient can sue the doctor or dentist; but it would appear from *Sidaway* that the patient sues for a breach by the doctor or dentist of the duty of care which they owe to their patients to disclose those risks inherent in the medical procedure which a responsible body of

1 'Even when his or her own life depends on receiving medical treatment, an adult of sound mind is entitled to refuse it': *St George's Healthcare NHS Trust v S; R v Collins, ex parte S* [1998] 3 WLR 936, [1998] 3 All ER 673, CA at 685 per Judge LJ.
2 *Canterbury v Spence* (1972) 464 F 2d 772.
3 [1985] AC 871, [1985] 1 All ER 643, HL (Lord Scarman dissenting).
4 On professional delictual liability, see Chapter 7 below.

medical or dental opinion would disclose, ie for an unintentional wrong and not an assault. In other words, the general principles of liability for *culpa* rather than assault apply to this particular issue. While *Sidaway* is an English case, it has been followed in Scotland.[1]

In practice, most patients simply sign a general consent form in respect of risks inherent in treatment. Nor is it clear when a reasonably prudent doctor should inform a patient of a particular risk inherent in a medical procedure. In *Sidaway* the risk of injury was slight, less than 1 per cent, but if it materialised the injury could have been severe. Yet the House of Lords took the view that since a majority of responsible medical practitioners would not have informed the patient of such a risk, no delictual liability was incurred.[2]

As we have seen, consent of the victim prevents delictual liability for assault from arising. This explains why there is no liability for assault in sports involving physical contact: boxing, rugby, soccer etc.[3] But the players give consent only to the physical contact inherent in the sport, so that there will be liability if injury is sustained as a result of conduct outwith the rules of the sport, if, for example, a rugby player punches, as opposed to tackles, an opponent. While an assault usually takes the form of physical contact this is not strictly necessary; thus to spit at a person or shake a fist in a threatening manner is an assault.

There is a complete defence to an action of assault if it was the result of an unavoidable accident or carried out in self-defence. If the assault took place as a result of the pursuer's provocation, the damages can be reduced. 'No verbal provocation whatever can justify a blow ... But ... verbal provocation is a good ground for mitigating damages ...'[4] The rationale is that since reparation for intentional wrong is based on *culpa*, the pursuer must come to the

---

1 *Moyes v Lothian Health Board* 1990 SLT 444. There it was observed by the Lord Ordinary (Caplan) at 447 that provided there was a failure to warn of risks, which amounted to a breach of a duty to care (ie that a responsible body of medical opinion would have disclosed some risks) it did not matter that the injury sustained by the pursuer was one the risk of which it was not necessary to disclose. However, the patient must show that he would not have agreed to the operation if the risks which should have been disclosed, had been disclosed.

2 It has been held that a significant risk of the order of 10 per cent should be disclosed, while a risk of 0.2 per cent need not be disclosed. See *Pearce v United Bristol NHS Trust* [1999] PIQR 53.

3 Cf non-physical sports, for example, golf: *Lewis v Buckpool Golf Club* 1993 SLT (Sh Ct) 43.

4 *Anderson v Marshall* (1835) 13 S 1130 at 1131 per the Lord President (Hope).

court with clean hands; if the pursuer's hands are not clean, the pursuer's damages can be reduced.[1]

One group of persons in Scotland remains without a remedy if assaulted. These are children who have been physically chastised by their parents. The force used by a parent when physically chastising a child must be reasonable but it is irrelevant that a parent loses his or her temper at the time.[2] Parents can delegate the right physically to chastise their children to persons who have *de facto* care of the child.[3] The Scottish Law Commission has recommended that parents should not have a defence to an action of assault on their children on the grounds that they were disciplining the child, if the child was struck with a stick, belt or other object, or in such a way as to cause or risk causing, pain or discomfort lasting more than a very short time.[4] It is also recommended that a person who has care and control of the child should have no greater right to discipline a child than a parent.[5] Moreover, in *A v United Kingdom*,[6] the European Court of Human Rights held that the parent's 'reasonable chastisement' defence was a breach of the child's right under article 3 to be protected from 'inhuman or degrading treatment or punishment': in this case a caning. It remains to be seen whether this decision will encourage the enactment of the Scottish Law Commission's recommendations.

Where an assault constitutes a crime, the victim may receive compensation under the Criminal Injuries Compensation Scheme.

(2) Seduction and entrapment

Closely related to assault is the delict of seduction. In a case of assault the essence of the delict is the invasion of a person's bodily integrity without consent. Thus, for example, rape is actionable as an assault because sexual intercourse was obtained without the woman's consent. Conversely, if a woman consents to sexual intercourse, no assault is committed as she has consented. In the case of seduction, the woman gives consent to sexual intercourse, but her consent is vitiated because it was obtained by the man as a

---

1 *Ross v Bryce* 1972 SLT (Sh Ct) 76.
2 *B v Harris* 1989 SCLR 644, 1990 SLT 208 (mother strapped her 7-year-old child who had called the mother 'a fucking bastard'). Cf *Cowie v Tudhope* 1987 GWD 12-395 (father hit 15-year-old son with the leg of a table).
3 *Stewart v Thain* 1981 JC 13, 1981 SLT (Notes) 2.
4 Report on Family Law (SLC no 135) rec 11(a).
5 Report on Family Law (SLC no 135) rec 11(b).
6 [1998] 2 FLR 959, (1998) Times, 1 October, ECHR.

result of deception or abuse of position. In the leading case of *Murray v Fraser*,[1] a young girl who was naive in sexual matters allowed a trusted member of the family to have sexual intercourse with her on his assurance that nothing would happen to her; in fact she became pregnant. The defender was held liable in seduction because he had abused a position of trust and had taken advantage of the girl's innocence. A common example of deception was where a girl allowed a man to have sexual intercourse with her because he promised to marry her but had no intention to do so.[2]

Entrapment arises when a person has been fraudulently induced to enter into a marriage which is void. The most common example is when the defender purports to marry the pursuer, knowing that he is already married to another and has therefore fraudulently misrepresented that he was in a position validly to marry the pursuer.[3]

(3) Enticement

It is a delict for A to entice B to leave B's family without justification. The most obvious reason why A would wish to entice B away from B's family is for sexual purposes but it could, for example, arise if A wished B to join A's religious sect. The pursuers are B's family.[4] However, there is now no longer delictual liability if A induces B to leave his or her spouse.[5] A *husband* no longer has the right to sue his wife's paramour in damages;[6] these damages were awarded as solatium to the husband in respect of the unlawful sexual intercourse, ie his wife's adultery with the defender. It is, however, arguable that a husband can still sue a man for solatium if he raped the husband's wife; the wife, of course, would sue the rapist in assault.

---

1   1916 SC 623.
2   It is thought that an action in seduction would continue to arise in these circumstances in spite of s 1(1) of the Law Reform (Husband and Wife) Scotland Act 1984 which declares inter alia that a promise to marry does not create any rights or obligations; this is because the delict of seduction does not arise solely from the breach of promise.
3   See, for example, *Burke v Burke* 1983 SLT 331, OH.
4   It has, however, been held that parents cannot sue for the loss of society of a child where the child has been removed from the parents as a result of intervention by the police in the interests of the child: *McKeen v Chief Constable, Lothian and Borders Police* 1994 SLT 93, OH. If the removal is not justified, the *child* may have the right to sue for infringement of liberty.
5   Law Reform (Husband and Wife) (Scotland) Act 1984, s 2(2).
6   Divorce (Scotland) Act 1976, s 10.

(4) Injuries to liberty

'Next to life is liberty; and the delinquence against it are restraint and constraint. And though liberty itself be inestimable, yet the damages sustained through these delinquencies are reparable'.[1] A slight infringement of liberty is prima facie actionable: so, for example, where a lady was alleged to have been detained against her will for a quarter of an hour by the manager of a hydropathic establishment, her action in delict was held to be relevant.[2] Thus, as a general principle, no one can be detained against his or her will; if this occurs, there is liability in delict. The loss suffered is both the loss of liberty and the affront caused to the pursuer. However, detention can be justified at common law if, for example, a store detective arrests a person suspected of shoplifting and detains that person for a reasonable time until the police arrive.[3]

In practice, cases of wrongful detention by ordinary members of the public are rare; instead, they arise when the person has been held under what purports to be lawful legal process. Even so, an action in delict may still arise, but there are formidable hurdles to success. This can be illustrated by *Henderson v Moodie*.[4] Medical laboratory scientific officers (MLSOs) staged a 'work in' at a hospital laboratory. When they refused to leave, the police were summoned. When they still refused to leave, the police broke down the door and arrested the MLSOs. They were taken to a police station where they were cautioned and charged; they were then placed in cells for one or two hours while the particulars they had given the police were checked. However, one of the men was handcuffed and a woman was required to remove her brassiere while in the cells. In an action for wrongful arrest and detention, it

1 *Stair* I, 9, 4.
2 *Mackenzie v Cluny Hill Hydropathic Co* 1908 SC 200, 15 SLT 518. In the course of his judgment, Lord Low said: 'It is averred that the manager detained this lady for fifteen minutes . . . and refused to let her go until she made an apology. If that be true it was an outrage . . .' (1908 SC 200 at 206).
3 Where, as in the example, the arrest is made without a warrant, the defender must establish that the suspicions were justified: *Pringle v Bremner and Stirling* (1867) 5 M (HL) 55; *Dahl v Chief Constable, Central Scotland Police* 1983 SLT 420, OH. If an arrest is made under authority of a warrant, it is presumed that the detention was lawful and the onus rests on the pursuer to show that the detention was not justified.
4 1988 SCLR 77, sub nom *Henderson v Chief Constable, Fife Police* 1988 SLT 361, OH.

was conceded that the handcuffing was unjustified. The Lord Ordinary (Jauncey) held that the arrests were justified, that the police were entitled to take the MLSOs to the police station and that it was reasonable to detain them in the cells while the particulars were checked, as it was a small police station. However, although it was normal police practice to ask women to remove their brassieres while in custody to prevent them harming themselves, it was unjustified in this case as the woman had been co-operative, had made no attempt to escape and was not mentally unbalanced so as to cause harm to herself or others. The request that she remove the garment was unjustified and therefore constituted an interference with her liberty. It should be noticed, however, that the onus rests on the pursuer to prove that the exercise by the police of their discretion was neither reasonable nor necessary and accordingly unjustified.[1]

Where a person is wrongfully imprisoned by a court, superior court judges are immune from liability. Inferior judges, such as justices of the peace or magistrates can, however, be liable if the sentence is imposed maliciously and without probable cause.[2] If, for example, a magistrate lacks jurisdiction, he will be acting ultra vires, but there is no liability for a bona fide error in relation to statutory interpretation of his jurisdiction. Before he can succeed the pursuer must also prove that the magistrate was acting maliciously.[3] Where there has been a miscarriage of justice by the superior courts, the Secretary of State may make an *ex gratia* award of compensation to the victim.

In certain circumstances, statute provides for the lawful detention of an individual. The most important, perhaps, are the provisions which allow the compulsory detention of a person in a mental hospital. An application is made to a sheriff by a mental welfare officer or the patient's nearest relative[4] with the recommendation of two doctors, one of whom must be a psychiatrist, that the patient is suffering from a mental illness and is a danger to himself or others.[5] If the sheriff agrees that the statutory criteria are satisfied, an order is made for the compulsory detention of the patient in a mental hospital for a period of up to

---

1 Ie that the detention was effected maliciously and without probable cause.
2 Criminal Procedure (Scotland) Act 1995, s 170(1).
3 *McPhee v Macfarlane's Exr* 1933 SC 163, 1933 SLT 148.
4 For the list of nearest relatives, see the Mental Health (Scotland) Act 1984, ss 53–55; usually the nearest relative is the relative who is the highest on the list.
5 Mental Health (Scotland) Act 1984, s 18.

six months. The patient's nearest relative has the power to object to an application by a mental welfare officer. The detention can be renewed for further periods without recourse to the sheriff, but the patient has the right to appeal to a sheriff. The nearest relative can seek the discharge of the patient, and if it is refused, the nearest relative has the right to appeal to the sheriff for the patient's discharge.

(5) Harassment

Every individual has a right to be free from harassment.[1] Where a person pursues a course of conduct which amounts to harassment, the victim can bring a civil claim against him: this is known as an action of harassment.[2] Before the pursuer will succeed it must be established that the defender intended his behaviour to amount to harassment, or his behaviour occurred in such circumstances that a reasonable person would conclude that it amounted to harassment.[3] The course of conduct can include speech and must have occurred on at least two occasions.[4] If the action is successful, the court can award damages:[5] these can include compensation for anxiety and financial loss caused by the harassment.[6] The court can also grant interdict or a non-harassment order.[7] Breach of a non-harassment order is a criminal offence.[8] It is a defence to an action of harassment that the course of conduct was authorised by law or was pursued for the purpose of preventing or detecting crime or was reasonable in the particular circumstances of the case.[9] Harassment is *not* defined in the legislation but 'includes causing the person alarm or distress'.[10]

1 Protection from Harassment Act 1997, s 8(1). It is arguable that conduct which deliberately caused fear and alarm, even in the absence of physical injury, was delictual at common law: *Ward v Scotrail Railways Ltd* 1999 SC 255. Such conduct could certainly be controlled by an interdict (molestation) and, in theory, should have been sufficient cause for a claim in damages.
2 Protection from Harassment Act 1997, s 8(2).
3 PHA 1997, s 8(1)(a), (b).
4 PHA 1997, s 8(3).
5 PHA 1997, s 8(5)(a).
6 PHA 1997, s 8(6).
7 PHA 1997, s 8(5)(b). Although an interim interdict is competent, an interim non-harassment order is not: *Heenan v Dillon* 1999 Fam LR 62.
8 PHA 1997, s 9.
9 PHA 1997, s 8(4).
10 PHA 1997, s 8(3).

C. INTENTIONAL DELICTS RELATING TO PROPERTY

(1) Heritable property

(a) Trespass

It is often wrongly assumed that Scots law does not recognise the delict of trespass. Indeed, it has been judicially opined that the word 'trespasser' means nothing more in Scots law than 'a person who intrudes on the lands of another without that other's permission'.[1] However, as we shall see, a person who deliberately enters another's land may be interdicted from doing so again and is liable to pay damages if he has caused any damage to the property. Trespass is a *temporary* intrusion into property owned by another, without the permission of the owner: for example, playing football in the owner's field or taking a short cut through his garden. Because heritable property is owned *a coelo usque ad centrum* (from the heavens to the centre of the earth) trespass protects an owner's air space as well as his land and the ground below his property. Thus, for example, the owner of a house successfully obtained an interdict preventing the respondent's crane from sweeping over his property, when the respondent was building on adjacent land.[2] Because of this, statute provides that aircraft may fly over a person's land without liability for trespass.[3]

The primary remedy for trespass is interdict. No damages are available unless there has been actual damage to the property as a result of the intrusion. There is therefore no liability for damages in Scots law merely for entering another's property. But the proprietor is entitled to use self-help to remove a trespasser provided it is reasonable in the circumstances; for example, the owner could ask a trespasser playing football in his field to leave but not threaten him with violence if the trespasser refuses to do so.[4] Interdict is an equitable remedy and is not granted automatically merely on proof of an unauthorised entry onto land. Before an interdict will be granted, further intrusions must be likely and the intention of the

---

1   *Dumbreck v Robert Addie & Sons (Colleries) Ltd* 1928 SC 547 at 554 per the Lord President (Clyde), 1928 SLT 341.
2   *Brown v Lee Constructions Ltd* 1977 SLT (Notes) 61, OH.
3   Civil Aviation Act 1982, s 76.
4   If the self-help is excessive and results in injury to the trespasser, the owner can be liable for assault or negligence: *Revill v Newberry* [1996] QB 567; [1996] 1 All ER 291 (owner shot the trespasser!)

trespasser is important. Any potential damage to the land as a result of the trespass will also be a relevant consideration. In *Winans v Macrae*,[1] for example, a shooting tenant of a lease of 200,000 acres was, perhaps understandably, refused an interdict to prevent a cottar's pet lamb from entering the property.

In summary, apart from specific statutory offences, in Scots law trespass is not per se criminal, does not give rise to an action in damages unless actual damage has been done to the property and will only result in an interdict if likely to recur again and any potential damage is not *de minimis*. However, the landowner is allowed a reasonable degree of self-help to remove the trespasser.

In this section, trespass has been defined as a *temporary* intrusion on to land. If a person enters on to another's property with the intention of occupying it for an indefinite period, for example, a squatter, he does commit a criminal offence under the Trespass (Scotland) Act 1865. If the owner is not in possession at the time, the squatter is liable for the delict of intrusion; if the owner is in possession and has been wrongfully removed by the squatter, the squatter is liable for the delict of ejection. The rightful owner can seek summary ejection, violent profits[2] and compensation for actual losses incurred.

(b) Aemulatio vicini

When A owns land (X) which adjoins B's land (Y), A will be liable to B if he uses his land (X) in such a way that is detrimental to B's enjoyment of his land (Y). Before A is liable for using his land *in aemulationem vicini*, A must use his land with the predominant motive of harming B and not to further A's legitimate interests. If A's predominant motive is not to harm B, then A cannot be liable for this delict but A's conduct may amount to nuisance.[3]

An example of use of land *in aemulationem vicini* would be where A intercepted water flowing below his land, with the predominant purpose of preventing the water percolating on to his neighbour, B's, land.[4] However, when these facts were litigated in the English

---

1 (1885) 12 R 1051.
2 Violent profits are the greatest profits the owner could have made if he was in actual possession of the land. It is thought that this should have been the remedy awarded in *Saeed v Waheed* 1996 SLT (Sh Ct) 39, 1995 SCLR 504, rather than damages for negligence.
3 On nuisance, see pp 182 ff below.
4 See Kames *Principles of Equity* (4th edn, 1800) p 42.

case of *Bradford v Pickles*,[1] the House of Lords held that *aemulatio vicini* was not part of English law. The case is important because Lord Watson, the Scottish Lord of Appeal in Ordinary, stated obiter that *aemulatio vicini* was also not part of Scots law.[2] This obiter dictum was, of course, contrary to institutional authority. In *Campbell v Muir*[3] where the defender spitefully exercised his right to fish from a boat in a river in such a way that it prevented anglers on the opposite bank from being able to cast their rods, the Lord President (Dunedin) held that the pursuer would have been entitled to interdict because 'the defender was on the particular occasion acting *in aemulationem vicini* against his neighbour's right, and that that was a just ground for complaint'.[4] In *More v Boyle*[5] it was accepted by the sheriff that the doctrine of *aemulatio vicini* is still part of Scots law.

As we have seen, liability arises only if it can be shown that the defender acted with the predominant motive of harming the pursuer. It is, of course, difficult to establish malice, so an objective assessment must be made of the defender's conduct in order to infer malice. But unlike nuisance, which is usually concerned with a continuing wrong,[6] liability for use of land *in aemulationem vicini* can arise from a single act of the defender, provided the predominant motive of harm to the pursuer can be established.

(2) Moveable property

(a) Trespass

In *Leitch v Leydon*[7] the complainers sold soda water to their customers. Since the bottles were more expensive than the contents, it was a term of their contract with their customers that the complainers retained the ownership of the siphons which should be returned to them when the contents were used. Instead, some customers went to the respondent to have the bottles filled with *his* soda water. The House of Lords held that the complainers were not entitled to an interdict preventing the respondent from

1 [1895] AC 587, HL.
2 [1895] AC 587 at 597–598.
3 1908 SC 387, 15 SLT 737.
4 1908 SC 387 at 393.
5 1967 SLT (Sh Ct) 38.
6 See pp 182 ff below.
7 1931 SC (HL) 1.

filling their bottles with soda water. While the complainers might have an action for breach of contract against their customers, the respondent had not incurred any delictual liability in filling the bottles with soda water at the request of the complainers' customers who had lawful possession of the siphons.[1] In the course of his speech, Viscount Dunedin said that the concept of trespass to moveables 'in a Scottish lawyer's mouth is a perfectly unmeaning phrase'.[2]

Nevertheless, where there have been 'sit-ins' on board a ship[3] or offshore oil installations,[4] it has been held that the delict of trespass was committed even although neither the ship nor off-shore oil installations constitute heritable property. The Lord Ordinary (Dunpark) maintained that 'Scots law offers remedies for the unlawful *occupation* of property, be it heritable or moveable'.[5] It would appear, therefore, that where the trespass consists of the unlawful occupation of moveable property, for example, a car or caravan, a ship or oil installation, there is delictual liability even though the property concerned is technically moveable rather than heritable. Where the moveable property cannot be occupied, like the soda siphons in *Leitch v Leydon*,[6] merely to handle the property does not per se constitute the delict of trespass.

(b) Wrongful interference with moveable property

As we have seen, unless moveable property is actually occupied, the delict of trespass is not available to the owner in Scots law. This does not mean that the owner of a moveable is without legal redress if a person wrongfully interferes with the property. However, the owner's remedy may lie in areas of the law other than the law of delict. Consider the following examples:

(1) A owns a horse. B steals the horse. Under the law of property, A is entitled to sue B for the return of the horse, ie A can vindicate (claim ownership of) the horse. If B had sold the horse to C, a bona fide purchaser for value, A can still vindicate against C because a *vitium reale* attaches to the horse.

1 Delictual liability would, however, arise if the respondent had intended to 'pass off' the soda water as that of the complainer. On passing off, see p 27 below.
2 1931 SC (HL) 1 at 12.
3 *Phestos Shipping Co Ltd v Kurmiawan* 1983 SC 165, 1983 SLT 388.
4 *Shell UK Ltd v McGillivray* 1991 SLT 667.
5 *Phestos Shipping Co Ltd v Kurmiawan* 1983 SLT 388 at 391.
6 1931 SC (HL) 1.

(2) A owns a horse. B steals the horse and sells it to C. C slaughters the horse and boils it down to make glue. Under the law of property, the glue belongs to C. A can no longer vindicate, since the horse, ie A's property, no longer exists. What remedies are available to A? First, if the delict still exists, A could sue B for spuilzie.[1] Second, he may have a delictual action against C on the general principles of *culpa*. If C knew the horse belonged to A, then A can sue C for intentionally destroying the horse. But even if C did not know that the horse belonged to A, A may be able to sue C if, in the circumstances, C was at fault in going ahead in boiling down the horse without inquiring whether or not B was the animal's true owner. Thus, in *Faulds v Townsend*,[2] a thief stole a horse which he sold in the middle of the night to the defender, who turned the unfortunate animal into chemicals. Because of the circumstances of the sale and the fact that the horse was in good condition, the court held that the defender was under a duty to inquire as to the ownership of the horse; he had not done so and was therefore at fault, and the owner could sue for damages under the general principles of *culpa*.[3] Finally, even if fault could not be established, A may have an action in unjustified enrichment against C, in so far as C is *lucratus* as a result of his mistake as to the ownership of the horse.

(3) The modern equivalent of the horse, is, of course, the motor car. As a general rule, the same principles would apply if A's car was stolen. However, difficulties can arise where A is technically the owner of a car, for example, a finance company, which is being purchased by B, a hirer, on a contract of hire purchase; what is A's remedy if B sells the car in breach of the hire contract to C, a third party? These difficulties are illustrated by *FC Finance v Langtry Investment Co Ltd*.[4] FC Finance owned a motor car which was hired to Allan under a contract of hire purchase. In breach of the contract, Allan sold the car to McKay who traded as Medwin Motors. McKay sold the car on hire purchase to Kennedy. The hire purchase was financed by Langtry Investment Co and Kennedy paid the instalments. Part III of the Hire Purchase Act 1964 provides an exception to the *nemo dat quod non habet*

---

1 See p 5 above. For an attempt to revive the delict see *FC Finance Ltd v Brown & Son* 1969 SLT (Sh Ct) 41.
2 (1861) 23 D 437, 33 SJ 224.
3 Ie because of his careless conduct in not satisfying himself as to the true ownership of the horse.
4 1973 SLT (Sh Ct) 11.

principle and Kennedy as an innocent private purchaser acquired a good title to the car. Therefore FC Finance could not vindicate against Kennedy. McKay was a man of straw. FC Finance had registered the car with HP Information Ltd; any finance company could telephone HP Information Ltd and discover, before buying the car, whether it was subject to an existing hire purchase agreement. These complex facts are summarised in the diagram on page 26 below.

FC Finance's primary remedy was to sue Allan for breach of contract. However, Allan had emigrated to Canada. In these circumstances, FC Finance sought redress against Langtry Investment. It was held that there was no duty on Langtry Investment to check with HP Information Ltd before financing Kennedy's hire purchase of the motor car. However, because Medwin Motors had offered them cars subject to subsisting hire purchase agreements on previous occasions, Langtry Investment should have been on their guard and were therefore at fault – like the defender in *Faulds v Townsend*[1] – for not making inquiries. Therefore they were liable on general principles of *culpa*. The parties agreed that if the defenders were liable, the measure of damages would be the balance of the outstanding hire purchase payments owed by Allan to FC Finance.

This decision is controversial. The pursuer's loss was purely economic – there was no physical damage to the car. As we shall see below, in cases of unintentional wrongs, the courts have been reluctant to allow recovery for pure economic loss. It is therefore doubtful whether there was sufficient proximity between the parties to impose a duty of care on the defender to prevent the pursuer suffering pure economic loss as a result of the defender's careless conduct. This might have been a case where spuilzie should have been resurrected, since the defender had wrongfully interfered with the possession of the pursuer's moveable property. Another solution might have been for the pursuer to have sued in unjustified enrichment for the amount that the defender was *lucratus* as a result of the mistaken dealings with the car. Whatever the solution, the case is an important example of how the law of delict cannot be treated in isolation from other areas of law when considering the difficult issues that can arise in modern commercial dealings.

---

1 (1861) 23 D 437, discussed at p 24 above.

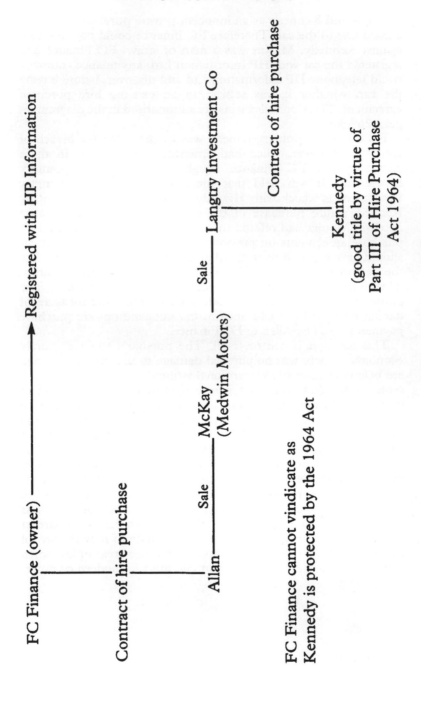

(c) Goodwill – passing off

The goodwill and reputation of a business can be a very valuable asset. Important elements of goodwill are the marketing devices used to enable customers to recognise the product and distinguish it from the products of competitors. These devices include trade names, personal and geographical names associated with a product, for example, Rennie Mackintosh jewellery[1] or Glenfiddich whisky,[2] and the 'get up' of the product, for example, a distinctive container.[3] If a competitor markets a product using a similar name or get up, this may cause confusion among actual or potential customers resulting in damage to the goodwill of the original trader through loss of custom or loss of reputation if the rival product is inferior. In order to protect a trader's goodwill, the delict of 'passing off' has been developed.

Goodwill consists of the features of a business which attract customers to trade with that business. Before there is an action for passing off it must be established that there is a close association between the trader and the particular device which identifies the product or services for existing or potential customers, ie that the device is part of the goodwill of the trader. It may be very difficult, particularly in relation to ordinary words, as opposed to invented words, to show that the word is a marketing device peculiar to the goodwill of a particular trader. Some words, such as hoover, may become part of ordinary usage and lose their distinctive quality of being associated with a particular manufacturer. On the other hand, other words, such as Scotch, while describing a geographical situation may, as in relation to whisky, acquire a secondary meaning peculiar to a particular product. Similar difficulties can arise if a trader claims that the shape of a product is sufficiently distinctive to constitute a protectable device; but a lemon-shaped container of lemon juice has been held to have a secondary meaning associated with a particular product.[4] Once it is established that the device is part of his goodwill, the law will protect the goodwill of the trader from being undermined by a competitor passing off his own product by using a similar name or get up.

The criteria of the delict were articulated by Lord Diplock in the

---

1 *Carrick Jewellery Ltd v Ortak* 1989 GWD 35–1624, OH.
2 *William Grant & Sons Ltd v William Cadenhead Ltd* 1985 SC 121, 1985 SLT 291.
3 *John Haig & Co Ltd v Forth Blending Co Ltd* 1954 SC 35, 1954 SLT 2, OH (Dimple bottle); *Reckitt and Colman Products Ltd v Borden Inc* [1990] 1 All ER 873, HL (Jif plastic lemon).
4 *Reckitt and Colman Products Ltd v Borden Inc* [1990] 1 All ER 873, HL.

leading case of *Erven Warnink BV v J Townend & Sons (Hull) Ltd.*[1]
Passing off consists of:

'(1) a misrepresentation (2) made by a trader in the course of trade, (3) to
prospective customers of his or ultimate consumers of goods or services
supplied by him, (4) which is calculated to injure the business or goodwill
of another (in the sense that this is a reasonably foreseeable consequence)
and (5) which caused actual damage to a business or goodwill of the trader by
whom the action is brought or (in a *quia timet* action) will probably do so.'[2]

The essence of the delict is that by using the same or similar
device which forms part of the goodwill of the pursuer, the defender
misrepresents his product as that of the pursuer thus causing actual
or potential damage to the pursuer's business. There is little
difficulty if the exact device is used, but an action of passing off will
lie even where there are differences, provided there is likelihood of
confusion among a substantial number of the pursuer's customers
or potential customers. If there is no likelihood of confusion, then
there is no passing off, even if, for example, the same name is used.[3]
Thus, in *Dunlop Pneumatic Tyre Co v Dunlop Motor Co*[4] it was held
that the pursuers, a large manufacturer of tyres, would not be
confused with a small family-owned garage of a similar name in
Kilmarnock. There is less likelihood of confusion where the
products do not belong to a 'common field of activity'. Accordingly,
in *Scottish Milk Marketing Board v Dryborough & Co Ltd*,[5] the
pursuer who marketed 'Scottish Pride' butter failed to interdict the
defender from selling 'Scottish Pride' lager, since it was unlikely
that the products – being so different – would be confused.
However, although confusion is more likely to be established where
there is a common field of activity, a common field of activity is not
essential where the device to be protected is, for example, a
household name.[6] If there is sufficient likelihood of confusion, it

---

1 [1979] AC 731 at 742, [1979] 2 All ER 927, HL. This approach was applied by
   the Second Division of the Inner House of the Court of Session in *Lang Bros Ltd
   v Goldwell Ltd* 1980 SC 237, 1982 SLT 309.
2 For a slightly different formulation, see also the speech of Lord Fraser of
   Tullybelton in *Erven Warnink BV v J Townend & Sons (Hull) Ltd* [1979] AC 731
   at 755 and 756, [1979] 2 All ER 927, HL.
3 *Harrods Ltd v Harrodian School* [1996] RPC 697, (1996) Times, 3 April, CA.
4 1907 SC (HL) 15, 15 SLT 362.
5 1985 SLT 253, OH.
6 In *Lego System A/S v Lego M Lemelstrich Ltd* [1983] FSR 155, a toy manufacturer
   successfully obtained an injunction preventing the manufacturers of irrigation
   equipment from using the name 'Lego' on the basis that their goodwill might be
   affected if they entered the same type of business as the defendant sometime in
   the future.

may not be permissible for the defender to use his own name.[1]

In *John Haig & Co Ltd v Forth Blending Co Ltd*[2] the pursuers established that a particular type of bottle (Dimple) was distinctive to their product's get up and successfully interdicted a rival from using a similar shaped bottle, in spite of its having a different label and stopper. The court was satisfied that when in use in a bar, there was a sufficient degree of likelihood of confusion to constitute passing off.

It has been held that manufacturers of Scotch whisky may interdict persons from exporting Scotch whisky, which they know will be mixed with local spirit abroad and passed off in the foreign country as the genuine article.[3] Similarly, passing off actions will lie where a spirit not distilled in Scotland is marketed as Scotch.[4] In *Lang Bros Ltd v Goldwell Ltd*[5] the defender manufactured 'Wee McGlen', a whisky Mac, a blend of Scotch whisky and ginger wine, made in England. This get up consisted of various words and phrases as well as a caricature of a betartaned Scotsman. The Lord Ordinary (Wheatley), a well-known teetotaller, held that the action was relevant. The get up could mislead the public into thinking that the whole product, ie the ginger wine as well as the whisky, was made in Scotland. This misrepresentation as to the origin of the ginger wine could endanger the reputation and goodwill which attaches to Scotch whisky because of its origins. This decision seems to push the delict to its limits since the defender was not misrepresenting his product as Scotch whisky, nor was the get up proved to be part of the exclusive goodwill of the pursuer.[6]

At one time it was thought that passing off was simply a particular aspect of the delict of fraud. This is no longer thought to be sound – at least if the only remedy sought is interdict as opposed to damages. However, the misrepresentation which constitutes passing off must be 'calculated to injure' the pursuer's business or goodwill. It is, however, enough if this is a reasonably foreseeable consequence of the misrepresentation.[7] In other words,

1 *Parker-Knoll Ltd v Knoll International* [1962] RPC 265, HL.
2 1954 SC 35, 1954 SLT 2, OH.
3 *John Walker & Sons Ltd v Douglas Laing & Co* 1993 SLT 156, OH.
4 *John Walker & Sons Ltd v Douglas McGibbon & Co Ltd* 1972 SLT 128, OH; *John Walker & Sons Ltd v Henry Ost & Co Ltd* [1970] 2 All ER 106, [1971] 1 WLR 917. Nevertheless, the author has noted that 'House of Lords' whisky, sold in the Crush Bar at Covent Garden, is manufactured in England!
5 1980 SC 237, 1982 SLT 309.
6 See, further, H L MacQueen 'Wee McGlen and the Action of Passing Off' 1982 SLT (News) 225.
7 *Erven Warnink BV v J Townend & Sons (Hull) Ltd* [1979] AC 731 at 742 per Lord Diplock.

'the calculated to injure' element is objectively ascertained. Nevertheless, it is thought that it remains appropriate to discuss passing off in the context of intentional delicts.

The primary remedy is interdict. Damages may be restricted to cases of actual fraud. However, it is extremely difficult to assess and quantify damages in respect of loss of custom, potential custom and goodwill.[1]

(d) Confidential information

Information can be very valuable. However, the law has not yet been prepared to regard information per se as a form of property.[2] Nevertheless, it is now clear that Scots law recognises a general obligation arising *ex lege* not to divulge information given in confidence.[3] But what is not clear is whether this obligation is delictual *stricto sensu* or whether, given the influence of equitable principles on the development of the obligation in English law,[4] it is better treated as an obligation *sui generis*. In these circumstances, only a basic outline of the law will be discussed in this section.[5]

The essence of the obligation is the duty not to disclose information given in confidence. There is generally no limit on the type of information which is protected; it is the fact that it is given in confidence which is important.[6] Information which has been protected includes sensitive government intelligence, trade secrets and personal information as to a person's sexual activities.

At first, the obligation not to disclose information given in confidence arose from a contractual relationship between the parties. The classic example is, of course, employer and employee. In *Duke of Argyll v Duchess of Argyll*[7] the Duke of Argyll obtained

---

1 On passing off generally, see 18 *Stair Memorial Encyclopaedia* paras 1451–1500.
2 *Grant v Allan* 1987 JC 71, 1988 SLT 11.
3 *Lord Advocate v Scotsman Publications Ltd* 1988 SLT 490 at 502–503 per Lord Justice Clerk (Ross), at 508–509 per Lord Dunpark and at 514 per Lord McDonald; 1989 SLT 705, HL at 708 per Lord Keith of Kinkel.
4 The view has been taken that the *substance* of the law is the same in both Scotland and England: *Lord Advocate v Scotsman Publications Ltd* 1989 SLT 705, HL at 708 per Lord Keith. It has been observed, however, that this is a developing area of Scots law and could evolve differently from the law in England: *Quilty v Windsor* 1999 SLT 346 at 356 per the Lord Ordinary (Kingarth).
5 For a full account, see 18 *Stair Memorial Encyclopaedia* paras 1451–1500.
6 However, an employee may use information given in confidence by a former employer provided it is not a trade secret and there is no valid restrictive covenant: *Faccenda Chicken Ltd v Fowler* [1987] Ch 117, [1986] 1 All ER 617, CA.
7 [1967] Ch 302, [1965] 1 All ER 611.

an interdict to prevent the Duchess divulging information as to his private life which he had given to her while they were married. While there is, of course, a contractual nexus between husband and wife, the obligation is also recognised where there is no contract between the parties but the relationship is clearly one of confidence, for example, doctor and patient, priest and parishioner, co-habitees whether heterosexual or homosexual or even friends.[1]

It is therefore clear that if A gives information to B, where there is a confidential relationship between the parties, then even if there is no contract between A and B, B is under an obligation not to divulge the information. If B divulges the information to C, the question then arises whether C owes an obligation to A not to disclose the information. At first, the Scottish courts were reluctant to impose an obligation on C, unless there was an agreement between A and C that the information was given in confidence.[2] However, it is now settled that C does owe an obligation to A if C knows or ought to have known that the information was confidential.[3] The test would appear to be that an obligation arises if a reasonable person would have realised in all the circumstances that he/she was bound to treat the information as confidential.

The reasonable person test explains not only why, in the example above, C owes an obligation to A not to disclose the information, but also why B owes a similar obligation to A. For where there is an agreement between A and B not to disclose the information, or where there is a confidential relationship with or without a contractual nexus, a reasonable person in B's position would realise that the information is given in confidence. It is therefore submitted that there should only be one test for determining whether a person owes an obligation not to disclose information, ie whether in all the circumstances a reasonable person in that position would have realised that the information was confidential. Factors to be considered would include the nature of the information itself, for example, love letters or government information; the relationship between the parties, for example, employer and employee or lovers; whether or not there is

---

1 *Stephens v Avery* [1988] Ch 449, [1988] 2 All ER 477; *Barrymore v News Group Newspapers Ltd* [1997] FSR 600, Ch D.
2 *Roxburgh v Seven Seas Engineering Ltd* 1980 SLT (Notes) 49, OH.
3 *Lord Advocate v Scotsman Publications Ltd* 1988 SLT 490, affd 1989 SLT 705, HL.

an express statement as to confidentiality[1] or an implied term as to confidentiality between the parties; whether or not the information was obtained by illegal or improper means, for example, industrial espionage or computer 'hacking'.[2] If the reasonable person test is satisfied, then the obligation not to divulge the information arises.

The obligation not to disclose information only continues if the information remains confidential. But merely because the information is known to some other people, for example, specialists in a scientific field, does not prevent the information being confidential. In *Exchange Telegraph Co Ltd v Giulianotti*,[3] the pursuer transmitted the results of races to subscribers. It was held that the information was still confidential even though the spectators at the event knew the result. But if the information is clearly in the public domain, it is no longer confidential and the obligation ceases to exist.[4] Thus, if A gives confidential information to B, and A later divulges the information to the world, B's obligation not to disclose the information comes to an end.[5] This principle has also been extended to the following situation: A gives information in confidence to B and B gives the information to C in circumstances where C as a reasonable person would realise it is confidential; if B divulges the information to the world, then C's obligation comes to an end. A will, of course, have a remedy in damages against B for breach of confidence.[6]

Although it has been held in England that there can be liability for unintentional breach of confidence,[7] it is thought that a pursuer would be unlikely to obtain damages in Scots law unless the defender intended to breach the confidence.[8]

1 The fact that the parties considered themselves to be under an obligation of confidence is, of course, important but it is not decisive. The test is ultimately objective: *De Maudsley v Palumbo* [1996] FSR 447, (1995) Times, 19 December, Ch D.
2 See further 'Breach of Confidence' (SLC no 90; Cmnd 9385 (1984)) p 64.
3 1959 SC 19, 1959 SLT 293, OH.
4 *Attorney-General v Guardian Newspapers Ltd (No 2)* [1990] 1 AC 109, [1988] 3 All ER 545, HL.
5 *O Mustad & Son v S Allcock & Co Ltd and Dosen* [1963] 3 All ER 416, [1964] 1 WLR 109, HL.
6 *Attorney-General v Guardian Newspapers Ltd (No 2)* above. A could not obtain an interdict against B to prevent further disclosure since the information was no longer confidential.
7 *Seager v Copydex Ltd* [1967] 2 All ER 415, [1967] 1 WLR 923, CA.
8 However, since the test of confidentiality is that of the reasonable person, ie an objective test, it is theoretically possible that a person could breach the obligation when he or she did not subjectively know that the information was confidential, ie because the person had not in fact reached the standard of the reasonable person.

The obligation not to disclose information given in confidence is not absolute. A defence is available if disclosure was in the public interest. Thus disclosure is justifiable if the information concerned the commission of a crime or a civil wrong.[1] Information disclosed to a public official or agency which could take appropriate action, for example, the police, is more likely to provide justification than simple disclosure to the media.[2] The courts must engage in a balancing exercise between the public interest in protecting confidential information and the public interest in access to information which should be known. In *X v Y*[3] a newspaper disclosed the identity of two doctors suffering from AIDS. The newspaper argued that it was in the public interest that patients should know the HIV status of their medical practitioners. In rejecting this defence, the court took the view that the public interest in maintaining confidentiality prevailed because it encouraged persons suffering from AIDS, including doctors, to seek treatment. In the case of government information, the Crown cannot obtain an interdict merely because the information is confidential: the public interest in open government will justify disclosure.[4] However, the public interest in disclosure will be 'trumped' if the disclosure of the information would be damaging to national security.[5]

The primary remedy for breach of confidence is interdict.[6] Damages are possible though difficult to assess. The person divulging the information may be required to account for any profits made from doing so.[7]

1 *Initial Services Ltd v Putterill* [1968] 1 QB 396, [1967] 3 All ER 145, CA.
2 *British Steel Corpn v Granada Television Ltd* [1981] AC 1096, [1981] 1 All ER 417, HL.
3 [1988] 2 All ER 648, [1988] RPC 379.
4 *Lord Advocate v Scotsman Publications Ltd* 1988 SLT 490, affd 1989 SLT 705, HL.
5 *Attorney-General v Guardian Newspapers Ltd (No 2)* [1990] 1 AC 109, [1988] 3 All ER 545, HL. Although the information in that case was prima facie damaging to national security, by the time the case reached the House of Lords knowledge of the material was so widespread that an injunction on further serialisation of the information was refused; in other words, the information was no longer confidential.
6 The general criteria for granting interdict must, of course, be present: see, for example, *Waste Systems International Inc v Eurocare Environmental Services Ltd* 1999 SLT 198, OH.
7 *Attorney-General v Guardian Newspapers Ltd (No 2)* [1990] 1 AC 109, [1988] 3 All ER 545, HL.

CHAPTER 2

The economic delicts and fraud

A. THE ECONOMIC DELICTS

(1) Introduction – the general principle

In a free market, competition is regarded as essential and in the public interest. This can result in one business being successful while another goes to the wall. The common law therefore took the view that A was entitled to harm B economically, provided A used lawful means, for example, undercutting the price of his product, in order to do so. However, towards the end of the nineteenth century and during the twentieth century, the courts developed a range of delicts which set parameters beyond which parties could not wield their economic and social power. These are known as the economic delicts. Since then, important statutory provisions and principles of EU law have been introduced directly to regulate competition, for example, the Office of Fair Trading. Competition law is outwith the scope of this book. However, the economic delicts remain important and will be treated in this chapter.

The basic principle was laid down by the House of Lords in *Allen v Flood*.[1] In this case boilermakers objected to the practice of employing shipwrights to repair ironwork on board ships. The plaintiffs were shipwrights who were employed to repair woodwork on certain ships. Members of the boilermakers' union discovered that they had previously been employed by another employer to repair ironwork on ships. Incensed, a trade union representative approached the current employer of the shipwrights and informed him that unless he dismissed the plaintiffs, his other employees would strike. This was done maliciously to punish the plaintiffs. The employer dismissed the plaintiffs who brought the action against the trade union representative.

Three points should be noticed. First, the case proceeded on the basis that there was no conspiracy, ie no agreement among the

1 [1898] AC 1, HL.

boilermakers that they would strike; it was simply the individual trade unionist who said that there would be a strike. Second, if there had been a strike, the employees would have terminated their contracts of employment lawfully. Third, when the employer dismissed the plaintiffs he did so by lawfully terminating their contracts. In other words, the individual trade unionist used lawful means (the threat of a lawful strike) to compel the employer to use lawful means (the lawful dismissal) to harm the plaintiffs economically (the loss of their employment). In these circumstances, the House of Lords held that no delict was committed even though the defendant had acted maliciously.

Accordingly, *Allen v Flood* is authority that an individual, A, can wield economic pressure to force B to act to his own or another's economic harm provided the means used by A are lawful. If, as in this case, the means used are lawful, no delict is committed even if A acts maliciously to harm B or another person, rather than to further A's economic interests. This result, while harsh, is an inevitable consequence of a free market economy. But if the means used are *not* lawful, as a result of later developments, delictual liability may arise. It is to these that we shall now turn.

(2) Inducing breach of contract – procuring breach of contract

If A induces B to break his contract with C, C can sue B for breach of contract. In addition, or as an alternative, C can sue A in *delict* for inducing B to break his contract with C. This delict was recognised as part of Scots law in *British Motor Trade Association v Gray*.[1] There Lord Russell approved counsel's concession that

'by the law of Scotland an actionable wrong is committed by one who intentionally and without lawful justification induces or procures someone to break a contract made by him with another, if damage has resulted to that other, provided the contract creates contractual relations recognised by law'.[2]

The delict can be represented by the diagram on page 37 below.

Thus if A, with the intention of harming C, induces B to break his contract with C, C can sue A in *delict* for inducing the breach, as well as suing B for breach of contract.

Before A is liable, A must know of the existence of the contract between B and C. It is not enough in Scots law that A was reckless

1   1951 SC 586, 1951 SLT 247.
2   1951 SC 586 at 603.

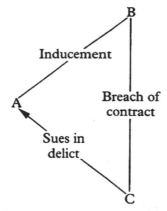

or turned a blind eye to whether or not a contract existed between B and C.[1] However, A does not need to know the specific terms of the contract between B and C. The court will readily infer that A knew of the existence of the contract if a reasonable person in A's position would know that a contract existed between B and C. A must intend that B should break his contract with C in order to harm C.[2] A must in fact induce B to break the contract.[3] It is not necessary that A's inducement takes the form of unlawful means, for example, threatening to assault B: A will still be liable to C if the means used are lawful and, indeed, beneficial to B, for example, giving B a gift to break his contract with C. C must suffer loss as a result of the inducement, but proof of specific damage is not required and once inducement of the breach is established, some damage will readily be inferred by the court.[4] Finally, A will have a defence if the inducement of the breach is justified, for example, inducing female artistes to break their contracts of employment to obtain better wages so that they do not have to resort to prostitution.[5]

1 *Rossleigh Ltd v Leader Cars Ltd* 1987 SLT 355, OH. Cf the position in England: *Emerald Construction Co Ltd v Lowthian* [1966] 1 All ER 1013, [1966] 1 WLR 691, CA.
2 While the point is controversial, the Court of Appeal has held that A does not have to intend to harm C. It is enough that A knows that her deliberate conduct vis-à-vis B will have as its probable consequence a breach by B of his contract with C: *Millar v Bassey* [1994] EMLR 44. Given that Scots law has rejected the notion of A's constructive knowledge of the contract between B and C, it is doubtful whether *Millar* would be followed in Scotland.
3 The inducement must be directed at B, the person in the contractual relationship with the victim, C: *Middlebrook Mushrooms Ltd v Transport and General Workers Union* [1993] ICR 612, (1993) Times, 18 January, CA.
4 *British Motor Trade Association v Gray* 1951 SC 586, 1951 SLT 247.
5 *Brimelow v Casson* [1924] 1 Ch 302.

We have been considering the situation where A induces or persuades B to break his contract with C. However, if B is unwilling to break his contract with C, A may nevertheless be able to procure the breach of contract by B. Before there is liability in this situation, A must use *unlawful* means to procure the breach. Procurement can arise directly if, for example, A steals B's tools with the result that B cannot fulfil his contract and breaks his contract with C: the theft constitutes the unlawful means. However, it is much more likely that procurement will be done indirectly, ie if A with the intention of harming C induces D to break his contract with B so that B cannot perform his contract with C. The delict can be represented as follows:

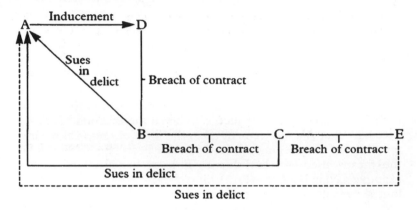

Here B could sue A in delict for directly inducing a breach of his contract with D. But C can also sue A for procuring a breach of C's contract with B: A's direct inducement of a breach of B's contract with D (ie a delict) constitutes the unlawful means used by A which are essential before A can be liable for procuring the breach of contract between B and C.[1] It should be emphasised that it does not matter whether the means used by A directly to induce D to breach her contract with B are lawful: direct inducement does *not* require unlawful means for delictual liability. But once A has directly induced the breach D–B, because direct inducement is a delict, it constitutes the unlawful means for the procurement of the breach B–C and so on.

Before there is liability, A must know of the existence of B's contract with C. If, as a result, C is unable to fulfil his contract

---

1 *Stratford (JT) & Son Ltd v Lindley* [1965] AC 269, [1964] 3 All ER 102, HL.

with E, E will also be able to sue A in delict provided A knows of C's contract with E and intended to harm E.[1] As we have emphasised, A must use unlawful means before there is liability for procurement. Justification can be a defence to procuring a breach of contract in the same way as in a case of direct inducement.

(3) Wrongful interference with performance of contract

Arising from the delict of inducement of breach of contract, the English courts have developed the delict of wrongful interference with performance of a contract, where there has technically been no breach. Like the delict discussed above this can take two forms – direct interference where unlawful means are not required and indirect interference where unlawful means are essential.

The origin of the delict is the case of *Torquay Hotel Co Ltd v Cousins*.[2] The Transport and General Workers Union (TGWU) attempted to organise the workforce at a Torbay hotel, but another union was recognised by the hotel. The TGWU brought its members at the hotel out on strike. The manager of the Imperial Hotel at Torquay who was the President of the Torquay Hotel Association, unwisely said that he wished to stamp out trade unions in hotels in Torquay. There were no members of the TGWU at the Imperial Hotel. The TGWU had members who were employed by Esso to deliver supplies of oil to the Imperial Hotel. The TGWU instructed those drivers not to deliver oil to the Imperial Hotel. The contract between the Imperial Hotel and Esso contained an exclusion clause under which Esso was not to be liable for failure to supply oil as a result of industrial action. The Imperial Hotel obtained a delivery of oil from Alternative Fuels. When the TGWU discovered this, the union informed Alternative Fuels not to enter any contract to supply the hotel with oil or else their drivers who were members of TGWU would boycott the hotel. In refusing to deliver oil to the hotel, the drivers were in breach of their contracts of employment with Esso and would have been in breach of their contracts of employment with Alternative Fuels. This complex factual situation can be shown by the diagram on page 41 below.

---

1 *Merkur Island Shipping Corpn v Laughton* [1983] 2 AC 570, [1983] ICR 490, HL. A's liability could continue indefinitely; for example, if E cannot fulfil his contract with F, F can sue A provided A has knowledge of the contract between E and F.
2 [1969] 2 Ch 106, [1969] 1 All ER 522, CA.

Although the TGWU had directly persuaded Esso not to perform the contract with the Imperial Hotel and had indirectly procured the non-performance of the contract by using unlawful means (the breach of the drivers' contracts of employment in refusing to deliver the oil to the hotel), the delicts of inducement or procurement of *breach* of contract were not applicable since there was no breach of contract by Esso in failing to perform, because of the exclusion clause in the contract. The Court of Appeal nevertheless held that it was not necessary to have a technical breach of contract before the TGWU was liable to Imperial Hotels.[1] It was enough that the TGWU had wrongfully interfered with Esso's performance of the contract with Imperial Hotel. Thus, a new delict, wrongful interference with performance of a contract, was born. As in the case of inducement/procurement of a breach of contract, the defender must know of the existence of the contract and intend to interfere with its performance. If there is direct interference, unlawful means are not required; if there is indirect interference, unlawful means are necessary. There is also the defence of justification.

It will be noticed that a contract to supply oil existed between the Imperial Hotel and Esso. While Alternative Fuels had made one delivery of oil, no contract to supply oil subsisted between the Imperial Hotel and Alternative Fuels. At most there was a prospective contract. Nevertheless, the Court of Appeal held that the TGWU was liable to the Imperial Hotel for indirectly interfering with its prospective contract with Alternative Fuels by using unlawful means (the breach of the drivers' contracts of employment with Alternative Fuel in refusing to deliver oil to the hotel). Again a new delict, preventing a person from entering into a contract by unlawful means, was born.

(4) Wrongful interference with business

As a result of the decision in the *Torquay* case, particularly in respect of the prospective contract with Alternative Fuels, the English courts have begun to argue that inducing or procuring a breach of contract, wrongful interference with the performance of a contract and preventing by unlawful means a person from

---

1 Esso could, of course, sue the TGWU for inducing its employees to breach their contracts of employment.

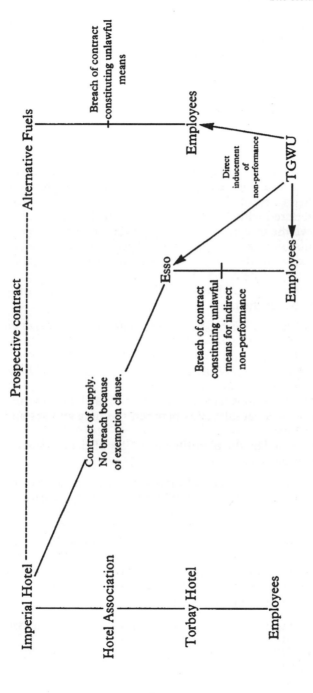

entering into a contract, are merely species of a more general delict, wrongful interference with business.[1]

The leading case is *Lonrho plc v Fayed.*[2] Lonrho was attempting a takeover of Harrods. The Secretary of State for Trade and Industry referred the matter to the Monopolies Commission and obtained an undertaking from Lonrho that it would not purchase any more shares before the Monopolies Commission reported. Before the Commission reported, Fayed made a bid. Induced by allegedly fraudulent misrepresentations made by Fayed as to its business reputation, the Secretary of State did not refer Fayed's bid to the Commission and Fayed took over the company. Lonrho argued that as a result of its allegedly fraudulent misrepresentations to the Secretary of State – unlawful means – Fayed had wrongfully interfered with Lonrho's business. If the Secretary of State had known the true position, he would have referred Fayed's bid to the Commission and Lonrho might have been able to make a successful bid when its undertaking was no longer applicable. The Court of Appeal held that Lonrho had an arguable case of wrongful interference with business. To succeed the following criteria have to be satisfied:

(1) the plaintiff has to establish that the defendant intended to harm the plaintiff's business; this intention does not, however, have to be the defendant's predominant intention or motive;
(2) the plaintiff has to establish that a business interest has been damaged by the defendant's conduct;
(3) the defendant's actions have to constitute unlawful means and there has to be a causal nexus between the unlawful act and the alleged loss;
(4) the loss sustained by the plaintiff has to be sufficient to sustain an action in damages.

Because of the need for *unlawful* means, the new delict can be distinguished from the general principle of non-liability for causing economic harm laid down in *Allen v Flood.*[3]

(5) Intimidation

Intimidation arises when A threatens B with an unlawful act unless B harms C economically. If B yields to the threat and harms C, C can sue A. The delict can be represented as follows:

1 See, in particular, *Merkur Island Shipping Corpn v Laughton* [1983] 2 AC 570, [1983] ICR 490, HL.
2 [1990] 2 QB 479, [1989] 2 All ER 65, CA.
3 [1898] AC 1, HL discussed at p 35 above.

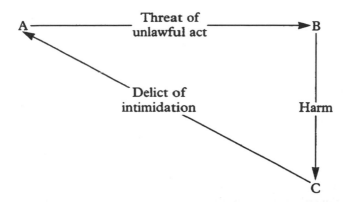

The existence of this delict was 'discovered' by the House of Lords in *Rookes v Barnard*.[1] British Overseas Airways Corporation (BOAC) and the draughtsmen's union, Association of Engineering and Shipbuilding Draughtsmen (AESD), had an informal 100 per cent union membership agreement (closed shop). Rookes was an employee of BOAC who had left the union. Two trade union officials who were employees of BOAC, and Silverthorne who was not an employee, told BOAC that unless Rookes was dismissed within three days, the AESD employees would withdraw their labour. As a result of a 'no strike' clause which had been incorporated from a collective agreement into the employees' contracts of employment, the threatened strike would have been a breach of the employees' contracts of employment. Under this pressure, BOAC lawfully dismissed Rookes. Rookes sued the three officials. This complex factual situation can be shown thus:

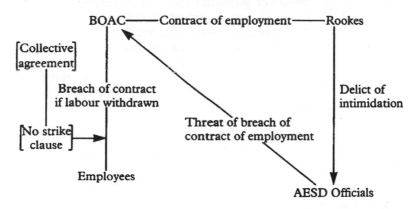

1 [1964] AC 1129, [1964] 1 All ER 367, HL.

The House of Lords held that Silverthorne and the other two employees were guilty of the delict of intimidation. By *threatening* a strike in breach of BOAC's employees' contracts of employment, they were threatening BOAC with *unlawful* means in order that BOAC should harm Rookes economically. As BOAC had yielded to the pressure and had dismissed Rookes, Rookes could sue the defendants on the basis of intimidation since the threat was made with the intention of harming Rookes.

To succeed the following criteria have to be satisfied:

(1) there has to be a threat as opposed to a warning;
(2) it must be a threat of unlawful means.[1] The means do not necessarily have to be within the power of all the defendants: Silverthorne was not an employee of BOAC. Unlawful means include threats of violence, delicts or a breach of contract;
(3) the threat must be made with the intention that the person threatened will harm the pursuer;
(4) the person threatened must yield to the threat and harm the pursuer; if he does not comply with the threat, it is not intimidation. If the person threatened resists and the threat is carried out, depending on the nature of the unlawful act, he may have a remedy in delict or for breach of contract.

There is always the possibility of the defence of justification: if, for example, Rookes had been a dealer in drugs who upset the rest of the workforce.

Rookes was concerned with three-party intimidation, ie A threatens B with unlawful means in order that B should harm C; if B yields, C can sue A for intimidation. The question arises whether there can be two-party intimidation, ie if A threatens B with unlawful means, can B sue A for intimidation? In the present writer's view, there is no delict of two-party intimidation because it is unnecessary. If A threatens B with violence, that is itself an assault and B can sue in delict. If A threatens B with breach of contract by A, that is an anticipatory breach of contract and B can sue A in contract. If A threatens B with other delictual conduct, then B must be robust and wait until the threat is carried out and then sue in delict; B cannot sue for an 'anticipatory' delict since he has not yet suffered any loss. If, however, the threat of unlawful

---

1 So, for example, if A threatened B that A would inform the Inland Revenue that B had failed to disclose all her income, that would not amount to intimidation because the conduct threatened is not unlawful.

means interferes with B's business, A could be liable for the delict of wrongful interference with B's business.[1]

(5) Conspiracy

Allen v Flood[2] was concerned with the situation where A uses lawful means to harm B economically. There it was held that A was not liable in delict to B, even if his predominant motive or intention was to harm B rather than further A's legitimate business interests. Only three years later, in *Quinn v Leathem*,[3] the House of Lords held that if A and B combine together with the intention to harm C, then A and B are liable in delict for harm caused to C as a result of their combination or conspiracy against him. The rationale of the delict of conspiracy is that while a person can be expected to withstand the harmful but lawful acts of another, he cannot be expected to withstand the harm caused by a combination or conspiracy of persons to harm him.[4] This rationalisation has been doubted, for a multi-national conglomerate or oil company may exercise far greater economic power than a combination of small businesses.[5]

The essence of conspiracy is therefore a combination of persons, who combine together with the intention of harming the pursuer economically. There are two types of conspiracy: (a) where the means used by the conspirators are lawful in the sense that they would not be actionable if carried out by one person alone (lawful means conspiracy); (b) where the means used by the conspirators are unlawful in the sense that *either* they would be actionable if carried out by one person alone, for example, if the means constitute a delict or breach of contract, *or* they involve a crime or a breach of statute which does not provide a civil remedy for breach (unlawful means conspiracy).

(a) Lawful means conspiracy

A combination of persons will be liable in conspiracy if they combine together with the predominant motive or intention of harming the pursuer rather than furthering their own legitimate

1 Discussed at p 42 above.
2 [1898] AC 1, HL. Discussed at p 35 above.
3 [1901] AC 495, HL.
4 *Mogul Steamship Co Ltd v McGregor, Gow & Co* (1889) 23 QBD 598, CA, at 616 per Bowen LJ.
5 *Lonrho Ltd v Shell Petroleum Co Ltd (No 2)* [1982] AC 173, [1981] 2 All ER 456, HL, at 464 per Lord Diplock; see also *Crofter Hand Woven Harris Tweed Co Ltd v Veitch* 1942 SC (HL) 1 at 8 per Viscount Simon LC, 1943 SLT 2.

interests. Thus, if A and B combine together with the predominant motive or intention to harm C, A and B are liable in conspiracy even if their actions, for example undercutting C's prices, would not be actionable in delict if carried out by A or B alone. It is the *combination* of A and B together *and* their predominant motive or intention of harming C which renders their conspiracy delictual. If the predominant motive or intention of A and B is not to harm C but to further their own legitimate interests, the conspiracy is not delictual even though C suffers economic loss as a result of the actions of A and B, provided these actions are lawful. Where lawful means are used, a conspiracy is delictual only if the predominant motive or intention of the conspirators is to harm the pursuer.

These principles were laid down in the leading case of *Crofter Hand Woven Harris Tweed Co Ltd v Veitch*.[1] Millowners on the Island of Lewis who made and sold tweed cloth from yarn spun on the island were unable to agree a 100 per cent union membership agreement (closed shop) with the TGWU because of competition from rival producers on the island (the pursuers) who obtained cheaper yarn from the mainland, wove it into cloth and sold it at a lower price than the millowners. The TGWU and the millowners combined together. They instructed the members of the TGWU who were employed at the port to refuse to handle the yarn being imported by the pursuers to the island from the mainland. The case proceeded on the basis that the dockers were not in breach of their contracts of employment with the port authority in refusing to handle the imported yarn because they were never asked by their employer to do so. The question was whether the combination amounted to an actionable conspiracy. This complex factual situation can be shown thus:

1   1942 SC (HL) 1, 1943 SLT 2.

The House of Lords held that since no unlawful means were used because the dockers were not in breach of their contracts of employment, ie there was no conduct which would be actionable if done by one person alone, the conspiracy would be delictual only if the pursuers could establish that the predominant motive or intention of the conspirators was to harm the pursuers. In this case, the predominant motive or intention was to further the union's legitimate interests, ie 100 per cent union membership. Harm to the pursuers was not their primary intention, it was only incidental to achieving their goal. Accordingly, the defenders were not liable.

It can, of course, be a very difficult issue of fact to establish whether the predominant purpose of the conspiracy is to harm the pursuer or whether the damage done to the pursuer is simply incidental to the furtherance of the conspirators' legitimate interests, be they commercial[1] or trade union interests, as in the *Crofter* case. In *Scala Ballroom (Wolverhampton) Ltd v Ratcliffe*[2] it was held to be legitimate for trade union officials to organise a boycott among their members from playing at a dance hall which operated a colour bar; although this objective did not bring any financial benefits to the members of the union, it was genuinely thought by them to be in the interests of the union.

To summarise: when the combination uses lawful means, ie means which would not be actionable if done by one person alone, then the conspiracy is not delictual unless the predominant motive or intention of the conspirators is to injure the pursuer. The onus rests on the pursuer to prove that the predominant purpose of the conspiracy was to harm the pursuer economically. Moreover, the pursuer must prove economic loss.[3]

(b) Unlawful means conspiracy

In considering unlawful means conspiracy, two situations have to be discussed. First is the case where the means used are unlawful in the sense that they would be actionable as a breach of contract

---

1 As in *Mogul Steamship Co Ltd v McGregor, Gow & Co* (1889) 23 QBD 598, CA.
2 [1958] 3 All ER 220, [1958] 1 WLR 1057, CA.
3 In *Lonrho plc v Fayed (No 5)* [1994] 1 All ER 188, [1993] 1 WLR 1489, CA, the Court of Appeal accepted that the defendants could be liable in conspiracy even if the statements they had made about the plaintiff were true, ie when they would have had a defence to an action of defamation. Since the means were lawful, their predominant motive would have had to have been harm to the plaintiff. Only damages for patrimonial loss would be recoverable; cf loss of reputation. On defamation, see Chapter 15 below.

or delict if committed by one person alone. So, for example, if the boycotting of the imported yarn in the *Crofter* case had involved a breach of the dockers' contracts of employment (unlawful means), the union would have been liable to the pursuers for procurement of a breach of their contract with the port authority to carry the imported yarn. Where the means are delictual or amount to a breach of contract, the pursuer will usually sue on the substantive delict or breach of contract without relying on the conspiracy.[1]

Second, the means may be unlawful but not actionable as a breach of contract or a delict if committed by one person alone. This will usually arise where the means used involve a breach of a statutory provision. While breach of some statutes gives rise to an action in delict,[2] not all breaches of statute give a person who suffers harm as a result the right to sue in delict. In particular, the pursuer will not generally have title to sue in delict unless the statute was specifically designed to protect the interests of a class of persons to which the pursuer belongs.[3] In this situation, since the means used do not constitute a substantive delict, conspiracy may be the only form of redress.

The criteria for an actionable unlawful means conspiracy have been the subject of two decisions of the House of Lords concerned with Lonrho. The first is *Lonrho Ltd v Shell Petroleum Co Ltd (No 2)*.[4] Lonrho owned a pipeline running from Beira in Mozambique to a refinery in Southern Rhodesia. The pipeline was operated under an agreement between Lonrho and oil companies, including Shell. When Southern Rhodesia declared unilateral independence, the British government made a sanctions order under the Southern Rhodesia Act 1965. As a result of the sanctions order, oil was no longer shipped to Beira, the pipeline ceased to be used and Lonrho lost profits. Before unilateral independence was declared, the oil companies gave assurances to the Rhodesian government that they would supply petroleum products to Rhodesia through South Africa. After independence had been declared, the defendants supplied the oil to Rhodesia in breach of the sanctions order. In an action of conspiracy against the defendants, Lonrho argued that the breach of the sanctions order enabled unilateral independence to last longer and thereby led to a loss of its revenue as a result of the prolonged non-use of its pipeline.

1 Similarly, in *Rookes v Barnard* [1964] AC 1129, [1964] 1 All ER 367, HL, Silverthorne was sued for the substantive delict of intimidation rather than conspiracy to break the employees' contracts. See p 43 above.
2 See Chapter 11 below.
3 *RCA Corpn v Pollard* [1983] Ch 135, [1982] 3 All ER 771, CA.
4 [1982] AC 173, [1981] 2 All ER 456, HL.

While the supply of the oil was a breach of the sanctions order, this was simply a criminal offence. In other words, the sanction order was not imposed for the benefit of persons, like Lonrho, who had traded with Rhodesia before independence. There was therefore no substantive delict arising from the defendants' breach of the order. The only delictual claim had to be based on conspiracy. Both the Court of Appeal and the House of Lords held that the conspiracy was not actionable because Lonrho had failed to establish that the defendants had *intended* to harm Lonrho when they breached the sanctions order. In the course of his speech in the House of Lords, Lord Diplock expressed the view that he did not wish to extend the delict of conspiracy beyond its existing limits.[1] Since the previous cases were concerned with lawful means conspiracy, where there is no liability unless the predominant motive or intention of the conspirators was to harm the pursuer, Lord Diplock's dicta were subsequently taken as authority that there was also no liability for an unlawful means conspiracy unless the primary aim of the combination was to harm the pursuer.[2]

The issue was purportedly clarified by the House of Lords in the second Lonrho case, *Lonrho plc v Fayed*.[3] In addition to the claim based on wrongful interference with business,[4] Lonrho also argued that the defendants had committed an unlawful means conspiracy against them, the alleged fraudulent misrepresentation to the Secretary of State constituting unlawful means. The House of Lords held that Lord Diplock's analysis in *Lonrho Ltd v Shell Petroleum Co Ltd (No 2)*[5] was not intended as a definitive account of the law relating to unlawful means conspiracy.[6] While accepting that a lawful means conspiracy was delictual only if the predominant motive or intention of the conspirators was to harm the pursuer, an unlawful means conspiracy was actionable if the pursuer could establish that the conspirators had *an* intention to harm the pursuer, even though that was not their *predominant* motive or intention. This intention could not be proved merely by showing that the defenders had used unlawful means: otherwise,

---

1 [1981] 2 All ER 456 at 464.
2 *Allied Arab Bank Ltd v Hajjar (No 2)* [1988] QB 944, [1988] 3 All ER 103; *Metall und Rohstoff AG v Donaldson Lufkin and Jenrette Inc* [1990] 1 QB 391, [1989] 3 All ER 14, CA.
3 [1991] 3 All ER 303, HL. For the facts, see p 42 above.
4 Discussed at p 42 above.
5 [1982] AC 173, [1981] 2 All ER 456, HL.
6 *Lonrho plc v Fayed* [1992] 1 AC 448, [1991] 3 All ER 303 at 312 per Lord Bridge; Lord Bridge had been a member of the House of Lords in *Lonrho Ltd v Shell Petroleum Co Ltd (No 2)* [1982] AC 173, [1981] 2 All ER 456, HL.

Lonrho should have succeeded in the *Shell Petroleum* case. However, if the conspirators have an intention to harm the pursuer, an unlawful means conspiracy is delictual even if the unlawful means used would not be actionable if done by one person alone.[1]

To summarise: if the means used are lawful, a conspiracy is delictual only if the *predominant* motive or intention of the conspirators is to harm the pursuer; if the means used are unlawful, a conspiracy is actionable if *an* intention of the conspirators was to harm the pursuer, even though that was not their primary purpose. Unlawful means include means which are delictual if done by one person alone or which constitute a breach of contract or amount to a breach of criminal law, even though this would not give rise to a delictual action if done by one person alone.

(7) Postscript

As we have seen, many of these economic delicts were developed in the context of industrial conflict between employers and trade unions. Most forms of effective industrial action will involve the commission of one or more of the economic delicts. In order to obtain a balance between the power of capital and labour for the purpose of collective bargaining, legislation has been passed to give immunity to trade unions and trade unionists from civil liability in respect of some, at least, of these delicts. Immunity arises only if the acts which prima facie constitute an economic delict are carried out in contemplation or furtherance of a trade dispute. There are now stringent balloting requirements of the members of a trade union which must be satisfied before the statutory defences are applicable; and the defences do not apply to some forms of secondary industrial action. The law has now been consolidated in the Trade Union and Labour Relations (Consolidation) Act 1992 and the reader seeking an account of the law relating to industrial action is referred to the textbooks on labour law.

1 In *Yukong Line Ltd of Korea v Rendsburg Investments Corpn of Liberia (No 2)* [1998] 1 WLR 294, [1998] 4 All ER 82, QBD (Comm Ct), Toulson J has suggested that the plaintiff in an unlawful means conspiracy must have title to sue on the unlawful means if committed by one person alone: otherwise, the conspiracy is not actionable unless the defendants' predominant motive was harm to the plaintiff. With respect, it is thought that this decision runs counter to the thrust of the decision of the House of Lords in *Lonrho plc v Fayed* [1992] 1 AC 448, [1991] 3 All ER 303.

B. FRAUD

Fraud is the paradigm example of an intentional delict in Scots law. It has been defined as 'a machination or contrivance to deceive'.[1] Fraud will usually cause pure economic loss to the pursuer. As we shall see, this provides a stark contrast to the situation where unintentional conduct results in pure economic loss; there the courts have been unwilling to allow recovery in delict. However, fraud is not restricted to economic loss. If A lies to B when A tells B that B's wife and children have been seriously injured with the result that B suffers nervous shock, B can recover damages from A for fraud.[2]

Much confusion has arisen in this area because the fraudulent conduct will often take the form of a misrepresentation which induces the misrepresentee to enter into a contract with the misrepresentor. In these circumstances, the misrepresentee may have two sets of remedies, ie contractual and delictual. If the fraudulent misrepresentation prevented the formation of the contract, the contract is null;[3] if, however, a contract is concluded but the misrepresentee was induced by the fraudulent misrepresentation to contract under essential error, the contract may be reduced provided *restitutio in integrum* is possible.[4] But, in addition, the misrepresentee can sue in *delict* for damages. Thus, if A lies to B to induce B to enter a contract with A, B will have contractual remedies against A, for example, reduction and the right to sue A for damages in delict. However, if A lies to B who as a result enters into a contract with C, B will have no contractual remedies against C (unless A was acting as C's agent) but B will be able to sue A in delict.

Although the institutional writers had a flexible view of the concept of fraud, as a result of developments in the nineteenth century fraud as a delict was confined to a relatively narrow range of situations where the defender intended to harm the pursuer. In

---

1 Erskine *Institute* III, 1, 16.
2 *Wilkinson v Downtown* [1897] 2 QB 57. Cf *Powell v Boladz* [1998] Lloyd's Rep Med 116, CA, (defendant had no intention to harm plaintiff by falsifying medical records). Similarly if A obtained sexual intercourse with B as a result of fraudulent misrepresentation.
3 *Morrisson v Robertson* 1908 SC 332, 15 SLT 697.
4 *Spence v Crawford* 1939 SC (HL) 52, 1939 SLT 305; *MacLeod v Kerr* 1965 SC 253, 1965 SLT 358.

effect, the Scots delict of fraud was equated with the English tort of deceit.[1]

Before delictual liability arises for fraud, there must be a positive act by the defender which causes loss to the pursuer. This will often take the form of a misrepresentation by words. However, positive conduct can amount to a fraudulent misrepresentation, for example, supplying reconditioned as opposed to new cash registers[2] or selling reproduction furniture 'got up' to look like antiques.[3] As a general rule, non-disclosure does not amount to a misrepresentation unless there is a fiduciary relationship between the parties or the contract is a contract *uberrimae fidei*.[4]

Before there is liability for fraud, the pursuer must establish that the defender had the requisite mental element, *mens rea*. In other words, the pursuer has to show that at the time of the misrepresentation the defender's state of mind was such that he did not, or could not, believe his statement was true. It is, of course, extremely difficult to prove this mental element; as a result, the law has developed liability for negligent – as opposed to fraudulent – misrepresentation where the defender's conduct can be tested objectively.[5]

What, then, will constitute the *mens rea* of fraud? The first situation is where the defender makes a statement which he knows is false. For example, A tells B there is a gold seam in A's garden when A knows that no seam is there. In these circumstances, A is lying. The second situation is where the defender makes a statement which he does not positively *know* is false but which he positively *believes* to be false. For example, A tells B there is a gold seam in A's garden; A has not dug up his garden and therefore does not know that there is no gold seam, but A believes no gold seam is there. If in fact there is no gold seam, then A can be sued by B for fraud. B will have great difficulty in proving that A believed his statement was false if A maintains he believed it was true. However, the court will infer fraud if the statement was destitute of all reasonable grounds for believing it was true or the least inquiry would immediately correct.[6]

---

1 On these developments see, generally, 11 *Stair Memorial Encyclopaedia* paras 701–789.
2 *Gibson v National Cash Register Co Ltd* 1925 SC 500, 1925 SLT 377.
3 *Patterson v H Landsberg & Son* (1905) 7 F 675, 13 SLT 62.
4 For example, a contract of insurance.
5 On these developments, see pp 79 ff below.
6 *Western Bank of Scotland v Addie* (1867) 5 M (HL) 80.

The final situation is where the defender makes a statement which he does not positively know is false and does not positively believe is false but is recklessly indifferent to whether it is true or false. If the matter is of no importance to speaker and listener, this is not dishonesty. But if it is a matter of importance between them, it is fraud, since the speaker has attempted to induce a belief in the listener, ie that the statement is true, which the speaker does not actually entertain.[1] For example, A tells B there is a gold seam in A's garden. A has done tests which establish that the strata are not inconsistent with a gold seam but A, nevertheless, has serious doubts whether a gold seam is actually there. Assuming B has an interest in the statement, although A does not positively know that the statement is false and does not positively believe that it is false, if he does not care whether it is true or false, he is liable in fraud to B if in fact there is no gold seam in the garden.[2] Proof of the requisite *mens rea* in this situation will be difficult, but again will be inferred if the statement was destitute of all reasonable grounds for believing it was true or the least inquiry would immediately correct.

To summarise,[3] *mens rea* for the purposes of fraud arises if the misrepresentor:

(1) positively knows the statement is false;[4] or
(2) positively believes the statement is false even though he does not positively know it is false: liability if in fact untrue;
(3) does not positively believe the statement is true, even though he does not positively know or believe it is false: liability if in fact untrue, provided both parties have an interest in what has been said.

There can, therefore, be no liability in fraud if the defender positively believes that the statement is true. However, in these circumstances, if he did not take reasonable care in making the statement, there may be liability for negligent misrepresentation.

Because fraud is an intentional delict, the pursuer is entitled to recover damages for all the losses directly arising from the fraud – even if the losses are not reasonably foreseeable by the defender.

---

1 *Lees v Tod* (1882) 9 R 807.
2 *H & JM Bennet (Potatoes) Ltd v Secretary of State for Scotland* 1986 SLT 665, OH (revsd on another point 1988 SLT 390).
3 The *locus classicus* is to be found in *Derry v Peek* (1889) 14 App Cas 337, HL, at 374 per Lord Herschell.
4 See, for example, *Henry Ansbacher & Co Ltd v Binks Stern* [1998] Lloyd's Rep Bank 1, (1997) Times, 26 June, CA.

Suppose, for example, A bought shares from B for £X. A was induced by B to purchase the shares as a result of B's fraudulent misrepresentation as to the value of the shares. In fact their value is £X–Y. However, unknown to A and B, at the time of the transaction the shares were overvalued at £X–Y, because of a fraud by C. When C's fraud is subsequently discovered, the shares fall in value to £(X–Y)–Z. A can recover the full extent of his loss from B, since A has been the victim of a fraudulent misrepresentation: B is liable for all A's losses directly arising from B's fraud, even though they were unforeseeable and, indeed, the result of the actions of a third party. In other words, A is put back into the position he would have been in if he had not entered the transaction.[1] It is not possible to exclude liability for fraud by an exemption clause.[2]

1 *Smith New Court Securities Ltd v Scrimgeour Vickers (Asset Management) Ltd* [1997] AC 254, [1996] 4 All ER 769, HL. The House of Lords indicated that B would not be liable for *all* A's losses if C's fraud had occurred *after* the transaction, on the basis that the causative influence of B's fraud on A's losses vis-à-vis C's fraud had faded: *sed quaere?*
2 Hence the necessity to plead fraud in *H & JM Bennet (Potatoes) Ltd v Secretary of State for Scotland* 1986 SLT 665, OH.

Part II

UNINTENTIONAL DELICT – GENERAL PRINCIPLES OF LIABILITY

Chapter 3.   The duty of care   57

Chapter 4.   Duty of care as a threshold device   69

Chapter 5.   Breach of a duty of care   111

Chapter 6.   Causation and related issues   129

CHAPTER 3

The duty of care

A. INTRODUCTION

In the first part of this book we examined the intentional delicts. *Culpa* or fault is the basis of delictual liability and is present in those delicts because the defender intended to harm the pursuer. Moreover, and this is important, the range of potential pursuers in those delicts is automatically restricted to those persons whom the defender intended to harm. However, in Scots law the concept of *culpa* also covers conduct which is merely careless, ie where the defender causes harm to the pursuer *unintentionally*. Immediately a difficulty arises. If A acts in a careless manner, ie his conduct fails to meet the standard of care demanded by society of a person in his position, then prima facie A is liable to anyone who suffers harm as a result of A's careless conduct.[1] In order to *limit* A's potential liability in delict to an indeterminate class of persons, the law has had to develop devices which restrict the number of persons who can claim damages for harm incurred by A's unintentional, but careless, conduct.

While there are many ways to restrict A's potential liability,[2] modern Scots law has accepted as a general principle that A will be liable for careless conduct only if he owed a duty of care to the person harmed by his actions. This duty of care must pre-exist the careless conduct. Whether a duty of care is owed by A to a particular person or class of persons, is ultimately a question of law to be determined by the courts. In deciding whether or not to recognise the existence of a duty of care in particular circumstances, the courts are influenced by issues of policy as well as legal principle. By recognising – or refusing to recognise – the existence of a duty of care, the courts in effect set the parameters of delictual liability for unintentional, but careless, conduct.

---

1 Cardozo J's phrase 'liability in an indeterminate amount for an indeterminate time, to an indeterminate class' elegantly summarises the point: *Ultramares Corpn v Touche* (1931) 255 NY 170 at 179.
2 For example, by developing a doctrine of proximate causation before A will be liable.

B. *DONOGHUE v STEVENSON*: THE NEIGHBOURHOOD PRINCIPLE

The starting point of any discussion of the duty of care is the famous case of *Donoghue v Stevenson*.[1] One Sunday evening, Mrs Donoghue went to visit a friend in Paisley.[2] They went to Wellmeadow Café at Wellmeadow Place, Paisley. The café was owned by Mr Minchella. They decided to have 'iced drinks', ie ice cream over which was poured lemonade. Mrs Donoghue's friend bought the ice cream and a bottle of 'ginger'.[3] The case proceeded on the assumption that Mrs Donoghue's friend had in fact bought a bottle of ginger beer, which would be contained in an opaque bottle. The friend poured some of the ginger beer over Mrs Donoghue's ice cream; but when, later in the evening, the friend poured the remainder of the contents of the bottle over Mrs Donoghue's melting ice, out floated the decomposing remains of a snail. The sight of the snail and her consumption of the snail-tainted iced drink resulted in Mrs Donoghue becoming ill. Mrs Donoghue sued Stevenson, the manufacturer of the ginger beer, in delict. The question before the courts was whether the manufacturer was liable to Mrs Donoghue in delict, even if she could prove the facts alleged and Stevenson had, in fact, been careless.

A most important point to notice is that there was no contractual nexus between Mrs Donoghue and Stevenson. The facts of the case can be shown thus:

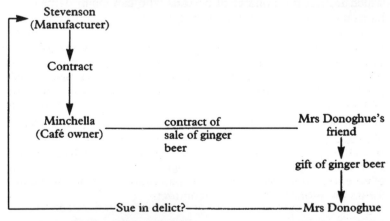

1 1932 SC (HL) 31, 1932 SLT 317. The literature on this case is voluminous, but see in particular A F Rodger 'Mrs Donoghue and Alfenus Varus' 1988 CLP 1.
2 The sex of the friend changes as the case proceeds through the courts!
3 In the parlance of the West Coast of Scotland at the time, 'ginger' was a generic term covering all kinds of aereated drinks.

Mrs Donoghue's friend could sue Minchella for breach of the contract of sale on the grounds that the ginger beer was not of merchantable quality; however, the friend's damages would be minimal since the friend did not suffer any ill-effects.[1] Mrs Donoghue could not sue Minchella, because she was not a party to the contract. Minchella could also have sued Stevenson in contract if he had suffered any loss. However, Mrs Donoghue had no contractual remedy. Therefore the issue before the House of Lords was whether *in the absence* of any contractual nexus between them, Mrs Donoghue, the ultimate consumer of the product, could sue the manufacturer in delict.

It was held by a majority of the House of Lords[2] that Mrs Donoghue was entitled to sue Stevenson in delict, because he owed her a duty of care; if he had in fact broken his duty towards her by his careless conduct and she had suffered loss, then she would succeed.[3] In other words, the relationship between the pursuer and defender was sufficiently proximate that the majority was prepared to hold that Stevenson owed Mrs Donoghue a duty of care for the purpose of liability in delict. Lord Atkin concluded:[4]

'... a manufacturer of products, which he sells in such a form as to show that he intends them to reach the ultimate consumer in the form in which they left him, with no reasonable possibility of intermediate examination, and with the knowledge that the absence of reasonable care in the preparation or putting up of the product will result in an injury to the consumer's life or property, owes a duty to the consumer to take that reasonable care'.

Lord Macmillan had

'no hesitation in affirming that a person, who for gain engages in the business of manufacturing articles of food and drink intended for consumption by members of the public in the form which he issues them, is under a duty to take care in the manufacture of these articles. That duty, in my opinion, he owes to those whom he intends to consume his produce ...'[5]

At its most specific level *Donoghue v Stevenson* is authority that a manufacturer of food and drink, which he intends to be used by the ultimate consumer without the opportunity of inspection or

1 For that reason it would have been pointless for the friend to have assigned his or her rights under the contract to Mrs Donoghue.
2 Lord Atkin, Lord Thankerton and Lord Macmillan; Lord Buckmaster and Lord Tomlin dissented.
3 After the decision of the House of Lords on the relevancy point, the case was settled and did not go to proof.
4 1932 SC (HL) 31 at 57.
5 1932 SC (HL) 31 at 71. On the genesis of Lord Macmillan's speech, see A F Rodger (1992) 168 LQR 236.

interference before use, owes a duty of care to the ultimate consumer to prevent him suffering injury to his person or property as a result of the manufacturer's carelessness when manufacturing the product. In other words, the relationship between manufacturer and ultimate consumer was sufficiently proximate in these circumstances that the court was prepared to impose a duty of care on the manufacturer towards the ultimate consumer. However, four years later, the Privy Council refused to interpret *Donoghue v Stevenson* in such a narrow way and held that the manufacturer of underpants owed a duty of care to the ultimate consumer even though the product was not for internal consumption, the underpants had been removed by the retailer from packets in which they had been delivered and they could have been – but had not been – washed by the ultimate consumer before use.[1] *Donoghue v Stevenson* thus becomes authority for the more general principle that a manufacturer of *any* product owes a duty of care to the ultimate consumer not to cause injury to his person or property as a result of a latent defect in a product which could not be discovered by inspection before use and was intended by the manufacturer to be used by the ultimate consumer in the same condition as it left the manufacturer. If, by his careless conduct, the manufacturer breaches this duty causing injury to the ultimate consumer's person or damage to his property, then he is liable in delict to make reparation for the harm suffered by the consumer.

Even at this more general level, there are two important limitations on the extent of the duty of care laid down in *Donoghue*:

(1) The duty only extends to *latent* defects; the bottle of ginger beer was opaque and the snail could not be seen before the contents were used.[2] If the defect is patent, ie obvious and the consumer chooses to use it, the manufacturer may escape liability because the chain of causation is broken[3] or, at least,

---

1 *Grant v Australian Knitting Mills Ltd* [1936] AC 85, PC. The plaintiff suffered dermatitis because free sulphites used in the manufacturing process had not been washed out of the garments before they were marketed. The fact that, unlike Mrs Donoghue, the plaintiff could have sued the retailer for breach of contract did not prevent recovery against the manufacturer in delict.

2 Similarly, the defect in the underpants in *Grant* was latent.

3 On causation, see Chapter 6 below. However, where the defect was originally latent, the chain of causation is not necessarily broken if the defect later comes to the attention of the consumer or that a third party had the opportunity, or indeed, an obligation to inspect the product. In the latter circumstances, the manufacturer and the third party can be jointly and severally liable: see *Grunwald v Hughes* 1964 SLT 94, OH, 1965 SLT 209; *Clay v A J Crump & Sons Ltd* [1964] 1 QB 533, [1963] 3 All ER 687, CA.

the damages will be reduced by the ultimate consumer's contributory negligence.[1]

(2) The duty is to prevent injury to the ultimate consumer's person or property. If A is injured by a defective product, carelessly manufactured by B, A can sue B for damages for pain and suffering (solatium). A can also sue B for economic loss which derives from his injuries (derivative economic loss), for example, loss of wages when in hospital, loss of wages in the future if A is permanently incapacitated and so forth.[2] If A's property is damaged by a defective product carelessly manufactured by B, then A can recover damages from B in respect of the damage to his property: for example, if A's dog dies as a result of contaminated dog food, or a defective vacuum cleaner damages A's carpet. But A is not able to sue B in delict if the only property damaged is the defective product itself. A cannot sue B in delict for the cost of repairing a defective car or for replacing a defective vacuum cleaner which blew up without injuring A's person or damaging any property, other than the vacuum cleaner itself. In these situations, A has suffered *pure*, as opposed to derivative, economic loss ie the cost of repair or replacement or the difference in value between the property with and without the defect. As we shall see, the courts are reluctant to allow a person to recover damages for pure economic loss in *delict*; A's remedy lies in *contract* against the person who sold him the goods, not the manufacturer.[3] Similarly, if the defect is discovered before there has been any damage done to A's person or property, the cost of repairing the defect is pure economic loss and cannot be recovered in delict.[4]

Donoghue is therefore an important decision in relation to product liability. But what makes the case remarkable is that two of the judges attempted to lay down criteria to determine the existence of a duty of care which would be applicable whenever an action for reparation as a result of unintentional, but careless, conduct arose. Lord Macmillan sets the scene:[5]

---

1 On contributory negligence, see pp 143 ff below.
2 On damages generally, see Chapter 16 below.
3 Of course A may not have a contract; for example, if the goods were a gift. But the purchaser could assign his contractual rights against the seller to A.
4 On economic loss, see further pp 78 ff below. There is no such restriction in the case of the intentional delicts.
5 *Donoghue v Stevenson* 1932 SC (HL) 31 at 70 (italics added).

'The law takes no cognisance of carelessness in the abstract. It concerns itself with carelessness only where there is a duty to take care and where failure in that duty has caused *damage*.[1] In such circumstances careless- ness assumes the legal quality of negligence and entails the consequences in law of negligence. What then are the circumstances which give rise to this duty to take care? In the daily contacts of social and business life, human beings are thrown into, or place themselves in, an infinite variety of relations with their fellows; and *the law can refer only to the standards of the reasonable man in order to determine whether any particular relationship gives rise to a duty to take care as between those who stand in relation to each other*. The grounds of action may be as various and manifold as human errancy; and the conception of legal responsibility may develop in adaption to altering social conditions and the changing circumstances of life. *The categories of negligence are never closed.* The cardinal principle of liability is that the party complained of should owe to the party complaining a duty to take care, and that the party complaining should be able to prove that he has suffered damage in consequence of a breach of that duty.'

Lord Macmillan is arguing that given changes in society, the courts, using as a yardstick the values of the reasonable man, may consider that new relationships are sufficiently proximate to impose a duty of care, breach of which gives rise to delictual liability for unintentional, but careless, conduct. *Donoghue v Stevenson* thus introduces a dynamic into the law which can extend the parameters within which there is delictual liability for careless conduct; this is done by the court deciding that a duty of care exists between parties in new social or economic relationships. Conversely, the court can refuse to extend the boundaries of delictual liability for careless conduct by deciding that a duty of care does not exist between parties in the circumstances of the case. As we shall see, during the period 1960–1980 the courts were prepared to expand the scope of delictual liability by recognising the existence of a duty of care in many new areas of social and economic life; but since the 1980s, the House of Lords has entered into a period of retrenchment and has refused to recognise the existence of a duty of care unless there is a direct precedent for doing so. Indeed, the House of Lords has overruled or distinguished earlier precedents where a duty of care had been

---

1 It cannot be emphasised enough that, in Scots law, there is no delictual liability unless a breach of a duty of care has caused damage: *damnum injuria datum*. Damage is a constituent of negligence as well as a consequence of negligence. We can owe a duty of care and be careless, but there is no liability unless our care- lessness has caused damage to the pursuer.

recognised on the basis that they extended liability too far.[1] It will be clear that in determining whether or not to impose a duty of care, the courts will be influenced by policy considerations as well as legal principle.

However, in *Donoghue v Stevenson* Lord Atkin attempted to provide a criterion for the existence of a duty of care which, at first sight, appears to be more objective. In a famous passage, he said:[2]

'The liability for negligence, whether you style it such or treat it as in other systems as a species of "*culpa*", is no doubt based upon a general public sentiment of moral wrongdoing for which the offender must pay. But acts or omissions which any moral code would censure cannot, in a practical world, be treated so as to give a right to every person injured by them to demand relief. *In this way rules of law arise which limit the range of complaints, and the extent of their remedy.* The rule that you are to love your neighbour becomes in law, you must not injure your neighbour; and the lawyer's question, Who is my neighbour? receives a *restricted* reply. You must take reasonable care to avoid acts or omissions which you can *reasonably foresee* would be likely to injure your neighbour. Who, then, in law, is my neighbour? The answer seems to be – persons who are so *closely and directly* affected by my act that I ought reasonably to have them in contemplation when I am directing my mind to the acts or omissions which are called in question.'

Thus, for Lord Atkin, a duty of care arises when it is reasonably foreseeable by the defender that a person in the position of the pursuer would be affected by the defender's acts or omissions. The neighbourhood principle therefore explains why a duty of care arises in many situations. A driver owes a duty of care to other road users because it is reasonably foreseeable that if he drives carelessly he may harm other road users. The occupier of property owes a duty of care to those who enter her property because it is reasonably foreseeable that they may be injured if the occupier is careless in the way she maintains the property. An employer owes a duty of care to his employee because it is reasonably foreseeable that if he is careless in the way he runs his system of working the employee may be injured. A manufacturer of a product owes a duty of care to the ultimate consumer because it is reasonably foreseeable that the ultimate consumer may be injured or suffer harm to his property if the product is defective.

It will be noticed, however, that in these examples the duty of care is to prevent *physical* harm to the pursuer or physical damage

1 See p 97 below.
2 1932 SC (HL) 31 at 44 (italics added).

to his property, and will enable the pursuer only to recover economic loss which is *derivative* from the injuries or damage sustained. But in situations where the pursuer does not suffer physical injury or damage to property, for example, pure economic loss, the courts tend to be reluctant to impose a duty of care even though the loss to the pursuer would have been reasonably fore-seeable by a person in the position of the defender. In other words, the reasonable foreseeability criterion, while a necessary condition for the existence of a duty of care, might not be sufficient to persuade the court to impose a duty of care in areas where no precedent for such a duty exists. Initially, in relation to recovery in delict for pure economic loss[1] the courts refused to impose a duty of care merely because the loss was reasonably foreseeable. Not only had loss to the pursuer to be reasonably foreseeable, but, in addition, there had to be a close degree of proximity between the parties *and* it had to be 'fair, just and reasonable' to impose a duty of care.[2]

This tripartite test was applied to a case of *physical* damage to property by the House of Lords in *Marc Rich & Co AG v Bishop Rock Marine Co Ltd, The Nicholas H*.[3] In this case, a surveyor (the defendant) advised the owner of a damaged vessel to continue on her voyage. The vessel sank and the cargo was lost. The House of Lords held that the surveyor did not owe a duty of care to the owner of the *cargo* (the plaintiff) to avoid damage to his property. This can be represented as follows:

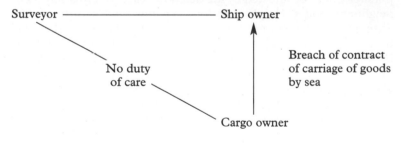

1 For full discussion, see pp 78 ff below.
2 *Caparo Industries plc v Dickman* [1990] 2 AC 605, HL, at 616–618 per Lord Bridge, at 628 per Lord Roskill, and at 633–634 per Lord Oliver. For full discussion see pp 81 below.
3 [1996] AC 211, [1995] 3 All ER 307, HL.

Although it was reasonably foreseeable that the surveyor's careless advice could result in *physical* harm to the plaintiff's property, nevertheless no duty of care arose, since the relationship between the parties was not sufficiently proximate and it would have been unfair, unjust and unreasonable to hold otherwise. To have imposed a duty of care in this case would have disturbed 'the intricate blend' of internationally accepted rules of shipping law, under which the owner of the cargo has a remedy against the owner of the ship in *contract*, but the amount of compensation is limited.[1]

The tripartite test has now been transplanted into Scots law to determine the existence of a duty of care in novel situations not governed by existing precedent. In *Coleridge v Miller Construction Ltd*,[2] the defender cut an electric cable supplying power to the pursuer's factory. The absence of electricity caused damage to the pursuer's furnace and to the glass being manufactured. Although the pursuer had sustained physical damage to his property, the Lord Ordinary (MacLean) held that the defender did not owe a duty of care. His reasoning was that although damage was reasonably foreseeable and there was sufficient proximity between the parties, it was not fair, just and reasonable to impose a duty of care, because this would upset the well-established liabilities of the parties' insurers.[3] The tripartite test has also been adopted where the pursuer has suffered personal injuries,[4] although it is accepted that in these circumstances 'it is self-evident that a civilised system of law should hold that a duty of care has been broken'.[5]

Put shortly, where the courts are being asked to extend delictual liability into hitherto uncharted waters, under the guise of determining whether or not there is a sufficient degree of proximity for the imposition of a duty of care and whether it is fair, just and

1 However, when a passenger was injured in an aircraft, it was held that a safety inspector owed him a duty of care on the basis of reasonable foreseeability of harm per se, without having to resort to the tripartite test. This was because it was not a novel situation, and it concerned personal injuries: *Perrett v Collins* [1998] 2 Lloyd's Rep 255, (1998) Times, 23 June, CA.
2 1997 SLT 485, OH.
3 See also *British Telecommunications plc v James Thomson & Sons (Engineers) Ltd* 1999 SC (HL) 9 (overruling decision at 1997 SC 59). The House of Lords, reversing the Second Division of the Court of Session, held that a domestic subcontractor did owe a duty of care to an employer whose insurance covered only nominated sub-contractors. Lord Mackay of Clashfern accepted that the tripartite test was appropriate: *British Telecommunicaions plc v James Thomson & Sons (Engineers) Ltd* 1999 (HL) 9 at 12.
4 *Gibson v Orr* 1999 SC 420, OH.
5 *Marc Rich & Co AG v Bishop Rock Marine Co Ltd, The Nicholas H* [1996] AC 211 at 235 per Lord Steyn.

reasonable to do so, the courts are undoubtedly influenced by policy considerations. In doing so they are governed by their concept of a fair distribution of risk in contemporary society – allowing the loss to be compensated in some areas, letting the risk lie where it has fallen in others.

To summarise: Lord Atkin's neighbourhood principle, based on reasonable foreseeability of harm, undoubtedly explains why a duty of care arises in many situations where there is the risk of physical harm to the pursuer or physical damage to the pursuer's property. But at the parameters of the field of existing delictual liability, the courts, for policy reasons, may refuse to extend the frontiers even though loss to the pursuer is reasonably foreseeable. On the other hand, there may be other factors present – as well as reasonable foreseeability of harm – which will persuade the courts that a duty of care should be imposed in the particular circumstances.

Although *Donoghue v Stevenson*[1] was a milestone in the development of the law of negligence, Lord Atkin's neighbourhood principle based on reasonable foreseeability of harm is no longer adequate as the touchstone for the impositiion of a duty of care. The tripartite test – the three elements of reasonable foreseeability, proximity and the 'fair, just and reasonable' criterion – has overtaken it in novel situations, ie those not governed by existing precedent. In *Gibson v Orr*, in the course of his judgment, the Lord Ordinary (Hamilton) said:[2]

'Although there is no authority directly binding on me, the three element test now falls . . . to be applied in Scotland in personal injury actions based on a duty of care as well as in other actions of damages so based. The more traditional approach in Scotland has been to apply the test laid down by Lord Atkin in *Donoghue v Stevenson*.[3] In *Dorset Yacht Co Ltd v Home Office* Lord Reid said that *Donoghue v Stevenson* might "be regarded as a milestone".[4] A milestone is an object encountered in the course of a journey. The relevant journey did not end in 1932 but went on, albeit not perhaps in a straight line . . . to the present day. Progress on that journey does not mean that milestones passed are no longer relevant; they remain important stages in the development of the law. However, I see no logical justification in modern circumstances and as the law has developed for applying a different test for the existence of a duty of care in respect of personal injury from that applicable relative to physical damage to property or to economic loss.'

1 1932 SC (HL) 32, 1932 SLT 317.
2 1999 SC 420, OH, at 431. For full discussion of this case, see pp 201 ff below.
3 1932 SC (HL) 31 at 44.
4 *Dorset Yacht Co Ltd v Home Office* [1970] AC 1004 at 1027, [1970] 2 All ER 294 at 297.

The fair, just and reasonable criterion expressly recognises that ultimately the imposition of a duty of care is an issue of policy and that any extension of delictual liability will occur on an incremental basis. In certain situations the tripartite test has itself been overtaken by other criteria for the imposition of a duty of care. In the next chapter, we shall consider some important examples of this process. The important point is that the concept of a duty of care is used as a *threshold* device, enabling the courts to extend the scope of delictual liability or to refuse to do so, depending on policy considerations. The duty of care allows the courts, if they so wish, to give an inch without fear that pursuers will take the proverbial mile.

CHAPTER 4

Duty of care as a threshold device

We shall now consider four examples of how the existence or non-existence of a duty of care has been used to extend or limit liability in delict for careless acts or omissions.

A. PURE OMISSIONS

A, a professor of law, is standing in the quadrangle of the university. He sees B, another professor, who is very shortsighted, walking with a white stick across the quadrangle. There is a banana skin lying in B's path. Instead of warning B, A merely stands and watches. B slips on the banana skin. A walks away giggling. Is A liable to B in delict for A's failure to warn B about the banana skin? The answer is no. Why? In spite of the fact that it is reasonably foreseeable by A that B may slip on the banana skin if A does not warn him, A does not owe B a duty of care. As a matter of policy, the law does not compel us to be good Samaritans. There must be additional factors creating a closer degree of proximity between the parties before the defender is liable in delict for an omission to act. Thus, for example, a parent is under a duty to rescue his child provided it is reasonable to do so; similarly, a nurse or a doctor owes a duty of care to tend their patients. But unless, as in these examples, there is some pre-existing relationship between the parties, the law does not impose a duty of care on the defender to rescue the pursuer or to act in such a way that the pursuer will avoid an accident.[1]

---

1 So, for example, in *Barrett v Ministry of Defence* [1995] 3 All ER 87, CA, the Court of Appeal held that the Royal Navy did not owe a duty of care to prevent an adult naval airman from becoming drunk off-duty. However, after the deceased had collapsed and was no longer capable of looking after himself, it was accepted that the Royal Navy had a duty to provide him with adequate medical care. The Royal Navy had broken that duty by not doing so: *sed quaere*? The deceased was held to be two-thirds contributorily negligent.

Returning to the example, it does not follow that B is without remedy. The university, as his employer, owes B a duty to take reasonable care for his safety at work;[1] moreover, as the occupier of the premises,[2] the university owes B a duty to take reasonable care that he is not harmed as a result of the state of the premises. If, of course, A deliberately dropped the banana skin in B's path, A would be liable for assault if A intended that B should slip. If A had carelessly dropped the banana skin, he could be liable since it is reasonably foreseeable that another person in the quadrangle could slip on the skin. But that duty of care is triggered by A's positive act in dropping the banana skin; it is no longer a case of a 'pure' omission.[3]

We must be careful to distinguish the cases of 'pure' omission where there is no liability, from the situation where there is a duty of care to prevent harm to the pursuer caused by the defender's careless conduct. In the latter situation, for example, in the case of the driver of a vehicle and other road users or the manufacturer of a product and the ultimate consumer, it is irrelevant for the purpose of the law of delict that the carelessness involves an omission to act, as opposed to a positive action. Overtaking without first checking in the mirror is just as careless as driving too fast: failing to check whether a product is infested by a snail is just as careless as giving the wrong instructions on how a product is to be used.

B. NERVOUS SHOCK

The law has long recognised that A can owe a duty of care to B to prevent B suffering nervous shock as a result of A's unintentional, but careless, conduct.[4] In order to succeed, the nervous shock must amount to a nervous illness, not simply a fright. However, initially at least, the duty of care arose only when the pursuer was in danger of suffering potential physical harm as a result of the defender's conduct. Put another way, where it was reasonably foreseeable by the defender that the pursuer could be physically injured as a result of the defender's conduct, it was also reasonably foreseeable that the pursuer might suffer a nervous shock if the defender's conduct did not actually cause physical injury to the

1 On employer's liability, see Chapter 12 below.
2 On occupier's liability, see Chapter 10 below.
3 For an interesting discussion of pure omissions, see T B Smith *A Short Commentary on the Law of Scotland* (Greens, 1962) p 672.
4 See, for example, *Dulieu v White & Sons* [1901] 2 KB 669.

pursuer but the pursuer had been terrified that it might do so. There was therefore a duty of care not to cause a nervous shock to a person who was within the area of risk of physical harm as a result of the defender's careless conduct. In the leading case of *Page v Smith*,[1] the plaintiff was involved in a road accident caused by the defendant's careless driving. The accident was not serious and the plaintiff suffered no physical injuries. However, the accident brought on a recurrence of the plaintiff's ME which had been in remission. The House of Lords held[2] that because the plaintiff was within the area of potential physical harm, he was to be regarded as a primary victim of the accident. In these circumstances, the defendant owed him a duty of care to prevent him suffering physical *or* psychiatric injury. It was irrelevant that he had not suffered physical injury or that psychiatric illness was not reasonably foreseeable because a person of ordinary fortitude would not have suffered a nervous shock in the circumstances. Thus a duty of care arises to prevent psychiatric illness, provided the pursuer is a primary victim, ie when it is reasonably foreseeable that she will suffer physical injury. It does not matter that she was not physically injured or that psychiatric injury was unforeseeable.

It is therefore important to determine when a person is a primary victim. Since the decision of the House of Lords in *White v Chief Constable of the South Yorkshire Police*,[3] the test is simply whether or not he had been exposed to physical danger.[4] In other words, whether or not the victim had been within the area of potential physical harm. Accordingly, persons who witnessed the death of fellow employees have been held not to constitute primary victims when they were not themselves in physical danger at the time of the accident.[5] Similarly, no duty of care is owed to prevent rescuers suffering nervous shock unless they are also in potential physical danger.[6]

1 [1996] AC 155, [1995] 2 All ER 736, HL.
2 Lords Ackner, Browne-Wilkinson and Lloyd; Lords Keith and Jauncey dissented.
3 [1999] 1 All ER 1, Lords Browne-Wilkinson, Steyn and Hoffmann; Lord Goff dissented and Lord Griffiths dissented in part.
4 Or had reasonable grounds to believe that he was in danger: see, for example, *Hunter v British Coal Corpn* [1999] QB 140, [1998] 2 All ER 97, CA.
5 *Robertson v Forth Road Bridge Joint Board* 1995 SC 364, 1996 SLT 263 (pursuer saw fellow employee blown off lorry on Forth road bridge); *McFarlane v EE Caledonia Ltd* [1994] 2 All ER 1 (plaintiff witnessed Piper Alpha explosion from a supply ship).
6 *White v Chief Constable of the South Yorkshire Police* [1999] 1 All ER 1. Cf *Chadwick v British Transport Commission* [1967] 2 All ER 945, [1967] 1 WLR 912, where the plaintiff was within the area of potential physical harm, and *Cullin v London Fire and Civil Defence Authority* (31 March 1999, unreported), QB.

If the pursuer is not a primary victim, she will be clasified as a secondary victim. For a long time, it was trite law that a defender did not owe a duty of care to a secondary victim to prevent her suffering psychiatric illness as a result of witnessing an accident. Here, the absence of a duty of care was being used by the courts as a threshold device to *limit* the defender's potential liability.

The leading case in Scots law is *Bourhill v Young*.[1] Young was a motorcyclist. Driving too fast, he overtook a stationary tramcar on its near side. He then crashed into a car which was turning right into a side street, some 50 feet from the tramcar. Young was killed. It was accepted that the accident was caused by Young's careless driving. At the time of the accident the pursuer, Mrs Bourhill, a fishwife, was on the far side of the tramcar putting her creel on her back. She therefore did not see the collision but she heard the crash and, after Young's body was removed, saw the blood on the road. She maintained that as a result of the accident she suffered a nervous shock which had caused her to miscarry. She sued Young's executor in delict. The complex factual situation can be shown as follows:

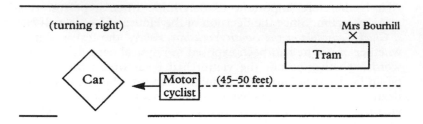

At the time of the accident Mrs Bourhill was 45–50 feet from the collision and on the far side of the tramcar. She was not within the area of risk of potential physical harm and – as we would say today – was therefore not a primary victim. In those circumstances, the House of Lords held that Young did not owe the pursuer a duty of care to prevent her suffering nervous shock as a result of his careless driving. It was accepted that a driver owes a duty of care to other road users or persons in premises adjoining the highway, but only when they were 'so placed' that they could reasonably be

1   1942 SC (HL) 78, 1943 SLT 105. For a discussion of this case, see W W McBryde '*Bourhill v Young*: the Case of the Pregnant Fishwife' in *Comparative and Historical Essays in Scots Law* (Butterworths, 1992) pp 66 ff.

expected to be injured by the defender's failure to take care.[1] Lord Macmillan stated that:[2]

'The duty to take care is the duty to avoid doing or omitting to do anything the doing or omitting to do which may have as its reasonable and probable consequence injury to others, and the duty is owed to those to whom injury may reasonably and probably be anticipated if the duty is not observed.'

But while Young owed such a duty to the occupants of the motor car, he did not owe it to Mrs Bourhill because she was outwith the area of risk of potential physical harm. As Lord Wright observed[3] she 'was completely outside the range of the collision. She merely heard a noise which upset her . . . She saw nothing of the actual accident, or indeed any marks of blood until later'. Lord Porter expressly articulated the policy considerations involved:[4]

'In the case of a civil action there is no such thing as negligence in the abstract. There must be neglect of the use of care towards a person towards whom the defendant owes the duty of observing care . . . The driver of a car or vehicle, even though careless, is entitled to assume that the ordinary frequenter of the streets has sufficient fortitude to endure such incidents as may from time to time be expected to occur in them, including the noise of a collision and the sight of injury to others, and is not to be considered negligent towards one who does not possess the customary phlegm.'

Thus, as a general rule, there was no duty of care to prevent a secondary victim from suffering a nervous shock: liability only extended to primary victims, ie persons who were placed in bodily danger or reasonably in fear of such danger as a result of the defender's careless conduct.

However, in *McLoughlin v O'Brian*[5] the House of Lords was persuaded to widen the scope of potential delictual liability for nervous shock. In this case, the plaintiff's husband and three children were involved in a road accident at 4 pm. They were taken to hospital where it was discovered that one child was dead. The plaintiff was told of the accident at 6 pm and went to the hospital where she saw the victims. She later suffered a psychiatric illness. The Court of Appeal took the view that while it was reasonably

---

1 1942 SC (HL) 78 at 86 per Lord Russell of Killowen.
2 1942 SC (HL) 78 at 88.
3 1942 SC (HL) 78 at 93.
4 1942 SC (HL) 78 at 98.
5 [1983] 1 AC 410, [1982] 2 All ER 298, HL. For an earlier example of liability to a secondary victim see *Hambrook v Stokes Bros* [1925] 1 KB 141, CA.

foreseeable that a wife and mother might suffer nervous shock in these circumstances, the defendant did not owe the plaintiff a duty of care because she was not present at the accident. In other words, since she was not within the area of potential physical harm, she was not a primary victim. The House of Lords rejected this argument and held that a duty of care existed in spite of the fact that the plaintiff had not witnessed the accident directly. While it was reasonably foreseeable that the spouse and mother of persons injured in an accident might suffer nervous shock, this in itself was not sufficient to create a duty of care. However, there were additional factors present in the case which provided the necessary degree of proximity between the parties from which a duty of care could be inferred. First, the plaintiff was with the victims shortly after the accident; accordingly, she had witnessed the aftermath of the accident. Second, she had personally *seen* the effects of the accident on her family and had not simply learned of the accident by letter or on television or from a third party.[1] It follows from *McLoughlin* that before a duty of care is owed to a secondary victim, not only must the risk of nervous shock to the pursuer be reasonably foreseeable but other factors must be present which show a sufficient degree of proximity between the parties. If these additional factors are *not* present, the court will not impose a duty of care.

These issues were further explored by the House of Lords in *Alcock v Chief Constable of South Yorkshire Police*.[2] Friends and relations of persons crushed to death at Hillsborough football ground brought claims for nervous shock. The House of Lords held that before a duty of care arose, it had to be reasonably foreseeable that the plaintiffs would suffer a nervous shock. The criterion was whether there was a close tie of love and affection between the plaintiff and the victim. This would be presumed if they were spouses or parent and child, but merely because they were related in some way would not per se be sufficient. Conversely, if they were not related, a plaintiff might still succeed if it could be shown that the requisite degree of love and affection *in fact* existed between the plaintiff and the victim.

In exceptionally horrific circumstances, a duty of care might arise even though the secondary victim did not fulfil the 'love and affection' criterion. However, this is difficult to prove. In *Robertson v Forth Road Bridge Joint Board*,[3] the fact that the pursuer, who had

1 *McLoughlin v O'Brian* [1983] AC 410 at 421–423 per Lord Wilberforce.
2 [1992] 1 AC 310, [1991] 4 All ER 907, HL.
3 1995 SC 364, 1996 SLT 263.

witnessed his fellow employee's death, had been a friend of the deceased and had socialised with him for many years was held not to be sufficient to constitute the necessary degree of 'love and affection'. The same kind of reasoning was applied in *McFarlane v EE Caledonia Ltd*,[1] where the plaintiff had witnessed the Piper Alpha explosion. So in this respect, *Alcock* has never been followed – what could have been more horrific than the accidents in *Robertson* and *McFarlane*?[2] In *Alcock*, the House of Lords held that reasonable foreseeability was not sufficient and the two *extra* factors for proximity had also to exist. Thus, the plaintiff had to witness the calamity or its aftermath (for example, by being at the stadium): identifying a dead relative or friend eight hours after the event was not enough. Secondly, the plaintiff must have seen or heard the accident: watching the event on television did not suffice since the defender knew that it was the policy of the television company in such circumstances to ensure that no specific person who was injured could be identified.

To summarise: a duty of care to prevent psychiatric injury to a secondary victim will arise if:

(1) there is a tie of love and affection between the secondary victim and the primary victim;
(2) the secondary victim was present at the accident or at its immediate aftermath; and
(3) the psychiatric injury was caused by direct perception of the accident or its immediate aftermath: it is not enough merely to have been informed of the accident.

The law now appears to be settled, but its application can lead to arbitrary results. In *Vernon v Bosley (No 1)*,[3] for example, two children were drowned when the car their nanny was driving crashed into a river. Their father was called to the scene and saw the unsuccessful attempts to rescue his children trapped in the car. The father's claim for damages for psychiatric injury was successful. The defendant owed him a duty of care because:

(1) he was the father of the primary victims; and
(2) he witnessed the aftermath; and
(3) his psychiatric illness arose from direct perception of the failed rescue attempt.

1 [1994] 2 All ER 1.
2 Similarly, the police constables in *White v Chief Constable of the South Yorkshire Police* [1999] 1 All ER 1, could not establish a sufficient tie of love and affection with the primary victims they were attempting to rescue: therefore the constables' claims as secondary victims failed.
3 [1997] 1 All ER 577.

But if, for example, he had not been able to be present at the rescue but was simply informed of his daughters' deaths by telephone, no duty of care would have arisen because of the absence of reasons (2) and (3). Similarly, Mrs Bourhill would still fail in her claim, since there was no tie of love and affection between her and Young's primary victims.[1]

In short, where the pursuer is not a primary victim, a claim for damages for psychiatric illness is likely to fail at the outset because of the difficulty of establishing a duty of care towards a secondary victim. Again, duty of care is being used as a threshold device.

C. WRONGFUL LIFE AND WRONGFUL BIRTH

It is generally accepted that a person owes a duty of care not to harm a foetus, ie a child *in utero*. If a foetus is injured in its mother's womb, if the child is subsequently born alive, the *child* can sue the defender in delict in respect of its physical damage, even though the injuries were sustained when the child was a foetus. However, in *McKay v Essex Area Health Authority*[2] a mother contracted rubella (German measles) during her pregnancy. When her child was born, the baby was badly deformed as a result of the mother's illness. The mother alleged that owing to the hospital's carelessness, she had not been informed that her baby might be born with deformities. Since no tests had been carried out, the mother had been denied the opportunity of a lawful termination of her pregnancy. The Court of Appeal held that the hospital may have been in breach of a duty of care towards the *mother* which would entitle her to damages for having to bring up a deformed child. However, the hospital did not owe a duty of care towards the *child*, to allow the child's mother the opportunity to terminate the pregnancy. A child has no right to be born whole or not at all. This denial of the existence of a duty of care towards a foetus to terminate the pregnancy, if the foetus is deformed, is clearly based on principles of public policy.[3] Thus the law has refused to recognise wrongful life actions by denying the existence of a duty of care: again, we see the duty of care being used as a threshold device.

---

1 But could she have sued if she had been related to Young, who was killed in the accident as a result of his own negligence? It is submitted that she could.
2 [1982] QB 1166, [1982] 2 All ER 771, CA.
3 Moreover, even if such a duty existed, the child's deformities were not caused by the careless conduct of the hospital, but by the rubella; on the necessity for causation, see Chapter 6 below. Of course, if the hospital had caused the injuries, it *would* have been liable to the child, if born alive.

While there will be no duty of care towards a foetus to terminate the pregnancy because it might be born deformed, the Court of Appeal emphasised that the defendant could have been in breach of its duty towards the *mother*, in not allowing her the opportunity of a termination. This has been accepted in Scots law. Thus a hospital owes a duty of care to the parents of a child to provide the mother with an opportunity to terminate her pregnancy if her child is likely to be born physically or mentally handicapped.[1]

In England, it has long been recognised[2] that a doctor owes a duty towards a man or a woman who undergoes sterilisation; if owing to the doctor's careless conduct, a child is conceived, the parents may sue in negligence for the birth of an unplanned child.

When this issue first arose in Scotland, the English approach was followed.[3] Then came the case of *McFarlane v Tayside Health Board*.[4] The pursuers sought damages for the birth of a healthy child who had been born as a result of a failed sterilisation on the father. The Lord Ordinary (Gill) admitted that the defenders owed a duty of care to the pursuers, who were their patients, but denied the pursuers' action of damages. Lord Gill argued that the parents had not sustained any reparable loss. He refused to classify pregnancy and labour as physical injury to the mother, and he did not regard the cost of rearing the child as economic loss, since such loss was outweighed by the inestimable benefits of being the parents of a healthy child.

This decision was reversed by the Second Division of the Inner House of the Court of Session.[5] There it was held that the parents' right not to have a child had been infringed, ie that the unplanned conception constituted the harm (*damnum*). This was a reparable interest in modern Scots law. Consequently, the mother could recover damages for pain and suffering caused by the pregnancy and birth; and both parents could recover compensation for the economic costs of bringing up the child whose birth had not been

---

1 *McLelland v Greater Glasgow Health Board* 1999 SC 305.
2 See, for examples, *Thake v Maurice* [1986] QB 644, [1984] 2 All ER 513; *Gold v Haringey Health Authority* [1987] QB 481, [1987] 2 All ER 888, CA. In *Goodwill v British Pregnancy Advisory Service* [1996] 2 All ER 161, CA, the Court of Appeal held that the duty of care did not extend to advising the future sexual partners of male patients that their vasectomy could undergo a spontaneous reversal. *Sed quaere*: counsel for Ms Goodwill was Ms Cherie Booth QC!
3 *Allan v Greater Glasgow Health Board* 1998 SLT 580, OH.
4 1997 SLT 211, OH. In *Anderson v Forth Valley Health Board* 1998 SLT 588, OH, the Lord Ordinary (Nimmo Smith) refused to follow *McFarlane*: in *Anderson*, the unplanned baby was handicapped.
5 1998 SLT 307.

planned. Moreover, their damages would not be reduced because the mother had refused to terminate the pregnancy.

D. PURE ECONOMIC LOSS

It is in the area of liability in delict for economic loss that the concept of a duty of care has been extensively used by the courts as a threshold device. *Donoghue v Stevenson*[1] is authority for the principle that a duty of care arises when it is reasonably foreseeable by the defender that his careless acts or omissions would cause physical injury to the pursuer or physical damage to the pursuer's property. However, the pursuer can recover damages for economic loss which derives from the pursuer's injuries or the physical damage to his property, for example, loss of earnings while in hospital and loss of earnings in the future when the pursuer is unable to work.[2] This is known as *derivative* economic loss, ie economic loss which derives from the pursuer's physical injuries or the physical damage to the pursuer's property. However, the law does not, as a general rule, allow recovery in *delict* where the pursuer only suffers economic loss as a result of the defender's careless conduct.[3] In the case of a defective product, for example, which has not physically injured the pursuer or damaged other property belonging to the pursuer, the cost of repair or the difference in value between a defective and non-defective product is not recoverable in *delict*. The pursuer has suffered pure economic loss and the courts have refused to impose a duty of care on the manufacturer in respect of such losses, even though such a loss is reasonably foreseeable. This is because the courts seek to protect the defender from potentially indeterminate liability.[4]

1 1932 SC (HL) 31, discussed at pp 58 ff above.
2 On damages, generally, see Chapter 16 below. Derivative economic losses may not be recoverable if they are too remote: see pp 265 ff below.
3 Where the defender has intended to cause economic loss, for example by fraud or by wrongful occupation of property, Scots law does provide compensation: see, for example, *Saeed v Waheed* 1996 SLT (Sh Ct) 39, 1995 SCLR 504. The reasoning in *Saeed* is controversial because Sheriff Principal Nicholson relied on English cases concerned with liability for pure economic loss arising from negligence. It is thought that the pursuer should have been awarded violent profits: see p 21 above.
4 So when a Scottish football team supporter claimed damages against FIFA and the Scottish Football Association for economic loss incurred as a result of the delay to a World Cup match between Scotland and Estonia, it was held that the SFA and FIFA did not owe the pursuer a duty of care to ensure that the match took place as scheduled: *Macdonald v Fédération Internationale des Football Associations* 1999 SCLR 59, OH.

Although reasonable foreseeability of pure economic loss is not sufficient for the imposition of a duty of care, the courts have, in certain situations, been prepared to hold that a duty of care does exist. However, there must be factors *in addition* to reasonable foreseeability of pure economic loss, which demonstrate that there is a sufficient degree of proximity between the parties so that it is fair, just and reasonable for a duty of care to be inferred. These additional requirements are, as we have seen,[1] simply a rationalisation by the courts of why they are, or are not, prepared to extend the parameters of liability in delict. It is the paradigm of the duty of care being used as a threshold device.

We shall now examine these developments in detail.

(1) Careless misrepresentation

A may make a statement to B which causes B physical injury or damage to B's property: for example, A tells B that it is safe to drink contaminated water. A will owe B a duty of care if it is reasonably foreseeable that B will suffer physical injury or damage to his property if A's statement is made carelessly. This is a simple application of the *Donoghue* neighbourhood principle.[2] However, A may make a statement to B which causes B pure economic loss. For example, A tells B that B should enter into a contract with C. Relying on A's advice, B enters into the contract with C. As a result, B loses money. Can B sue A in delict for the pure economic loss B has suffered, if A's statement was made carelessly?[3] The answer depends on whether A owes a duty of care to B not to make careless statements which cause B pure economic loss.

The criteria for the existence of such a duty were laid down by the House of Lords in *Hedley Byrne & Co Ltd v Heller & Partners Ltd*.[4] The plaintiffs through their bankers asked E's bankers, the defendants, whether E was a respectably constituted company. E's bankers replied that E was. On reliance of this statement, the plaintiffs became E's advertising agents. E later went into liquidation. As a result, the plaintiffs suffered economic loss. The facts of the case can be shown as follows:

1 See pp 64 ff above.
2 For full discussion, see pp 58 ff above.
3 Cf if A made the statement fraudulently, when, of course, A is liable for fraud. On fraud, see pp 51 ff above.
4 [1964] AC 465, [1963] 2 All ER 575, HL.

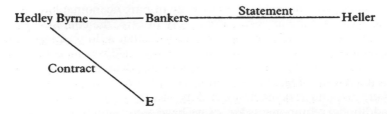

It will be clear that there was no contract between Hedley Byrne and Heller. The question was whether the plaintiffs could sue the defendants in delict. The House of Lords held that the defendants owed a duty of care to the plaintiffs, if the defendants had undertaken responsibility for the accuracy of the statement and knew or ought to have known that the plaintiffs would rely on that statement. If the duty was broken as a result of the statement being made carelessly, the defendants could be liable for the plaintiffs' pure economic loss. In the course of his speech, Lord Devlin stated[1] that before there was liability, the plaintiffs had to show that the defendants owed the plaintiffs 'a special duty' to take care. The categories of relationships where this duty arose included not only contractual relationships (ie where there was a contract between the parties) or fiduciary relationships (for example, parent and child, trustee and beneficiary) but also relationships which were the 'equivalent to contract'. One example of this would be where the defender had voluntarily assumed responsibility for the accuracy of the statement and knew or ought to have known that the pursuer would rely on the information. The paradigm situation is where the defender is a professional business man, for example a banker, solicitor or accountant, who in the absence of a contract between them, gives advice to the pursuer in the course of the defender's business, knowing that it will be relied on by the pursuer.

It is important to notice that reasonable foreseeability of loss to the pursuer is not per se sufficient to establish a duty of care. There must be additional factors present from which the courts will infer the necessary proximity of relationship between the parties. These factors include the defender's knowledge of the identity of the pursuer, either as an individual or as a member of an identifiable class; and the defender's knowledge that the information will be communicated to and used by the pursuer in connection with a particular transaction or transactions of a particular kind.

1 [1963] 2 All ER 575 at 610.

These limitations on *Hedley Byrne v Heller* liability were recognised by the House of Lords in *Caparo Industries plc v Dickman*.[1] The auditor of a company carelessly carried out an audit showing that the company was in a better financial position than was in fact the case. It was reasonably foreseeable (a) that potential investors in reliance on the audit would invest in the company to their loss; and (b) that existing shareholders, in reliance on the audit, would purchase more shares in the company to their loss. This, in fact, happened. Although the auditor had a contract with the company, he did not have a contract with existing and potential shareholders. Although the losses which had been incurred were reasonably foreseeable, the House of Lords held that the auditor did not owe a duty of care to the shareholders or potential shareholders to prevent them suffering economic loss as a result of the careless audit. The reasons were that their relationships were not sufficiently proximate and that it was not fair, just and reasonable to impose a duty of care. In other words, the factors additional to reasonable foreseeability did not exist in this case. Lord Bridge explained:[2]

'The salient feature of all these cases [ie where a *Hedley Byrne v Heller* duty of care was recognised] is that the defendant giving advice or information was fully aware of the nature of the transaction which the plaintiff had in contemplation, knew that the advice or information would be communicated to him directly or indirectly and knew that it was very likely that the plaintiff would rely on that advice or information in deciding whether or not to engage in the transaction in contemplation. In these circumstances the defendant could clearly be expected ... specifically to anticipate that the plaintiff would rely on the advice or information given by the defendant for the very purpose for which he did in the event rely on it. So also the plaintiff ... would in that situation reasonably suppose that he was entitled to rely on the advice or information communicated to him for the very purpose for which he required it. The situation is entirely different where a statement is put into more or less general circulation and may foreseeably be relied on by strangers to the maker of the statement for any one of a variety of different purposes which the speaker has no specific reason to anticipate. To hold the maker of the statement to be under a duty of care in respect of the accuracy of the statement to all and sundry for any purpose for which they may choose to rely on it is not only to subject him, in the classic words of Cardozo CJ to "liability in an indeterminate amount for an indeterminate time to an indeterminate class",[3] it is also to confer on the world at large a quite unwarranted entitlement to

---

1 [1990] 2 AC 605, [1990] 1 All ER 568, HL.
2 [1990] 1 All ER 568 at 576.
3 *Ultramares Corpn v Touche* (1931) 255 NY 170 at 179.

appropriate for their own purposes the benefit of the expert knowledge or professional expertise attributed to the maker of the statement.'

Accordingly, the House of Lords held that an auditor did not owe a duty of care to a member of the public at large who relied on the audit to purchase shares or increase an existing shareholding in the company: such a duty would arise only if the auditor knew that his statement would be communicated to the plaintiff and relied upon by the plaintiff in a particular transaction of a particular kind.[1]

Hedley Byrne v Heller was an English case. The principle has been accepted as part of Scots law.[2] One area where it has been applied is in relation to the liability of surveyors. Consider the following example. A wishes to purchase a house from B. He approaches a building society for a loan. Before it can give the loan the building society must obtain a report on the value of the property from a surveyor. It is a term of A's contract with the building society that A will pay the surveyor's fee. Instead of obtaining an independent survey, A relies on the valuation report commissioned for the building society and goes ahead with the purchase. The house turns out to have faulty foundations which will cost £20,000 to repair. The facts of the case can be represented in the diagram on page 83 below.

Since A has not been physically injured and the faulty foundations have not caused physical damage to any other property owned by A, A has suffered only pure economic loss. This is either the cost of repairs or the difference in value between the house with faulty foundations and the house if the foundations were sound. Although A has a contract of sale with B, the seller of heritage does not usually warrant that a house built on the land conveyed is sound. Therefore A has no *contractual* remedy against B. Moreover, although A paid for the survey, he has no contract with the surveyor: the surveyor's

1 In *Nordic Oil Services Ltd v Berman* 1993 SLT 1164, OH, the Lord Ordinary (Osborne) held that directors of a company did not owe a duty of care to creditors of the company to prevent them suffering economic loss as a result of the acts or omissions of the company. In *Reeman v Department of Transport* [1997] 2 Lloyd's Rep 648, CA, it was held by the Court of Appeal that before a duty of care could arise by virtue of *Caparo*, the defendant's statement had to be plaintiff-specific, purpose-specific and transaction-specific. Thus if an auditor is aware that a particular identified bidder or lender would rely on the audited accounts and the auditor intends that the bidder or lender should rely on them, he owes that party a duty of care: *Galoo Ltd (in liquidation) v Bright Grahame Murray* [1994] 1 WLR 1360, [1995] 1 All ER 16, CA.
2 *John Kenway Ltd v Orcantic Ltd* 1979 SC 422, 1980 SLT 46, OH; *Eastern Marine Services (and Supplies) Ltd v Dickson Motors Ltd* 1981 SC 355, OH; *Twomax Ltd v Dickson, McFarlane and Robinson* 1982 SC 113, 1983 SLT 98, OH. The last decision must now be read in the light of the limitations laid down in *Caparo Industries plc v Dickman* [1990] 2 AC 605, [1990] 1 All ER 568, HL.

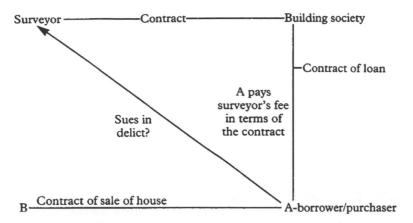

Surveyor ——————Contract——————Building society

—Contract of loan

A pays
surveyor's fee
Sues in   in terms of
delict?   the contract

B——Contract of sale of house——————A-borrower/purchaser

contract is with the building society. However, it has been held that the surveyor owes a duty of care to A, if the surveyor knows that the report will be used by A and will be relied upon by A to purchase the house.[1] As well as reasonable foreseeability of loss to A, the surveyor's knowledge of A and the particular transaction, A's reliance on the report and the fact that A paid for the report, provide the additional factors which create a sufficient degree of proximity between A and the surveyor for a *Hedley Byrne v Heller* duty of care to arise. Accordingly, if the report was made carelessly, A can recover damages for pure economic loss from the surveyor. If, however, A later sold the house to C and C relied on the valuation report rather than commission a new survey, the surveyor would not owe a duty of care to C. For although it is reasonably foreseeable that the report would be relied on by a singular successor of A (ie a subsequent purchaser of the house), since the surveyor did not know the identity of C at the time of the survey and C did not pay the fee, the additional factors are not present and the duty of care does not arise.[2]

1 *Martin v Bell-Ingram* 1986 SC 208, 1986 SLT 575; *Smith v Eric S Bush and Harris v Wyre Forest District Council* [1990] 1 AC 831, [1989] 2 WLR 790. See also *Smith v Carter* 1994 SCLR 539, 1995 SLT 295, OH, where the survey was commissioned by A acting as the undisclosed agent of B. It was held that a duty of care was owed to B because it is not uncommon for one person to commission a report on behalf of joint purchasers.
2 This would follow from the *ratio* of *Caparo Industries plc v Dickman* [1990] 2 AC 605, [1990] 1 All ER 568, HL. Similarly, the absence of such additional factors prevented the surveyor owing a duty of care to the owner of the lost cargo in *Marc Rich & Co AG v Bishop Rock Marine Co Ltd, The Nicholas H* [1994] 3 All ER 686, [1994] 1 WLR 1071, CA (affd [1995] 3 All ER 307, HL) discussed at p 64 above.

Although the existence of a duty of care to prevent economic loss to the plaintiff was recognised in *Hedley Byrne & Co Ltd v Heller & Partners Ltd*,[1] in fact the plaintiff did not obtain damages in that case. When they provided the information, the defendants expressly stated that it was given 'without responsibility on the part of the bank'. The House of Lords held that this disclaimer was effective to protect the defendants from liability. After their potential delictual liability towards purchasers of property was established, surveyors started to insert a similar disclaimer in their valuation reports or in the building society's contract with the borrower/purchaser. Provided the disclaimer came to the notice of the purchaser before the purchaser entered into the contract of sale,[2] for a time these disclaimers were effective to protect the surveyor from liability in delict.[3] However, where the disclaimer is a term of the purchaser's contract with the building society,[4] it cannot be relied on unless it satisfies the requirement of reasonableness under the Unfair Contract Terms Act 1977.[5] Moreover, the controls in UCTA 1997 now extend to disclaimers which are not contractual terms.[6] This includes any disclaimers in the surveyor's valuation report. Accordingly, a surveyor cannot escape delictual liability by relying on a disclaimer, unless it satisfies the requirement of reasonableness. In *Smith v Eric S Bush; Harris v Wyre Forest District Council*,[7] the House of Lords, applying the parallel English provisions of the Unfair Contract Terms Act 1977, held that a disclaimer was not reasonable when the purchaser was of limited means and buying domestic property. If the purchaser was wealthy or the property bought was commercial, then a surveyor might be able to establish that the disclaimer was

1 [1964] AC 465, [1963] 2 All ER 575, HL.
2 If it did not come to the purchaser's notice before the contract of sale was agreed, the disclaimer was not effective: *Martin v Bell-Ingram* 1986 SC 208, 1986 SLT 575.
3 *Robbie v Graham and Sibbald* 1989 SCLR 578, 1989 SLT 870, OH.
4 *Melrose v Davidson and Robertson* 1993 SC 288, 1993 SLT 611.
5 UCTA 1977, s 16. See *Melrose v Davidson and Robertson* 1993 SC 288, 1993 SLT 611.
6 Law Reform (Miscellaneous Provisions) (Scotland) Act 1990, s 68.
7 [1990] 1 AC 831, [1989] 2 All ER 514, HL.

reasonable.[1] It is thought that a similar view would be taken by the courts in Scotland.[2]

The classic example of *Hedley Byrne v Heller* liability is where A makes a misrepresentation to B which B relies on to enter a contract with C. A owes B a duty of care which enables B to sue A in *delict* for pure economic loss. However, does A owe B a *Hedley Byrne v Heller* duty of care when A makes a misrepresentation to B which induces B to enter a contract with A? For many years, as a result of the decision in *Manners v Whitehead*,[3] B was denied a remedy in delict against A unless A's misrepresentation was fraudulent.[4] The rule in *Manners v Whitehead* has been abolished.[5] Accordingly, provided the *Hedley Byrne v Heller* criteria are established,[6] A will owe B a duty of care so that B can sue A in *delict* if the misrepresentation was made carelessly and caused B pure economic loss. In addition or as an alternative, B will have contractual remedies, for example, reduction, arising from the misrepresentation.[7] There has, as yet, been no reported decision in Scotland where an action for negligent misrepresentation in delict has been successfully brought against the other party to the contract.[8]

(2) *Henderson v Merrett* – A general duty of care to prevent pure economic loss?

An attempt to rationalise the law on delictual liability for pure economic loss was made by the House of Lords in *Henderson v*

1 As happened, for example, in *Omega Trust Co Ltd v Wright Son & Pepper (No 1)* [1997] 1 EGLR 120, CA.
2 The House of Lords in *Smith v Eric S Bush; Harris v Wyre Forest District Council* [1990] 1 AC 831, [1989] 2 All ER 514, HL, also rejected the argument that the disclaimer prevented a duty of care arising in the first place. Instead, it held that the duty of care existed in spite of the disclaimer and that the disclaimer was therefore an exemption clause purporting to exclude liability. Where the disclaimer satisfies the requirement of reasonableness, no duty of care arises: *McCullagh v Lane Fox and Partners* [1996] 1 EGLR 35, (1995) Times, 22 December, CA.
3 (1898) 1 F 171.
4 On fraud, see pp 51 ff above.
5 Law Reform (Miscellaneous Provisions) (Scotland) Act 1985, s 10.
6 And it is submitted that in this situation they usually are.
7 These are the same as the contractual remedies available after a fraudulent misrepresentation, discussed at p 51 above.
8 An attempt failed in *Palmer v Beck* 1993 SLT 485, OH on the ground that s 10 of the LR(MP)(S)A 1985 was not retrospective. See also *Clelland v Morton Fraser Milligan* 1997 SLT (Sh Ct) 57, where an action under s 10 failed because it was not brought against the other party to the pursuer's contract.

Merrett Syndicates Ltd.[1] Actions for damages were brought by 'Lloyd's names' against Lloyd's members' agents and managing agents of syndicates. The 'names' alleged that they had suffered losses as a result of the negligence of the agents. Under contracts with their members' agents, the names gave the agents the exclusive right to undertake risks and reinsurance on their behalf. This was done directly through the members' agents or indirectly by the members' agents delegating the tasks to managing agents through a sub-agency contract. This can be illustrated as follows:

CONTRACT

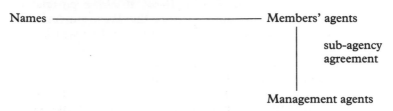

Names ———————————————————— Members' agents

sub-agency
agreement

Management agents

The obvious remedy was for the names to sue the members' agents for breach of contract. Unfortunately, this action was time-barred. So an action against them and the management agents could lie only in tort/delict. The question before the House of Lords was whether the management agents and the members' agents owed a duty of care to the names. Their Lordships held that they did. Why?

Lord Goff of Chieveley maintained that a duty of care arises to prevent the plaintiff suffering pure economic loss when the defendant has voluntarily assumed responsibility for the economic interests of the plaintiff, with the knowledge that the plaintiff is relying on the defendant's expertise. This assumption of responsibility covers the provision of services as well as information, careless omissions and careless actions. When the parties are linked directly or indirectly by contracts, the terms of the contracts may exclude liability in delict, but to be effective any such exemption clauses will have to satisfy the requirements of reasonableness under the Unfair Contract Terms Act 1977.

Like Lord Atkin with his neighbourhood principle,[2] Lord Goff was laying down a general duty of care: if the two criteria are satisfied, ie voluntary assumption of responsibility and concomitant reliance, then a duty of care exists and it is not necessary to

1 [1995] 2 AC 145, [1994] 3 All ER 506, HL.
2 See *Donoghue v Stevenson* 1932 SC (HL) 31, 1932 SLT 317.

consider whether or not it is fair, just and reasonable to impose a duty of care.[1]

To summarise: a general duty of care to prevent pure economic loss will arise if:

(1) the defender has voluntarily assumed responsibility for the economic interests of the pursuer;
(2) the defender knows that the pursuer is relying on the defender's professional expertise; and
(3) the terms of any contract linking the pursuer and defender does not negative delictual liability.

A couple of points should be noted. First, although the defender must voluntarily assume responsibility for the pursuer's economic interests, the test is objective, in that any provision purporting to exclude delictual liability must satisfy the requirements of reasonableness in the Unfair Contract Terms Act 1977. Thus, in the case of the negligent surveyor,[2] he will be held to have assumed voluntarily responsibility for the financial interests of the purchaser of a domestic building because any exemption clause will not satisfy the requirement of reasonableness. Second, the defender must know that the pursuer does or will rely on his expertise. The necessity for 'concomitant reliance' by the pursuer, which is known to the defender, provides an element of mutuality between the parties which restricts the defender's potential delictual liability.

It is submitted that the *Henderson v Merrett* criteria provide a rationale for the liability for negligent misrepresentations discussed in the previous section. However, they also explain other situations where delictual liability for pure economic loss has been recognised. In *Spring v Guardian Assurance plc*,[3] for example, the House of Lords held that an employer owed a duty of care to a former employee when providing a reference for him. Because of the defendant's carelessness, the plaintiff had been unable to obtain a job. By agreeing to provide a reference, the employer had voluntarily assumed responsibility for Spring's financial interests, knowing that he would rely on them to prepare the reference carefully.[4]

---

1 The general nature of the duty was emphasised by the House of Lords in *Williams v Natural Life Health Foods Ltd* [1988] 2 All ER 577, HL, at 581 per Lord Steyn. A director of a company was held not to owe a duty of care to the plaintiff in this case because he had not assumed personal responsibility for the plaintiff's financial interests: the *company* was, of course, liable.
2 For discussion, see pp 82 ff above.
3 [1995] 2 AC 296, [1994] 3 All ER 129, HL.
4 See also *Donlon v Colonial Mutual Group (UK Holdings) Ltd* 1998 SC 244, 1997 SCLR 1088 (failure by employer to exercise reasonable care in ensuring that facts communicated to third parties were acccurate).

A bank's liability to its customers will depend on the scope of the responsibility it has voluntarily assumed.[1] Before the director or an employee of a company can be personally liable to a customer of the company's, there must be evidence from their dealings that he or she assumed personal responsibility for the financial interests of the customer.[2]

It remains to be seen whether the Scottish courts will follow and develop the *Henderson v Merrett* general duty of care. It is the present writer's view that the concepts of voluntary assumption of responsibility and concomitant reliance do provide the basis for a general duty of care to prevent pure economic loss. As a result of the defender's carelessness, the pursuer is prevented from entering into prospective contracts[3] or induced to enter an uneconomic contract, or an existing contract becomes less profitable. We can call this interference with the pursuer's contracts 'relational economic loss'. The defender's liability arises from his assumption of responsibility *and* his knowledge of the pursuer's reliance – which provides the necessary proximity.

However, the courts are still attracted to the *Caparo* tripartite criteria,[4] and appear reluctant to forego the 'incremental' approach[5] in favour of a *Henderson v Merrett* general duty of care to prevent relational economic loss.[6]

(3) Liability arising from defective performance of a contract

A enters a contract with B. In order to fulfil his contract with A, B enters into a contract with C. C's performance of his contract with

1 See *Verity v Lloyds Bank plc* [1996] Fam Law 213 (bank owes duty when advising on the prudence of a specific transaction); *Gold Coin Joailliers SA v United Bank of Kuwait* [1997] 6 Bank LR 60, (1996) Times, 4 November, CA (bank does not owe a duty to the recipient of a standard reference, that he is dealing with the bank's customer and not a rogue).
2 See *Williams v Natural Health Foods Ltd* [1998] 2 All ER 577, HL.
3 As in *Spring v Guardian Assurance plc* [1995] 2 AC 296, [1994] 3 All ER 129, HL.
4 Discussed at p 81 above.
5 *Weir v National Westminster Bank plc* 1994 SLT 1251 (extending bank's liability to detect and report forged signatures to include the agent of a disclosed principal, who under a power of attorney was the sole signatory on the account).
6 See, for example, the approach of the Court of Appeal in *Peach Publishing Ltd v Slater & Co; Slater & Co v Sheil Land Associates Ltd* [1998] BCC 139, CA; *Bank of Credit and Commerce International (Overseas) Ltd (in Liquidation) v Price Waterhouse (No 2)* [1998] Lloyd's Rep Bank 85, (1998) Times, 4 March, CA (tripartite test, incremental approach and assumption of responsibility all used to determine the existence of a duty of care).

B is carried out carelessly. As a result, A suffers pure economic loss. The facts can be represented as follows:

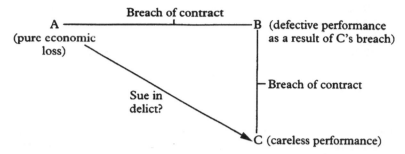

A's obvious remedy is to sue B for breach of contract. But if this is not possible (for example, if there is an exemption clause in A's contract with B) or not desirable (for example, if B is bankrupt) can A sue C in delict?

If C's careless performance of his contract with B had caused physical injury to A or physical damage to A's property, C would owe A a duty of care provided A's injury or damage to A's property was reasonably foreseeable: ie the *Donoghue v Stevenson* neighbourhood principle would apply.[1] Since A suffers only pure economic loss, reasonable foreseeability of such loss is not sufficient to give rise to a duty of care. But A, B and C are connected by a series of contracts. If C had broken his contract with B, with the intention of harming A, A can sue C in *delict* for wrongful interference with B's performance of his contract with A and can recover for pure economic loss.[2] In this case, however, C has not broken his contract with B in order to harm A. Instead, C has by his *careless* conduct broken his contract with B with the result that B's performance of his contract with A is defective, causing A economic loss. In these circumstances, does C owe a duty of care to A not to perform his contract with B in a careless manner, if it will cause A economic loss to do so?

In *Junior Books Ltd v Veitchi Co Ltd*,[3] the House of Lords held that such a duty of care could exist. The pursuers entered into a contract with Ogilvie (Builders) Ltd (the main contractor) for the construction of a factory. The pursuers' architects nominated Veitchi, a floor specialist, to lay a floor in the factory. In other

1 *Donoghue v Stevenson* 1932 SC (HL) 31, 1932 SLT 317. For discussion, see pp 58 ff above.
2 On the relevant delicts see pp 35 ff above.
3 1982 SC (HL) 244, 1982 SLT 492.

words, Veitchi was a nominated sub-contractor. However, Veitchi's contract to lay the floor was with the main contractor, not Junior Books. The floor laid was seriously defective and had to be replaced by the pursuers. There was no averment that the floor laid was dangerous so as to be likely to cause physical injuries to any persons in the factory or damage to the pursuers' property. The pursuers sought damages from the defenders for the cost of replacing the floor. This complex factual situation can be illustrated as follows:

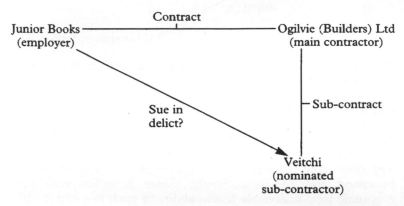

Although nominated by Junior Books' architect, Veitchi had no contractual relationship with Junior Books. Although Junior Books could have sued the main contractor for breach of contract, they chose not to do so. Their only remedy against Veitchi, therefore, lay in delict. Since there was no danger of any physical injury to persons in the factory or damage to the pursuer's property, the case fell outside the neighbourhood principle of reasonable foreseeability of harm laid down in *Donoghue v Stevenson*.[1] In other words, the case was concerned with the recovery of pure economic loss, ie the cost of replacing the defective floor. Nevertheless, the House of Lords held[2] that, in the circumstances, there was sufficient proximity between the parties for a duty of care to arise: the defenders were under a duty to prevent loss to the pursuers as a

1 However, Lord Keith of Kinkel took the view (1982 SC (HL) 244 at 267) that if such a danger was present, the neighbourhood principle in *Donoghue* was wide enough to cover the cost of averting such a danger. This is doubtful after the decision of the House of Lords in *Murphy v Brentwood District Council* [1991] 1 AC 398, [1990] 2 All ER 908, HL, discussed at pp 97 ff below.
2 Lords Fraser of Tullybelton, Russell of Killowen, Keith of Kinkel and Roskill; Lord Brandon dissented.

result of the defenders' careless performance of their contract with Ogilvie (Builders) Ltd.

Lord Roskill identified eight factors from which the requisite proximity for a duty of care could be inferred:[1]

'(1) The appellants [Veitchi] were nominated sub-contractors. (2) The appellants were specialists in flooring. (3) The appellants knew what products were required by the respondents [Junior Books] and their main contractors and specialised in the production of those products. (4) The appellants alone were responsible for the composition and construction of the flooring. (5) The respondents relied upon the appellants' skill and experience. (6) The appellants as nominated sub-contractors must have known that the respondents relied upon their skill and experience. (7) The relationship between the parties was as close as it could be, short of actual privity of contract. (8) The appellants must be taken to have known that if they did the work negligently (as it must be assumed that they did) the resulting defects would at some time require remedying by the respondents expending money upon the remedial measures as a consequence of which the respondents would suffer financial or economic loss.'

Several points should be noted. First, the defender and the pursuer are connected by a series of contracts which are subsisting at the time of the defenders' careless acts (ie the installation of the defective floor). Second, Veitchi had been nominated by the pursuers' architect. This is important because as a nominated sub-contractor, Veitchi must have known the identity of the employer, Junior Books, who was contracting with the main contractor, Ogilvie (Builders) Ltd. Third, because Veitchi knew that Junior Books required their services, knew that Junior Books relied upon their expertise, and knew that careless performance of their contract would require the floor to be repaired by Junior Books, Veitchi must have *known* that careless performance by them of their contract with Ogilvie (Builders) Ltd would cause *economic* loss to the pursuer.

Thus, for a *Junior Books* duty of care to arise, the pursuer A and defender C must be connected by a series of contracts: A–B–C.[2] In addition to reasonable foreseeability of loss as a result of his careless acts, C must know the identity of the pursuer A, know that A has a contract with B and know that A will suffer economic loss as a result of C's careless performance of his contract with B, since this will, in turn, render defective B's performance of his contract with A. In establishing this degree of knowledge, the fact that C is

---

1 *Junior Books Ltd v Veitchi Co Ltd* 1982 SC (HL) 244 at 277.
2 *Comex Houlder Diving Ltd v Colne Fishing Co Ltd (No 2)* 1992 SLT 89, OH; *Scott Lithgow Ltd v GEC Electrical Products Ltd* 1989 SC 412, 1992 SLT 244, OH.

a nominated sub-contractor is important but not necessary.[1] However, A's reliance on C's expertise etc is important. It provides *evidence* that C knows that his careless performance will cause A economic loss. The crucial point is that C must know that the careless performance of his contract with B will cause A economic loss as a result of B's consequent defective performance of his contract with A.[2]

Thus, it is the present writer's submission that *Junior Books* liability should be seen as an extension of the economic delict of wrongful interference with performance of a contract. If, in the above example, C broke his contract with B with the result that B renders defective performance of his contract with A, it is long settled that A can sue C in delict for pure economic loss if C broke his contract with B *with the intention* of harming A. *Junior Books* goes a step further by providing that A can sue C in delict where C carelessly performs his contract with B with the result that B renders defective performance of his contract with A, provided C *knew* that his careless performance of his contract with B would cause economic loss to A; ie C owes a duty of care to A not to perform his contract with B in a careless manner.

Read this way, the duty of care held to exist in *Junior Books* is kept within the narrowest of limits. First, it only applies where the parties are connected by contracts which are *existing* at the time of the defender's careless acts. In *D & F Estates Ltd v Church Commissioners for England*,[3] the Church Commissioners owned a block of flats built by the main contractors. The main contractors sub-contracted the plaster work to sub-contractors. The plaster was defective but was not a source of danger. *After* the flats were built, a flat was leased to the plaintiffs. The plaintiffs sued inter alios the main contractors in delict for the cost of repairing the plaster work. The House of Lords held that the main contractors and the sub-contractors were not under a duty of care to prevent economic loss to the plaintiffs as a result of the defective plaster.[4]

---

1 In *Scott Lithgow Ltd v GEC Electrical Products Ltd* 1989 SC 412,1992 SLT 244, OH, the Lord Ordinary (Clyde) thought at 250 ff that it would be enough if the defender had been approved by the pursuer.
2 On the other hand, if A's reliance on C's expertise is held to be necessary, and given that C must know that A will suffer economic loss by C's careless performance of the contract, it could be argued that *Junior Books* liability is simply an example of the general *Henderson v Merrett* duty of care to prevent relational economic loss.
3 [1989] AC 177, [1988] 2 All ER 992, HL.
4 For discussion of the absence of a duty of care to prevent economic loss arising from a defective product, see pp 95 ff below.

In the present writer's view, there was also no possibility of a *Junior Books* duty of care in this case because there was no contractual nexus between the plaintiffs and the main contractor or sub-contractor at the time of the careless act, as illustrated below:

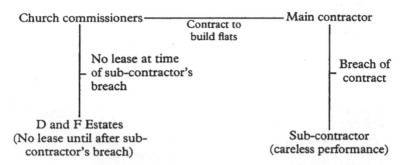

Second, even if there is an existing contractual nexus, no *Junior Books* duty of care will arise unless the defender knows the identity of the pursuer; this will therefore prevent such a duty of care arising in most cases involving mass production. For example, if A manufactures components for B who uses them to produce products which he sells to C, a distributor, who sells them to X, Y and Z etc, A does not owe a *Junior Books* duty of care to X, Y or Z to prevent *economic loss*[1] due to A's careless performance of his contract with B in supplying B with defective components. This is because A will generally not know of the contracts between C and X, Y, and Z:

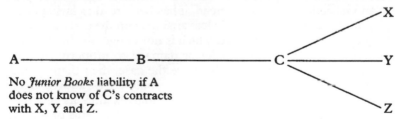

Third, even if there is an existing contractual nexus and the defender knows the identity of the pursuer, the terms of the contracts between the parties, for example exemption or indemnity clauses, may indicate that the parties intended to exclude potential liability in delict. In those circumstances, the court is

---

1 Of course, A may owe a *Donoghue v Stevenson* duty of care to X, Y and Z to prevent them suffering physical injury or damage to their property as a result of A's careless manufacture of the components.

unlikely to find the existence of a *Junior Books* duty of care. Finally, the defender must anticipate loss to the particular pursuer as a result of the defender's defective performance.[1]

The limitations which are inherent in the *Junior Books* duty of care are therefore sufficient to keep potential liability for economic loss within relatively narrow parameters. Once again we see the duty of care operating as a threshold device.

If it is accepted that the *Junior Books* duty of care is simply an extension of the delict of wrongful interference with the performance of a contract, so as to trigger liability as a result of the defender's careless conduct as well as conduct intended to harm the pursuer, then it is thought that there is a future for *Junior Books* liability.

Although it has been followed in Scotland, *Junior Books Ltd v Veitchi Co Ltd*[2] has been consistently distinguished in cases south of the border. In *D & F Estates Ltd v Church Commissioners for England*[3] Lord Bridge opined[4] of *Junior Books*:

'The consensus of judicial opinion, with which I concur, seems to be that the decision of the majority is so far dependent on the unique, albeit non-contractual, relationship between the pursuer and the defender in that case and the unique scope of the duty of care owed by the defender to the pursuer arising from that relationship that the decision cannot be regarded as laying down any principle of general application in the law of tort or delict.'

The reason for this scepticism is that *Junior Books* has *not* been regarded as a case which is only concerned with wrongful interference with the pursuer's existing contracts (ie recovery of relational economic loss). Instead, it has been read as laying down potential liability for economic loss arising from the careless manufacture of a defective product, which is not dangerous in the sense of causing injury to the pursuer or damage to property (ie non-relational economic loss). If this were the case, then there would, indeed, be cause for concern. But if analysed as above, *Junior Books* liability does not have this potential. Within its relatively narrow sphere, *Junior Books* is both an important and principled decision.[5]

---

1 *Simaan General Contracting Co v Pilkington Glass Ltd (No 2)* [1988] QB 758, [1988] 1 All ER 791, CA.
2 1982 SC (HL) 244, 1982 SLT 492.
3 [1989] AC 177, [1988] 2 All ER 992, HL.
4 [1988] 2 All ER 992 at 1003.
5 *Junior Books* has been approved by the Court of Appeal in Singapore: see *RSP Architects Planners and Engineers v Ocean Front Pte Ltd* (1998) 14 Const LJ 139, CA (Sing).

(4) Liability arising from defective products and buildings

As we have seen, A owes a duty of care to B when it is reasonably foreseeable that B will suffer physical injury or physical harm to his property as a result of A's careless acts or omissions. In *Donoghue v Stevenson*[1] it was held that the manufacturer of a product owed a duty of care to the ultimate consumer to prevent the consumer suffering personal injury or physical damage to his property as a result of a defect in the product caused by the manufacturer's carelessness. The consumer is entitled to damages not only for pain and suffering but also for economic loss which derives from the injury or damage to his property, ie derivative economic loss.

There is an important limitation on the scope of *Donoghue v Stevenson* liability. The duty of care extends only to physical injuries to the pursuer or damage to the pursuer's property caused by the defective product. The damage must be done to property other than the defective product itself. For example, if a defective vacuum cleaner explodes and burns the pursuer or burns the pursuer's carpet, there is *Donoghue v Stevenson* liability. But if the defective vacuum simply does not work or it explodes and does not injure the pursuer or does not damage any other property of the pursuer there is no *Donoghue v Stevenson* liability. Why? In these circumstances, the pursuer has suffered only *pure* economic loss, ie the cost of repairing the vacuum cleaner or the difference in value between a defective and non-defective cleaner. The courts have consistently refused to allow the pursuer to recover compensation in *delict* for such losses. Instead, the pursuer must resort to the law of contract to obtain compensation:

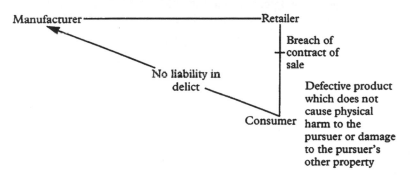

1 1932 SC (HL) 31, 1932 SLT 317, discussed at pp 58 ff above.

The consumer cannot sue the manufacturer in delict because the consumer has suffered only pure economic loss. The consumer must sue the retailer for *breach of contract* to recover any loss suffered as a result of the product being defective. If the ultimate consumer does not have a contract with the retailer, if, for example, the defective product was a gift from a third party, the consumer has prima facie no remedy. However, the third party could assign his rights under *his* contract with the retailer to the consumer, thus enabling the consumer to recover damages for breach of contract.

It should also be noticed that there will generally be no possibility of *Junior Books* liability in this situation. This is for two reasons: (1) no contractual chain or nexus exists between the manufacturer and the consumer at the time of the careless act since the consumer will only enter into a contract with the retailer *after* the product has been manufactured; and (2) the manufacturer will not know the identity of the consumer.[1] Similarly, there is no *Henderson v Merrett* general duty of care[2] to prevent relational economic loss, because the defender manufacturer does not voluntarily assume responsibility for the ultimate consumer's financial interests and there is no concomitant reliance on the consumer's part.

This principle of non-liability for economic loss also applies to the provision of services. In *D & F Estates Ltd v Church Commissioners for England*[3] the plaintiffs incurred expense in repairing defective plasterwork. The defective plasterwork was not a danger to the plaintiffs' person or property. The House of Lords held that the plaintiffs could not sue the defendants, who were responsible for the defective plasterwork, in *delict* because they had only suffered pure economic loss, ie the cost of repair. The plaintiffs' only remedy could be in contract.

However, at one time there appeared to be an exception in respect of defective buildings. Local authorities are under a duty to ensure that buildings conform to building regulations and bye-laws: this is done by a local authority engineer approving the plans

---

1 It might, of course, be different in both respects if the manufacturer were supplying a product specifically designed for the consumer.
2 See *Henderson v Merrett Syndicates Ltd* [1995] 2 AC 145, [1994] 3 All ER 506, HL, and pp 85 ff above.
3 [1989] AC 177, [1988] 2 All ER 992, HL. There was no *Junior Books* liability in this case. See p 92 above.

and the design of the proposed building. In *Anns v Merton London Borough Council*[1] the defendants approved the design of the foundations of a building. After it was built, the foundations were discovered to be defective. The House of Lords held that the local authority owed the owner[2] of the house a duty of care in this situation and that damages could include the cost of repair. It was also decided that the builder owed a similar duty of care to the owner of the property. The fact that the plaintiff had only suffered pure economic loss appeared to be irrelevant. The concept of the duty of care was clearly being used as a threshold device significantly to extend the parameters of delictual liability for pure economic loss. In a famous passage, Lord Wilberforce explained:[3]

'The position has now been reached that in order to establish that a duty of care arises in a particular situation, it is not necessary to bring the facts of that situation within those of previous situations in which a duty of care has been held to exist. Rather the question has to be approached in two stages. First one has to ask whether, as between the alleged wrongdoer and the person who has suffered damage there is a sufficient relationship of proximity or neighbourhood such that, in the reasonable contemplation of the former, carelessness on his part may be likely to cause damage to the latter, in which case a prima facie duty of care arises. Secondly, if the first question is answered affirmatively, it is necessary to consider whether there are any considerations which ought to negative, or to reduce or limit the scope of the duty or the class of person to whom it is owed or the damages to which a breach of it may give rise.'

Applying these principles, Lord Wilberforce held that the local authority owes a duty of care to the owner of a building which was subject to latent defects in construction when the plans were inspected and approved by the local authority. The fact that the owner may suffer only pure economic loss was not sufficient to deny the existence of the duty on policy grounds, since the class of potential plaintiffs was restricted to the owners or lessees of the property.

This was to prove to be the high-water mark of the extension of the parameters of delictual liability for defective buildings. The courts thereafter refused to use Lord Wilberforce's two-stage test further to extend the scope of liability. At length, *Anns* itself came to be doubted and was ultimately overruled in *Murphy v Brentwood*

---

1 [1978] AC 728, [1977] 2 All ER 492, HL.
2 Technically, the plaintiff in this case was a lessee of the property.
3 [1978] AC 728 at 751–752.

District Council.[1] In this case, a builder laid foundations of a house in accordance with designs approved by the local authority. The foundations proved to be defective. The owner could not afford the £45,000 required for repairs; instead he sold the house for £35,000 less than its market value would have been if the foundations had been sound. The owner sued the local authority for the loss of the value of the house. The House of Lords held that *Anns* was wrongly decided. Neither a local authority nor a builder owes the owner of a house a duty of care in respect of pure economic loss arising from the defective construction of the property; and pure economic loss includes the cost of repairs or the loss of the property's value.

The House of Lords was also sceptical of what is known as the 'complex structure' doctrine. It can be argued that the foundations should be regarded as separate from the rest of the house. If they are defective and cause physical damage to another part of the house, for example, by cracks in the walls, this is damage to 'other' property and falls within the *Donoghue v Stevenson* duty of care. The view was taken that this approach is unrealistic:[2]

'The reality is that the structural elements in any building form a single indivisible unit of which the different parts are essentially interdependent. To the extent that there is any defect in one part of the structure it must to a greater or lesser degree necessarily affect all other parts of the structure. Therefore any defect in the structure is a defect in the quality of the whole and it is quite artificial, in order to impose a legal liability which the law would not otherwise impose, to treat a defect in an integral structure, so far as it weakens the structure, as a dangerous defect liable to cause damage to "other property".'

But where a distinct item, such as a central heating boiler, is incorporated into the structure of a building there can be *Donoghue v Stevenson* liability if, as a result of a defect, it causes damage to

---

1 [1991] 1 AC 398, [1990] 2 All ER 908, HL. The House of Lords doubted the value of Lord Wilberforce's two-stage test for the existence of a duty of care. Instead, it should only be imposed by analogy with earlier precedents ie it is an incremental process. In this respect, *Murphy* has been followed in Scotland: *Nordic Oil Services Ltd v Berman*. '[I]n determining the existence and scope of a duty of care in a context in which a claim is made for economic loss, the court must have particular regard to the traditional categorisation of situations in which duties may or may not have been recognised in particular circumstances': 1993 SLT 1164 at 1171 per the Lord Ordinary (Osborne). *Murphy* has not been followed in Australia or New Zealand: see *Bryan v Maloney* (1995) 11 Const LJ 274, HC (Aus); *Invercargill City Council v Hamlin* [1996] AC 624, [1996] 1 All ER 756, PC.
2 *Murphy v Brentwood District Council* [1990] 2 All ER 908 at 928 per Lord Bridge.

the house. The owner in these circumstances could sue the manufacturer of the boiler for physical damage to his 'other' property, ie his house.

It is important to examine the implications of *Murphy* for purchasers of heritable property. Consider the following example. A, a company, enters into a contract with B to build a block of flats. After the flats are completed, A feus the flats to various purchasers (vassals), including C. After a few years, cracks appear in C's flat. It is discovered that the foundations are unsound and that it will cost approximately £10,000 to have them repaired:

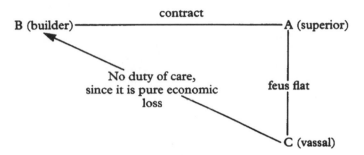

As a result of *Murphy*, C has no delictual remedy against B because C has only suffered pure economic loss; ie B does not owe C a duty of care in respect of the cost of repairs.[1] Although there is a contractual relationship between A and C, this will not help C because a superior does not warrant the quality of the buildings on the land feued.[2] Similarly, if B enters into a contract to build a house for A who later sells the house to C (a singular successor), B does not owe C a duty of care to prevent C suffering pure economic loss as a result of defects in the building:

1 If C was injured or any property of C's other than the house was damaged, C can sue B in delict as B owes C a duty of care under the *Donoghue v Stevenson* neighbourhood principle.
2 But cf *Stevenson v A & J Stephen (Builders) Ltd* 1996 SLT 140, OH, where the builders were the pursuer's feudal superiors. They had obtained completion certificates on the basis that there was a fire stop between the pursuer's house and his garage. This had in fact not been done. The pursuer sued the builder when fire spread from the garage and destroyed the pursuer's house. Even if damage to the house were treated as economic loss, a duty of care might be owed because of the feudal relationship between the parties. It should be noted that the feudal system is to be abolished: Abolition of Feudal Tenure etc (Scotland) Bill 1999.

B (builder)————contract to build————A————contract of sale————C (singular
↑   successor)
└——————————————No duty of care, because——————————————┘
                        pure economic loss

Again, although there is a contract between A and C, C will have
no contractual remedy against A because A does not usually
warrant the quality of the buildings on the land disponed.

Moreover, B does not owe a *Junior Books* duty of care[1] to C in
either of these examples. This is because there is no contractual
nexus between B and C at the time of the careless act, since C only
purchases the property *after* it is built. Even if C had an option
from A to purchase a flat while it was being built, a *Junior Books*
duty of care will not arise unless B knows the identity of the
purchaser, C. Similarly, there is no *Henderson v Merrett* general
duty of care[2] to prevent relational economic loss because there is
no voluntary assumption of responsibility and concomitant
reliance.

Because of the absence of a delictual claim against B or a
contractual claim against A, in order to protect his interests C
should obtain an independent survey *before* purchasing the
property. If as a result of the surveyor's carelessness the defects are
not discovered, C can sue the surveyor for breach of contract. And,
as we have seen,[3] even if C relied upon a survey carried out on
behalf of C's bank or building society for the purpose of obtaining
a loan, C may be able to sue the surveyor in delict on the grounds
of careless misrepresentation, where damages for pure economic
loss are recoverable.

(5) Non-liability for secondary economic loss

We have been considering the situation where the defender has
directly caused pure economic loss to the pursuer. However, there
is a second situation where pure economic loss can arise. This is
where the defender has caused physical harm to A or A's property,
and as a result B suffers economic loss. This will most often arise
where a contract which B had with A cannot be fulfilled or is no
longer profitable. This is known as secondary economic loss.

1 See *Junior Books Ltd v Veitchi & Co Ltd* 1982 SC(HL) 244, 1982 SLT 492, and
  pp 88 ff above.
2 See *Henderson v Merrett Syndicates Ltd* [1995] 2 AC 145, [1994] 3 All ER 506,
  HL, and pp 85 ff above.
3 See pp 82 ff above.

In *Reavis v Clan Line Steamers Ltd*[1] Mrs Reavis and her orchestra were involved in a collision at sea which was caused inter alia by the fault of the defender, the owner of the ship in which they were sailing. Some members of the orchestra were drowned and the orchestra had to be disbanded. Mrs Reavis claimed that the services of the players had been secured by contracts of employment and she sought damages from the defender for the loss of profits she had sustained as a result of the deaths and injuries of her employees.

The court held that she was not entitled to recover. An employer is not entitled to sue in delict in respect of secondary economic loss sustained as a result of the death or injury of an employee caused by the negligence of a third party. In other words, the defender did not owe Mrs Reavis a duty of care to prevent her suffering economic loss as a result of her employees being no longer able to perform their contracts of employment with her. If Mrs Reavis had been injured, she could, of course, recover for derivative economic loss arising from her *own* injuries – but she could not sue in respect of the death or injury of her employees. (The injured employees and the families of the deceased employees, would, of course, have separate claims in delict against the defender).

Thus, where a person is injured or property is damaged, prima facie it is only the injured person or the owner of the property who has title to sue. Third parties who suffer economic loss as a result of the injuries or damage to the property are not entitled to sue for secondary economic loss because the defender does not owe them a duty of care. Thus, for example, in *Dynamco Ltd v Holland and Hannen and Cubitts (Scotland) Ltd*[2] the defender's excavator damaged an underground electric supply cable owned by the South of Scotland Electricity Board. As a result, there was a power cut at the pursuer's factory which lasted for 15½ hours. The pursuer sued for the loss of profits while the factory was closed. The court held that although the defender owed a duty of care to the electricity board not to damage its property, ie the cable, the defender did not owe a duty to the pursuer in respect of secondary economic loss, even though such loss was reasonably foreseeable. In *Coleridge v Miller Construction Ltd*,[3] the power cut physically damaged the glass that the pursuer manufactured in his factory.

1 1925 SC 725, 1925 SLT 386, OH.
2 1971 SC 257, 1972 SLT 38.
3 1997 SLT 485, OH.

The Lord Ordinary (MacLean) held that the test for the existence of a duty of care should be the same whether or not the pursuer suffered physical damage to his property or pure economic loss. In the absence of avements that the defender knew that the pursuer required a continuous supply of electricity, it was not reasonably foreseeable that the pursuer would suffer damage to his products if an electric cable were cut. Moreover, it was not fair, just and reasonable to impose a duty of care in these circumstances, even if damage had been reasonably foreseeable, because the pursuer should have insurance to cover any losses arising from power cuts howsoever caused. Thus secondary physical damage is irrecoverable, as well as secondary economic loss.[1]

In the important case of *Nacap Ltd v Moffat Plant Ltd*,[2] the pursuers entered into a contract with British Gas to lay a pipeline owned by British Gas in the North Sea. During the work, the defenders damaged the pipeline. As a result, Nacap was unable to complete the work in the time agreed in their contract with British Gas and consequently suffered economic loss. The Inner House held that the pursuers had no title to sue because they were not the owners of the pipeline. In other words, they could not sue in delict for the secondary economic loss they had suffered as a result of the damage to property owned by a third party, ie British Gas.

This approach has been followed in England. In *Candlewood Navigation Corpn Ltd v Mitsui OSK Lines Ltd, The Mineral Transporter*[3] the plaintiffs time-chartered a vessel from the owners of a ship. The vessel was damaged by the defendants. The Privy Council held that the plaintiffs could not recover damages for the hire charges they had to continue to pay and the loss of profits they had incurred while the ship underwent repairs. The defendants did not owe a duty of care to the plaintiffs in respect of the secondary economic loss they had suffered as a result of their contract with the owners becoming less profitable:

---

1 In *Skerries Salmon Ltd v The Braer Corpn* 1999 GWD 1–63, the Lord Ordinary (Gill) held that the defender did not owe the pursuers a duty of care to prevent them from having to sell their salmon at low prices. The pursuers alleged that this was caused by a loss of public confidence in the quality of Shetland salmon after the Braer oil tanker had run aground. In the absence of any evidence that the pursuers' fish had been contaminated with oil, this was a case of secondary economic loss and no duty was owed. See also *Landcatch Ltd v The Braer Corpn*; *Landcatch Ltd v International Oil Pollution Compensation Fund* 1999 GWD 20–962.
2 1987 SLT 221, reversing 1986 SLT 326.
3 [1986] AC 1, [1985] 2 All ER 935, PC.

Owner of ship ◄───────────── Defendants damage ship

Charterparty

Plaintiffs – contract becomes less profitable

In this and the previous cases, a *Junior Books* duty of care does not arise because there is no contractual nexus between the parties. Even if, in *Dynamco Ltd v Holland and Hannen and Cubitts (Scotland) Ltd,*[1] the defender had been engaged on a contract with the electricity board, who had, of course, a contract with its customer, Dynamco, *Junior Books* liability would still not have arisen because the defender would not have known the identity of the pursuer. Similarly, no *Henderson v Merrett* general duty of care arises because in none of these cases did the defender voluntarily assume responsibility for the financial interests of the pursuers.

Nevertheless, in other circumstances, it is thought that there could be sufficient proximity between the parties for a *Junior Books* or *Henderson v Merrett* duty to arise. In *Leigh and Sillavan Ltd v Aliakmon Shipping Co Ltd, The Aliakmon,*[2] the plaintiff (the buyers) entered into a cost and freight (c & f) contract for the purchase of steel coils. Under a c & f contract the seller arranges for the shipping of the goods and obtains a bill of lading from the shipper. The bill of lading is the contract of carriage of the goods. The buyer becomes the owner of the goods when the bill of lading is indorsed by the seller and delivered to the buyer against payment by the buyer of the price. On indorsement, the buyer 'steps into the shoes' of the seller in relation to the bill of lading issued by the shipper. Accordingly, if the goods are damaged in transit, the buyer can sue the shipper for breach of contract. This did not happen in this case because the c & f contract was varied by the parties with the effect that the seller remained owner even though the risk of damage to the goods passed to the buyers. The bill of lading was not indorsed, so that the buyers did not have title to sue the shippers for breach of contract. When they eventually became

---

1 1971 SC 257, 1972 SLT 38.
2 [1986] AC 785, [1986] 2 All ER 145, HL, affirming [1985] 2 All ER 44, CA. The contractual position has now been overtaken by the Carriage of Goods Act 1992, which makes it easier for the buyer who undertakes the risk to sue the shipper for breach of contract.

the owners of the goods, the plaintiff attempted to sue the shippers in delict. The complex facts can be shown thus:

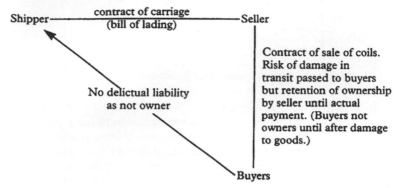

Shipper ——— contract of carriage
              (bill of lading) ——— Seller

No delictual liability
as not owner

Contract of sale of coils.
Risk of damage in
transit passed to buyers
but retention of ownership
by seller until actual
payment. (Buyers not
owners until after damage
to goods.)

Buyers

Because the buyers assumed the risk under the contract of sale, they had no right to sue the seller for breach of contract when the goods were damaged. As a result of the variation, the buyers could not use the usual remedy in a c & f situation of suing the shipper for breach of contract. The House of Lords held that the buyers could not sue the shipper in delict, because they were not the owners of the goods at the time the goods were damaged. *Junior Books Ltd v Veitchi & Co Ltd*[1] was distinguished on the grounds that the pursuer in that case was the owner of the floor when it was carelessly laid.[2] However, if *Junior Books* had been argued as a wrongful interference with contracts case, there could have been liability if the shipper had known the identity of the buyers and the existence of the c & f contract when they carelessly performed their contract with the sellers. However, such an argument would probably have failed, because the shipper had no knowledge of the variation of the contract between the sellers and the buyers, and the buyers had consequently not become the owners of the goods in the usual way.[3]

---

1 1982 SC (HL) 244, 1982 SLT 492.
2 *Leigh and Sillavan Ltd v Aliakmon Shipping Co Ltd, The Aliakmon* [1986] 2 All ER 145 at 155 per Lord Brandon.
3 For similar reasons, it would be unlikely that the shipper had voluntarily assumed responsibility for the financial interests of the buyers. But if, in *Reavis v Clan Line Steamers Ltd* 1925 SC 725, 1925 SLT 386, OH, Mrs Reavis had been killed or injured with the result that her employees suffered economic loss, it is submitted that there would now be a possibility of their recovering damages for economic loss under *Junior Books* if the defender, who had a contract of carriage with Mrs Reavis, had known the identity of her employees and the existence of the contracts of employment.

In the *Aliakmon* case,[1] an attempt was made to circumvent the principle of non-recovery in delict for secondary economic loss by invoking the doctrine of 'transferred loss'. In the Court of Appeal Goff LJ formulated the doctrine thus:[2]

'Where A owes a duty of care in tort [delict] not to cause physical damage to B's property, and commits a breach of that duty in circumstances in which the loss of or physical damage to property will ordinarily fall on B but (as is reasonably foreseeable by A) such loss or damage, by reason of a contractual relationship falls on C, then C will be entitled, subject to the terms of any contract restricting A's liability to B, to bring an action in tort against A in respect of such loss or damage to the extent that it falls on him, C.'

This would have enabled the plaintiff to succeed in *Aliakmon* provided such loss was reasonably foreseeable by the defendant; it is submitted that it would have been reasonably foreseeable as in a normal c & f contract the buyer would have an action to sue on the bill of lading if the goods were damaged in transit. Similarly, in *Nacap Ltd v Moffat Plant Ltd*[3] the pursuer could have relied on this doctrine, although it might have been more difficult to establish that the loss suffered as a result of the contract with British Gas was reasonably foreseeable.[4] However, the introduction of the principle of transferred loss into English law was vigorously rejected by the House of Lords.[5] It is thought, after *Nacap*, that the principle would not fare any better north of the border.

Thus, it appears that the courts have set their face against recovery in delict for secondary economic loss by restricting title to sue to the person injured or the owner of the damaged property. However, where a person has a possessory title to the property, he may be able to sue. For example, if A pledges his watch worth £500 to B in return for a loan of £300, B, the pledgee, has a possessory title to the watch. If the watch is damaged by C, B can sue C in delict to the extent of his interest in the watch, ie up to £300.

1 See *Leigh and Sillavan Ltd v Aliakmon Shipping Co Ltd, The Aliakmon* [1986] AC 785, [1986] 2 All ER 145, HL, affirming [1985] 2 All ER 44, CA.
2 [1985] 2 All ER 44 at 77.
3 1987 SLT 221, discussed at p 102 above.
4 Goff LJ expressly stated ([1985] 2 All ER 44 at 77) that the doctrine would not have helped the plaintiff in *Candlewood Navigation Corpn Ltd v Mitsui OSK Lines Ltd, The Mineral Transporter* [1986] AC 1, [1985] 2 All ER 935, PC; the present writer would have thought that loss to a time-charterer from a collision would be reasonably foreseeable by a shipowner: see p 102 above.
5 [1986] 2 All ER 145 at 157 per Lord Brandon.

Cases of possessory title apart, it is clear from *Nacap* that merely to have lawful possession of the property is not sufficient, since the pursuers in that case had lawful possession of the pipeline which they were laying. In *North Scottish Helicopters Ltd v United Technologies Corpn Inc (No 2)*,[1] however, the pursuers were allowed to sue in respect of economic loss sustained as a result of damage to a helicopter which they leased but did not own. Under the lease agreement with the owner, a finance company, the second pursuer had to maintain the helicopter, indemnify the finance company if the helicopter was damaged or destroyed and replace or repair the helicopter at the pursuer's expense. It was agreed with the finance company that the helicopter could be flown by the first pursuer, a subsidiary company of the second pursuer. The finance company had no obligation to provide a replacement if the helicopter was not operational. Owing to a fault in the manufacturing process, the helicopter went on fire and was destroyed. The pursuers sought damages for the economic loss sustained in indemnifying the finance company in terms of the lease, and loss of profits sustained due to the absence of a helicopter. The complex facts can be shown thus:

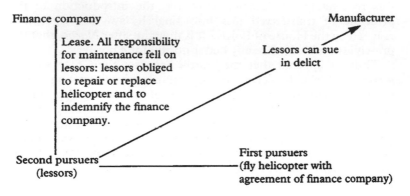

The Lord Ordinary (Davidson) held that because of the onerous terms of the lease and the fact that the finance company had agreed that the helicopter could be flown by the first pursuers, the second pursuers were 'owners' of the helicopter as a matter of substance even if, technically, the finance company was the owner as a matter of law. In other words, the pursuers had far more than

1 1988 SLT 778n, OH.

lawful possession of the helicopter and this gave them title to sue, in spite of not being the legal owner of the property. Thus it appears that there can be exceptional circumstances when a non-owner has title to sue.

It was assumed in this case that the manufacturer owed a duty of care to the pursuer. However, it should be noticed that the destruction of the helicopter was pure economic loss: the defective product did not cause physical injury to the pursuers or any other property owned by the pursuers – it only destroyed itself. The manufacturer's duty of care could therefore not have arisen by virtue of the *Donoghue v Stevenson* neighbourhood principle.[1] Nor could there be a *Junior Books* duty of care[2] owing to the absence of a contractual nexus between the pursuer and defender at the time of the fault in the manufacturing process. The action could therefore have been defended on the ground that the defender did not owe a duty of care to prevent pure economic loss arising to the pursuers and, indeed, the finance company, rather than the absence of the pursuers' title to sue for secondary economic loss.

In the cases we have been discussing, the only remedy available to a person who has suffered secondary economic loss is to obtain an assignation of the owner's rights against the defender. In Scots law, delictual rights as well as contractual rights can be assigned. For example in *Nacap Ltd v Moffat Plant Ltd*,[3] British Gas could have assigned to the pursuer its rights as owner of the pipeline to sue the defender in delict. The difficulty here is that British Gas's loss arising from damage to its pipeline is not the same as the losses incurred by Nacap in being unable to perform their contract on time. But where, as in *Aliakmon*,[4] the owner has a contractual remedy against the defender, the assignation of the contractual rights to the pursuer will provide a just solution provided, of course, the owner is prepared to assign his rights.

E. CONCLUSION

In this chapter, we have been considering how the concept of a duty of care has been used as a threshold device to set the

---

1 See *Donoghue v Stevenson* 1932 SC (HL) 31, 1932 SLT 317.
2 See *Junior Books Ltd v Veitchi Co Ltd* 1982 SC (HL) 244, 1982 SLT 492, CA.
3 1987 SLT 221.
4 See *Leigh and Sillavan Ltd v Aliakmon Shipping Co Ltd, The Aliakmon* [1986] AC 785, [1986] 2 All ER 145, HL.

parameters of liability in delict. Four important areas have been examined: pure omissions, nervous shock, wrongful life and birth actions, and economic loss. The last has been treated in depth because it has been an area of extensive judicial activity and controversy and, in addition, is conceptually difficult. There are, of course, other areas where the duty of care is used as a threshold device and some of these, at least, will be treated later in this book.[1]

At the end of the day, the imposition of a duty of care is a matter of policy for the courts. As a final example, this is graphically illustrated by the decision of the House of Lords in *Hill v Chief Constable of West Yorkshire*.[2] There, the mother of the last victim of the Yorkshire Ripper brought an action against the Chief Constable of West Yorkshire on the grounds that the police had been careless in their investigation of the earlier murders and should have apprehended the killer before her daughter was murdered. The House of Lords held that the police did not owe a duty of care to individual members of the public to identify and apprehend an unknown criminal, even though it was reasonably foreseeable that a member of the public would be harmed if the criminal was not detected and apprehended. Lord Keith of Kinkel held[3] that on the facts the victim had been at no special distinctive risk as compared with other potential victims and therefore the police did not owe her a duty of care.[4] But he expressly stated that the imposition of such a duty of care was contrary to public policy as it would involve the courts in an elaborate examination of the conduct of a police investigation and would waste valuable police time in defending such actions.[5] As Lord Templeman observed:[6]

'. . . if this action lies, every citizen will be able to require the court to investigate the performance of every policeman. If the policeman concentrates on one crime, he may be accused of neglecting others. If the policeman does not arrest on suspicion a suspect with previous convictions, the police force may be held liable for subsequent crimes. The threat of litigation against the police force would not make a policeman more efficient. The necessity for defending proceedings, successfully or

1 For example, delictual liability of public authorities: see pp 198 ff below.
2 [1989] AC 53, [1988] 2 All ER 238, HL.
3 [1988] 2 All ER 238 at 243.
4 Of course, an action in delict is available against the criminal.
5 [1988] 2 All ER 238 at 239.
6 [1988] 2 All ER 238 at 245.

unsuccessfully, would distract the policeman from his duties. This action is, in my opinion misconceived and will do more harm than good.'

A duty of care will therefore be imposed only when in the view of the courts it would achieve more good than harm to do so.[1]

---

1 In *Elguzouli-Daf v Commissioner of Police of the Metropolis; McBrearty v Ministry of Defence* [1995] QB 335, [1995] 1 All ER 833, CA, it was held that the Crown Prosecution Service did not owe a duty of care in respect of the detention of prisoners whose trials were later abandoned. The police *do* owe a duty of care to informants to keep their information confidential so that they will not be harmed by the third party in respect of whom they supplied the information: *Swinney v Chief Constable of Northumbria Police* [1997] QB 464, [1996] 3 All ER 449, CA. In so far as *Hill v Chief Constable of West Yorkshire* [1989] AC 53, [1988] 2 All ER 238, HL, was thought to lay down a 'blanket' immunity for the police, it is contrary to Article 6 of the European Convention on Human Rights: *Osman v United Kingdom* 5 BHRC 293, (1998) Times, 5 November, ECHR.

CHAPTER 5

Breach of a duty of care

A. INTRODUCTION

We have been considering situations where an action in delict fails at the outset because there is no duty of care owed by the defender to prevent harm to the pursuer as a result of the defender's unintentional, but careless, conduct. This is done by the courts utilising the concept of a duty of care as a threshold device, and the decision whether or not to recognise the existence of a duty of care in particular circumstances ultimately involves issues of policy. The duty of care enables the courts to determine the parameters of liability in delict for unintentional, but careless, conduct.

However, even where it is recognised that the defender owes the pursuer a duty of care, a pursuer is not entitled to succeed unless it can be shown that the harm sustained by the pursuer arose as a result of a *breach* by the defender of the duty of care which he owed to the pursuer. In this chapter we shall examine the criteria which must be satisfied before the defender's act or omission will constitute a *breach* of the duty of care which, *ex hypothesi*, the defender owes to the pursuer. Only when these criteria are satisfied, ie when there is a breach by the defender of the duty of care he owes to the pursuer, will the defender be liable to make reparation to the pursuer for harm sustained as a result of the defender's breach of duty.[1]

B. THE CRITERIA USED TO ESTABLISH A BREACH OF A DUTY OF CARE

(1) Voluntary act or omission of the defender

Before there is a breach by the defender of a duty of care owed to the pursuer, the relevant act or omission must be voluntary on the

1 In this chapter, I owe an immense debt to W A Wilson, 'The Analysis of Negligence' in *Introductory Essays on Scots Law* (2nd edn, 1984) pp 126–148.

part of the defender. In *Waugh v James K Allan Ltd*[1] a lorry driver, Gemmell, suffered symptoms consistent with a gastric attack. When he felt he had recovered, he drove the lorry. In fact, the symptoms were the onset of thrombosis and he shortly thereafter died at the wheel. The lorry swerved and seriously injured a pedestrian. Although the lorry driver clearly owed the pursuer a duty of care, it was held that there was no breach of duty in this case. On the medical evidence, the driver had no reason to anticipate the onset of the thrombosis and had therefore acted reasonably in driving the lorry after he felt better. Accordingly, the driver's act which injured the pursuer, ie his death, was involuntary and there was therefore no breach of the duty of care. If, however, the driver should have realised that he was seriously ill, then the act of driving while unfit to do so would have been a voluntary act which could have amounted to a breach of duty. But, in the circumstances, Lord Reid observed:[2]

'I am therefore of opinion that the appellant [the pursuer] has failed to prove that Gemmell acted rashly or negligently in driving off so soon after his illness, and no other fault can be imputed to him. One must have great sympathy with the appellant who has suffered so severely through no fault of his own, but I find it impossible to blame Gemmell. Accordingly, I would dismiss this appeal.'

(2) The defender's act or omission must have as its reasonable and probable consequence harm to the pursuer

Before there is a breach of a duty of care, harm to the pursuer must be a reasonable and probable consequence of the acts or omissions of the defender. The leading case is *Muir v Glasgow Corpn.*[3] Members of the Milton Free Church were having a Sunday school picnic in King's Park, Glasgow. Although it was a June afternoon, it began to rain. Mrs Alexander, the manageress of a tea room/sweet shop in the park, gave permission to the party to have their tea in the tea room. Access to the tea room was through a narrow passage where the sweet shop was situated. Some of the children were queuing in the passage to purchase sweets from the shop. When two members of the party carried a tea-urn full of

1 1964 SC (HL) 102, 1964 SLT 269. The pursuer was suing the driver's employer as vicariously liable for the employee's delict: on vicarious liability, see pp 209 ff below.
2 1964 SC (HL) 102 at 106.
3 1943 SC (HL) 3, 1944 SLT 60.

boiling water through the passage in order to gain entry to the tea room, the tea-urn dropped, scalding several children. It was never established how the urn was upset. We can illustrate the case as follows:

Clearly the persons carrying the urn owed a duty of care to the injured children but no action in delict was brought against them, either because of difficulty in establishing the cause of the accident or, more likely, because they had no assets. Instead, an action was brought against the Glasgow Corporation on the basis that, as Mrs Alexander's employer, the corporation was vicariously liable for any delicts she committed in the course of her employment.[1] It was accepted that as manageress of the tea room Mrs Alexander owed a duty of care to any persons she allowed to enter the premises. But, in order to succeed, the pursuer had to show that by allowing the urn to be carried through the passage crowded with children, Mrs Alexander was in breach of the duty of care she undoubtedly owed to them. The House of Lords took the view that Mrs Alexander could only be liable for those consequences of her actions which a reasonable person in her position would have had in contemplation in the circumstances of the case. Lord Thankerton said:[2] '. . . it has long been held in Scotland that all that a person can be held bound to foresee are the reasonable and probable consequences of the failure to take care, judged by the standard of the ordinary reasonable man [sic]'. Lord Wright considered[3] that:

'It is not, of course, a question of what she [Mrs Alexander] actually thought at the moment, but what the hypothetical reasonable person could have foreseen. That is the standard to determine the scope of her duty. This involves the question: Was the operation of carrying the tea-urn

1 On vicarious liability, see pp 209 ff below.
2 1943 SC (HL) 3 at 8.
3 1943 SC (HL) 3 at 15.

something which a reasonable person in Mrs Alexander's position should have realised would render the place in which it was performed dangerous to the children in the circumstances? This is the crucial issue of fact and the acid test of liability.'

The House of Lords held that the answer to this question was no. Mrs Alexander was entitled to assume that the tea-urn would be carried by responsible persons and that if carried with reasonable care would cause no harm to the children. A reasonable person in her position would not therefore have foreseen as a possibility, let alone a probability, that the urn would slip and the children would be scalded. Thus, because injury to the children could not have been foreseen as a *reasonable* and *probable* consequence of allowing the urn to be carried through the passage, Mrs Alexander had not broken the duty of care she owed the children.[1]

Muir v Glasgow Corpn is therefore authority that before a breach of a duty of care can arise, the defender's acts or omissions must have as their *reasonable* and *probable* consequence injury to the pursuer or damage to the pursuer's property. The test is the reasonable foresight of the hypothetical reasonable person in the position of the defender, as opposed to what the particular defender actually foresaw. But since the hypothetical reasonable person is in effect the court, it will be obvious that the scope of the duty of care in a particular case is, to some extent at least, determined by the judges.[2]

Thus, for example, in *Malcolm v Dickson*[3] a painter who was working on a house set the house on fire. A guest who was staying there attempted to save some of the property. As a result of his exertions, the guest collapsed and died. The court held that the painter had not broken the duty of care he owed to the deceased because it could not have been anticipated by a reasonable person

---

1 Lord Wright thought it would have been different if, for example, Mrs Alexander had allowed lions or tigers to be taken through the passage: 1943 SC (HL) 3 at 16.
2 In *Mullin v Richards* [1998] 1 All ER 920, CA, the Court of Appeal held that a reasonable 15-year-old schoolgirl could not foresee as a probable consequence of play fighting with plastic rulers that her friend (the plaintiff) could lose her eye as a result of the plastic snapping. See too *McDougall v Strathclyde RC* 1996 SLT 1124 (PE instructor not in breach of his duty to assist a pupil when pupil chose to perform an exercise not previously performed without supervision, during teacher's absence to assist another pupil: not reasonably foreseeable as a probable consequence of instructor's absence that pupil would try out the difficult exercise).
3 1951 SC 542, 1951 SLT 357.

in the defender's position that an occupant of the house would die as a result of trying to salvage furniture. As Lord Patrick said:[1]

'It would not occur to the ordinary reasonable man that a reasonable and probable consequence of his being careless in burning paint from a window frame would be that some intervener would suffer a substantial injury through over-exertion, strain and excitement in carrying furniture from the house.'

It is important to note in this case that the deceased died from a heart attack. If he had died as a result of the fire, for example, suffocated by smoke, it is submitted that there would have been a breach of the duty of care, because it is foreseeable as a reasonable and probable consequence of carelessly setting a house on fire that an occupant might die from the smoke.

Since policy considerations are inevitably involved in determining what the hypothetical reasonable person can be deemed to foresee, it should occasion little surprise that, as a general rule, the courts take the view that when a person causes an accident, it is a reasonable and probable consequence of his carelessness that a rescuer may appear on the scene and be injured.[2]

In determining whether or not the injury was a reasonable and probable consequence of a careless act or omission, the scientific knowledge available to the hypothetical reasonable person at that time can be crucial. In *Roe v Minister of Health*[3] a patient was given a spinal anaesthetic. As was ordinary practice at the time, the phials containing the anaesthetic were kept in a solution of phenol. Unknown to the hospital, the phials developed invisible cracks and the anaesthetic became impregnated with phenol. As a result of the phenol in the anaesthetic, the patient was paralysed. The court held that the defendant had not broken the duty of care owed to the plaintiff: given the state of scientific knowledge at the time, a reasonable medical practitioner could not have foreseen that paralysis of a patient was a reasonable and probable consequence of storing the phials in phenol.

Before there is a breach of the duty of care, the act or omission must have as its reasonable and probable consequence injury to the *pursuer*. In *Bourhill v Young*,[4] for example, even if Young had

---

1 1951 SC 542 at 556.
2 See, for example, *Steel v Glasgow Iron and Steel Co Ltd* 1944 SC 237, 1945 SLT 70; *Videan v British Transport Commission* [1963] 2 QB 650, [1963] 3 WLR 374, CA.
3 [1954] 2 QB 66, [1954] 2 All ER 131, CA.
4 1942 SC (HL) 78, 1943 SLT 105: for full discussion see pp 72 ff above.

owed Mrs Bourhill a duty of care, he did not breach that duty in respect of her because a reasonable motor cyclist could not have foreseen as a reasonable and probable consequence of his careless driving that a pedestrian who was 50 feet or so away from the collision, ie outwith the area of potential physical danger, would be injured.

Mrs Bourhill was, of course, a secondary victim. In *Page v Smith*,[1] the House of Lords held that the defender was in breach of his duty of care to a primary victim even though the psychiatric illness was not reasonably forseeable as a probable consequence of the defendant's careless driving. This can only be justified on the basis that *physical* injury was reasonably foreseeable, since otherwise the plaintiff would not have been a primary victim. However, when the pursuer is a secondary victim, psychiatric illness will only be treated as a reasonably foreseeable, probable consequence of the defender's carelessness if a person of ordinary phlegm would have suffered psychiatric harm in the circumstances.

It is not, however, necessary reasonably to foresee the *extent* of the pursuer's injuries; it is enough that the injuries actually sustained by the pursuer are of a *kind* which would be foreseeable as a reasonable and probable consequence of the defender's careless conduct. Nor does every aspect of the accident have to be reasonably foreseeable. These points were settled by the House of Lords in the important decision, *Hughes v Lord Advocate*.[2] In order to work on underground cables, Post Office workers uncovered a manhole. They erected a canvas shelter over the manhole. At 5 pm, when it was dusk, they left the manhole unattended; they also left outside the shelter a ladder, a rope, and paraffin warning lamps. Two boys[3] saw the shelter and decided to explore. They carried the ladder, the rope and a paraffin lamp inside the tarpaulin. One boy tripped over the lamp which fell into the manhole. The paraffin spilled from the lamp, was vaporised by the heat and there was an explosion. There was a rush of flame and one of the lads fell into the manhole and suffered severe burns.

It was agreed by expert witnesses that in the circumstances[4] an explosion was not reasonably foreseeable. But it was accepted that the workmen were careless in leaving the manhole unattended.

1 [1996] AC 155, [1995] 2 All ER 736, HL.
2 1963 SC (HL) 31, 1963 SLT 150.
3 The pursuer, aged 8, and his 10-year-old *uncle*!
4 Cf if they had been working on a gas main.

The House of Lords held that it was foreseeable as a reasonable and probable consequence of leaving the manhole unattended that a child might enter the tent with a lamp, that the paraffin might spill and the child suffer a burn, ie that a boy might be burned by the lamp. This was sufficient to establish a breach of the duty of care which the workmen undoubtedly owed to prevent physical harm to pedestrians by leaving the manhole unattended. The fact that there had been an unforeseeable explosion and that the child's burns were therefore much worse than could have been reasonably anticipated, was irrelevant. As Lord Morris of Borth-y-Gest explained:[1]

'The circumstances that an explosion as such could not have been contemplated does not alter the fact that it could reasonably have been foreseen that a boy who played in and about the canvas shelter and played with the things that were thereabouts might get hurt and might in some way burn himself. That is just what happened. The pursuer did burn himself, though his burns were more grave than would have been expected. The fact that the features and developments of an accident may not reasonably have been foreseen does not mean that the accident itself was not foreseeable. The pursuer was, in my view, injured as a result of the type or kind of accident or occurrence that could reasonably have been foreseen.'

Hughes v Lord Advocate is therefore authority that a breach of a duty of care will occur when the pursuer suffers the kind or type of injury which is a reasonable and probable consequence of the defender's careless act or omission; the fact that the injuries sustained are greater than could have been reasonably foreseen and/or that some of the causes of the accident were unforeseeable is irrelevant, as long as the type of injury suffered by the pursuer and the fact that an accident could occur as a result of the defender's carelessness are reasonably foreseeable.[2]

Finally, there can be difficulties if a defender has been careless but the damage to the pursuer has been caused as a result of the

---

1 *Hughes v Lord Advocate* 1963 SC (HL) 31 at 43–44.
2 In *Galbraith's Curator ad Litem v Stewart (No 2)* 1998 SLT 1305, the Lord Ordinary (Nimmo Smith) held that it was enough that it was reasonably foreseeable that children would be attracted to pipes left unsecured overnight and that they might suffer personal injuries when playing with them: the precise nature of the accident which had occurred did not have to be reasonably foreseeable. Cf *Jolley v Sutton London Borough Council* [1998] 3 All ER 559, CA, where it was held that an accident to a child while attempting to repair an abandoned boat left near a block of council flats was not reasonably foreseeable. See also *Doughty v Turner Manufacturing Co Ltd* [1964] 1 QB 518, [1964] 1 All ER 98, CA.

NB: HL reversed.
[2000] 3 All ER 409

intervention of a third party. As a general rule, there will be no breach by the defender of his duty of care in these circumstances unless it is foreseeable as a reasonable and probable consequence of the defender's carelessness that a third party would intervene and harm the pursuer. In *Maloco v Littlewoods Organisation Ltd*[1] the defender owned an empty cinema. Vandals broke in and started a fire which damaged neighbouring property. While the defenders owed the pursuers, as neighbouring proprietors, a duty of care not to damage their property, the House of Lords held that there had been no breach of the duty in the circumstances. The defenders did not know that vandals were trespassing on their property and kindling fires there. Accordingly, it was not foreseeable that the defenders' failure to mount a 24-hour guard on the property would have as a reasonable and probable consequence the destruction by fire of neighbouring properties. As Lord Mackay of Clashfern explained:[2]

'While no doubt in this case . . . it was probable that children and young persons might attempt to break into the vacated cinema, this by no means establishes that it was a probable consequence of its being vacated with no steps being taken to maintain it lockfast that it would be set on fire with consequent risk of damage to neighbouring properties.'[3]

On the other hand, in *Dorset Yacht Co Ltd v Home Office*[4] borstal boys were working on the Isle of Wight under the custody and control of three borstal officers. The officers went to bed leaving the boys to their own devices. Seven boys decided to escape. They went on board a yacht moored off the island, which collided and damaged the plaintiff's yacht. The House of Lords held that the borstal officers owed a duty of care to the plaintiff, which they had broken in the circumstances. The officers were responsible for the boys. It was foreseeable as a reasonable and probable consequence of leaving the boys alone that they would try to abscond. Since the only means of escape was by sea, it was also reasonably foreseeable as a probable consequence that they would steal a yacht and, being

1 1987 SC (HL) 37, 1987 SCLR 489, 1987 SLT 425: discussed in the context of delictual liability of owners of heritage at pp 178 ff below.
2 1987 SLT 425 at 431.
3 Cf *Nolan v Iceland Frozen Foods* (3 December 1997, unreported), CC (Liverpool), where a supermarket was held liable for damage caused by children misusing abandoned trolleys – not an unusual occurrence.
4 [1970] AC 1004, [1970] 2 All ER 294, HL.

inexperienced mariners, collide with another vessel.[1] It should be noted, however, that there was a special relationship between the officers and the third party who caused the damage, ie the boys; for the officers were under a duty to guard the lads. It therefore remains a general principle that a person is not liable in delict for damage caused as a result of the deliberate acts of third parties.

(3) The standard of care – negligence

Before a defender is in breach of a duty of care, it must be established that the careless act or omission which caused harm to the pursuer constituted *culpa*. In modern terminology, the careless act or omission must amount to *negligence*. What the law requires is that the defender's conduct should not fall below the standard of the reasonable person in the position of the defender. If the defender's act or omission does not fall below the standard of the reasonable person, ie he is not negligent, there is no breach of duty even though damage to the pursuer was foreseeable as a reasonable and probable consequence of the defender's conduct. The law demands reparation only when the defender has been negligent, ie when his conduct has not met the standards of the reasonable person in the position of the defender. The law does not expect the defender to go beyond the standards of the reasonable person. The defender is only obliged not to be negligent: he is not expected to ensure that his acts or omissions never harm the pursuer. This point was forcibly made in *Muir v Glasgow Corpn*,[2] where the House of Lords held that the duty of the manageress was only to take reasonable care, and not to prevent any accident occurring on the premises.

How then do we determine the standard of care of a reasonable person in any particular circumstance? Once again, since the standard of care is that of the hypothetical reasonable person in the position of the defender, the issue is ultimately a question for the

---

1 It is important to note that the duty was owed to the plaintiff only because it was reasonably foreseeable that damage might be caused to his yacht because the only method of effecting escape was by sea. If the boys had broken into a shop to steal food and drink, it is unlikely the court would have imposed a duty of care on the officers towards a member of the general public who suffered damage as a result of the acts of an absconding criminal. In other words, the duty of care would be used as a threshold device to prevent delictual liability as in the case of *Hill v Chief Constable of West Yorkshire* [1989] AC 53, [1988] 2 All ER 238, HL discussed at pp 108–109 above.
2 1943 SC (HL) 3, 1944 SLT 60, discussed at pp 112 ff above.

court. What the judges do is to consider a number of relevant factors and then determine what steps a reasonable person would have taken to prevent a foreseeable risk of harm to the pursuer. If the defender did not take these steps – or their equivalent – then she has been negligent and has broken the duty of care which she owed to the pursuer, always provided that harm to the pursuer is a reasonable and probable consequence of her failure to do so.

This involves a balancing process. The relevant factors to be considered include the probability of injury, the seriousness of the injury, the practicability of precautions, the cost of the precautions and the utility of the defender's activities. The practice of other persons in the same type of business or profession as the defender can also be important. The court then balances the costs of preventing harm to the pursuer against the risk of injury to the pursuer. By such a calculus of risk, there emerges the standard of the reasonable person in the position of the defender. If the defender's conduct has *in fact* not reached that standard, she has been negligent and therefore in breach of the duty of care owed to the pursuer.

Considering the factors in more detail:

(a) Probability of injury to the pursuer

Even if injury to the pursuer is foreseeable, a defender who causes such an injury is not negligent in failing to take precautions to avoid such injury, if the risk of such an injury is so improbable that a reasonable person in the position of the defender would not have taken any precautions. Thus, for example, in *Bolton v Stone*[1] the plaintiff was injured by a cricket ball which had been hit out of a cricket ground. This had happened on six occasions in the previous thirty years and no one had been injured. The House of Lords held that the defendants had not been negligent in failing to take precautions, since the risk of injury was so slight in the circumstances that a reasonable person in the position of the defendants would not have taken any precautions. Lord Reid explained:[2]

'In my judgment, the test to be applied here is whether the risk of damage to a person on the road was so small that a reasonable man in the position of the appellants [the defendants], considering the matter from the point

1 [1951] AC 850, [1951] 1 All ER 1078, HL.
2 [1951] 1 All ER 1078 at 1086. See in relation to golf balls 'driven' off course where the pursuer succeeded *Whitefield v Barton* 1987 SCLR 259, Sh Ct.

of view of safety, would have thought it right to refrain from taking steps to prevent the damage. In considering the matter I think that it would be right to take into account, not only how remote is the chance that a person might be struck, but also how serious the consequences are likely to be if a person is struck, but I do not think that it would be right to take into account the difficulty of remedial measures. If cricket cannot be played on a ground without creating a substantial risk, then it should not be played there at all.'

In *Gillon v Chief Constable of Strathclyde Police*,[1] it was held that the risk of a police officer being injured by a player at a football match was so small that a reasonable employer – and the football club – were not required to take any precautions.

(b) Seriousness of injury to potential pursuer

As Lord Reid indicated in the passage cited above, the seriousness of the consequences for a person if he is injured is a relevant factor. In *Paris v Stepney Borough Council*,[2] a mechanic who had the use of only one eye was not supplied with goggles. When he was removing a rusty bolt from a car with a hammer, a chip of metal flew into his good eye and as a result he became totally blind. The employer had known that the plaintiff had only one eye. It was accepted that it was not the practice in the industry to supply goggles to workers engaged on the plaintiff's tasks. The question, however, was whether the employer had been negligent in failing to provide goggles for an employee whom they knew was already partially sighted. In the Court of Appeal,[3] the plaintiff's claim failed. Asquith LJ took the view that while the greater risk of injury was a relevant factor, the risk of greater injury was not. The House of Lords[4] held, however, that the seriousness of the consequences of an injury for a particular plaintiff was a relevant consideration. Since the consequences of an eye injury for an already partially sighted person could be total blindness, the court held that the employer had been negligent in failing to provide him with goggles. It was irrelevant that the defendants might not have been negligent in failing to provide goggles to two-eyed workers. Lord Normand observed:[5]

---

1 1997 SLT 1218, (1996) Times, 22 November, OH.
2 [1951] AC 367, [1951] 1 All ER 42, HL.
3 [1949] 2 All ER 843, CA.
4 [1951] AC 367, [1951] 1 All ER 42, HL.
5 *Paris v Stepney Borough Council* [1951] 1 All ER 42 at 49.

'The court's task of deciding what precautions a reasonable and prudent man would take in the circumstances of a particular case may not be easy. Nevertheless, the judgment of the reasonable and prudent man should be allowed its common every day scope, and it should not be restrained from considering the foreseeable consequences of an accident and their seriousness for the person to whom the duty of care is owed . . . the seriousness of the injury or damage risked and the likelihood of its being in fact caused may not be the only relevant factors. For example Asquith LJ in *Daborn v Bath Tramways Motor Co Ltd and Smithey*[1] pointed out that it is sometimes necessary to take account of the consequences of not assuming a risk.'

(c) Utility of the activity

Daborn v Bath Tramways Motor Co Ltd and Smithey[1] concerned an ambulance with a left-hand drive, which was used during the Second World War. The plaintiff had put a sign at the back of the vehicle which said, 'Caution – Left hand drive – No signals'. When she was turning to the right, having given a hand signal, she collided with a bus which she could not see was trying to overtake her. The plaintiff was injured. The defendant argued that the plaintiff, as well as the bus driver, had been negligent and that her damages should be reduced on the grounds of her contributory negligence.[2] The Court of Appeal held that the plaintiff had not been negligent. In the course of his judgment Asquith LJ said:[3]

'I think that the plaintiff did all that in the circumstances she could reasonably be required to do if you include in those circumstances, as I think you should: (i) the necessity in time of national emergency of employing all transport resources which were available and (ii) the inherent limitations and incapacities of this particular form of transport. In considering whether reasonable care has been observed, one must balance the risk against the consequences of not assuming that risk, and in the present instance that calculation seems to me to work out in favour of the plaintiff.'

Thus, the social utility of the activities which it is foreseeable may cause injury must be taken into account. In *Watt v Hertfordshire County Council*[4] a woman was trapped under a vehicle. The fire service sent a lorry with a jack. During the attempt to rescue the

1 [1946] 2 All ER 333, CA.
2 On contributory negligence, see pp 143 ff below.
3 [1946] 2 All ER 333 at 336.
4 [1954] 2 All ER 368, [1954] 1 WLR 208, CA.

woman, the jack slipped and a fireman was injured. He claimed that the defendants, his employers, were negligent in not using a specially adapted lorry. The court held that given the emergency the employers were justified in using the vehicle which was available, ie a reasonable employer would have used the vehicle. They had not therefore fallen below the standard of the reasonable person in their position and therefore had not broken the duty of care which they owed to their employee.

(d) Practicality of precautions

The hypothetical reasonable person in the position of the defender will – indeed, can – only take such precautions as are practicable to avoid the risk of harm. In *Quinn v Cameron and Roberton Ltd,*[1] for example, the pursuer developed pneumoconiosis as a result of prolonged exposure to silica dust where he was working. His case against his employers failed on the basis that since the danger to employees from silica dust in iron foundries was not appreciated during the period when the pursuer was working for the employer (nine years prior to 1951), the defenders were not in breach of their duty of care by not providing precautions. However, another reason why they had not been negligent was that effective dust-extraction appliances were not available to the employers until 1950. The Lord President (Clyde) explained:[2]

'The Lord Ordinary has held it proved that the provision of dust-extraction appliances at plough buffs was not general practice between 1946 and 1951, and the expert evidence is really unanimously in favour of this conclusion. Indeed any apparatus to cope with the dangerous dust only seems to have come into the market in 1950, and went into general practice thereafter.'

(e) Cost of precautions

The hypothetical reasonable person in the position of the defender will take into account the cost of precautions and balance this against the probability of risk of harm and the seriousness of any injuries likely to be sustained. The defender's duty is not to be

---

1 1956 SC 224, 1957 SLT 2. See also *Smith v P & O Bulk Shipping Ltd* [1998] 2 Lloyd's Rep 81, QBD (employer could not have known about danger from asbestos when plaintiff was employee).
2 1956 SC 224 at 233.

negligent; it is not to act to eliminate all risks of injury to the pursuer. Thus, for example, in *Latimer v AEC Ltd*[1] a factory floor became slippery as a result of a phenomenal rainstorm. In an attempt to avoid accidents, the employer spread three tons of sawdust on the floor. Nevertheless, an employee slipped and was injured on a part of the floor *not* covered by sawdust.[2] The plaintiff argued that the employer should have closed down the factory while the floor was properly cleaned, thus eliminating the risk of employees slipping. This would, of course, have involved loss of production. The House of Lords held that the employer did all that a reasonable person would have done and was therefore not negligent. For Lord Tucker[3] the only question was:

'Has it been proved that the floor was so slippery that, remedial steps not being possible, a reasonably prudent employer would have closed down the factory rather than allow his employees to run the risks involved in continuing work? . . . The absence of any evidence that anyone in the factory during the afternoon or night shift, other than the appellant, slipped, or experienced any difficulty, or that any complaint was made by or on behalf of the workers, all points to the conclusion that the danger was, in fact, not such as to impose on a reasonable employer the obligation [to close down the factory].'

In *Charlton v Forrest Printing Ink Co Ltd*[4] it was one of the tasks of a group of employees to collect the wages for the workforce from a bank and take them to the factory. The employer had warned them of the possibility of being robbed and advised them to vary the times – and the transport used – when they went to collect the wages. Nevertheless, there was a robbery and the plaintiff was blinded by acid which had been thrown in his face. The Court of Appeal held that the employer had taken reasonable precautions and had not been negligent in failing to use the services of Securicor to uplift the wages, which could have been done at a very modest cost. This case illustrates graphically the importance of the cost of precautions in determining the standard of care of the hypothetical reasonable person in the position of the defender.

---

1 [1953] AC 643, [1953] 2 All ER 449, HL.
2 In spite of using three tons, some areas were left uncovered!
3 [1953] 2 All ER 449 at 455.
4 [1980] IRLR 331, CA. The case was concerned with an employer's *contractual* duty to take reasonable care for the safety of employees; however, the point is also applicable in respect of the employer's *delictual* duty of care towards his employees.

(f) Practice of other persons in the same business, trade or profession as the defender

The standard to be reached is that of the hypothetical reasonable person in the position of the defender. Accordingly, the practice of other persons in the same business, trade or profession as the defender will be at least an indication of the standard expected by a reasonable person in that situation. This was recognised by the Lord President (Dunedin) in *Morton v Wm Dixon Ltd.*[1] There a miner sued his employer on the basis that the employer had been negligent in failing to provide a 'shielding contrivance' to prevent coal falling between a cage and the side of the mine shaft. In determining whether the employer was negligent and in breach of his duty of care, Lord Dunedin said:[2]

'I look upon this matter as one of great importance not merely for this particular case, but for cases of this sort generally. Where the negligence of an employer consists of what I may call a fault of omission, I think that it is absolutely necessary that the proof of fault of omission should be one of two kinds, either – to shew that the thing which he did not do was a thing which was commonly done by other persons in like circumstances, or – to shew that it was a thing which was so obviously wanted that it would be folly in anyone not to provide it.'

While the determination whether the particular defender has fallen below the requisite standard is a question of fact, the standard of care demanded is that of the hypothetical reasonable person and is ultimately the standard which the court decides is appropriate in a particular situation. If, for example, an employer does not take certain precautions, the court may still take the view that he did not reach the standard of care of the reasonable person in that situation, even though he was following the usual practice in his trade or business in not taking the precautions. In *Cavanagh v Ulster Weaving Co Ltd*[3] an employee who was wearing rubber boots slipped off a roof ladder while carrying cement. No handrail was provided on the ladder. There was evidence that it was not the practice in the building trade to provide a handrail in these circumstances. The House of Lords held that evidence of the practice, while important, was not conclusive in establishing the requisite standard of care: that remained the standard of the reasonable person in the defendant's position. Given the circumstances of this

1 1909 SC 807, 1909 1 SLT 346.
2 1909 SC 807 at 809.
3 [1960] AC 145, [1959] 2 All ER 745, HL.

case, including the fact that the employee's boots were two sizes larger than they should have been, a reasonable employer would have supplied a handrail and therefore the defendant was negligent. Lord Dunedin's formula in *Morton v Wm Dixon Ltd*,[1] while important, was not 'intended to depart from or modify the fundamental principle that an employer is bound to take reasonable care for the safety of his workmen'.[2]

Conversely, where the defender has not followed the usual practice in his trade or profession, he may nevertheless have taken reasonable care. In *Brown v Rolls Royce Ltd*[3] it was common practice in the defenders' industry to supply workers in the position of the pursuer with a barrier cream. The defenders considered that barrier cream was ineffective and instead took other precautions advised by a medical officer. The pursuer contracted dermatitis. The House of Lords held that while the defenders' failure to follow the usual practice was prima facie evidence of negligence, it was not conclusive. Because the defenders had taken other precautions against the risk of their employees suffering dermatitis, the defenders had not failed to take reasonable care. In relation to Lord Dunedin's formula, Lord Keith of Avonholm observed:[4]

'As has been said before in this House, Lord Dunedin was laying down no proposition of law; nor did he say that, if a practice was averred and proved which might have avoided the accident, this was necessarily conclusive of negligence on the part of an employer who had not followed the practice. The ultimate test is lack of reasonable care for the safety of the workman in all the circumstances of the case.'

The standard of care required of professional men and women, such as members of the medical and legal professions, is discussed later in the book.[5]

(4) Remoteness of injury

In some earlier Scottish cases, delictual liability has been rejected on the ground that the injury suffered by the pursuer was 'too remote'. In *Reavis v Clan Line Steamers Ltd*,[6] for example, the court

---

1 1909 SC 807 at 809.
2 *Cavanagh v Ulster Weaving Co Ltd* [1959] 2 All ER 745 at 751 per Lord Keith of Avonholm.
3 1960 SC (HL) 22, 1960 SLT 119.
4 1960 SC (HL) 22 at 26.
5 See Chapter 7 below.
6 1925 SC 725, discussed at pp 101 ff above.

denied Mrs Reavis compensation for the loss of her orchestra on the simple basis that this loss was 'too remote'. It is submitted that the better analysis is that the defender did not owe her a duty of care to prevent her suffering secondary economic loss. Similarly, in *Bourhill v Young*,[1] it was argued by some of the judges that the pursuer could not sue in delict because the nervous shock she sustained was too remote. Again it is submitted that Mrs Bourhill's claim failed because Young did not owe her a duty of care in respect of inflicting nervous shock because she was a secondary victim. Conversely, *Hughes v Lord Advocate*[2] has been treated as a case where the pursuer's injuries were not regarded as too remote. But it is thought that that decision is better analysed as an example of how a breach of duty occurs. In other words, since injury to the pursuer was foreseeable as a reasonable and probable consequence of the defender's carelessness, there was a breach of duty even though the extent of the pursuer's injuries could not have been reasonably foreseen. Accordingly, it is thought that the concept of remoteness of injury has no part to play in determining the existence of a duty of care or the breach of such a duty in the modern Scots law of delict.

Remoteness of injury must not be confused with remoteness of damages. Where there has been a breach of a duty of care and the pursuer has suffered harm, the pursuer may not be able to recover for all the losses suffered as a result of the defender's negligence. Some losses may be considered by the court to be too remote. For example, if A injures B as a result of negligent driving, B is entitled to damages for pain and suffering and derivative economic loss, such as loss of wages, loss of future earnings etc. But if as a result of the accident, B was unable to post his football coupon, could he recover damages from A if he would have won a fortune if the coupon had been sent? In other words, is the loss of the winnings too remote to be compensated by A? This is a question of remoteness of damages and is discussed later in the book.[3]

C. CONCLUSION

In this chapter we have been discussing when a breach of a duty of care arises. The defender's act or omission must be voluntary;

---

1 1942 SC (HL) 78, 1943 SLT 105, discussed at pp 72 ff above.
2 1963 SC (HL) 31, 1963 SLT 150, discussed at pp 116 ff above.
3 See pp 265 ff below.

harm to the pursuer must be foreseeable as a reasonable and probable consequence of the defender's act or omission, and, finally, the act or omission must constitute negligence, ie the defender must have failed to reach the standard of care of the hypothetical reasonable person in the position of the defender. Where these criteria are satisfied, there is a breach of the duty of care owed to the pursuer and a delict is committed when the pursuer sustains harm as a result of the defender's breach of the duty of care. Even though there has been a breach of the duty of care, it is important to appreciate that the delict is only completed and delictual liability is only incurred when harm is sustained by the pursuer.[1] There must be a concurrence of *damnum* (loss or harm sustained) and *injuria* (breach of the duty of care) before delictual liability arises (*damnum injuria datum*).[2] If there is no harm or loss to the pursuer as a result of the defender's breach of a duty of care which he owes to the pursuer, then there is no delictual liability. Harm to the pursuer is a constituent of, as well as a consequence of, negligence.

However, before the pursuer can succeed, she must prove that the harm or loss suffered was caused by the defender's breach of a duty of care owed to her. It is to the difficulties inherent in the concept of causation that we now turn.

---

1 *Watson v Fram Reinforced Concrete Co (Scotland) Ltd and Winget Ltd* 1960 SC (HL) 92, 1960 SLT 321.
2 Thus, for example, the prescriptive period will only begin to run from the date that the pursuer suffers harm, not the date of the breach of duty: for example, when Mrs Donoghue became ill, not when Stevenson manufactured the ginger beer negligently.

CHAPTER 6

Causation and related issues

Before there is liability in delict, the pursuer must prove that the defender's breach of her duty of care was the cause of the loss or harm suffered by the pursuer. The concept of causation is a complex and difficult subject raising fundamental philosophical as well as legal issues. In a work of the present compass, only an outline of the relevant issues is given.[1]

A. FACTUAL CAUSATION

The first essential is that the defender's acts or omissions are a cause of the pursuer's injury or loss. This is a question of fact. If the defender's conduct is not a factual cause of the pursuer's injury or loss, there is no liability even if the defender has broken a duty of care which he owed to the pursuer. To use Latin terminology, the defender's breach of duty must be a *causa sine qua non* of the pursuer's injury or loss. In other words, 'but for' the defender's conduct, the pursuer would not have suffered harm. If the pursuer would have suffered the same injury notwithstanding the defender's breach of duty, then the defender's conduct is not a factual cause of the harm, ie it is not a *causa sine qua non*. Accordingly, to determine whether the defender's breach of duty is a factual cause of the pursuer's injury, we must ask ourselves whether 'but for' the breach of duty, would the pursuer's injury have occurred? If it would *not* have occurred, the defender's act or omission is a factual cause of the pursuer's injury:[2] if it would still have occurred, the defender's act or omission is *not* a factual cause

---

1 For a superb account of the subject, see Hart and Honoré *Causation and the Law* (2nd edn, 1985). The book is an excellent example of the constructive use to which linguistic philosophy can be put in the context of law.
2 It is enough if it can be shown that 'but for' the defender's act or omission it was probable that the injury would not have occurred: *Porter v Strathclyde Regional Council* 1991 SLT 446.

of the pursuer's injury. The onus of satisfying the 'but for' test rests on the pursuer.[1]

Two cases illustrate the application of the 'but for' test. In *Barnett v Chelsea and Kensington Hospital Management Committee*[2] the plaintiff's husband drank a cup of tea and became violently ill because the tea had been poisoned. The hospital doctor refused to treat the husband, telling him to see his own doctor. The husband died. It was held that although the defendant may have been in breach of a duty of care, the hospital was not liable because the husband would still have died of the poison, even if he had been treated by the hospital doctor, ie the husband did not die 'but for' the hospital's negligence. Accordingly, the breach of duty was not a *causa sine qua non* of the husband's death and the plaintiff's action failed.

In *Kay's Tutor v Ayrshire and Arran Health Board*[3] a child was brought into hospital suffering from meningitis. He was given a massive overdose of penicillin.[4] The child thereupon suffered severe convulsions but as a result of treatment recovered. However, the child was left deaf. In an action against the hospital, the defenders admitted that they were in breach of their duty of care in administering the overdose of penicillin. But the hospital denied that this breach of duty had caused the child's deafness. The House of Lords held that the onus lay on the pursuer (the child's father) to prove that 'but for' the overdose, the child would not be deaf. In the absence of evidence to show that an overdose of penicillin caused deafness in a patient and, given that deafness is common in patients who suffer meningitis, the pursuer failed to establish that 'but for' the breach of duty, deafness would not have occurred. The breach was therefore not a *causa sine qua non* of the child's deafness and the pursuer's action failed.

This concept was taken a stage further by the House of Lords in *Bolitho v City and Hackney Health Authority*.[5] It was accepted that a

---

1 See, for example, *Dingley v Chief Constable of Strathclyde Police (No 1)* 1998 SC 548, OH (pursuer failed to establish on the balance of probabilities that a whiplash injury sustained in a road accident had triggered the onset of symptomatic multiple sclerosis); *Pickford v ICI plc* [1998] ICR 673, [1998] 3 All ER 462, HL (onus was on plaintiff to prove that her condition had an organic cause: the employer's failure to prove that the condition was psychogenic was no more than a relevant factor in determining whether or not the plaintiff had discharged the burden of proof. In the circumstances, the plaintiff had failed to do so).
2 [1969] 1 QB 428, [1968] 1 All ER 1068.
3 1987 SC (HL) 145, 1987 SLT 577, HL, affirming 1986 SLT 435.
4 30 times the prescribed amount.
5 [1998] AC 232, [1997] 4 All ER 771, HL.

doctor had been in breach of her duty of care by failing to attend her patient, a child. The child died. It was also accepted that the only way in which the child's life could have been saved was by intubation. However, evidence was led that a responsible body of medical opinion would not have intubated in the circumstances. In other words, if the doctor had attended her patient, she would not have been negligent if she had not attempted to save the child's life by intubating her. Consequently, the child would still have died if the doctor had attended her.

The logic appears strained, but it is nevertheless compelling. Since the patient would still have died even if she had received reasonable care, ie no intubation, the doctor's negligence in failing to attend her was not a factual cause of her death.[1] Where the treatment of a patient would have had less than a 50 per cent chance of success, the failure to treat is not regarded as the cause of the pursuer's injuries or illness: in other words, the chances of success must be more than 50 per cent.[2]

Another striking example of the 'but for' test is *McWilliams v Sir William Arrol & Co and Lithgows Ltd.*[3] The pursuer's husband, a steel erector, was killed. It was held that the defenders were in breach of their duty of care towards McWilliams in failing to provide him with a safety belt. However, it was also established that even if they had provided him with a safety belt, McWilliams would not have worn it. In these circumstances, the pursuer failed to prove that 'but for' the defenders' breach of duty, the accident would not have occurred. The defenders' breach was not a *causa sine qua non* of McWilliams' death and the pursuer's action failed.

Where the pursuer suffers loss which he would have suffered anyway, but, as a result of the defender's breach of duty, he suffers the loss at an earlier date, the Scottish courts have held that the 'but for' test is satisfied and an action will lie in delict.[4] Conversely, where a pursuer is injured as a result of the defender's breach of duty but later suffers an accident or disease unrelated to the defender's conduct, the fact that he would have been debilitated by the later accident or disease is taken into account in assessing the pursuer's loss.[5]

1 It would still be very difficult to explain to the child's parents why their action failed, given the doctor's admitted negligence in not attending their child.
2 See *Kenyon v Bell* 1953 SC 125, 1952 SLT (Notes) 79, OH; *Hotson v East Berkshire Area Health Authority* [1987] 2 All ER 909, HL.
3 1962 SC (HL) 70, 1962 SLT 121.
4 *Sutherland v North British Steel Group Ltd* 1986 SLT (Sh Ct) 29 (accelerated hernia operation).
5 See *Jobling v Associated Dairies Ltd* [1982] AC 794, [1981] 2 All ER 752, HL.

Difficulties arise where there is more than one potential cause of the pursuer's injuries, ie the defender's breach of a duty of care and another source of danger which is not the responsibility of the defender. The starting point of the discussion is *Wardlaw v Bonnington Castings Ltd*.[1] A workman contracted pneumoconiosis from breathing dust in the atmosphere of his workplace. Some of the dust was caused by a hammer in relation to which there was no known or available precautions which could be taken to prevent the employee breathing contaminated air. Therefore the defender was not in breach of the duty of care owed to the pursuer in respect of the dust caused by the hammer. However, there were other machines in the workshop which also produced dust for which adequate extraction plant was available, and the employers were held responsible for not adequately maintaining the extracting plant.[2]

There were therefore two possible sources of the dust which had caused the pursuer's illness, for only one of which the defender was delictually liable, ie the dust from the other machines. The House of Lords held that the onus lay on the pursuer to show that on the balance of probabilities, the dust from the machines was a *causa sine qua non* of his illness. In the situation of two potential sources of danger, the pursuer would discharge the onus if he could show that the source for which the defender was responsible had materially contributed to his injury. Lord Reid observed:[3]

'It appears to me that the source of his [the pursuer's] disease was the dust from both sources, and the real question is whether the dust from the swing grinders [the other machines] materially contributed to the disease. What is a material contribution must be a question of degree. A contribution which comes within the exception *de minimis non curat lex* is not material but I think that any contribution which does not fall within that exception must be material.'

In this case, the dust from the machines did materially contribute to the pursuer's illness and the pursuer was successful. Thus, where there are two or more sources of harm to the pursuer which operate concurrently, the source for which the defender is responsible will be regarded as a *causa sine qua non* of the pursuer's injury if it materially contributed to the injury.

1 1956 SC (HL) 26, 1956 SLT 135.
2 This was a breach by the employer of their statutory duty under the Grinding of Metals (Miscellaneous Industries) Regulations 1925, SR & O 1925/904. On breach of statutory duty, see Chapter 11 below.
3 *Wardlaw v Bonnington Castings Ltd* 1956 SC (HL) 26 at 32.

The concept of factual causation was taken a considerable step further in *McGhee v National Coal Board*.[1] The pursuer worked all day in a hot and dusty kiln. He had to cycle home unwashed because the defender failed to provide on-site washing facilities. After several days, the pursuer contracted dermatitis. It was admitted that the dermatitis was attributable to the work the pursuer did in the brick kiln, but the defender was not in breach of a duty of care in allowing the pursuer to work there. The breach of duty was the failure to provide on-site washing facilities. This omission only resulted in the pursuer cycling home unwashed: clearly, it did not relate to the hours he spent working in the kiln. Common sense would suggest that it was far more likely that the dermatitis was contracted when he was working in the kiln, for which the employer was not delictually liable, rather than during the short time he cycled home. But the expert evidence could not establish how dermatitis was actually contracted. *Wardlaw v Bonnington Castings Ltd*[2] could therefore not provide a solution, since it could not be proven that the additional exposure to injury caused by cycling home unwashed had materially contributed to his injury. *Wardlaw v Bonnington Castings Ltd* is concerned with two sources of danger operating *concurrently*; but *McGhee v National Coal Board* is concerned with two sources of danger operating *consecutively*, where the defender was responsible only for the later one. Therefore, it can be argued that the pursuer in *McGhee* would have to prove – which on the evidence he could not – that the later source of danger had caused, or, at least, materially contributed, to his dermatitis.

However, the House of Lords was prepared to take a broader view of causation. The medical evidence suggested that the fact that the pursuer had to cycle home caked with grime and sweat added materially to *the risk* that the disease might develop, although it could not explain why this was so. In the view of the House, materially to increase the risk of the pursuer's injuries was to be regarded as a material contribution to the injury. Lord Reid opined:[3]

'But it has often been said that the legal concept of causation is not based on logic or philosophy. It is based on the practical way in which the ordinary man's mind works in the every-day affairs of life. From a broad and practical viewpoint I can see no substantial difference between saying that

---

1   1973 SC (HL) 37, 1973 SLT 14.
2   1956 SC (HL) 26, 1956 SLT 135.
3   *McGhee v National Coal Board* 1973 SC (HL) 37 at 53–54.

what the defender did materially increased the risk of injury to the pursuer and saying that what the defender did made a material contribution to his injury.'

Lord Salmon observed:[1]

'In the circumstances of the present case,[2] the possibility of a distinction existing between (a) having materially increased the risk of contracting the disease and (b) having materially contributed to causing the disease may no doubt be a fruitful source of interesting academic discussions between students of philosophy. Such a distinction is, however, far too unreal to be recognised by the common law'!

Thus, where there are two or more sources of danger, for only one of which the defender is delictually liable, factual causation will be established if the pursuer can prove on the balance of probabilities *either* that the defender's breach of duty materially contributed to his injury *or* that the defender's breach of duty materially increased the risk of the pursuer sustaining injury. It does not matter if the sources of danger operate concurrently or consecutively.[3]

However, there is an important limitation on this principle. While the *sources* of danger may be different, it must be established that each source could have in fact been the cause of the pursuer's injuries. In both *Wardlaw* and *McGhee* it was clear that dust caused the pursuers' diseases: the only question was whether the defenders' breach of duty had materially contributed to, or increased the risk of, the pursuers' illnesses. By way of contrast, in *Kay's Tutor v Ayrshire and Arran Health Board*,[4] there was no evidence that the defender's breach of duty in giving the overdose of penicillin could in fact have caused the child's deafness. In these circumstances, *Wardlaw* and *McGhee* are irrelevant. As Lord Griffiths explained:[5]

---

1 1973 SC (HL) 37 at 62.
2 Given the defender's admitted breach of a duty of care.
3 The implications of *McGhee* are remarkable. For example, suppose A smokes cigarettes and B, her employer, allows C and D, fellow employees, to smoke in a room occupied by A. A contracts lung cancer. Since A's passive smoking of C and D's cigarette smoke materially increases the risk of A contracting lung cancer, C and D's smoking (and B's allowing them to smoke) could be treated as the cause of A contracting the disease. But common sense would suggest that A contracted the disease as a result of her own smoking habit. A would, of course, be contributorily negligent: see pp 143 ff below.
4 1987 SC (HL) 145, 1987 SLT 577. Discussed at p 130 above.
5 1987 SLT 577 at 581.

'The principle in *McGhee* would only fall for consideration if it was first proved that it was an accepted medical fact that penicillin in some cases caused or aggravated deafness. The question would then arise whether when there are two competing causes of deafness, namely meningitis and penicillin, the law should presume in favour of the plaintiff (sic) that the tortious (sic) [delictual] cause was responsible for the damage.'[1]

B. LEGAL CAUSATION

For the purpose of liability in delict, it is not enough that the defender's breach of duty is a factual cause or *causa sine qua non* of the pursuer's harm or loss. While factual causation is a necessary condition of delictual liability, it is not sufficient. In addition, the defender's breach of duty must be the legal cause of the pursuer's injury. To use Latin terminology, it must be the *causa causans*. Various terms are used to describe legal causation: these include the direct, decisive, proximate, real, dominant, efficient, effective and substantial cause of the pursuer's loss or harm.

For example, A drops a brick on B's foot, breaking his toe. B is taken to hospital in an ambulance. The ambulance is driven carelessly and B is killed in a road accident. A's breach of duty is a *causa sine qua non* of B's death since 'but for' A's dropping the brick on his toe, B would not have been in the ambulance in which he died. But should A be delictually liable for B's death which was caused by the ambulance driver's careless driving? The answer is no. A's breach of duty, although a *causa sine qua non* of B's death, is not treated as the legal cause, ie it is not the *causa causans*. The *causa causans* is the ambulance driver's careless driving. We can say that the chain of causation between A's breach of duty has been broken as a result of the careless act of the ambulance driver, which prevents A's breach of duty from being the legal cause of B's death. To use legal terminology, the ambulance driver's conduct is a *novus actus interveniens* which breaks the chain of causation so that A is not delictually liable for B's death, although A remains liable for B's broken toe.

In this example, the *novus actus interveniens* was the conduct of a third party, the ambulance driver. But the conduct of the victim

1 See also *Wilsher v Essex Area Health Authority* [1988] AC 1074, [1988] All ER 871, HL (child's condition could have been caused by defendant's negligence or by four other conditions. The plaintiff's evidence of the defendant's failure to take preventative measures against one of the five possible conditions was not proof of which of the five caused the injury).

may also break the chain of causation. So, for example, if A drops a brick on B's foot, breaking his toe, whereupon B cuts his own throat to put himself out of pain, A will not be delictually liable for B's death. B's action has broken the chain of causation and, as a result, A's breach of duty is not regarded as the legal cause, the *causa causans*, of B's death.

When, then, will an act of a third party or the act of the victim constitute a *novus actus interveniens*, breaking the chain of causation? Since we are concerned with determining legal causation, this is ultimately a question for the courts: the judges will *evaluate* whether or not in the circumstances it is fair to relieve the defender of his delictual liability. At one time, this was a crucial decision where the victim had contributed to his own injuries: for if the court decided that the pursuer's conduct was a *novus actus interveniens* so that the defender's breach of duty was not the *causa causans*, the pursuer was denied any compensation. However, as a result of the Law Reform (Contributory Negligence) Act 1945, the court now has the power to reduce the damages awarded to the pursuer in proportion to the pursuer's responsibility for her own injuries.[1] Although the 1945 Act has, in so far as the pursuer's conduct is concerned, reduced the importance of determining a single cause or *causa causans*, the court still retains the power of limiting a defender's delictual liability for breach of a duty of care. It does this by deciding that the breach is not the legal cause of the pursuer's injuries, for example, because of the intervention of a third party. Therefore, the determination of legal causation remains important.

The decision as to whether or not a breach of duty constitutes the *causa causans* of the pursuer's injuries 'must be dealt with broadly and upon common sense principles as a jury would probably deal with it'.[2] Two factors are important, as we shall now see.

(1) Foreseeability

Where there has been a breach of duty by the defender, the act of a third party or the victim will not generally break the chain of causation if it was reasonably foreseeable that the subsequent act

---

1 On contributory negligence, see pp 143 ff below.
2 *Admiralty Comrs v SS Volute* [1922] AC 129, HL, at 144 per Birkenhead LC. See also *Galoo Ltd (in liquidation) v Bright Grahame Murray* [1995] 1 All ER 16, CA at 29 per Glidewell LJ, quoting an Australian decision: 'The answer in the end is "By the application of the court's common sense"'.

would take place. Thus, for example, in *Sayers v Harlow Urban District Council*[1] the plaintiff entered a cubicle in a public lavatory maintained by the defendant. Owing to a fault in the lock, she could not reopen the door. She banged on the door and put her hand out of the window in unsuccessful attempts to attract attention. After 15 minutes, she tried to escape through the space between the top of the door and the roof. She put her left foot on the lavatory seat, her right foot on the toilet roll holder, one hand on the lavatory cistern and the other hand on the top of the door. When she found it impossible to squeeze through the space, she proceeded to come down, but because of her weight, the toilet roll holder rotated, she lost her balance and fell. The court held that it was reasonably foreseeable that a person in Mrs Sayers' position would try to escape and that this was not a hazardous enterprise. Accordingly, her attempted escape was not a *novus actus interveniens* and the defendant's breach of duty was the *causa causans* of the accident. However, when she found she could not escape, she was careless in putting so much weight on the toilet roll holder: although this did not break the chain of causation, it did constitute contributory negligence and her damages were reduced by 25 per cent.[2]

Even if the subsequent act of a third party or the pursuer is reasonably foreseeable, it may break the chain of causation if it was hazardous for the third party or the pursuer to act in such a way. In *McKew v Holland and Hannon and Cubitts (Scotland) Ltd*,[3] the pursuer injured his ankle as a result of the defender's breach of duty. Because of the fracture, his leg was liable to 'give way' from time to time. After the accident, the pursuer went to see a flat. The stairway leading to the flat had no handrail. Although he knew that his leg was likely to give way at any time, after visiting the flat the pursuer went down the stairs in a normal manner, ie he did not go down slowly so that he could sit on a step if his leg 'gave way'. His leg gave way and in panic the pursuer jumped down 10 steps and was injured.

The court held that the defender was not liable for the second injury. Although it was reasonably foreseeable that the pursuer might climb stairs which had no handrail, he had acted in a hazardous manner in walking down the stairs in the normal way without assistance. The defender's breach of duty which had

---

1 [1958] 2 All ER 342, [1958] 1 WLR 623, CA.
2 On contributory negligence, see pp 143 ff below.
3 1970 SC (HL) 20, 1970 SLT 68.

caused the injury to the pursuer's ankle was not the *causa causans* of the pursuer's second injury. Instead, the pursuer's carelessness in walking down the stairs without assistance constituted hazardous conduct on the pursuer's part which broke the chain of causation between the defender's breach of duty and the pursuer's second injuries.

In *Sabri–Tabrizi v Lothian Health Board,*[1] the pursuer became pregnant as a result of a failed sterilisation. She had a termination. Knowing that she was fertile, she had sexual intercourse with her husband on several occasions. She fell pregnant again. Although the defenders admitted liability for the first pregnancy, they denied liability for the second. The Lord Ordinary (Nimmo Smith) agreed:[2]

'The alleged negligence resulted in the pursuer's being still fertile, just as she would have been had the failed sterilisation operation never been carried out. The pursuer knew this, and consequently knew that there was a risk of her becoming pregnant if she had sexual intercourse with her husband . . . She avers that she took precautions, but in so far as there remained a residual risk, in a question between her and the defenders I think that it is unreasonable of her to expose herself to that risk. Accordingly I regard her decision to have sexual intercourse in the knowledge that she was not sterile as constituting a *novus actus interveniens*, breaking the chain of causation, with the result that the defenders cannot be held liable for the second pregnancy and the consequences thereof.'

(2) The order of events

The order of events may be important in determining whether or not the defender's breach of duty is the *causa causans* of the pursuer's injuries. In *Donaghy v National Coal Board,*[3] the defender broke the duty of care which was owed to the pursuer, by leaving a detonator lying around the workplace. The pursuer took the detonator home and hit it with a hammer. As a result he was injured. The court held that the pursuer's conduct amounted to a *novus actus interveniens*: it was unforeseeable, unreasonable, ie hazardous, and was the last act which had led to the accident. On

1 1998 SC 373, 1998 SLT 607.
2 1998 SC 373, at 378.
3 1957 SLT (Notes) 35.

the other hand, in *Davidson v City of Glasgow District Council*,[1] the second defender supplied the pursuer's employer, the first defender, with planks which were too short for a particular task. The employer rejected the planks, but owing to the employer's alleged carelessness one of the short planks was not rejected. As a result of the plank being too short, there was an accident and the pursuer was injured. The pursuer sued the employer (first defender) and the supplier (the second defender). The second defender argued that the employer's failure to reject all the planks constituted a *novus actus interveniens*. The court held that merely because the employer's conduct was the 'last act' that led to the accident, this did not necessarily mean that it amounted to a *novus actus interveniens*:

'Even although there was in effect an intermediate inspection, and assuming in the alternative that the first defenders [the employer] failed to discover that one of the planks remained and was inadvertently used, it does not follow that that was negligence or that it broke the chain of causation and was the sole cause of the accident.'[2]

Thus, where an accident is caused to A as a result of a breach of duty by B *and* a breach of duty by C, the mere fact that B's breach of duty arose after C's breach of duty will not necessarily break the chain of causation to exonerate C from delictual liability. In *Grant v Sun Shipping Co Ltd*,[3] ship repairers working on a ship left hatches uncovered. By doing so, they were in breach of a duty of care owed to dock labourers on the ship. The ship owners also failed to ensure that the hatches were covered and did not provide an adequate system of lighting: this constituted a breach of their duty of care to dock labourers on the ship. The pursuer, a dock labourer, fell through an unlighted hatch. The House of Lords held that the shipowner's breach of duty did not constitute a *novus actus interveniens* breaking the chain of causation between the accident and the ship repairers' breach of duty of care towards the pursuer by leaving the hatches uncovered. Instead, both the shipowners and the ship repairers were jointly liable in delict.[4] Where there is joint liability, under s 3 of the Law Reform (Miscellaneous Provisions) (Scotland) Act 1940, the court has the power to apportion the damages between the defenders.[5]

---

1 1993 SLT 479, OH.
2 1993 SLT 479 at 482 per Judge D B Robertson QC.
3 1948 SC (HL) 73, 1949 SLT 25.
4 See also *Davidson v City of Glasgow District Council* 1993 SLT (Notes) 35, discussed above.
5 On joint liability, see p 146 below.

(3) Conclusion

Where A's breach of a duty of care is a *causa sine qua non* of B's injuries, the courts appear unwilling to be persuaded that a subsequent act – even if careless – constitutes a *novus actus interveniens* unless it is so unusual or unexpected that it could not have been reasonably foreseeable, or so hazardous on the part of B, that it would be unreasonable to hold A liable. If the subsequent act is that of a third party, C, and constitutes a breach of duty owed by C to B, A and C will be held jointly liable in delict to B. If the subsequent act is that of B, A remains liable, ie B's act will not break the chain of causation, but instead it will lead to a reduction of damages on the grounds of contributory negligence. Although this will be the usual result, there can, of course, still be exceptional cases where the chain of causation is broken and A's breach of duty is not treated as the *causa causans* of B's injuries. So, for example, if A injured B's foot and B suffered an infection in hospital, the chain of causation would not be broken as it is reasonably foreseeable that B might get an infection in hospital. But if the surgeon in the hospital is careless and amputates B's uninjured foot, the chain of causation is broken, since the surgeon's conduct is so unusual and unexpected that it is not reasonably foreseeable and therefore it constitutes a *novus actus interveniens*. This exonerates A from delictual liability in respect of the amputation, but not, of course, in respect of the original injury to B's foot.

The chain of causation is not broken by an act of a third party where the defender's duty of care was to prevent the third party from causing injury or damage to the pursuer.[1] But as a general rule, A does not owe B a duty of care to prevent B from being injured as a result of the deliberate conduct of a third party, C.[2] Here, of course, it is the absence of a duty of care which prevents A from being liable to B in delict.

---

1   *Dorset Yacht Co Ltd v Home Office* [1970] AC 1004, [1970] 2 All ER 294, HL, discussed at p 118 above.
2   There are, of course, exceptions. See, for example, *Empress Car Co (Abertillery) Ltd v National Rivers Authority* [1998] 1 All ER 481, HL (a person causes a pollutant to enter controlled waters even if a necessary condition of the actual escape is the act of a third party, provided the third party's act is an act of normal life, eg vandalism, and not extraordinary).

C. RELATED MATTERS

(1) *Volenti non fit injuria*

The chain of causation will, however, be broken if the pursuer has voluntarily undertaken the risk of harm created by the defender's breach of duty. This is the doctrine of *volenti non fit injuria*. Because the chain of causation is broken and the defender's breach of duty is no longer the *causa causans* of the pursuer's injuries, the doctrine of *volenti* provides the defender with a complete defence to an action in delict. The theoretical basis of *volenti* is that by knowing acceptance of the risk, the pursuer has absolved the defender of the consequences of the defender's breach of the duty of care owed to the pursuer. In other words, the defender still owes the pursuer a duty of care but the chain of causation is broken by the pursuer voluntarily undertaking the risk.[1]

Before the defender will succeed in the defence of *volenti non fit injuria* the defender must prove that before or at the same time as the negligent act or omission,[2] the pursuer knowingly and willingly undertook the risk of danger created by the defender's breach of duty. In *Titchener v British Railways Board*[3] the defender failed to maintain a fence made of sleepers which was positioned along a railway track. A 15-year-old girl climbed through the fence and went up the embankment to take a short cut across the railway line to a piece of waste ground where she intended to have a kiss and cuddle with her boyfriend. She was injured by a train when she was crossing the line. As we shall see,[4] the House of Lords held that in the circumstances the defender did not owe the pursuer a duty of care. But the House indicated that even if a duty of care had been owed and there had been a breach of duty, the defender would have had the defence of *volenti* since the pursuer knew and accepted the risk of being injured by a train when she crossed the line.

Because the pursuer must have knowledge of, and be *willing*, to accept the risk, the courts are unlikely to accept a plea of *volenti* in an action between employee and employer. Nevertheless, the

---

1 See *Winnick v Dick* 1984 SC 48, 1984 SLT 185.
2 See *Sabri-Tabrizi v Lothian Health Board* 1998 SC 373, 1998 SLT 607.
3 1984 SC (HL) 34, 1984 SLT 192. See also *Devlin v Strathclyde Regional Council* 1993 SLT 699, OH.
4 Page 190 below.

defence succeeded in *ICI v Shatwell*.[1] Contrary to their employer's instructions, the plaintiff and his brother, who were experienced shotfirers, agreed to test their detonators without first returning to a safety shelter. There was an explosion; the plaintiff was injured and his brother was killed. It was held that the employer had not been in breach of a duty of care towards the plaintiff.[2] However, the plaintiff sued the employer as vicariously liable for his brother's careless act in testing the detonator.[3] The House of Lords held that since the plaintiff had agreed with his brother to run the risk of injury by testing the detonators without first returning to a place of safety, the employer could successfully plead the defence of *volenti*.

The defence of *volenti* does not apply in the case of a rescuer. By virtue of s 149 of the Road Traffic Act 1988, the defence of *volenti* does not apply to a claim by a passenger against the driver of a vehicle which has compulsory third party insurance. Thus, if a passenger accepts a lift from a drunken driver and the car has compulsory third party insurance, the driver cannot plead *volenti* if the passenger is injured as a result of the driver's breach of duty. The passenger's damages could, of course, be reduced on the grounds of contributory negligence.

Where the duty of care is to *prevent* the defender from acting in a particular way, it would make nonsense of the existence of the duty if *volenti* could be used when the defender does the act the pursuer should have prevented. For example, the police owe a duty of care to prevent prisoners from harming themselves while on remand: if, in breach of their duty, a prisoner is able to injure or kill himself, the defence of *volenti* cannot be used.[4]

It is sometimes argued that the reason why a spectator at a dangerous sport, such as motor racing, cannot sue a participant who injures him by crashing into the crowd at high speed, is that the spectator is *volens* of the risk of harm inherent in the sport. However, it is thought that the better way to analyse the situation is to argue that in the circumstances the participant does not owe the spectator a duty of care to avoid the possibility of such an accident. The organiser of the event may owe the spectator a duty of

---

1 [1965] AC 656, [1964] 2 All ER 999.
2 Or in breach of any statutory duty.
3 On vicarious liability, see pp 209 ff below.
4 *Commissioner of Police for the Metropolis v Reeves* (15 July 1999, unreported), HL (Lord Hoffman, Lord Mackay, Lord Jauncey and Lord Hope; Lord Hobhouse dissented).

care, if, for example, the circuit was not suitable for racing or the safety precautions were inadequate, and the spectator will not be *volens* of these risks simply by attending the event.[1]

Where a participant in a dangerous sport is injured by another participant, again it is thought the reason an action in delict will not be successful is not that the pursuer was *volens*, but that the defender does not owe a duty of care to the pursuer to protect him from injuries the risk of which are inherent in the sport, for example being bruised when tackled at rugby football.[2] If the injury arises from conduct which is contrary to the rules of the game, the pursuer's remedy lies in assault, rather than in a breach of the duty of care.

(2) Contributory negligence

As we have seen, where the defender's breach of duty to the pursuer is a *causa sine qua non* of the pursuer's injuries, the courts are reluctant to accept that the pursuer's subsequent conduct is a *novus actus interveniens* or amounts to *volenti*, so that the defender is exonerated from delictual liability. This is particularly the case where the pursuer has acted in the 'agony of the moment', ie reacts carelessly in a situation caused by the defender's breach of duty, for example, jumps out of a window to escape a fire caused by the defender's negligence. Instead, the court will hold that the pursuer's conduct was a contributory cause of the injury. The effect of a finding of contributory negligence is to reduce the damages which would otherwise have been awarded to the pursuer, to reflect the pursuer's responsibility for the damage or injury sustained. Section 1(1) of the Law Reform (Contributory Negligence) Act 1945 provides:

'Where any person suffers *damage as the result partly of his own fault* and *partly due to the fault of any other person or persons*, a claim in respect of that damage shall not be defeated by reason of the fault of the person suffering the damage, but the *damages recoverable* in respect thereof *shall be reduced* to such an extent as the *court thinks just and equitable* having regard to the *claimant's share in the responsibility* for the damage.' [emphasis added]

---

1 See *Wooldridge v Sumner* [1963] 2 QB 43, [1962] 2 All ER 978, CA; *Lewis v Buckpool Golf Club* 1993 SLT (Sh Ct) 43.
2 However, a referee owes a duty of care to the players. When the referee has been negligent, an injured player is not *volens* merely by participating in the game: *Smoldon v Whitworth* [1997] PIQR P133, (1996) Times, 18 December, CA.

Before the 1945 Act applies, the pursuer must have suffered damage partly as a result of his own *fault*.[1] Fault covers the pursuer's deliberate as well as negligent actions.[2] In relation to the latter, the pursuer's act must fall below the standard of the reasonable person in the pursuer's position. The onus rests on the defender to prove that the pursuer was at fault. Although, for example, a passenger injured in a motor accident will usually be at fault if he or she fails to wear a seat belt, in *Mackay v Borthwick*[3] the pursuer was held not to be contributorily negligent for failing to wear a seat belt since it was uncomfortable for her to wear it, because she was suffering from a hiatus hernia. In *Pace v Culley*[4] the pursuer, who was a taxi driver, failed to wear a seat belt because he had been advised by the police not to do so, in the event that he might be attacked by his passengers. Although he accepted that failure to wear a seat belt could amount to contributory negligence, the Lord Ordinary (Weir) thought that the driver's conduct in this case was a misjudgment rather than a failure to take care for his own safety.[5] In *Blackhall v MacInnes*,[6] the pursuer was injured while she was changing the offside wheel of her motor car. She was held to be 20 per cent contributorily negligent because – contrary to the Highway Code – she had made no attempt to get the vehicle off the road, although it was practicable to drive on the verge.

The defender must also prove that the pursuer's fault contributed to the injuries sustained, ie 'but for' the pursuer's fault, the injuries or damage suffered would not have been as bad as actually occurred. In other words, the defender must establish that the pursuer's fault was a factual cause, a *causia sine qua non*, of the injuries or harm sustained. Thus, contributory negligence was established when the defender proved, on the balance of prob-

---

1 Fault is defined in s 5(a) of the Law Reform (Contributory Negligence) Act 1945 as: 'wrongful act, breach of statutory duty or negligent act or omission which gives rise to liability in damages . . .'.
2 *Commissioner of Police for the Metropolis v Reeves* (15 July 1999, unreported), HL (prisoner killed himself: family's damages reduced by 50 per cent as a result of his suicide).
3 1982 SLT 265, OH.
4 1992 SLT 1073, OH.
5 The contributory negligence, if any, would have been *de minimis* in respect of the total claim and could therefore be ignored.
6 1997 SLT 649, OH.

abilities, that the pursuer would have suffered less severe neck injuries if she had worn a seat belt.[1]

When contributory negligence is established, the proportion to be deducted from the damages is a matter for the discretion of the judge, ie what the judge considers just and equitable having regard to the pursuer's share in the responsibility for the damage. This can vary from as little as five per cent in 'agony of the moment' cases to as much as 80 per cent.[2] It is submitted that 100 per cent deduction is not possible under the Law Reform (Contributory Negligence) Act 1945 since in those circumstances the pursuer would be solely responsible and not 'share in the responsibility for the damage'.[3] A drunken pedestrian run down by a careless driver has had his damages reduced by 50 per cent as a result of contributory negligence.[4] Similarly, a guest injured at a party has had his damages reduced by 50 per cent because he had been drinking heavily.[5]

As a matter of public policy, if the pursuer is participating in a criminal activity at the time he is injured, he may be barred from obtaining reparation: for example, if A and B steal a car and A is injured as a result of B's careless driving.[6] However, the bar is not automatic and depends on the circumstances. In *Weir v Wyper*[7] the pursuer was not barred when she was injured in a car crash even though she knew that the driver had only a provisional licence. When the action is not barred, the pursuer's damages could, of course, be reduced on the ground of contributory negligence.[8]

---

1 *Hanlon v Cuthbertson* 1981 SLT (Notes) 57, OH. Cf *Neill v Docherty and Akram* (23 May 1996, unreported), HC, where the plaintiff's injuries were sustained on initial impact, ie *before* she was ejected from the taxi because she was not wearing a seat belt.
2 *Uddin v Associated Portland Cement Manufacturers Ltd* [1965] 2 QB 582, [1965] 2 All ER 213, CA.
3 If the pursuer is solely responsible, the defender will escape liability because either his breach of duty is not the *causa causans* or the pursuer is *volens*: see *ICI v Shatwell* [1965] AC 656.
4 *Malcolm v Fair* 1993 SLT 342, OH.
5 *Brannan v Airtours* (18 January 1999, unreported), CA. Although there is no duty to prevent an adult from becoming drunk, there may be a duty to look after the drunk person if she becomes incapable of looking after herself. When there is such a duty and it is broken, the plaintiff's damages can be reduced on the grounds that she got inebriated: *Barrett v Ministry of Defence* [1995] 3 All ER 87, CA (two-thirds contributorily negligent).
6 *Duncan v Ross Harper & Murphy* 1993 SLT 105n, OH.
7 1992 SCLR 483, 1992 SLT 579, OH.
8 *Taylor v Leslie* 1998 SLT 1248, 1998 Rep LR 110, OH (defender drove car while unlicensed, uninsured and underaged. Passenger killed. Conduct not regarded as reprehensible by the community of Shapinsay, a remote island. The deceased had encouraged the defender to speed. Damages reduced by 50 per cent).

(3) Joint fault

Joint fault arises where harm is caused to the pursuer as a result of the conduct of more than one defender. This is known as joint liability, if the harm has been caused as a result of a breach by each defender of a duty of care owed to the pursuer; in the case of other delicts, it is known as joint wrongdoing. Before there can be joint liability, each breach of duty must have materially contributed to, or materially increased the risk of, the *same* delict to the pursuer. Thus, for example, in *Anderson v St Andrew's Ambulance Association*[1] a passenger in a bus was injured in a collision between the bus and an ambulance. The bus driver had failed to observe a 'slow' sign; the ambulance driver had failed to observe a 'halt' sign. The court held that this was a case of joint liability, for both drivers were responsible for the same wrong suffered by the pursuer. Conversely, in *Fleming v McGillivray*[2] the court held that it was not a case of joint liability where an injured pursuer sued a van driver for careless driving and the owner of the van for failing to have compulsory third party insurance: the driver was being sued for breach of his duty of care (delict 1), while the owner was being sued for breach of statutory duty in not having insurance (delict 2). Since they were not responsible for the same delict, this was not a case of joint liability or joint wrongdoing.

If A and B are jointly liable, the pursuer may sue A or B or both. If the pursuer sues only A and obtains a decree, if A pays the damages, the pursuer cannot then sue B; but if A does not pay the damages, the pursuer can sue B. If the pursuer successfully sues both A and B, he will be awarded a joint and several decree. This entitles the pursuer to obtain *all* the damages from either A or B. Where A has paid all the damages, the court can apportion the damages between A and B; and if B was not sued in the original action, A can, nevertheless, recover from B the proportion of the damages which the court deems attributable to B's conduct.[3] Where the pursuer is contributory negligent, the total damages to be paid by A or B will be reduced to reflect the pursuer's responsibility for the injury or harm suffered.

1 1943 SC 248, 1943 SLT 258.
2 1946 SC 1, 1945 SLT 301.
3 Law Reform (Miscellaneous Provisions) (Scotland) Act 1940, s 3. The proportions *inter se* the defenders is what the court, or jury, considers just in the circumstances: see, for example, *BOC v Groves* 1993 SLT 360, OH (75 per cent and 25 per cent).

Part III

DELICTUAL LIABILITY IN SPECIFIC SOCIAL AND ECONOMIC CONTEXTS

Chapter 7.   Professional liability   149

Chapter 8.   Product liability   157

Chapter 9.   Delictual liability for animals   169

Chapter 10.   Delictual liability arising from ownership or
                   occupation of property   177

Chapter 11.   Breach of statutory duty and public law issues   193

Chapter 12.   Employers' liability and vicarious liability   205

Chapter 13.   Delict and the family   221

Chapter 14.   Delict and road trafic   235

Chapter 15.   Defamation and verbal injury   243

Introduction

Having discussed the general principles of delictual liability, it is now proposed to examine the law of delict as it operates in certain specific social and economic contexts. As we shall see, the general principle of delictual liability for harm caused to the pursuer as a result of the defender's *culpa* is often supplemented by other common law principles, for example, nuisance and vicarious liability. More importantly, perhaps, in certain areas common law delictual liability has been supplemented or supplanted by statutory liability. It is thought that these developments are better understood if discussed in the context of the particular social and economic relationships in which they occur.

CHAPTER 7

Professional liability

The general principles of the law of delict apply where a person causes harm to another in the course of his trade, business or profession. Often, of course, the person harmed will be a client or a customer of the defender; if this is so, the pursuer's primary remedy will be to sue the defender in contract. Almost inevitably, the defender will have assumed responsibility for the interests of the client or customer: the customer or client will almost inevitably have relied on the defender's expertise. Accordingly, unless the terms of their contract negative delictual liability, the defender will also owe the pursuer a *Henderson v Merrett*[1] duty of care to prevent economic loss arising from the defender's negligence. Put another way, where the client and professional are directly linked by contract, concurrent liability in contract and delict can arise. If, however, there is no direct contractual relationship between the parties, liability can lie only in delict.

Where the pursuer suffers physical injury or harm to his property, the defender will be liable in delict if the injury or harm was caused intentionally or as a result of a breach of a duty of care owed by the defender to the pursuer. The existence of such a duty of care will be determined by the *Donoghue v Stevenson* neighbourhood principle.[2] Where the pursuer has suffered pure economic loss, liability will lie in delict if the defender intended to harm the pursuer or if a *Henderson v Merrett* duty of care exists. A duty of care could also arise if, for example, the *Caparo* tripartite test is satisfied,[3] or *Junior Books* liability exists.[4]

---

1 See *Henderson v Merrett Syndicates Ltd* [1995] 2 AC 145, [1994] 3 All ER 506, HL, discussed at p 85 above.
2 See *Donoghue v Stevenson* 1932 SC (HL) 31, 1932 SLT 317.
3 *Caparo Industries plc v Dickman* [1990] 2 AC 605, [1990] 1 All ER 568, HL. See, for example, *Weir v National Westminster Bank plc* 1993 SC 515, 1994 SLT 1251.
4 *Junior Books Ltd v Veitchi Co Ltd* 1982 SC (HL) 244, 1982 SLT 492.

In determining whether or not there has been a breach of a duty of care, the defender's conduct is judged by the standard of care expected in his or her profession. In other words, in order to establish that the defender was negligent, the pursuer must prove that the defender's conduct fell below that of the reasonable accountant, architect, lawyer, medical practitioner or surveyor etc. Accordingly, while ultimately a question of law,[1] the usual practice of persons in the same trade, business or profession as the defender will be significant in determining whether or not the defender was negligent.

It can, however, be particularly difficult to establish negligence where the defender's conduct involves an exercise of professional judgment. Often there will be several courses of action open to the defender. In these circumstances, the defender will *not* be negligent if she adopted a course of action which resulted in harm to the pursuer, unless no reasonable professional person in her position would have chosen that option. Nor does it matter that the course of action chosen was *not* the normal practice in the profession. In the leading case of *Hunter v Hanley*[2] the pursuer alleged that the defender, a doctor, was negligent in using a needle which was unsuitable for treating the patient. In discussing the standard of care appropriate to a doctor, the Lord President (Clyde) observed:[3]

'. . . in regard to deviation from ordinary professional practice . . . such deviation is not necessarily evidence of negligence. Indeed it would be disastrous if this were so, for all inducement to progress in medical science would then be destroyed. Even a substantial deviation from normal practice may be warranted by the particular circumstances. To establish liability by a doctor where deviation from normal practice is alleged, three facts require to be established. First of all it must be proved that there is a normal practice; secondly it must be proved that the defender has not adopted that practice; and thirdly (and this is of crucial importance) it must be established that the course which the doctor adopted is one which no professional man of ordinary skill would have taken if he had been acting with ordinary care.'

Thus it is not enough that the defender's conduct deviated from normal practice: it must be demonstrated that no professional man of ordinary skill would have followed the course taken by the

---

1 *Bolitho v City and Hackney Health Authority* [1998] AC 232, [1997] 4 All ER 771, HL.
2 1955 SC 200, 1955 SLT 213.
3 1955 SC 200 at 206. Lord Clyde's approach was approved by McNair J in the leading English case, *Bolam v Friern Hospital Management Committee* [1957] 2 All ER 118, [1957] 1 WLR 582.

defender. Even if the pursuer can establish that a responsible body of medical opinion regards the defender's decision or conduct as wrong, the defender will not be regarded as having been negligent if there is also a responsible body of medical opinion which regards the defender's decision or conduct as reasonable in the circumstances.[1] This test applies not only to medical treatment[2] but also to diagnosis[3] and advice.[4]

Gordon v Wilson[5] provides an illustration of the formidable difficulties facing a pursuer in an action of medical negligence. In that case, the pursuer argued that a doctor was negligent in delaying to refer a patient to a specialist. Although the pursuer established that there was a responsible body of medical opinion which took the view that a reasonable doctor would have referred the patient to a specialist at an earlier stage, the court held that the defender was not negligent because the defender could show that there was also a responsible body of medical opinion to the effect that a reasonable doctor would not have referred the patient to a specialist until the defender had done so. Accordingly, the pursuer's action failed. Professional negligence cannot be established by preferring one body of professional opinion to another; instead the pursuer must prove that no reasonable doctor exercising his ordinary clinical skills would have taken the defender's course of action in the circumstances of the particular case.[6]

1 *Maynard v West Midlands Regional Health Authority* [1985] 1 All ER 635, [1984] 1 WLR 634, HL. The number of specialist doctors who accept the defender's practices need not be substantial, provided they are responsible: *Defreitas v O'Brien* [1995] 6 Med LR 108. If there is no recognised standard practice, the court must determine whether or not the defender took reasonable care in all the circumstances: *AB v Tameside and Glossop Health Authority* [1997] 8 Med LR 91, CA (defendant sent a secret letter to patients informing them that a health worker who had treated them was HIV positive: defendant not negligent simply because they sent a standard letter, rather than organising face-to-face disclosure of the tiny risk of infection).

2 *Whitehouse v Jordan* [1981] 1 All ER 267, [1981] 1 WLR 246, HL.

3 *Maynard v West Midlands Regional Health Authority* [1985] 1 All ER 635, [1984] 1 WLR 634, HL.

4 *Gold v Haringey Health Authority* [1987] QB 481, [1987] 2 All ER 888, CA. The same criteria apply to the duty to inform a patient of risks inherent in a medical procedure even if it is carried out properly: *Sidaway v Bethlem Royal Hospital Board of Governors* [1985] AC 871, [1985] 1 All ER 643, HL.

5 1992 SLT 849n, [1992] 3 Med LR 401, OH.

6 In *Bolitho v City and Hackney Health Authority* [1998] AC 232, [1997] 4 All ER 771 HL, it was stressed by the House of Lords that the body of medical opinion must be reasonable and responsible. In other words, there must be a logical basis for the opinion the experts support. Although this is ultimately a question of law, it would only be in rare cases that the court would reject the medical experts' views as unreasonable.

These cases were concerned with the medical profession. However, as indicated above, the tests for establishing the requisite standard of care are applicable in relation to other professions where an exercise of professional judgment is involved.[1]

The position of the legal professions requires further treatment. Where a solicitor takes instructions from her client, liability can arise in contract and delict. The contract may stipulate a higher standard of care than that required by the law of negligence, ie strict liability rather than a failure to take reasonable care.[2] As a general rule, the solicitor owes a duty of care to her client: she does not owe a duty of care to a third party, for example, a person who would benefit from an *inter vivos* transaction.[3] However, where a solicitor gives advice or information to a person who is not a client, ie who does not have a contractual relationship with the solicitor, the solicitor may be liable in delict provided the *Henderson v Merrett* criteria for a duty of care exist. In other words, there must be voluntary assumption of responsibility by the solicitor and concomitant reliance on the third party's part.[4] In *Midland Bank plc v Cameron, Thom, Peterkins & Duncans*,[5] the Lord Ordinary (Jauncey) observed:[6]

'. . . I have no hesitation in concluding . . . that situations can arise in which a solicitor owes a duty not only to his client but to a third party who relies upon what the solicitor tells him. In my opinion four factors are relevant to the determination of the question whether in a particular case a solicitor, while acting for a client, also owes a duty of care to a third party: (1) the solicitor must assume responsibility for the advice or information furnished to the third party; (2) the solicitor must let it be known to the third party expressly or impliedly that he claims, by reason of his calling, to have the requisite skill or knowledge to give the advice or furnish the information; (3) the third party must have relied upon that advice or information as a matter for which the solicitor has assumed personal responsibility; and (4) the solicitor must have been aware that the third party was likely so to rely.'

---

1 See, for example *Gaughan v Bedfordshire Health Authority* [1997] 8 Med LR 182, QBD (midwives); *Henderson v Merrett Syndicates Ltd (No 2)* [1997] LRLR 265, QBD (Comm Ct) (underwriting agents); *Sneesby v Goldings* [1995] 2 EGLR 102, CA (surveyors); *Scott v Lothian Regional Council* 1999 Rep LR 15 (guidance teachers).
2 *Mortgage Corpn Ltd v Mitchells Roberton* 1997 SLT 1305, OH.
3 *Tait v Brown & McRae* 1997 SLT (Sh Ct) 63.
4 Before *Henderson v Merrett Syndicates Ltd* [1995] 2 AC 145, [1994] 3 All ER 506, HL, liability would arise if *Hedley Byrne & Co Ltd v Heller & Partners Ltd* [1964] AC 465, [1963] 2 All ER 575, HL, were applicable.
5 1988 SCLR 209, 1988 SLT 611, OH.
6 1988 SLT 611 at 616.

Where such a duty exists, the pursuer will, of course, succeed only
if it can be established that the solicitor was negligent in giving the
advice, ie that a reasonable solicitor would not have given that
advice in the circumstances.[1]

Midland Bank is concerned with a duty of care in giving advice
or information to a person who is not a client. It is not concerned
with the situation where a solicitor acts on the instructions of a
client but as a result of the solicitor's carelessness does not give
effect to the client's instructions, with the result that a third party
suffers loss. Normally, no duty of care is owed to the third party.[2]
An important exception may exist when the third party is a 'disappointed legatee'.

Consider the following problem. A instructs a solicitor to draw
up a will under which B is the principal beneficiary. As a result of
the solicitor's carelessness the will is invalid and B does not obtain
the legacy. There is no contractual relationship between B and the
solicitor. Therefore B's remedy, if any, lies in delict against the
solicitor. B has suffered pure economic loss and before there is
delictual liability the solicitor must owe B a duty of care to prevent
B suffering such loss. Unlike in the advice and information situations, B has not relied on the solicitor's expertise: B will probably
not know the solicitor's identity. Even if the solicitor can be said to
have assumed responsibility for B's interests, the *Henderson v
Merrett* duty of care will not normally arise because of the absence
of concomitant reliance on B's part. We have therefore a situation
where the courts must be prepared on policy grounds to impose a
duty of care before the solicitor can be liable in delict.[3] For many
years, the Scottish courts refused to recognise such a duty of care.
In *Robertson v Fleming*[4] Lord Campbell LC observed:[5]

'I never had any doubt of the unsoundness of the doctrine . . . that A
employing B, a professional lawyer, to do any act for the benefit of C, A
having to pay B, and there being no intercourse of any sort between B and
C – if through the gross negligence or ignorance of B in transacting the
business, C loses the benefit intended for him by A, C may maintain an

1 On the standard of care for professional persons, see pp 150 ff above.
2 *Bristol and West Building Society v Aitken Nairn* 1999 SLT 43, OH. There are
very rare cases where a duty can arise because of exceptional degrees of proximity
between the parties: *Mortgage Corpn Ltd v Mitchells Roberton* 1997 SLT 1305,
OH.
3 Ie the duty of care is being used as a threshold device: see Chapter 4 above.
4 (1861) 23 D (HL) 8, 4 Macq 167.
5 (1861) 4 Macq 167 at 177.

action against B and recover damages for the loss sustained. If this were law a disappointed legatee might sue the solicitor employed by a testator to make a will in favour of a stranger, whom the solicitor never saw or before heard of, if the will were void for not being properly signed or attested. There must be privity of contract between the parties. I am clearly of opinion that this is not the law of Scotland, nor of England, and it can hardly be the law of any country where jurisprudence has been culti- vated as a science.'

Robertson v Fleming was a decision of the House of Lords in a Scottish appeal. In *Weir v J M Hodge & Son*[1] the Lord Ordinary (Weir) took the view that the case was authority that a duty of care did not exist between a solicitor and a disappointed legatee. Although he considered that the decision in *Robertson* was 'out of sympathy with the modern law of negligence',[2] Lord Weir felt he was bound to follow its ratio because it constituted a binding precedent.[3]

On the other hand, in England, the courts have refused to follow *Robertson*. The issue was fully explored by the House of Lords in *White v Jones*.[4] After a family quarrel, a father struck his daughters out of his will. Later he relented. In spite of the family's attempts to encourage their father's solicitor to fulfil the old man's instruc- tions, the father died before the will was altered in favour of the daughters. By a majority,[5] the House of Lords held that the solicitor owed a duty of care to the disappointed legatees. For Lords Goff and Browne–Wilkinson it was enough that the solicitor had assumed responsibility for the potential beneficiaries: this was implicit when accepting their father's instructions. Concomitant reliance was not necessary to impose a duty of care in the case of disappointed legatees. Lord Nolan found actual reliance, since the defender had acted as a solicitor for the family, not merely the father. Lord Mustill dissented, owing to the absence of concomi-

---

1 1990 SLT 266.
2 1990 SLT 266 at 270.
3 See also *MacDougall v Clydesdale Bank Trustees* 1993 SCLR 832, sub nom *MacDougall v MacDougall's Executors* 1994 SLT 1178, OH. In this case, the Lord Ordinary (Lord Cameron of Lochbroom) also denied the existence of a duty of care; but here the pursuer was not the disappointed legatee, but the legatee of the beneficiary who would have inherited under the invalid will. Even if there was a duty to a disappointed legatee, it is doubtful if it would extend to his legatees.
4 [1995] 2 AC 207, [1995] 1 All ER 691, HL.
5 Lord Goff of Chieveley, Lord Browne–Wilkinson and Lord Nolan; Lords Mustill and Keith of Kinkel dissented.

tant reliance which he felt was constitutive of a *Henderson v Merrett* duty of care.[1]

It is quite clear that the majority in *White v Jones* felt that a negligent solicitor *should* be liable in this situation. But, although we may be sympathetic to the policy, the reasoning is less than happy. In particular, the absence of the need for reliance makes it impossible to fit *White v Jones* within the *Henderson v Merrett* general duty of care to prevent economic loss. In spite of its difficulties, *White v Jones* has been consistently followed in England[2] and appears to have been accepted as Scots law by the Second Division of the Inner House of the Court of Session.[3] Given that the potential pursuer falls into a restricted class, ie the 'legatee' named in the instructions and therefore known to the solicitor, it is thought by the present writer that a duty of care should exist in these circumstances.[4]

Where there has been a breach of a duty of care by a solicitor, there may be difficulties in quantifying the pursuer's loss. In *Kyle v P & J Stormonth Darling WS*[5] the defender failed to lodge the pursuer's appeal in time with the result that the pursuer lost the opportunity to appeal. In rejecting the defender's argument that the pursuer was entitled to damages only if it could be established on the balance of probabilities that the appeal would have been successful, the Lord Ordinary (Prosser) said:[6]

'where there has been deprivation of a legal right, that will in itself constitute a completed wrong, and one will be entitled, as a matter of valuation, to take into consideration all reasonable prospects of success, if they exceed nuisance value, even if they fall short of probability.'

Advocates are not liable in delict in respect of the conduct and management of a case in court or any preliminary work connected with conducting such a case.[7] However, an advocate can be liable for giving negligent advice, for example, an opinion on a point of law.[8] It has been suggested that the same immunity extends to

1 See *Henderson v Merrett Syndicates Ltd* [1995] 2 AC 45, [1994] 3 All ER 506, HL.
2 *Carr–Glynn v Frearsons* [1998] 4 All ER 225, [1998] 3 FCR 487, CA.
3 *Robertson v Watt & Co* (4 July 1995, unreported). I am indebted to Professor Hector MacQueen for this reference.
4 A better solution, perhaps, would be to allow the court to rectify the will so that it would correspond to the testator's final intentions, evidence of which would have to be very convincing!
5 1993 SC 57, 1994 SLT 191, affirming 1992 SLT 264, OH.
6 1992 SLT 264 at 268.
7 *Rondel v Worsley* [1969] 1 AC 191, [1967] 3 All ER 993, HL.
8 *Saif Ali v Sydney Mitchell & Co* [1980] AC 198, [1978] 3 All ER 1033, HL.

solicitors in respect of court work,[1] but there is Scottish authority that solicitors could, nevertheless, be liable.[2] Where a solicitor has acted on counsel's advice, it has been argued that the solicitor should enjoy immunity, if counsel would have been immune.[3]

The delictual liability of surveyors has been discussed in the context of liability for careless misrepresentation.[4]

1 *Saif Ali v Sydney Mitchell & Co* [1980] AC 198, [1978] 3 All ER 1033, HL.
2 *Murray v Reilly* 1963 SLT (Notes) 49, OH.
3 *Reid v Edinburgh Acoustics Ltd (No 2)* 1995 SCLR 791n, 1995 SLT 982, OH.
4 See pp 82 ff above.

CHAPTER 8

Product liability

A. INTRODUCTION

The basis of product liability in Scots law was, of course, laid down in *Donoghue v Stevenson*.[1] There it was held that the manufacturer of a product owes a duty of care to the ultimate consumer, when a product is manufactured which is intended to reach the ultimate consumer in the form in which it left the manufacturer, without the possibility of intermediate examination. If the product was manufactured carelessly, with the result that the ultimate consumer suffered injury or harm to his property, the manufacturer is liable in delict. However, the onus lies on the pursuer to prove that there was a breach of duty by the manufacturer, ie that the manufacturer was negligent.[2] If negligence cannot be established, the action fails.

Apart from the difficulty of establishing negligence, other factors could operate to prevent the pursuer from succeeding. Where, for example, a manufacturer has provided an adequate warning that a product is potentially dangerous and this is ignored by the ultimate consumer, then there will be no liability because the pursuer's failure to heed the warning will constitute a *novus actus interveniens* which breaks the chain of causation.[3] Where the product is a complex structure made up of components manufactured by various persons, an action may fail if the pursuer is unable to identify the person who was responsible for the defect in the product. For example, in *Evans v Triplex Safety Glass Co Ltd*,[4] the plaintiff was injured when the windscreen of his motor car disintegrated.

---

1 1932 SC (HL) 31, 1932 SLT 317. Discussed at pp 58 ff above.
2 If it is established that a product has failed because of a specified defect in the manufacturing process, it is open to a judge to hold that on the balance of probabilities this was due to the manufacturer's negligence: *Carroll v Fearon* [1998] PIQR P416, CA.
3 *Kubach v Hollands* [1937] 3 All ER 907, KB. On causation generally, see Chapter 6 above.
4 [1936] 1 All ER 283.

The manufacturer of the car fitted a windscreen made by the defendant. Evans failed to establish whether the accident was the result of the windscreen being fitted carelessly by the manufacturer of the car or whether it was due to a defect in the windscreen caused by the negligence of the defendant. In these circumstances, his action was dismissed. Finally, there is no liability under *Donoghue v Stevenson* if the only loss suffered by the pursuer arises from the fact that the product itself is defective, ie the cost of repair or the difference in value between a defective and non-defective product. This is pure economic loss and is prima facie not recoverable in delict.[1]

B. STATUTORY REGULATION

Because of these difficulties, but particularly the fact that the onus of proof of negligence lies on the ultimate consumer, the law has now imposed a statutory regime of strict liability in respect of product liability. What this means is that provided the case falls within the statutory provisions, the defender is liable in delict to compensate the pursuer without the pursuer having to prove that the defender was negligent. The strict liability regime for defective products is to be found in Part I of the Consumer Protection Act 1987. This statute implements EC Directive No 85/374/EEC and it is expressly enacted that it should be interpreted to comply with the Directive.[2] The general idea of the Act is simple: it is to place the primary responsibility for injury or damage caused by a defective product on the producer and to enable the consumer who has been injured by the defective product or whose property has been damaged by the defective product to obtain compensation from the producer without having to prove fault. However, as we shall see, the provisions of the statute are hideously complex. Before considering them, however, it should be noted that where the statutory regime is not applicable, common law liability remains[3] and the pursuer may bring an action based on a breach of the *Donoghue v Stevenson* duty of care but will, of course, have to prove negligence if he is to be successful.

1 For full discussion, see pp 78 ff above.
2 Consumer Protection Act 1987, s 1(1). The Act came into force on 1 March 1988. It is not retrospective. References in this section are to CPA 1987 unless otherwise stated.
3 CPA 1987, s 2(6).

The Consumer Protection Act 1987 imposes strict liability on the producer of a product 'where any damage is caused wholly or partly by a defect in a product'.[1] Damage is defined as 'death or personal injury or any loss of or damage to property (including land)'.[2] Thus, if a person is killed or injured by a defective product, or his land or other property is damaged by a defective product, the producer of the product is liable to pay compensation without proof of fault. In other words, the producer is strictly liable.

(1) Exceptions to strict liability

However, damage to certain types of property is excluded from the statutory regime:

(a) loss or damage to the defective product itself.[3] Thus, the cost of repair or the difference in value between a defective and non-defective product is not recoverable under the Consumer Protection Act 1987. Nor is it recoverable in delict at common law since it is pure economic loss. Where the product is a complex structure, loss or damage to the whole or part of the product caused by a defective component is also excluded. Thus, for example, if a motor car (complex product) is damaged as a result of a defective wheel (component), the damage to the car is excluded but not, of course, injury to the driver or damage to other property;

(b) property damaged or lost as a result of a defective product, where the property *damaged or lost* is not for private use.[4] Property is not for private use if it is not of a description of property ordinarily intended for private use, occupation or consumption *and* it is not intended by the person suffering the loss or damage mainly for his own private use, occupation or consumption. What this means is that before the Act applies and there is strict liability, the property damaged must be 'consumer' property, ie of a kind ordinarily intended for private use which the person suffering the loss or damage intended to be used for private use. For example, if A produces a defective vacuum cleaner, the Act will apply if it damages the carpet in B's home but not if it damages the

---

1 Consumer Protection Act 1987, s 2(1).
2 CPA 1987, s 5(1). Personal injury includes any disease and any other impairment of a person's physical or mental condition: CPA 1987, s 45(1).
3 CPA 1987, s 5(2).
4 CPA 1987, s 5(3).

carpet in B's office or factory. It is important to note that it is the property which is damaged which must be 'consumer' as opposed to 'business' property. If A produces a defective lorry which is used in B's business, the Act *will* apply if the defective lorry damages C's family motor car, but the Act will not apply if the defective lorry damages C's van which he uses for his business. When the Act is excluded because the property damaged is not 'consumer' property, resort will have to be made to delictual liability at common law when negligence will have to be established;

(c) property damaged or lost as a result of a defective product, where the loss or damage does not exceed £275.[1] Where such loss or damage occurs, resort must again be made to delictual liability at common law when negligence will have to be established.[2] It should be noted that this exception only applies to damage to property. If, for example, A cuts his finger as a result of B's defective product, the Act still applies and B is strictly liable even if A's damages are less than £275.

(2) Definition of product

Strict liability applies where damage is caused wholly or partly by a defect in a product. A product is defined[3] as any goods or electricity. It includes – and this is important – components and raw materials which are parts of a complex product. So, for example, if there is a complex product such as a motor car and a component of the car, for example a windscreen, is defective, that component, as well as the motor car is regarded as a product for the purpose of the Consumer Protection Act 1987. Thus the problem which arose in *Evans v Triplex Safety Glass Co Ltd*[4] will not arise under the Act. Goods also include 'substances, growing crops and things comprised in land by virtue of being attached to it and any ship, aircraft or vehicle'.[5] Substance means any natural or artificial substance, whether in solid, liquid or gaseous form or in the form of vapour and includes substances which are comprised in or mixed with other goods, for example, a cylinder of gas. Things comprised in land by virtue of being attached to it include, for

---

1 Consumer Protection Act 1987, s 5(4). This includes interest.
2 Such an action would be brought under the small claims procedure.
3 CPA 1987, s 1(2).
4 [1936] 1 All ER 283, discussed at pp 157 ff above.
5 CPA 1987, s 45(1).

example, the window frames of a house, a garden shed or a swing. Ship includes any boat or vessel used for navigation; aircraft includes gliders, balloons and hovercraft; vehicle is not defined. Game or agricultural produce do not constitute products for the purpose of the Act unless they have undergone an industrial process.[1] Thus, A will be strictly liable under the Act if he produces defective smoked salmon which causes illness to the consumer but he will not be strictly liable if he supplies contaminated 'fresh' salmon:[2] this is because smoked salmon has undergone an industrial process. The victim of the contaminated 'fresh' salmon must resort to delictual liability at common law and establish that A was negligent in supplying fish in that condition.

(3) Parties liable

As mentioned above, prima facie strict liability is imposed on the producer of the product. A producer is defined as the person who manufactured the product[3] or who won or abstracted the substance.[4] Where a product is not manufactured, won or abstracted but its essential characteristics are attributable to an industrial or other process, the producer is the person who carried out the process: for example, where the product is pasteurised milk, the producer is the person who carried out the pasteurisation process.[5] A person who merely packages goods is not a producer. Any person who puts his own name on a product, or uses a trade mark on a product, is liable under the Consumer Protection Act 1987 if by so doing he holds himself out to be the producer.[6] This provision brings 'own branders' within the strict liability regime. Similarly, any person who imports products from abroad with a view to distributing them within the EU is liable under the Act.[7] This clearly is to protect ultimate consumers in EU member states from having to sue a producer outwith the EU. The importer may, of course, have a remedy, for example in contract, against the non-EU producer. The producer of a component or of raw materials

1 Consumer Protection Act 1987, s 2(4).
2 It does not matter if the salmon is farmed as opposed to wild, because agricultural produce means any produce of the soil, of stock-farming or of fisheries: CPA 1987, s 1(2).
3 CPA 1987, s 1(2)(a).
4 CPA 1987, s 1(2)(b).
5 CPA 1987, s 1(2)(c).
6 CPA 1987, s 2(2)(b).
7 CPA 1987, s 2(2)(c).

used in a complex product is prima facie jointly and severally liable with the producer of the complex product if it is defective.

Although strict liability falls on the producer, own brander or importer of a defective product, as a fall back position a supplier of the product may also be liable. Thus all parties in the distribution chain from the producer to the own brander or importer are potentially liable under the Act:

Producer————Wholesaler————Retailer————Purchaser

In this example, the wholesaler and retailer are suppliers within the meaning of the Act. However, a supplier will be liable only if the person who suffered the damage asked the supplier within a reasonable time of the damage being sustained to identify the producer or a supplier further up the chain of distribution and the supplier failed to provide the information within a reasonable time, provided it was not reasonably practicable for the person suffering the damage to identify the producer. Thus, in order to escape potential strict liability under the Act, the supplier must keep records of his suppliers or producers.[1]

A supplier will not be strictly liable if the defective goods were not supplied in the course of business.[2] Thus, A will not be strictly liable if A sells his washing machine to his neighbour B in a private transaction or if A gives B the washing machine as a birthday present. Of course, A may be liable for breach of contract or in delict at common law if the washing machine is defective and injures B or damages B's property. Where we are dealing with a producer, own brander or importer, they will escape strict liability under the Act only if the goods were supplied otherwise than with a view to profit.[3] Thus if A makes lemon curd which is *donated* to the local church sale of work, A is not liable, although he is a producer, because the goods were not supplied with a view to A's profit. But if A *sells* the lemon curd to the sale of work, A will remain liable under the Act. In both cases, the church will not be liable under the Act, since the only potential liability is as a supplier and the lemon curd was not sold in the course of a business. The church could, of course, be liable at common law.[4]

1 Consumer Protection Act 1987, s 2(3).
2 CPA 1987, s 4(1)(c)(i).
3 CPA 1987, s 4(1)(c)(ii).
4 If A supplies a 'free gift' when selling another product, A will be strictly liable under the Act if the gift is given away in the course of A's business.

(4) Meaning of defective product

In order to attract strict liability the damage must be caused 'wholly or partly' by a *defect* in the product.[1] What then is a defective product? A product is defective 'if the safety of the product is not such as persons are entitled to expect'.[2] For these purposes, 'safety shall include safety in the context of risks of damage to property as well as in the context of risks of death or personal injury'.[3] It will be noted that the test is what the *consumer* is entitled to expect in terms of the safety of the product: if it falls below the *consumer*'s expectations then the product is defective. This, in theory at least, is in marked contrast to the concept of negligence at common law which is tested by the standards of the hypothetical reasonable person in the position of the manufacturer.[4] Moreover, although the Consumer Protection Act 1987 is concerned with products which are dangerous because badly manufactured or incompetently designed, it also applies to products which are superbly designed and excellently manufactured but which are inherently dangerous if not used carefully, for example, drugs, guns etc. Such products will be defective if there are inadequate warnings, instructions as to use, etc.

In determining what the consumer is entitled to expect, the court must consider all the circumstances of the case.[5] These include:

(a) the purposes for which the product was marketed, its 'get up', any mark in relation to the product and any instructions or warnings.[6] Instructions or warnings are of particular importance where the product is inherently dangerous. Obviously if no warning is given, the product will be defective. But if there is an adequate warning, for example, in respect of drug dosage, will that satisfy the consumer's expectation of safety or must the container of the drug be, for example, child proof?;

(b) what might reasonably be expected to be done with or in relation to the product.[7] Theoretically, this should be what the *consumer* might *reasonably* expect to be done with the product rather than what the producer expects it to be used for.

1 Consumer Protection Act 1987, s 2(1).
2 CPA 1987, s 3(1).
3 CPA 1987, s 3(1).
4 For discussion, see pp 119 ff above.
5 CPA 1987, s 3(2).
6 CPA 1987, s 3(2)(a).
7 CPA 1987, s 3(2)(b).

Ultimately, however, it will be the court's view of reasonable expectation which will prevail. The test is clearly objective. So, for example, it is unlikely that a freezer which cannot be opened from within would be held to be defective even though a child climbed into the freezer and could not get out: freezers cannot reasonably be expected to be hiding places for toddlers!;

(c) the time when the product was supplied by its producer to another.[1] The relevant time for assessing the standard of safety of a product is the time at which it was supplied by the producer: the fact that products which are put on the market after that date have more safety features does not per se mean that the earlier product was defective at the time it was supplied.

At the end of the day, the test is sufficiently open that it will be left to the courts to determine the requisite standard of safety, and in spite of the fact that it is the consumer's expectation of safety that is in issue, the courts will no doubt consider the factors, for example, costs, with which they are familiar in establishing negligence at common law.[2]

Before there is strict liability under the Act, the pursuer has to show that the damage was '*caused* wholly or partly by a defect in a product'.[3] Therefore, as in the case of delictual liability at common law, the claim may fail unless there is a sufficient causative link between the damage and the defective product.[4] However, provided there are no causation problems, the pursuer who has suffered damage is entitled to compensation from the producer, own brander, importer or supplier without having to establish negligence. In other words, there is strict liability.

(5) Defences to claim of strict liability

The Consumer Protection Act 1987 does, however, provide the defender with the following defences to a claim based on *strict* liability:

---

1 Consumer Protection Act 1987, s 3(2)(c).
2 See pp 119 ff above.
3 CPA 1987, s 2(1) (emphasis added).
4 Although CPA 1987 applies when a defective product causes psychiatric illness, it will probably not apply to secondary victims, since their illnesses are caused by their reactions to the injuries of primary victims, rather than by the defective product which injured the primary victim concerned. On delictual liability for nervous shock, see pp 70 ff above.

(a) the defect in the product is attributable to the defender's compliance with statutory or EU obligations;[1]
(b) the defender did not at any time supply the product to another, for example, the product was stolen;[2]
(c) the defect did not exist in the product at the relevant times.[3] In the case of a producer, own brander or importer this will be the time he first supplied the product to another; in the case of a supplier, when the product was last supplied by a producer, an own brander or an importer into the EU. So in the case of the producer etc, he will escape strict liability if the product was not defective when it entered circulation, but subsequently becomes defective. There can, of course, still be delictual liability at common law. The supplier will escape strict liability if the product was not defective when it was last supplied by a producer etc even though the defect was subsequently caused by the supplier himself. For example, if a retailer keeps processed food which was edible when he obtained it from the producer but sells it when it has gone off, the retailer will not be liable. This is, to say the least, an odd result but, of course, the retailer will be liable in contract to the purchaser and at common law in delict to the ultimate consumer, when negligence will readily be inferred;
(d) the state of scientific and technical knowledge at the relevant time[4] was not such that a producer of products of the same description as the product in question might be expected to have discovered the defect if it had existed in his products while they were under his control.[5] This is known as the 'state of the art' defence. It is controversial in that a producer can escape *strict* liability if the defect in his product would not have been known by manufacturers of a similar product, given the state of scientific and technical knowledge at the time. This defence is, of course, similar to the common law principle that a defender cannot be liable in delict if, as a result of the scientific knowledge available to the hypothetical reasonable person at the time, injury to the pursuer was not a reasonable and probable consequence of the defender's conduct.[6] Moreover,

---

1 Consumer Protection Act 1987, s 4(1)(a).
2 CPA 1987, s 4(1)(b).
3 CPA 1987, s 4(1)(d).
4 See discussion immediately above.
5 CPA 1987, s 4(1)(e).
6 *Roe v Minister of Health* [1954] 2 QB 66, [1954] 2 All ER 131, CA, discussed at p 115 above.

the defence expressly refers to the awareness of producers of similar products. This is similar to the important role that the practice of persons in the same trade, business or profession of the defender plays in establishing a breach of a duty of care at common law.[1] Thus, the state of the art defence re-introduces negligence into the regime of strict liability laid down in the Consumer Protection Act 1987.

In many cases, the defence will not be available to the producer simply because, given the state of scientific and technical knowledge at the time, he[2] should have known the product was defective. Where the defence could be used is in the production of drugs whose side effects could not have been discovered given the state of scientific knowledge which existed at the time they were produced; it may take years before the side effects of certain drugs become apparent in patients. In these circumstances, the defence could be used by the defender. It is somewhat ironic that one of the reasons for the move towards a strict liability regime for defective products was to avoid the shortcomings of the law of negligence which became apparent in the thalidomide tragedy. The European Court of Justice has held that the scope of the Consumer Protection Act 1987, s 4(1)(e) is not in conflict with EU law;[3]

(e) if the defective product is a complex product, the producer of a component or of any raw materials contained in the complex product has a defence if the defect in the complex product is wholly attributable to the design of the complex product or to the fact that he complied with the instructions of the producer of the complex product;[4] otherwise, of course, both the producer of the complex product and the producer of the component or raw materials are jointly and severally liable;[5]

(f) contributory negligence.[6] Liability under the Consumer Protection Act 1987 cannot be excluded by an exemption clause.[7]

1 See pp 125 ff above.
2 Or, technically, producers of similar products.
3 *Commission of the European Communities v United Kingdom* (C300/95) [1997] All ER (EC) 481, ECJ (Fifth Chamber).
4 Consumer Protection Act 1987, s 2(4)(f).
5 See p 161 above.
6 CPA 1987, s 6(4).
7 CPA 1987, s 7.

This discussion of product liability is important because it illustrates how the common law of delictual liability based on the defender's *culpa* was thought to be inadequate to protect the interests of consumers who might be injured or whose property might be damaged by defective products. Accordingly, a regime of strict liability was introduced by statute so that the ultimate consumer would no longer have to prove fault before obtaining compensation. However, as we have seen, the Consumer Protection Act 1987 is not comprehensive and it will still be necessary on occasion for a pursuer to resort to delictual liability at common law, when, of course, negligence will have to be established.

CHAPTER 9

Delictual liability for animals

A. DELICTUAL LIABILITY AT COMMON LAW

Where the defender owes the pursuer a duty of care, the defender can be liable where the pursuer's injuries or damage to property is caused by an animal. In *Henderson v John Stuart (Farms) Ltd*[1] an employee was killed by a bull when cleaning out its box. The employer was held to be negligent in failing to fit the box with baffles or escape gaps. In other words, the employer had broken the duty of care he owed to his employee by failing to provide a safe working environment.[2] Similarly, in *Hill v Lovett*[3] an employee of the defenders, who were veterinary surgeons, was bitten by one of their West Highland terriers when she went into the garden to clean the windows of the surgery. As a result, the unfortunate pursuer eventually had to have her leg amputated. The Lord Ordinary (Weir) held that the defenders had broken the duty of care they owed to the pursuer both as employers and occupiers of the garden,[4] in failing to take reasonable care to ensure that the pugnacious dogs were not in the garden when the pursuer was there.

An unusual case in *Cameron v Hamilton's Auction Marts Ltd*.[5] The defenders were driving cattle along the highway. A cow escaped, climbed the stairway of a property adjoining the road, turned on a tap, and fell through the floor into the pursuer's shop causing flooding and damage. Clearly the defender owed a *Donoghue v Stevenson* duty of care[6] to the pursuer as the owner of property adjacent to the highway. In these circumstances, the sheriff held that the defenders would be liable for breach of their duty of care if the cow had escaped because of their negligence.[7]

---

1 1963 SC 245, 1963 SLT 22, OH.
2 On employers' liability, see Chapter 12 below.
3 1992 SLT 994, OH.
4 On occupiers' liability, see pp 186 ff below.
5 1955 SLT (Sh Ct) 74, 71 Sh Ct Rep 285.
6 See *Donoghue v Stevenson* 1932 SC (HL) 31, 1932 SLT 317.
7 See also *Swan v Andrew Minto & Son* 1998 Rep LR 42.

These cases, then, are examples of breach of an existing duty of care as a result of the defender's carelessness: the fact that the injuries and damage were caused by an animal is largely irrelevant. They are simply examples of common law delictual liability for negligence.

However, at common law, certain animals were regarded as *ferae naturae*, ie as having vicious propensities. These included, for example, lions, tigers and elephants. If such an animal caused injury or damage to a person, the person in charge of the animal was strictly liable, ie there was no need to prove fault. Strict liability applied even though the animal had not shown any vicious propensities before.[1] On the other hand, certain animals were regarded as *domitae naturae*, ie as having no vicious propensities. These included, for example, dogs, cats and cattle, including bulls. If such an animal had *in fact* shown vicious propensities before the pursuer suffered injury or damage, then strict liability would attach to the defender. But as in *Henderson v John Stuart (Farms) Ltd*[2] and *Hill v Lovett*,[3] where the bull and the dog had not hitherto shown vicious tendencies so that strict liability could not be imposed, the defenders were nevertheless successfully sued in negligence for breach of their duty of care.[4]

B. LIABILITY UNDER THE ANIMALS (SCOTLAND) ACT 1987

(1) Introduction

The common law on *strict* liability for injuries or damage caused by animals was regarded as unsatisfactory. For injury or damage caused by an animal after 10 June 1987, the common law on *strict* liability has been replaced by the provisions of the Animals (Scotland) Act 1987.[5] However, common law liability for injury or damage caused by an animal as a result of the defender's *negligence* has *not* been

---

1 See the English case of *Behrens v Bertram Mills Circus Ltd* [1957] 2 QB 1, [1957] 1 All ER 583, where the defendants were held strictly liable for the injuries caused to a midget by an elephant which had hitherto appeared docile.
2 1963 SC 245, 1963 SLT 22.
3 1992 SLT 994, OH.
4 Special rules applied to dogs under the Dogs Acts 1906–1928; damage done by straying cattle was governed by the Winter Herding Act 1686.
5 Animals (Scotland) Act 1987, s 1(8). References in this section are to the Animals (Scotland) Act 1987 unless otherwise stated.

replaced by the provisions of the 1987 Act[1] and a pursuer is there-fore able to sue on the general principles of *culpa* if his case does not fall within the strict liability regime imposed by the 1987 Act.

Where the Animals (Scotland) Act 1987 applies, the defender's liability is strict, ie the defender is liable without the pursuer having to prove that the defender was negligent. The person who is liable is the *keeper* of the *animal* 'at the time of the injury or damage complained of'.[2] The keeper of an animal for the purposes of the Act is defined as follows:[3]

(a) the owner of the animal: remains the owner, even if the animal has been abandoned or has escaped, until someone else becomes the owner;[4]
(b) the person with possession of the animal:[5] remains in posses-sion, even if the animal has been abandoned or has escaped, until someone else obtains possession.[6] However, a person is not a keeper of an animal by virtue of possession if he is detaining the animal to prevent it from causing injury or damage on his land[7] or is 'temporarily detaining it for the purpose of protecting it or any other person or other animal or restoring it as soon as is reasonably practicable to its owner or a possessor of it';[8]
(c) a person with 'actual care and control of a child under the age of 16' who is the owner or has possession of the animal.[9] Thus, for example, a parent of a child under the age of 16 is regarded as the keeper of any animal owned by the child, provided the parent has actual care and control of the child.

Where an animal is owned by A but in the possession of B, A and B can be jointly and severally liable under the Act.

(2) Meaning of animal

What animals fall within the Animals (Scotland) Act 1987? For strict liability to apply, the animal must be of 'a species whose

1 See the Animals (Scotland) Act 1987, s 1(8).
2 A(S)A 1987, s 1(1).
3 A(S)A 1987, s 5(1)(a).
4 A(S)A 1987, s 5(2)(b). The Crown does not become the owner if an animal is abandoned: A(S)A 1987, s 5(2)(c).
5 A(S)A 1987, s 5(1)(a).
6 A(S)A 1987, s 5(2)(b).
7 A(S)A 1987, s 3.
8 A(S)A 1987, s 5(2)(a).
9 A(S)A 1987, s 5(1)(b).

members generally are by virtue of their physical attributes or habits likely (unless controlled or restrained) to injure severely or kill persons or animals, or damage property to a material extent'.[1] Read literally, this definition is potentially very wide indeed. Although bulls can clearly fall within the definition,[2] it could, for example, include a domestic cat, since a cat by virtue of its physical attributes or habits is likely to injure severely or kill animals like birds or mice! It will ultimately be for the court to decide whether or not a certain species falls within the statutory criteria.

For the purpose of s 1(1)(b) of the Animals (Scotland) Act 1987, certain animals are deemed to be likely (unless controlled or restrained) to injure severely or kill persons or animals by biting or otherwise savaging, attacking or harrying. These are dogs and dangerous wild animals within the meaning of s 7(4) of the Dangerous Wild Animals Act 1976.[3] Therefore all types of dogs are regarded as animals for the purpose of the 1987 Act so that strict liability is imposed on their keepers, even if the dog concerned has never shown any vicious tendencies in the past. Before strict liability arises, the dog must have caused the injuries or damage by 'biting or otherwise savaging, attacking or harrying'. Thus there was no strict liability when a woman was 'knocked down' by an overly affectionate labrador.[4]

Where an animal is a dangerous wild animal within the meaning of the 1976 Act, it is regarded as an animal for the purpose of strict liability under the 1987 Act. Dangerous wild animals include wild dogs, wolves, jackals, coyotes, foxes (but not the common red fox), cassowaries, Old World monkeys, crocodiles and alligators, emus, poisonous snakes, lions and tigers, cheetahs and panthers, Gila monsters and Mexican beaded lizards, gibbons, orangutans, gorillas and chimpanzees, ostriches and bears.[5] Again, strict liability only arises when the dangerous wild animal has caused the injuries or damage by 'biting or otherwise savaging, attacking or harrying'. In addition, cattle, horses, asses, mules, hinnies, sheep,

---

1 Animals (Scotland) Act 1987, s 1(1)(b).
2 *Foskett v McClymont* 1998 SC 96, 1998 SLT 892, OH. It is a question of fact whether the particular animal fulfils the statutory criteria.
3 A(S)A 1987, s 1(3)(a).
4 *Fairlie v Carruthers* 1996 SLT (Sh Ct) 56. The court, of course, cannot look into a dog's mind to determine *mens rea*! The test is objective after considering what actually happened. There was also no liability for negligence in this case, since the defender had no grounds to believe that the dog would knock the pursuer over.
5 Dangerous Wild Animals Act 1976, s 7(4) and Sch 3.

pigs, goats and deer *in the course of foraging* are deemed to be likely (unless controlled or restrained) to damage to a material extent land or the produce of land for the purpose of s 1(1)(b) of the 1987 Act.[1]

As a result of these provisions a wide range of species are deemed to be animals for the purpose of the Animals (Scotland) Act 1987. But if an animal is not deemed to fall within the definition in s 1(1)(b), it is, of course, possible to argue that it is nevertheless of a species which by virtue of the physical attributes or habits of its members is likely to injure severely or kill persons or other animals, or damage property to a material extent. In assessing whether this is so, the age and sex of the animal is relevant.[2] Thus, a non-foraging cow is unlikely to fall within the definition in s 1(1)(b), while a non-foraging bull could.[3] The 1987 Act expressly *excludes* from the definition of animal, viruses, bacteria, algae, fungi and protozoa.[4]

Where the animal falls within the definition in the Animals (Scotland) Act 1987, s 1(1)(b) or is deemed to do so by virtue of s 1(3)(a) or (b), its keeper is strictly liable, ie liable without establishing *culpa*, for any damage or injury suffered by the pursuer which is directly referable to the animal's dangerous attributes or habits.[5] In other words, the damage or injury sustained must arise from the particular attributes or habits of the species which bring the animal within the definition in s 1(1)(b). So, for example, the keeper of a red setter dog is strictly liable under the 1987 Act if the dog bites the pursuer, since the injury is directly referable to a dog's attribute or habit to bite.[6] But if the pursuer's injury is sustained as a result of falling over the red setter dog, the keeper is not strictly liable under the 1987 Act, although the keeper could be liable if he owed a duty of care to the pursuer and negligence could be established.[7]

---

1 Animals (Scotland) Act 1987, s 1(3)(b). In *Foskett v McClymont* 1998 SC 96, 1998 SLT 892, OH, the bull was not automatically deemed to be an animal for the purpose of the Act, since the damage did not occur in the course of foraging, and personal injury as opposed to property damage was involved.
2 A(S)A 1987, s 1(2)(a).
3 *Foskett v McClymont* 1998 SC 96, 1998 SLT 892, OH.
4 A(S)A 1987, s 7.
5 A(S)A 1987, s 1(1)(c).
6 So if a domestic cat was a dangerous animal, its keeper would only be liable if, for example, it killed the pursuer's pet bird. In other words, the injury must be referable to the attributes or habits of a domestic cat which bring the cat under the statutory definition.
7 For discussion, see pp 169 ff above.

Strict liability does not apply to injury or damage caused by the
mere fact that the animal in question was present on a road or in
any other place.[1] Thus, if a motorist was injured while trying to
avoid running over a dog, the keeper is not strictly liable under the
Animals (Scotland) Act 1987, but may, of course, be liable at
common law if a breach of a duty of care towards the pursuer can
be established. The 1987 Act does not apply if the injury caused by
the animal consists of a disease which was transmitted by means
which were unlikely to cause severe injury other than disease.[2] So,
for example, if A is savaged by a rabid dog and contracts rabies, the
keeper is strictly liable under the 1987 Act, because the disease was
transmitted by means which were likely to cause severe injury, ie
the dog's bites. But if the animal had merely licked the pursuer
thereby transmitting the disease, the keeper is not strictly liable
under the 1987 Act, since the means, ie the licking, was unlikely to
cause severe injury other than the disease. In the latter situation, of
course, the keeper could still be liable at common law provided
there was a breach of a duty of care owed to the pursuer, ie
provided that negligence could be established.

(3) Defences to liability under the Animals (Scotland) Act 1987

Even where the Animals (Scotland) Act 1987 applies and the
keeper is prima facie strictly liable, there are several possible
defences:

(a) if the injury or damage was due wholly to the fault of the
     person sustaining it or, in the case of an injury sustained to
     another animal, the keeper of that animal.[3] This will cover the
     situation where, for example, the pursuer has goaded a docile
     animal which attacks the pursuer in defence;
(b) if the person sustaining the injury or damage, or a keeper of the
     animal sustaining the injury, willingly accepted the risk of it as
     his.[4] The classic example is a person who willingly puts his
     head in a lion's mouth. This defence is, of course, a statutory
     form of *volens non fit injuria*;[5]

1 Animals (Scotland) Act 1987, s 1(5).
2 A(S)A 1987, s 1(4).
3 A(S)A 1987, s 2(1)(a).
4 A(S)A 1987, s 2(1)(b).
5 For discussion of the *volens* doctrine, see pp 141 ff above.

(c) if the person who was injured or suffered damage was a trespasser, ie was not authorised to be on the keeper's property.[1]
The effect of this provision is only to remove *strict* liability from
the keeper. As we shall see,[2] the keeper of the animal as occupier of property owes a duty of care to any person who enters
on to the property, including a trespasser. Thus, although the
keeper is not *strictly* liable under the 1987 Act to the trespasser
who has been injured by an animal, the keeper may be liable as
occupier of the property if negligence can be established. Strict
liability in relation to a trespasser is *not* removed by s 2(1)(c) of
the Animals (Scotland) Act 1987, if the animal which caused
the injury or damage was there for the purpose of protecting
persons or property. But the keeper will get the benefit of s
2(1)(c) if it is shown that it was reasonable to keep such an
animal there and that the use made of the animal was reasonable.[3] Consider the following example:

(i) If A, a trespasser, is injured by B's goose,[4] prima facie
s 2(1)(c) of the Animals (Scotland) Act 1987 applies and
B is not strictly liable. But if the goose was on the land to
protect B's warehouse, then s 2(1)(c) is disapplied and B
is strictly liable. But if B can show it is reasonable to have
a goose as a 'guardbird', s 2(1)(c) is reapplied and B is not
strictly liable. It is thought that B would succeed in this
case since it is reasonable to have a goose as opposed to a
tiger as a 'watch animal'.[5]

Where the animal concerned is a guard dog, the keeper
remains strictly liable to a trespasser, ie s 2(1)(c) of the 1987
Act is disapplied, unless the keeper can show that he has
complied with the provisions of s 1 of the Guard Dogs Act
1975.[6] Under this section, *either* the dog's handler must be
present and have the dog under his control, *or* the dog must be
secured so that it is not at liberty to go freely about the
premises. In addition, notices of the dog's presence must be
displayed at every entrance to the property.

---

1 Animals (Scotland) Act 1987, s 2(1)(c). In the case of injury to another animal,
   if the keeper of that animal was not entitled to have the animal on the land.
2 On occupiers' liability, see pp 186 ff below.
3 A(S)A 1987, s 2(2).
4 Assuming, of course, that a goose is an animal for the purpose of A(S)A 1987,
   s 1(2)(b).
5 A(S)A 1987, s 2(2).
6 A(S)A 1987, s 2(2).

Consider the following example:

(ii) If A, a trespasser, is injured by B's guard dog, prima facie
s 2(1)(c) of the Animals (Scotland) Act 1987 does not
apply and B remains strictly liable. But if B can show that
he complied with the provisions of s 1 of the Guard Dogs
Act 1975, then s 2(1)(c) of the 1987 Act is reapplied and
B is not strictly liable.

In both examples (i) and (ii), B would be liable to A if he was in
breach of the duty of care he owes to A as occupier of the property.
To be successful, A would have to prove that B did not take
reasonable care to protect him from the danger arising from having
the animal on the land,[1] ie that B was negligent.

Where the Animals (Scotland) Act 1987 applies, there is no
defence on the ground of *damnum fatale* or, for example, of intervention by a third party which caused the animal to escape. This is
because liability is strict. However, the pursuer's damages may be
reduced on the grounds of contributory negligence.[2]

In this chapter we have seen how the general principles of
delictual liability for negligence apply where damage or injury has
been caused by an animal. However, even at common law it was
thought to be in the interests of society that the owner of a
dangerous animal should be liable without proof of fault. These
rules were, however, unclear and, in so far as strict liability is
concerned, they have been replaced by the regime imposed by the
1987 Act. But where a case does not fall within the statutory
regime of strict liability, the keeper may still be liable if he was in
breach of a duty of care which he owed to the pursuer, but in these
circumstances the onus rests on the pursuer to prove that the
keeper was negligent.

1 On occupiers' liability, see pp 186 ff below.
2 The keeper's statutory liability is treated as fault for the purposes of the Law
Reform (Contributory Negligence) Act 1945: Animals (Scotland) Act 1987,
s 1(6). On contributory negligence, see pp 143 ff above.

CHAPTER 10

Delictual liability arising from ownership or occupation of property

A. DELICTUAL LIABILITY AT COMMON LAW

The owner or occupier of property may be liable under general principles of *culpa* if a person is injured or if property is damaged as a result of the state of the defender's property. In a case of unintentional acts or omissions, it will be necessary for the pursuer to show that the owner or occupier owed him a *Donoghue v Stevenson* duty of care[1] and that the defender was in breach of that duty.[2] In order to establish a breach of duty, it will, of course, be necessary to show that the defender was negligent. So, for example, if a slate falls off the defender's roof and injures a pedestrian who is using the highway or damages a motor car, the defender may be liable for breach of a duty of care owed to the pedestrian or the owner of the car[3] if the pursuer can establish negligence.[4]

Although it is clear that the owner of property does not act at his peril, ie is not strictly liable,[5] the court will readily infer negligence if the defender has built a structure on his land which if unsafe would cause serious damage. In *Kerr v Earl of Orkney*,[6] the defender built a dam on his land across a stream on which the pursuer had a mill about half a mile lower down. Four months later, after several days of heavy rain, the dam burst and the pursuer's house and his mill were swept away. The court held that the defender was liable unless he could show that the dam had collapsed as a result of a *damnum fatale*, for example, an earthquake as opposed to several days of heavy rain. The fact that the

---

1 See *Donoghue v Stevenson* 1932 SC (HL) 31, 1932 SLT 317, and Chapter 3 above.
2 See Chapter 5 above.
3 It is thought that as a general principle the owner or occupier of property adjoining the highway would owe a duty of care to a pedestrian or motorist.
4 *MacColl v Hoo* 1983 SLT (Sh Ct) 23.
5 *McLaughlan v Craig* 1948 SC 599, 1948 SLT 483.
6 (1857) 20 D 298, 30 SJ 158.

178   *Delictual liability arising from ownership or occupation of property*

dam had burst shortly after it had been built implied that the defender was at fault. Liability arises either because the *opus manufactum* could not be constructed so as to avoid harm to the neighbouring property, in which case there was fault in building the structure at all, or the work was built negligently.[1] While achieving a similar result in cases such as *Kerr*, Scots law does not accept the English doctrine laid down in *Rylands v Fletcher*[2] that the owner of land is strictly liable for damage caused by the escape of dangerous things brought on to his property as a consequence of the defendant's non-natural use of his land.[3] In *RHM Bakeries (Scotland) Ltd v Strathclyde Regional Council*,[4] Lord Fraser of Tullybelton was adamant that *Rylands v Fletcher* 'has no place in Scots law, and the suggestion that it has, is a heresy which ought to be extirpated'.[5]

Although reasonable foreseeability of injury to the pursuer or harm to his property is the usual criterion for the imposition of a duty of care on the owner or occupier of property, in one situation at least the duty of care has been used as a threshold device to restrict the potential delictual liability of proprietors.[6] The question is whether the owner or occupier of property owes a duty of care to owners or occupiers of adjacent property, to prevent damage to their property as a result of the acts of third parties. For example, does the owner of derelict property owe a duty of care to adjacent proprietors, to prevent vandals from entering the derelict property and starting a fire which spreads and damages the adjacent properties? Or does the owner of a flat owe a duty of care to the owner of the shop below the flat, to prevent a thief from entering the flat in order to gain access and steal from the shop?

These difficult issues were explored by the House of Lords in *Maloco v Littlewoods Organisation Ltd*.[7] It was accepted by the court that the owner or occupier of property owed a duty to proprietors

1 *GA Estates Ltd v Caviapen Trustees Ltd (No 1)* 1993 SLT 1037, OH, at 1041 per the Lord Ordinary (Coulsfield).
2 (1868) LR 3 HL 330. The scope of *Rylands v Fletcher* liability was re-examined by the House of Lords in *Cambridge Water Co v Eastern Counties Leather plc* [1994] 2 AC 264, [1994] 1 All ER 53, HL.
3 In Scots law liability does not arise simply because a dangerous thing escapes, but from the construction of the *opus manufactum*: see *GA Estates Ltd v Caviapen Trustees Ltd (No 1)* 1993 SLT 1037, OH.
4 1985 SLT 214, HL.
5 1985 SLT 214 at 217.
6 On the duty of care as a threshold device, see Chapter 5 above.
7 1987 SC (HL) 37, 1987 SCLR 489, 1987 SLT 425; for facts, see discussion at p 118 above.

of adjacent property to take reasonable care of his property so that it did not cause them physical injury or damage to their property. But there was no general duty to take reasonable care of property to prevent a *third party* from using the premises to cause physical injury or damage to neighbouring proprietors. Using the duty of care as a threshold device, the House of Lords held that no such duty arose even if it was reasonably foreseeable that a third party could enter the defender's property and cause harm to the adjacent proprietor. Thus, while it is reasonably foreseeable that if a person leaves his flat unlocked a thief may enter the premises and gain access to an adjacent flat or shop, the owner of the flat does not owe a duty to take reasonable care to prevent this occurrence. In these circumstances, the owner of the adjacent flat or shop must seek redress against the thief, ie against the third party.

However, Lord Mackay was prepared to accept that a duty of care could be imposed on the owner or occupier of property if in the circumstances it was highly probable – as opposed to reasonably foreseeable – that a third party would cause harm to an adjacent proprietor.[1] Lord Goff took the view that this could arise if the owner 'negligently causes or permits a source of danger to be created on his land, and can reasonably foresee that third parties may trespass on his land and, if interfering with the source of danger, may spark it off, thereby causing damage to the person or property'.[2] For example, a duty of care would arise if A kept explosives in his house, told persons that the explosives were there, but took no precautions to prevent trespassers from having access to the premises. Similarly, a duty of care would arise if the owner had allowed his property to become a fire hazard, knew persons had been trespassing on the premises and had already started fires, but did not take reasonable precautions to prevent access.[3] As we have seen,[4] no duty arose in the *Littlewoods* case, since the defenders did not know that the derelict cinema had, in fact, become a fire hazard: derelict buildings are not, per se, fire hazards.

Lord Goff doubted[5] whether the owner or occupier of property ever owes a duty of care to adjacent proprietors to prevent a thief from gaining access to their premises:

1 *Maloco v Littlewoods Organisation Ltd* 1987 SLT 425 at 429.
2 1987 SLT 425 at 439.
3 *Thomas Graham & Co Ltd v Church of Scotland General Trustees* 1982 SLT (Sh Ct) 26.
4 Page 118 above.
5 *Maloco v Littlewoods Organisation Ltd* 1987 SLT 425 at 441.

'. . . I do not think that liability can be imposed on an occupier of property in negligence simply because it can be said that it is reasonably foreseeable, or even (having regard, for example, to some particular temptation to thieves in adjacent premises) that it is highly likely that, if he fails to keep his property lockfast, a thief may gain access to his property and thence to the adjacent premises. So to hold must presuppose that the occupier of property is under a general duty to prevent thieves from entering his property to gain access to neighbouring property, where there is a sufficient degree of foresight that this may occur. But there is no general duty to prevent third parties from causing damage to others, even though there is a high degree of foresight that they may do so. The practical effect is that everybody has to take such steps as he thinks fit to protect his own property, whether house or flat or shop, against thieves.'

Although obiter, this dictum is a remarkable example of the duty of care being used as a threshold device to deny delictual liability for reasons of policy.[1] As a result, the decision of the Inner House in *Squires v Perth and Kinross District Council*[2] must be regarded as unsound. There the pursuers, who were jewellers, successfully sued building contractors who were working on a flat above their shop for not adequately securing the flat against entry by a thief who gained access to their shop and stole jewellery. In the light of Lord Goff's dictum, the case should have been dismissed *in limine* because of the absence of a duty of care.[3]

The occupier of property owes the owner a duty of care to prevent damage to the premises. Since there is usually a contract between them, this duty is usually contractual. However, it was held in *Fry's Metals Ltd v Durastic Ltd*[4] that the defenders were liable in *delict* for failing to maintain an alarm system after their lease with the pursuer had expired. Their duty of care arose because they had retained the keys and were the only persons who had access to the building to operate the alarm. Moreover, they were liable for the damage caused by vandals who had broken into the premises because, in the circumstances, it was highly probable that this would occur if the alarm system was not working.

---

1 For full discussion, see Chapter 5 above.
2 1986 SLT 30.
3 Even if there was a duty of care it is doubtful whether the defender should have been liable. In his evidence, the thief claimed that although he got the idea of gaining access to the shop via the flat when he saw the defender's scaffolding and the open windows, he in fact entered the flat from the back by going up a drain pipe and entering an open door. The chain of causation between the defender's carelessness and the theft is therefore very fragile – provided, of course, we believe the thief.
4 1991 SLT 689n, OH.

B. THE *ACTIO DE EFFUSIS VEL DEJECTIS* AND THE *ACTIO DE POSITIS VEL SUSPENSIS*

As we have seen, the owner or occupier of property may be liable in delict for injury or damage caused by the defective state of the property on general principles of *culpa*. To be successful the pursuer must establish fault on the part of the defender. In Roman law, however, in two situations actions were available in which an owner or occupier was strictly liable, ie where there was no need to establish *culpa*. These were the *actio de effusis vel dejectis* where something was poured or thrown out of a building causing harm to the victim, and the *actio de positis vel suspensis* where something placed on or suspended from a building fell, causing harm to the victim. Under these *actiones* the owner or occupier was strictly liable for personal injuries or damage to property. Given its civilian background, it has been argued that these *actiones* are part of Scots law.[1]

Although there is no authoritative decision of the Court of Session or House of Lords, attempts to rely on the *actiones* have not been successful. In *Gray v Dunlop*[2] the pursuer's son had the contents of a pot of urine poured over him from a window of a hostel for the indigent. In an action against the occupier of the premises, it was argued that the *actio de effusis vel dejectis* was applicable and the defender was strictly liable. But the court held that the *actio* did not apply and the pursuer's case failed because fault could not be established. Similarly, in *MacColl v Hoo*[3] the *actio de positis vel suspensis* was held not to apply when the pursuer's car was damaged by a slate which fell off the defender's roof. The defender was therefore not strictly liable and in order to succeed the pursuer would have to establish that the slate fell off the roof because the defender had failed to take reasonable care in respect of the maintenance of the property, ie that the defender was negligent.

C. *AEMULATIO VICINI*

If the proprietor uses his land in such a way as to interfere with his neighbour's use or enjoyment of his property, then the conduct may be actionable *in aemulationem vicini*. Before there is liability, it

1 See, for example, DM Walker, *The Law of Delict in Scotland* (2nd edn, 1981, Greens) p 284.
2 1954 SLT (Sh Ct) 75, 70 Sh Ct Rep 270.
3 1983 SLT (Sh Ct) 23.

must be shown that the defender's use of his property was done with the intention of interfering with the neighbour's use or enjoyment of his land. A single incident is sufficient to establish liability. This delict has been fully discussed in the context of the intentional delicts.[1]

D. NUISANCE

The owner of property[2] must not use his land in such a way as to disturb his neighbour's enjoyment of his property or cause damage to his neighbour's land.[3] If a person does so, he may be liable in nuisance. Nuisance is usually a continuing wrong, ie there is more than one act. But delictual liability for nuisance arises even if the defender did not intend to cause inconvenience to the pursuer's enjoyment of his land or damage to the pursuer's property. The delict can be summarised in the brocard, *sic utere tuo ut alienum non laedas*, ie use your own property in such a way that you do not do harm to others.

Common examples of nuisance are noise, smells, the emission of fumes and burst pipes. The existence of a building per se does not constitute a nuisance even if it interferes with another person's enjoyment of her land, for example, by causing interference with her television signal.[4] The essence of the delict is that as a result of the defender's actions on his property, the pursuer has suffered more than he could reasonably be expected to tolerate: *plus quam tolerabile*. Whether this has been established is a matter of fact and degree in the particular circumstances of the case. For instance, the smell of dung may be acceptable in the countryside but not in the confines of a city tenement. Regularly to play CDs of Wagner at full blast may be acceptable in a large detached house, but not in a two-bedroomed semi-detached. Even if the defender is a professional musician who has to practise 12 hours a day, if the noise disturbs his neighbour more than the neighbour can be expected to tolerate, it is a nuisance and the fact that it is a normal and familiar use of a musician's home is no defence. Nor can it be

---

1 See p 21 above.
2 This can include the owner of a servitude right. Persistent use of a servitude right which involves a serious risk of damage to the servient tenement can constitute a nuisance: *Cloy v Adams & Sons* 1999 GWD 19-908.
3 *Watt v Jamieson* 1954 SC 56 at 58 per the Lord President (Cooper).
4 *Hunter v Canary Wharf Ltd* [1997] AC 655, [1997] 2 All ER 426, HL. The building must, of course, satisfy planning controls.

argued that the pursuer came to the nuisance. So if in our example, the musician's previous neighbour enjoyed hearing him practise, this is no defence to an action of nuisance brought by the new proprietor of the neighbour's house, if the continual practising is driving the pursuer mad!

Noise caused by normal domestic use of a family home does not amount to nuisance, provided it would not seriously disturb or substantially inconvenience an average reasonable person living in the locality.[1] To constitute a nuisance, the defender's use must amount to offensive conduct, the effects of which are *intolerable*: it is not enough that they merely cause discomfort to the pursuer.[2]

If the use of the defender's property is in the public interest, this is no defence if it would otherwise constitute nuisance. In *Webster v Lord Advocate*[3] the pursuer had bought a flat in Edinburgh near the Castle. As the Edinburgh Festival approached, the enjoyment of her flat was disturbed by the noise of workmen erecting the grandstand for the military tattoo. The court held that this was a prima facie case of nuisance: it was irrelevant that the noise could be reduced if the pursuer closed her windows or installed double glazing. While accepting that the tattoo was a valuable and profitable part of the Festival, the court decided that this 'greater good' argument was not sufficient to prevent it from ordering that the nuisance should cease. Accordingly, the court granted declarator that a nuisance was established and that the defender should take steps to ensure that the grandstand was constructed by using less noisy techniques. It is a defence, however, to an action that the conduct constituting the nuisance was carried out with statutory authority.[4]

Because nuisance usually involves *continuing* acts or omissions, the primary remedy is interdict, ie an order that the defender's act or omission should cease. In determining whether or not to grant interdict, the court is concerned with the position of the pursuer, ie whether the pursuer should have to continue to suffer the nuisance. Whether or not the nuisance was caused by conduct

---

1 *Davidson v Kerr* 1997 Hous LR 11, 1996 GWD 40-2296, Sh Ct. In *Murdoch v Glacier Metal Co Ltd* [1998] Env LR 732, [1998] EHLR 198, CA, the noise from the defendant's factory did not constitute a nuisance even though it exceeded the maximum level recommended by the World Health Organisation.
2 *Anderson v Dundee City Council* 1999 GWD 1-52.
3 *Webster v Lord Advocate* 1985 SC 173, 1985 SLT 361.
4 A planning authority has no jurisdiction to authorise a nuisance unless it has a statutory power to permit a change in the character of the neighbourhood and the nuisance was an inevitable consequence of the change: *Wheeler v JJ Saunders Ltd* [1995] 2 All ER 697, [1995] 3 WLR 466, CA.

which amounted to *culpa* on the part of the defender is largely irrelevant. Thus, in the context of granting interdict, the defender's liability for nuisance is strict, ie there is no need to aver or prove fault.

However, where the nuisance has caused damage to the pursuer's property, no claim for damages will be successful unless the pursuer avers and proves that the nuisance arose as a result of the defender's *culpa*. This was settled by the House of Lords in *RHM Bakeries (Scotland) Ltd v Strathclyde Regional Council.*[1] The pursuer's premises were flooded as a result of the collapse of a sewer, the maintenance of which was the responsibility of the defender. Food and packing materials stored in the bakery were damaged. Even if the failure to maintain the sewer adequately amounted to nuisance, the House of Lords held that the pursuer's action in damages failed because they had not averred, let alone proved, that the collapse of the sewer was due to the negligence of the defender. Thus, before the pursuer can obtain damages for harm caused by nuisance, *culpa* on the part of the defender must be established.

But what constitutes *culpa* in this context? This issue was explored in *Kennedy v Glenbelle Ltd.*[2] The pursuer sought damages for harm sustained to his property as a result of the removal of a wall within the defender's premises. The Lord President (Hope) held[3] that *culpa* would arise if:

(1) the defender deliberately intended to damage the pursuer's property (malice); or
(2) the defender knew that her act or omission would damage the pursuer's property; or
(3) the defender was reckless, ie she had no regard to the question whether or not her conduct might be likely to damage the pursuer's property; or
(4) the defender's conduct had such potentially hazardous consequences for the pursuer's property that knowledge that her conduct would damage the pursuer's property is presumed; or
(5) the defender's acts or omissions were carried out carelessly, ie negligence.

In cases (1) to (4), *culpa* arises because the defender knows (or is deemed to know) that the conduct which constitutes the nuisance will damage the pursuer's property, ie it is intentionally caused

1 1985 SC (HL) 17, 1985 SLT 214.
2 1996 SC 95.
3 1996 SC 95 at 100 ff.

harm. It is quite irrelevant that the defender's actions were carried out carefully. The fault lies in the fact that the defender knows (or is deemed to know) that her conduct will harm the pursuer's property. Given that the defender's conduct must satisfy the *plus quam tolerabile* test before it will constitute a nuisance, it is thought that in case (5) damages will lie if the pursuer can show that the defender's conduct fell below the standard of reasonable care: it is not necessary that the defender owed the pursuer a pre-existing duty of care.

Because of the difficulty of proving *culpa*, in *RHM Bakeries* Lord Fraser expressed the view that the court would readily infer *culpa* from the fact that the sewer had collapsed causing serious damage.[1] Although this may be the case where the defender has built a dangerous *opus manufactum* on his property, it is doubtful that negligence will be inferred from the mere fact that the pursuer has sustained harm. In *Argyll and Clyde Health Board v Strathclyde Regional Council*[2] the Lord Ordinary (McCluskey) held that in an action for damages it was not sufficient for the pursuers simply to aver that a pipe running below their field had burst causing damage. Instead the pursuers had to have specific averments showing why the defenders were at fault: for example, that they were negligent in failing to inspect the pipe and carry out regular maintenance. The fact that the pipe had burst causing damage to the pursuers did not have the effect that the onus automatically shifted to the defenders to show that they were not negligent in maintaining the pipe.

In the *RHM Bakeries* case the House of Lords did not overrule its earlier decision in *Caledonian Rly Co v Greenock Corpn*.[3] In that case, Greenock Corporation had altered the channel of a burn to make a paddling pool. After heavy rainfall, the pursuer's property was flooded. The House of Lords awarded the pursuer damages without the need to prove fault, ie the defender was held to be strictly liable. This decision was distinguished in *RHM Bakeries* on the ground that it was concerned with the alteration of the natural direction of a stream not with damage caused by 'unnatural' use of property. It is submitted that the distinction is tenuous and that, at the very least, the decision in the *Caledonian Rly* case rests uneasily with the ratio in *RHM Bakeries* where it was held that when a

---

1 *RHM Bakeries (Scotland) Ltd v Strathclyde Regional Council* 1985 SC (HL) 17 at 45.
2 1988 SCLR 120, 1988 SLT 381, OH.
3 1917 SC (HL) 56, 1917 2 SLT 67.

nuisance has damaged property, compensation is available only if *culpa* on the part of the defender can be established.[1]

It is now clear that if nuisance is established an interdict can be granted without proof of fault, whereas damages are awarded only on proof of *culpa*. The question arises whether this distinction is sensible. Where, for example, the nuisance is fumes emanating from the defender's factory, the effect of an interdict may mean that the defender has to close the factory while extensive – and expensive – repairs are carried out; yet, in theory at least, the defender may not have been negligent. But given that nuisance is often a continuing wrong, even where the nuisance has caused damage, the defender still remains obliged to ensure that the nuisance stops, ie the defender could be interdicted if it were to continue. It is therefore submitted that the defender should not have to meet the *additional* obligation of compensating the pursuer unless *culpa* is established: *culpa* is, after all, the basic tenet of the obligation to make reparation in Scots law.

Finally, the function of the law of nuisance is to protect the pursuer's interest in his land. Therefore only a person with a recognised interest in heritable property has title to sue.[2] Moreover, damages are awarded only to compensate the pursuer for any diminution in the value of her *property* caused by a nuisance. Where *personal injuries* are involved, the pursuer, even if she is the owner of the land, must sue either for intentional wrongdoing or in negligence, where the defender will not be liable unless he has breached a pre-existing duty of care which he owed to the pursuer. Nuisance is a *proprietary remedy* and compensation is only available in respect of harm to the pursuer's heritable property.[3]

E. OCCUPIERS' LIABILITY

We have been considering cases where, as a result of acts or omissions on his property, the owner/occupier of property causes harm

---

1 The exception in relation to altering the natural flow of a stream was accepted by the Lord Ordinary (Coulsfield) in *GA Estates Ltd v Caviapen Trustees Ltd (No 1)* 1993 SLT 1037 at 1041.

2 *Harvie v Robertson* (1903) 5 F 338, 10 SLT 581; *Hunter v Canary Wharf Ltd* [1997] AC 655, [1997] 2 All ER 426, HL. See also *Dundee (City of) District Council v Cook* 1995 SCLR 559.

3 For an authoritative statement of the law of nuisance see 14 *Stair Memorial Encyclopaedia* paras 2001–2168.

to persons who are not on his property, for example, adjacent proprietors, neighbouring proprietors, pedestrians or motorists on the highway who pass the defender's property. In this section, we shall consider the delictual liability of the occupier of property towards persons who *enter* upon the property.

Scots common law was strongly influenced by English law. As a result of the decision of the House of Lords in *Dumbreck v Robert Addie & Sons*,[1] the duty of care towards a person entering on to property depended on the status of the person who was injured, ie whether he was a licensee, for example, a lodger or member of the occupier's family; an invitee, for example, a guest; or a trespasser. In the case of a trespasser, liability was restricted to intentional, as opposed to negligently caused, injury. However, as a matter of law, these classifications were swept away by the Occupiers' Liability (Scotland) Act 1960.[2]

The general thrust of the Act is that occupiers of property owe a duty to take such care in respect of persons entering their land or premises as is reasonable in all the circumstances of the case. The statutory obligation rests on the person 'occupying or having control of land or other premises' who is referred to in the Act as the 'occupier of premises'.[3] Where the owner of the property is also the occupier of the premises, the statutory obligation lies with him. If, however, the owner is not the occupier, he will not be liable under the 1960 Act, but may incur liability under the general duty of care incumbent on owners of property, provided *culpa* is established.[4] A person occupies the land or other premises if he is in possession of the property, for example, he is a tenant. But he will also be treated as the occupier if he has control of the land or other premises. A person has 'control' if he is entitled to take the steps in relation to the land or property which the statute requires in order to fulfil the duty of taking reasonable care of the premises. So, for example, the owner of derelict property who is not *in fact* in possession is nevertheless the occupier because he has control of the premises. The determination whether a defender has sufficient

---

1 1929 SC (HL) 51, 1929 SLT 242. See T B Smith 'Full Circle: The Law of Occupiers' Liability in Scotland' in *Studies Critical and Comparative* (1962, Greens) p 154.
2 In this section, references are to the Occupiers' Liability (Scotland) Act 1960 unless otherwise stated.
3 Occupiers' Liability (Scotland) Act 1960, s 1(1). The common law rules for determining whether or not a person is an occupier for these purposes is expressly reserved in the Act: s 1(2).
4 See pp 177 ff above.

possession or control to be an occupier is one of fact and degree in the light of the circumstances of the particular case.[1]

While land is self-explanatory, 'premises' are not defined in the 1960 Act. They would include houses, flats, sheds, garages, shops etc; land would include gardens. Moreover, the statutory obligation to take such care as is reasonable in all the circumstances expressly applies to occupiers of 'any fixed or moveable structure, including any vessel, vehicle or aircraft'.[2] Thus, the 1960 Act applies to a wide range of property: for example, ships, barges, oil rigs, buses, caravans, cars, tractors, helicopters, planes and hovercraft. It is *not* therefore restricted to heritable property.

Section 2(1) of the Occupiers' Liability (Scotland) Act 1960 lays down the nature and extent of the statutory duty:

'The care which an occupier of premises is required, by reason of his occupation or control of the premises, to show towards a person entering thereon in respect of dangers which are due to the state of the premises or to anything done or omitted to be done on them and for which the occupier is in law responsible shall . . . be such care as in all the circumstances of the case is reasonable to see that that person will not suffer injury or damage by reason of any such danger.'

It will be noted that the 1960 Act imposes a positive duty on the occupier to take such care as is reasonable in all the circumstances to ensure that a person entering the premises will not suffer injury or damage by reason of any danger on the premises. Nevertheless, the onus lies on the pursuer to show that the occupier did not take the care that was reasonable in the circumstances: it is not enough simply to aver that there was a danger and that the pursuer suffered injury or damage as a result.[3] In *McGuffie v Forth Valley Health Board*,[4] for example, the pursuer slipped on snow on the defender's premises which had not been removed by the defender. The pursuer's action failed because she had not specified the period in which it would have been reasonable for the defender to have removed the snow or instructed its employees to do so. On the other hand, in *Porter v Strathclyde Regional Council*,[5] the pursuer slipped on food which had been spilled on the floor of a nursery

---

1 *Feely v Co-operative Wholesale Society* 1990 SCLR 356, 1990 SLT 547, OH. The main contractor on a building site may be 'in control' of the premises for the purpose of the 1960 Act: *Keane v Walker Contracts (Scotland) Ltd* 1999 GWD 9-410.
2 Occupiers' Liability (Scotland) Act 1960, s 1(3)(a).
3 *Wallace v City of Glasgow District Council* 1985 SLT 23; *McDyer v Celtic Football and Athletic Co Ltd* 1999 SLT 2.
4 1991 SLT 231.
5 1991 SLT 446.

under the control of the defender. She was able to establish that the defender did not have a system of working whereby an employee would mop up the mess soon after it was spilled. The failure to have such a system was held to be a breach of the occupier's statutory duty to take reasonable care to prevent the pursuer from slipping on the floor as it was probable that the accident would not have occurred if such a system had been in operation.[1]

The Occupiers' Liability (Scotland) Act 1960 applies where the injury or damage arose from dangers 'which are due to the state of the premises *or* to anything done or omitted to be done on them'.[2] Dangers due to the state of the premises clearly covers dangers such as dry rot arising from dilapidated buildings. It would also include uneven roads,[3] slippery floors and unsafe furniture or plenishings. In *Taylor v Glasgow Corpn,*[4] where a child died as a result of eating poisonous berries which were growing in the Glasgow Botanic Gardens, the poisonous berries constituted a danger due to the state of the premises. But the statutory duty also applies to dangers which are due to anything done or omitted to be done on the premises. Thus the 1960 Act would apply to dangers caused by the occupier's failure to provide adequate lighting or to secure a fence, as well as by his positively creating a hazard. As we have seen, the failure to ensure that a pursuer would not enter a garden to clean windows while pugnacious West Highland terriers were also there, has been held to be a breach of the 1960 Act.[5]

It is important to appreciate that the occupier's statutory obligation is only to take such care as is reasonable in all the circumstances to prevent injury or damage from such dangers: it is not to eliminate the risk that an accident might happen. Accordingly, in determining whether or not the occupier has taken reasonable care, the calculus of risk is relevant. The court will consider such factors as the nature of the danger, the occupier's knowledge of the danger,[6] the extent of the injury or harm, the probability of

---

1 However, the pursuer's damages were reduced by 50 per cent as a result of her contributory negligence.
2 Occupiers' Liability (Scotland) Act 1960, s 2(1) (italics added).
3 *Beggs v Motherwell Bridge Fabricators Ltd* 1998 SLT 1215, 1997 SCLR 1019, OH.
4 1922 SC (HL) 1, 1921 2 SLT 254. This was, of course, a case before the 1960 Act.
5 *Hill v Lovett* 1992 SLT 994, OH, discussed in the context of liability for animals, p 169 above.
6 It would appear that the defender must know of the danger: *Keane v Walker Contracts (Scotland) Ltd* 1999 GWD 9-410. *Sed quaere?* It is surely enough that the defender ought reasonably to have known of the danger.

the injury or harm arising, the age of the person injured, whether or not the pursuer was permitted on to the premises and the cost of eliminating the danger. Thus, in *McGlone v British Railways Board*,[1] the defender was held to have taken reasonable care in respect of the danger of a 12-year-old child being burnt by a transformer. The defender had put up warnings and surrounded the transformer with a barbed wire fence which had proved not to be impenetrable. Nevertheless, the House of Lords held that to provide an impenetrable and unclimbable fence went beyond what was reasonable in the circumstances, given that a 12-year-old child should have realised the danger he would incur if he climbed through the barbed wire. In the circumstances, the defender had discharged its duty of reasonable care by erecting an obstacle which a 12-year-old would take some trouble to overcome before he would be in danger. If the fence could have been penetrated by a 3-year-old, then there might well have been a breach of the duty to take reasonable care in respect of a child of that age. The fact that the pursuer was a trespasser was also held to be a relevant factor in assessing whether or not reasonable care had been taken.[2]

A similar approach can be discerned in *Titchener v British Railways Board*.[3] A young man was killed by a train and his 15-year-old girlfriend was seriously injured. The couple had taken a short cut over the line to have a 'kiss and a cuddle' in a derelict brickworks. The defender had provided a fence made of sleepers but there were gaps in the fence through which it was possible for persons to reach the railway line. It was argued that the Board had been in breach of its duty of reasonable care in failing to maintain the fence and thus ensure that there were no gaps providing access to the railway. The House of Lords held that the statutory duty was owed to the particular pursuer, ie a 15-year-old girl who knew the danger involved in crossing a railway line. Accordingly, in determining whether or not the defender had taken reasonable care, the pursuer's age and knowledge were relevant factors. In these

---

1 1966 SC (HL) 1, 1966 SLT 2.
2 In *Platt v Liverpool City Council* CCRTF 97/0072/C, CA the court described as 'absurd' the contention that the defendant had not taken reasonable care to prevent children from entering dangerous premises, when it had put an eight-foot high corrugated metal fence around the property.
3 1984 SC (HL) 34, 1984 SLT 192. See also *Devlin v Strathclyde Regional Council* 1993 SLT 699, OH (no breach of duty in respect of injuries to a 14-year-old child deliberately jumping on a skylight cover on a roof: the child was also a trespasser).

circumstances, the fence – even with gaps – gave adequate warning to a girl of 15 who knew the danger of crossing the line. Indeed, Lord Fraser thought[1] that the defender would have taken reasonable care in respect of the pursuer if there had been no fence at all! It would therefore appear that the more obvious and greater the danger, the *less* by way of warning is required for the average person; conversely *more* is required if the pursuer is, for example, a young child.

The defence of *volenti non fit injuria* can be used by the defender.[2] Thus, if there had been a breach of duty in *Titchener*, the House of Lords indicated that *volenti* would have been a defence.[3] Damages may be reduced on the ground of contributory negligence. The parties are free to vary the statutory duty by *agreement*.[4] This enables the occupier to undertake a more onerous or less onerous obligation. Where, however, the premises are used for business, any exemption clause excluding or limiting the occupier's liability for death or personal injuries is void and any clause restricting liability for other kinds of damage is unenforceable unless it satisfies the requirement of reasonableness.[5]

By s 3 of the Occupiers' Liability (Scotland) Act 1960, a landlord who is responsible for the maintenance or repair of premises which have been let, owes a similar obligation to persons who enter the premises, in respect of dangers arising from the landlord's failure to maintain or repair the property. The statutory obligation extends to anyone lawfully on the premises, such as the tenant's child.[6] The landlord is not obliged to *improve* the premises.[7]

The Occupiers' Liability (Scotland) Act 1960 was necessary to sweep away the common law rules which were based on the artificial distinctions between licensee, invitee and trespasser. In their place, the Act imposes on an occupier a statutory duty to take reasonable care that a person entering the premises does not suffer injury or damage from any dangers thereon. This is a statutory duty but the wording of the provision is not without its difficulties. Given the way in which it has been interpreted, perhaps the time

---

1 1984 SLT 192 at 195.
2 Occupiers' Liability (Scotland) Act 1960, s 2(3). On *volenti* see pp 141 ff above.
3 *Volenti* would also have been a defence in *Devlin v Strathclyde Regional Council* 1993 SLT 699, OH.
4 Occupiers' Liability (Scotland) Act 1960, s 2(1). A non-contractual notice is therefore ineffective.
5 Unfair Contract Terms Act 1977, s 16.
6 *Guy v Strathkelvin District Council* 1997 SCLR 405, OH.
7 *Scott v Glasgow City Council* 1997 Hous LR 107, Sh Ct.

has come to repeal the Act, so that the delictual liability of an occupier of property towards a person entering his premises will be determined by the general principles of intentional and unintentional delictual liability.

CHAPTER 11

Breach of statutory duty and public law issues

A. BREACH OF STATUTORY DUTY

The common law principle of delictual liability may be supplemented or supplanted by delictual liability for breach of a statutory
duty. Provided the pursuer can establish that he was injured or
suffered damage to his property as a result of the defender's breach
of statutory duty, the pursuer will obtain reparation: it is not necessary for the pursuer to establish delictual liability at common law.
The statutory duty may be similar to the common law standard of
reasonable care as, for example, in the case of the Occupiers'
Liability (Scotland) Act 1960.[1] More often, however, the statute
may impose a standard which is higher than that expected of the
reasonable person at common law, ie the statute imposes strict
liability on the defender. We have seen examples of this in Part I of
the Consumer Protection Act 1987[2] and in the Animals (Scotland)
Act 1987.[3]

These statutes expressly stipulate that breach of the statutory
duty gives rise to a civil remedy in delict for reparation.
Conversely, some statutes expressly stipulate that a breach of
statutory duty does not give rise to a civil remedy for reparation
even if a person is injured as a result.[4] But there are many statutes
which are silent on whether or not a person is entitled to seek reparation in a civil action if he or she suffers injury or loss as a result of
a breach of statutory duty. Yet it has long been recognised that
even where a statute is silent on the matter, a person who has
suffered loss may still be able to seek reparation in a delictual

---

1 Discussed in Chapter 10 above.
2 Discussed in Chapter 8 above.
3 Discussed in Chapter 9 above.
4 For example, the Health and Safety at Work etc Act 1974, s 47.

action for breach of statutory duty. Thus, for example, where an employee was injured at work and the injury arose as a result of a breach of the employer's statutory duty to maintain machinery, the court held that the employer was liable to compensate the employee for breach of statutory duty, even though the statute provided criminal sanctions for breach.[1]

What criteria are used by the courts to determine whether or not a breach of statutory duty gives rise to a civil action in delict where the statute is silent on the matter? The answer appears to be that it is a question of construction of the particular statute to discover whether Parliament intended to confer on the pursuer the right to obtain reparation for breach of statutory duty. This gives the courts considerable discretion, albeit within the confines of the language of the statute. And, like the use of the duty of care as a threshold device,[2] the decision whether or not to allow the pursuer an action for breach of statutory duty will ultimately turn on policy considerations, ie whether or not such an action makes social or economic sense. That said, there are certain presumptions which are used by the courts when construing a statute in order to determine whether a civil remedy lies for breach of statutory duty and these will now be briefly considered.

As a general principle, where a statute provides a specific mode of enforcement of the statutory duties, the presumption is that Parliament did not intend that a civil action for damages in delict was necessary as an *additional* sanction if the statutory obligation is breached. Conversely, if the statute does not provide a specific mode of enforcement of the statutory duties, then there is a presumption that Parliament did intend that a civil action for damages would lie. So, for example, in *Dawson v Bingley Urban District Council*,[3] the defendant's breach of statutory duty in failing to provide a notice indicating the position of a fire plug, with the result that there was a delay in putting out a fire at the plaintiff's premises, was held to be actionable by the plaintiff in a civil action. The statute did not provide a penalty or other remedy for breach of the statutory obligations.

Where, however, the pursuer would already have a private law remedy against the defender if the statute was broken, for example, for breach of contract, it is presumed that Parliament did not

---

1 *Groves v Lord Wimborne* [1898] 2 QB 402, CA.
2 For further discussion, see Chapter 4 above.
3 [1941] 2 KB 149, CA.

intend that the pursuer should have the additional remedy of suing in delict for breach of statutory duty. Although the position is not clear, it is submitted that the existence of a right to seek judicial review should not be presumed to exclude the possibility of a civil remedy for breach of statutory duty: judicial review is simply a procedure and damages are available only if the pursuer has a private law remedy. Accordingly, the right to seek judicial review, while a factor to be taken into consideration by the courts, should not be conclusive in deciding whether or not Parliament intended that the pursuer should also have the private law remedy of suing in delict for breach of statutory duty.[1]

The general presumption is that, where a statute provides a penalty for breach of statutory duty, Parliament did not intend that there should be the additional sanction of delictual liability for breach of statutory duty. However, there are two exceptions to this rule.[2]

First, if it is apparent that the statutory obligations were passed for the protection of a particular class of individuals, then a delictual action for breach of statutory duty may lie if the pursuer belongs to that class and has suffered injury or loss. This explains how employees have been able to sue for breach, for example, of the Factories Acts, even though this legislation imposed criminal penalties on employers who were in breach.[3] Similarly, performers whose work was recorded by record companies without their permission in breach of the Dramatic and Musical Performers' Protection Act 1958 were held to have been intended by Parliament to be able to pursue private law remedies for breach of statutory duty, in spite of the fact that the statute also provided criminal sanctions.[4] But it must be clear that the pursuer falls within the class. So, for example, in *RCA Corpn v Pollard*[5] it was held that companies who had exclusive recording contracts with performers could not sue for breach of statutory duty under the 1958 Act.

---

1 *Hague v Deputy Governor of Parkhurst Prison* [1992] 1 AC 58, [1991] 3 All ER 733, HL, at 752 per Lord Jauncey.
2 *Lonrho Ltd v Shell Petroleum Co Ltd (No 2)* [1981] 2 All ER 456 at 461 per Lord Diplock.
3 See also *Littlejohn v Wood & Davidson Ltd* 1997 SLT 1353, OH (Merchant Shipping Act 1988, s 31(1) intended to protect a particular class of persons, ie persons on board ship: civil claims for damages allowed in spite of existence of criminal sanctions).
4 *Ex parte Island Records Ltd* [1978] Ch 122, [1978] 3 All ER 824, CA.
5 [1983] Ch 135, [1982] 3 All ER 771, CA.

If the statute is not designed to protect a particular class and provides penalties for breach, no action for breach of statutory duty will lie. But it may be difficult to determine whether or not the legislation was designed to protect a particular class. In *Cutler v Wandsworth Stadium Ltd (in liquidation)*,[1] for example, the appellant brought proceedings against a licensed dog track to compel it to allow him space at the track to carry on his profession as a bookmaker. Statute provided that the occupier of a licensed track 'shall take such steps as are necessary to secure that . . . there is available for the bookmakers space on the track where they can conveniently carry on bookmaking in connection with dog races run on the track'. The House of Lords held that the purpose of the legislation was to protect those members of the public who wished to place bets by ensuring that there was a choice of bookmakers at the track: it was not to give bookmakers the right of a place at the track. Accordingly, the appellant was not entitled to a remedy for breach of statutory duty. But it could equally be argued that it was Parliament's intention to protect the rights of bookmakers to earn their living. The decision in *Cutler* was ultimately a matter of policy. It is interesting to note that the courts are more prepared to construe statutes as giving a delictual remedy for breach of statutory duty where the pursuer has been physically injured[2] than, as in *Cutler*, where the pursuer has only suffered pure economic loss as a result of the breach of the statutory obligations.

Nevertheless, in the leading Scottish case of *Pullar v Window Clean Ltd*,[3] the Inner House of the Court of Session refused to accept that planning legislation which inter alia provided that window sashes should be so constructed to enable the window to be cleaned from the inside, was intended to protect window cleaners. There was therefore no breach of statutory duty when a window cleaner fell from the outside sill because the sashes had not been constructed in accordance with the legislation: 'The solution in each case must depend upon what the intention of Parliament was in enacting the obligation in question, and what persons consequently have a right to enforce it or to found upon it as a basis for a claim in damages'.[4]

Even when the legislation is designed to protect a particular class, there may be other factors which deny an action for breach of statutory duty, albeit that the statute does *not* provide criminal

1 [1949] AC 398, [1949] 1 All ER 544, HL.
2 As in the case of the Factories Acts.
3 1956 SC 13, 1956 SLT 17.
4 1956 SC 13 at 20 per the Lord President (Clyde).

sanctions for its breach. In *X (minors) v Bedfordshire County Council*,[1] children sued a local authority (i) for personal injuries sustained by being removed from their parents in care proceedings, and (ii) for personal injuries sustained by not being removed from their parents in care proceedings. Although the children were clearly within the class of persons the care legislation was designed to protect, the House of Lords held that Parliament did not intend that the children should have a private law right to sue for breach of the statute. This was because the legislation involved an administrative system designed to promote the social welfare of the community, and the local authority's duties were expressed in broad language. Moreover, Parliament could not possibly have intended that a local authority should be liable, without proof of fault, merely because a court subsequently decided that children should not have been taken into care and vice versa. In short, given the discretion inevitably involved in child care legislation, bona fide mistakes would arise and such mistakes were not to be compensated in the absence of fault.[2]

In *Lonrho Ltd v Shell Petroleum Co Ltd (No 2)*[3] Lord Diplock maintained that there was a second exception where a private law remedy could arise for breach of statutory duty, even though the statute provided criminal penalties for its breach:

'The second exception is where the statute creates a public right (ie a right to be enjoyed by all those of Her Majesty's subjects who wish to avail themselves of it) and a particular member of the public suffers . . . "particular, direct and substantial" damage other and different from that which was common to all the rest of the public.'[4]

However, the extent of this exception is not as yet developed and need not be discussed further.

Once it has been decided as a matter of construction that Parliament intended that a delictual action should lie for breach of statutory duty, a person who has suffered harm must show that the statute was intended to protect a person in his position, ie that the pursuer falls within the class to be protected and that the damage sustained is of the kind that the statute was designed to prevent. In *Gorris v Scott*,[5] for example, statutory regulations required that sheep or cattle being shipped from a foreign country to the United

1 [1995] 2 AC 633, [1995] 3 All ER 353, HL.
2 See also, for example, *O'Rourke v Camden London Borough Council* [1998] AC 188, [1997] 3 All ER 23, HL.
3 [1982] AC 173, [1981] 2 All ER 456, HL.
4 [1981] 2 All ER 456 at 461.
5 (1874) LR 9 Exch 125.

Kingdom had to be put in pens. The defendant failed to provide
the pens and, as a result, the plaintiff's sheep were washed overboard in a storm. The plaintiff's action for breach of statutory duty
failed because the court held that the purpose of the pens was to
prevent animals from being infected by contagious diseases, not to
prevent them from being swept overboard. If the sheep had died as
a result of a contagious disease, a delictual claim for breach of
statutory duty would have been successful.

The defender must, of course, have broken a statutory duty
which was incumbent upon him. Whether or not the defender's
conduct constitutes a breach will depend on the interpretation of
the particular provision. Statutes may impose absolute liability,
strict liability, or reasonable practicability. If a breach of the statutory duty is established, ie the defender has broken the duty,[1] there
is no need for the pursuer to prove fault. The pursuer must establish that the breach of statutory duty caused the injury or harm.[2]
Unless, as in the case of the Occupiers' Liability (Scotland) Act
1960,[3] the defence is expressly stated to be available, *volenti non fit
injuria* cannot be pleaded.[4] This is because a person cannot agree
to take a risk of injury or harm which Parliament has legislated to
prevent arising. However, the pursuer's damages may be substantially reduced as a result of contributory negligence.[5]

B. PUBLIC LAW ISSUES[6]

Ministers of the Crown, local authorities and other governmental
agencies are often given statutory powers to implement policy.
This will often involve the exercise of discretion. Consider the
following examples:

(1) A minister is given the power to send some criminals to an
    open prison: if such a criminal should escape, steal and
    damage a person's motor car, is the minister liable in delict?[7]

1 For examples see discussion of Part I of the Consumer Protection Act 1987, the
  Animals (Scotland) Act 1987 and the Occupiers' Liability (Scotland) Act 1960,
  above.
2 On causation generally, see Chapter 6 above.
3 Occupiers' Liability (Scotland) Act 1960, s 2(3).
4 See, for example, *Wheeler v New Merton Board Mills Ltd* [1933] 2 KB 669, CA.
5 For discussion, see pp 143 ff above.
6 I am grateful to W Green for allowing me to quote extensively in this section
  from my article, 'Delictual Liability of State Agencies – Further Confusion' 1999
  SLT (News) 245.
7 Of course, the criminal will be liable in delict.

(2) A local authority is given the power to inspect and approve the plans of buildings: if the local authority approves the plans for the foundations of a house, is the local authority liable to the owner of the house if the foundations were unsuitable and have to be repaired?

(3) A minister is empowered to give information to the public on the risks of HIV infection: is the minister liable to a person who contracts HIV through injecting heroin if the information only disclosed the risk of infection from sexual contact and omitted the danger of infection from drug abuse?

In *X (minors) v Bedfordshire County Council*,[1] the House of Lords recognised that if a state agency exercised its statutory powers carelessly, there could be liability at common law in negligence. But before there can be liability in negligence, the careless exercise of the statutory powers must amount to a breach of a pre-existing duty of care owed by the agency to the pursuer. Traditionally, the courts have been reluctant to impose a duty of care on a state agency to exercise its powers carefully. Before such a duty will be imposed, three hurdles must be overcome:

(1) If the agency's statutory discretion involves broad issues of policy, the issue is non-justiciable. The paradigm is when an authority has to allocate scarce resources. If, for example, a local authority chose to spend resources on library provision rather than on increasing the number of fire engines, a person who suffered burns in a fire which could not be contained because of the absence of the fire brigade would be unable to sue, because the issue of whether more resources should have been spent on fire engines as opposed to books is non-justiciable.

(2) Where the statutory discretion operates at an operational as opposed to a broad policy level, a duty of care cannot be imposed unless the purported exercise of the power is beyond the ambit of the statutory discretion. In determining this issue, the courts have adopted – while occasionally denying they are doing so – quasi-administrative law principles. In particular, this hurdle is said only to be overcome if the exercise of the discretion was such that no reasonable state agency would have acted in this way. In other words, where the mistake, albeit careless, was one which a reasonable state agency or local authority could have made in the bona fide exercise of its powers, a duty of care will not be imposed, and

---

1 [1995] 2 AC 633, [1995] 3 All ER 353, HL.

accordingly liability at common law for negligence cannot lie. So, for example, if a fire authority prioritised calls, provided the prioritisation was not unreasonable, the decision would fall within the ambit of the statutory discretion and no liability would arise even if, with hindsight, the prioritisation was mistaken.

(3) Even if the 'public law' hurdle in (2) is satisfied, the *Caparo* criteria for a duty of care have to exist, namely reasonable foreseeability of harm to the pursuer, proximity between the pursuer and defender, and that it is fair, just and reasonable to impose the duty.[1] Again, the courts have tended to decline to impose the duty of care either because of the absence of proximity or on the broader 'fair, just and reasonable' criteria. Thus, for example, in *Hill v Chief Constable of West Yorkshire*,[2] the House of Lords held that the chief constable did not owe a duty of care to the mother of the last victim of the Yorkshire ripper. Not only was there no proximity, but also Lord Templeman considered that it would not be fair, just and reasonable to impose a duty of care on the chief constable in relation to his function of investigating crime. Similarly, in *X (minors) v Bedfordshire County Council*[3] itself it was not thought fair, just and reasonable to impose a duty of care on social workers, because child care decisions were interdisciplinary, a local authority might become overcautious and more appropriate alternative remedies were to be found in the child care legislation.[4]

However, where the carelessness takes place at a more basic, operational level, the courts are prepared to impose a duty of care. In *Barrett v Enfield London Borough Council*,[5] for example, the House of Lords refused to strike out a claim against a local authority brought by a man who had spent his childhood in care. The plaintiff alleged that he now suffered psychiatric illness as a

---

1   See *Caparo Industries plc v Dickman* [1990] 2 AC 605, [1990] 1 All ER 568, HL.
2   [1989] AC 53, [1988] 2 All ER 238, HL. See also *Palmer v Tees Health Authority* (1999) Times, 6 July (mental hospital not liable to victim of a discharged patient).
3   [1995] 2 AC 633, [1995] 3 All ER 353, HL.
4   See also *Forbes v City of Dundee District Council* 1997 SLT 1330, 1997 SCLR 682, OH (not fair, just and reasonable to impose a duty of care on a local authority to ensure that steps were built in accordance with building regulations: the pursuer could, of course, sue the owner/occupier of the building); *Onifade v Secretary of State for Social Security* 1999 GWD 17-819 (no duty of care to prevent pursuer from suffering economic loss as a consequence of an erroneous decision by an adjudication officer refusing the pursuer income support).
5   [1999] 3 WLR 79.

result of the authority's failure to provide suitable care for him, for example by placing him for adoption. In Lord Slynn's view[1] *X (minors) v Bedfordshire County Council*[2] established that 'decisions by local authorities whether or not to take a child into care with all the difficult aspects that involves and all the disruption which may come about are not ones which the courts will review by way of a claim for damages in negligence'. However, once a child had been taken into care, a local authority could owe the child a common law duty of care to prevent him from suffering mental illness caused by their carelessness in providing suitable support: it was irrelevant that the local authority's decisions involved the exercise of discretion on the part of professional social workers. Their 'protection' arises at the next stage, ie whether or not there has been a breach of the duty of care, not in denying the existence of a duty. It can be very difficult to establish professional negligence.[3] The pursuer must establish that the negligence caused the illness, ie that he was worse off as a result of the carelessly delivered service than if the service had not been provided at all.

In *Gibson v Orr*,[4] a bridge carrying a public road collapsed. The police assumed control of the hazard. They coned off the north side and positioned a police vehicle on the bridge as a warning to drivers on the south side. After an hour, they left without having received confirmation that any barrier or warning was in place on the south side. The pursuer was injured when the car in which he was a passenger was driven on to the bridge from the south side and fell into the river. In a fully reasoned speech, the Lord Ordinary (Hamilton) held that the police authority owed the pursuer a duty of care. By purporting to take control of the hazard, the police constables entered into proximate relationships with those road users likely to be immediately and directly affected by that hazard. Moreover, unlike the case of the investigation of crime, there were no policy reasons why it would not be fair, just and reasonable to impose the duty. The policy/operational distinction is at the forefront of the reasoning. The difficulty is that the accident would have happened in exactly the same way, even if the service had not been provided at all. However, the whole point of the defender's duty was to prevent an accident occurring after the officers had taken control. If the duty of care had been performed, the accident in which the pursuer was injured would not have happened.

1 [1999] 3 WLR 79 at 94.
2 [1995] 2 AC 633, [1995] 3 All ER 353, HL.
3 On professional liability, see Chapter 7 above.
4 1999 SC 420.

This is quite different from the situation where, owing to its operational carelessness, a fire brigade increases the risk of damage to the pursuer's life or property, ie when the pursuer's position is worse off as a consequence of the careless delivery of the service. In *Duff v Highland and Islands Fire Board*,[1] it was held that a fire brigade did owe a duty of care not to be careless when engaged in fire fighting. There the defender had attended to a fire in the pursuer's chimney which restarted after the brigade had left, causing the destruction of the pursuer's house.[2]

We have been considering potential liability in negligence for the careless exercise of statutory powers. A similar approach has been taken when a local authority or state agency has failed to use a statutory power which it was not obliged to exercise under the legislation. In *Stovin v Wise and Norfolk County Council*,[3] a local authority had a statutory power to direct a landowner to remove a wall which was a danger to users of the highway. Before the plaintiff was injured in a road accident, the local authority had known the wall was a hazard but had not exercised the power to have the danger removed. The House of Lords held that the local authority had a public law duty to consider whether or not to exercise the power, but this did not automatically confer a common law right on an individual to obtain damages if injured as a consequence of the authority's decision not to exercise its powers. A common law duty of care would only arise from such an omission if (i) the local authority's failure to exercise the power was irrational (the 'public law' hurdle), and (ii) it was the policy of the legislation to give a person damages if she suffers injury if the power is not exercised. Although the public law hurdle is similar to that which obtains in delictual liability for a careless exercise of a statutory power, it is difficult to see the relevance of the second hurdle given that we are considering a common law duty of care, not breach of statutory duty. It is submitted that if the public law hurdle can be crossed, a

---

1 1995 SLT 1362.
2 In *Capital and Counties plc v Hampshire County Council* [1997] QB 1004, [1997] 2 All ER 865, CA, the Court of Appeal held that a fire brigade did not owe a duty of care to a member of the public to answer calls for help because there was no proximity at that stage. However, once the brigade had turned up and begun fighting the fire, a duty of care arose not to increase the risk of injury or damage caused by the original fire as a result of carelessness in carrying out the operations. In *Duff v Highland and Islands Fire Board* 1995 SLT 1362, it was not thought to be necessary that the damage sustained should be worse as a result of the defender's negligence: *sed quaere?*
3 [1996] AC 923, [1996] 3 All ER 801, HL.

duty of care will arise if the *Caparo* criteria[1] are satisfied: the policy
of the legislation may, of course, be relevant in determining
whether or not it is fair, just and reasonable to impose a duty of
care.[2]

Further difficulties can be anticipated as a consequence of the
decision of the European Court of Human Rights in *Osman v
United Kingdom*.[3] There the Court of Appeal struck out a claim for
damages arising from the alleged negligence of a police authority in
the detection and prevention of crime. As we have seen, in *Hill v
Chief Constable of Yorkshire*,[4] the House of Lords had refused to
impose a duty of care in these circumstances on the basis that it
was not fair, just and reasonable to do so. The European Court
held, however, that such a 'blanket' immunity was a breach of the
plaintiff's right under art 6 of the Convention. Article 6 provides
that 'In the determination of his civil rights and obligations . . .
everyone is entitled to a fair and public hearing'. The European
Court held that the plaintiff had been denied access to a court to
determine in the light of the evidence whether or not the defender
should owe a duty of care to the plaintiff on the facts of this particular case. It would appear, therefore, that in every situation where
the English and Scottish courts have held as a matter of law that
the defender does not owe a duty of care to the pursuer on public
policy grounds, namely that it is not fair, just and reasonable to
impose a duty, there is a potential breach of art 6 if the pursuer is
not allowed to adduce evidence that such immunity is not propor-
tionate to the harm suffered by the pursuer in the particular case.
In these circumstances, the courts in England may now be more
reluctant to strike out such claims against state agencies: similarly,
courts in Scotland may be even more reluctant to dismiss such
cases as irrelevant and, instead, allow proof before answer.

It is important to appreciate that in this section we have been
concerned with the possibility of delictual liability arising from the
exercise of a discretionary power by a minister of the Crown, a
local authority or another governmental agency. Where, however,

1 See *Caparo Industries plc v Dickman* [1990] 2 AC 605, [1990] 1 All ER 568, HL.
2 In *McKnight v Clydesdale Buses Ltd* 1999 GWD 4-213, the Lord Ordinary (Lady
Cosgrove) allowed a proof before answer when the pursuer alleged that an accident occurred as a result of a local roads authority's failure to provide warning
signs in respect of a low bridge. The authority had a duty to remedy a situation
of foreseeable danger and it was not certain in the absence of evidence that this
was simply a case of mere omission to exercise a statutory power: *Stovin* was
distinguished.
3 5 BHRC 293, ECHR.
4 [1989] AC 53, [1988] 2 All ER 238, HL discussed at p 108 above.

there is no degree of discretion involved, then the 'public law' hurdle withers away. The driver of a ministerial motor car or a local authority bus, for example, owes the same *Donoghue v Stevenson* duty of care[1] to a fellow road user as an ordinary driver and will be liable in delict if the duty of care is breached. In other words, the defender owes the pursuer a duty of care independent of her status as an employee of a state agency. In these circumstances, the state agency will be vicariously liable for the delict of its employee provided, of course, the employee was acting within the scope of her employment at the time the accident occurred.[2]

1 See *Donoghue v Stevenson* 1932 SC (HL) 31, 1932 SLT 317.
2 On vicarious liability see Chapter 12 below.

CHAPTER 12

Employers' liability and vicarious liability

A. EMPLOYERS' LIABILITY

It is an implied term of the contract of employment that an employer will take reasonable care for the safety of his employees. If an employer does not take reasonable care, he will be in material breach of contract. In these circumstances, an employee may withdraw his labour and sue for damages. An employer may be in breach of his contractual obligations even if the employee has not suffered any injury. However, in addition to his contractual obligations, an employer owes a *Donoghue v Stevenson* duty of care[1] to his employees to prevent them from suffering physical injury or harm as a result of the employer's negligent conduct. Accordingly, an employee who is injured may sue his employer in delict as well as for breach of contract; but the employee cannot be compensated twice for the same loss.

The obligation to take reasonable care for the safety of his employees is personal to the employer, ie it cannot be delegated by the employer to senior employees or a third party.[2] However, in a modern industrial context, in order to *fulfil* the obligation of reasonable care, an employer may have to appoint a safety officer and/or safety committee. The scope of the duty incumbent on an employer includes taking reasonable care to supply the employee with proper plant and equipment, to select competent fellow workers and to provide a safe system of working; however, it is a *general* duty to take reasonable care. Thus, for example, an employer can be liable for failure to *devise* a safe system of working: *McGregor v AAH Pharmaceuticals Ltd.*[3] Where an employer fails to instruct an employee to use protective devices or clothes, or fails to

---

1 See *Donoghue v Stevenson* 1932 SC (HL) 31, 1932 SLT 317, and Chapter 3 above. The existence of a contract between the employer and employee is an important factor in establishing the 'foreseeability of injury or harm' criterion.
2 *Hislop v Durham* (1842) 4 D 1168.
3 1996 SLT 1161, OH.

provide adequate training, a breach of the duty to take reasonable care can arise: *Pickford v ICI plc*.[1] An employer may also have to train employees to protect themselves from violent third parties they may meet in the course of their employment, for example, schoolchildren![2]

Moreover, it cannot be overemphasised that at common law the employer is only expected to maintain the standards of the reasonable person in his position ie it is only to take reasonable care. An employer is not expected to ensure that an employee is never injured. In assessing whether or not a particular employer has taken reasonable care, the calculus of risk will be relevant.[3] The court will therefore consider such factors as the nature of the danger, the employer's knowledge of the danger, the extent of the injury or harm, the probability of the injury or harm arising and the cost of eliminating the risk.[4]

In *Davie v New Merton Board Mills Ltd*,[5] for example, an employee was injured when a piece of a chisel he was using broke and a splinter entered into his eye. The defect in the chisel was latent and arose as a result of the metal used for the chisel not having been tempered properly by the manufacturer. The employer had bought the chisel from a reputable retailer who had in turn bought it from a reputable wholesaler who had purchased it from the manufacturer. In these circumstances, the House of Lords held that the employer had taken reasonable care and the employee's action against the *employer* failed. The employee could, of course, have sued the manufacturer in delict for breach of the manufacturer's *Donoghue v Stevenson* duty of care which he owed to the ultimate consumer of the product.[6] However, the view was taken that this was placing too heavy an onus on an employee. Accordingly, under the Employers' Liability (Defective Equipment) Act 1969,[7] if an employee suffers personal injury as a result

---

1 [1996] ICR 566, [1996] IRLR 622, CA.
2 *McLeod v Aberdeen City Council* 1999 GWD 23-1115.
3 *Brisco v Secretary of State for Scotland* 1997 SC 14; *McErlean v J & B Scotland Ltd* 1997 SLT 1326, 1997 GWD 6-253, OH. On the calculus of risk generally, see pp 119 ff above.
4 *Latimer v AEC Ltd* [1953] AC 643, [1953] 2 All ER 449, HL.
5 [1959] AC 604.
6 See *Donoghue v Stevenson* 1932 SC (HL) 31, 1932 SLT 317. On product liability generally, see Chapter 8 above.
7 Employers' Liability (Defective Equipment) Act 1969, s 1(1).

of a defect in equipment[1] provided by the employer and the defect is attributable wholly or partly to the fault of a third party,[2] for example, the manufacturer, then the defect is deemed to be also attributable to negligence on the part of the employer. In other words, the employee can sue the employer without the need to prove that the employer was negligent. The *employer* will then seek redress against the third party either in contract or, theoretically at least, in delict.

The employer has to take reasonable care in selecting competent workers who will not cause injury or harm to the other employees. If the employer fails to do so and an employer is injured as a result, the employee can sue the employer for breach of the duty of care.[3] Again it must be emphasised that the employer is only expected to take reasonable care. Before the employer can be negligent, he must know that the employee he has appointed could be a danger to fellow workers.[4] The contract of employment is not a contract *uberrimae fidei*; the employer must therefore make reasonable enquiries to determine whether or not an aspirant employee would be a source of danger to fellow employees if he were to be engaged. For example, the employer should ask whether or not an applicant for a job as a van driver has a clean driving licence and whether or not he has been convicted of careless or reckless driving.[5]

The duty to provide a safe system of working is owed to the particular employee. Thus, for example, if an employer knows that an employee is an epileptic or has only one eye, the standards required to constitute reasonable care may be greater in respect of that employee than the other workers. Accordingly, the employer may be negligent vis-à-vis that employee even if his conduct would

---

1 The courts have taken a wide view of the meaning of 'equipment' in order to protect employees: see, for example, *Knowles v Liverpool City Council* [1993] 4 All ER 321, [1993] WLR 1428, HL (council employee injured by a defective flagstone: flagstone held to constitute equipment).

2 The pursuer is not obliged to identify the third party who was at fault: *Edwards v Butlins Ltd* 1998 SLT 500, 1997 GWD 21-1052.

3 The duty extends to providing adequate supervision of employees whose behaviour at work might injure a fellow worker: *Gibson v British Rail Maintenance* 1995 SC 7, 1995 SLT 953 (pursuer injured by a ball which was being used in a game played by two other employees: employer liable, because foreman was absent when the game was being played).

4 See, for example, *Hudson v Ridge Manufacturing Co Ltd* [1957] 2 QB 348, [1957] 2 All ER 348.

5 Subject to the offences being spent under the Rehabilitation of Offenders Act 1974.

not amount to negligence if the employee were not epileptic or had two eyes.[1]

In *Walker v Northumberland County Council*,[2] the plaintiff, a social worker, suffered a nervous breakdown. Upon his return to work, the employee was offered no additional support in spite of the fact that his workload had increased. The plaintiff suffered a second breakdown. Given that the employer knew that the employee was susceptible to mental illness as a result of pressure at work, it was held that the employer was in breach of its duty of reasonable care in failing to reduce his workload or provide assistance. It was irrelevant that the employee had suffered mental illness as opposed to physical injury, because mental illness was reasonably foreseeable as a probable consequence of the failure to reduce pressure at work.[3]

The employer must provide a safe environment in which his employee works. Where an employee works at a place which is not under the control of his employer, the employer can still be liable for failing to inspect the premises to ensure that the employee is not exposed to unnecessary risks.[4] It has been held that there can be a breach of the duty if the employer has not taken reasonable steps to protect an employee from the risk of illness arising from passive smoking.[5]

At common law the onus lay on the employee to prove that the injury or harm sustained was a breach of the employer's duty of care, ie that the employer was negligent. Since the nineteenth century, safety at work has been the subject of statutory regulations. These provide detailed safety requirements for machinery, particular processes and operations. Although earlier statutes provided criminal sanctions in cases of breach, the courts allowed an employee who was injured as a result to sue the employer in delict for breach of statutory duty. Moreover, as the statutes often

---

1 *Paris v Stepney Borough Council* [1951] AC 367, [1951] 1 All ER 42, HL, discussed at p 121 above.
2 [1995] 1 All ER 737, [1995] IRLR 35, CA. See also *Ward v Scotrail Railways Ltd* 1999 SC 255, where an employee suffered psychiatric illness as a result of a fellow employee's sexual molestation. The Lord Ordinary (Reed) held that the employer could be in breach of the duty to the pursuer in failing to stop the harassment. It must be reasonably foreseeable that the fellow employee's conduct will lead to psychiatric illness (cf emotional distress) before the employer is liable: *Rorrison v West Lothian College* (1999, unreported), OH, per the Lord Ordinary (Reed).
3 The plaintiff's *known* susceptibility to mental illness distinguishes this case from the 'nervous shock' decisions, discussed at pp 70 ff above.
4 *Crombie v McDermott Scotland Ltd* 1996 SLT 1238, 1996 Rep LR 122, OH.
5 *Rae v Strathclyde Joint Police Board* 1999 GWD 12-571.

imposed strict liability, an employee who sued for breach of statutory duty did not have to establish negligence. But, of course, the employee had to show that the employer was in breach of the statutory obligations and this could involve complex issues of statutory construction.[1]

The Health and Safety at Work etc Act 1974 lays down the minimum standards required of employers for safety at the workplace. It is, however, a criminal statute and it is expressly enacted that its breach does not give rise to a private law remedy for breach of statutory duty. Confusingly, the morass of safety legislation, in particular the Factories Act 1961, continued in force for a while and breach of these provisions did give rise to an action for breach of statutory duty. But now much of this legislation has been repealed and replaced by statutory regulations implementing EU directives.[2] Breach of these detailed regulations will in, general, continue to give rise to delictual liability. Discussion of these regulations is outside the compass of this current work.[3] Nevertheless, where an employee is injured as a result of a breach of these regulations, it is important to remember that he will still be able to sue for breach of statutory duty and plead the employer's negligence at common law in the alternative. As in all cases of breach of statutory duty, *volens* is not a defence unless expressly allowed in the statutory regulations, but the employee's damages may be reduced on the grounds of contributory negligence.[4]

An employer may owe the employee a duty of care under the Occupiers' Liability (Scotland) Act 1960[5] as well as the general duty of care owed to employees at common law.[6]

B. VICARIOUS LIABILITY

(1) Introduction

In certain circumstances a person may be liable for the delicts committed by another. This is known as vicarious liability.

1 See, for example, *Hunter v British Steel Corpn* 1980 SLT 31.
2 See, for example, the Manual Handling Operations Regulations 1992, SI 1992/2793, implementing Council Directive 90/269/EEC: *Cullen v North Lanarkshire Council* 1998 SC 451, 1998 SLT 897. The regulations are not to be interpreted restrictively.
3 For an excellent account of the law, see Craig and Miller *The Law of Health and Safety at Work in Scotland* (2nd edn, 2000).
4 On contributory negligence, see pp 143 ff above.
5 On occupiers' liability, see pp 186 ff above.
6 *Hill v Lovett* 1992 SLT 994, OH.

Although the doctrine arises out of several relationships,[1] the most common by far is that of employer and employee. An employer is vicariously liable for the delicts committed by the employee in the course of his employment. This arises when the employee concerned injures or harms a third party or another employee, provided the delict was committed in the course of employment. Although the employer and employee are jointly and severally liable,[2] in practice the pursuer will sue the employer, who is more likely to have funds or be insured. Where it is an employee who has been injured, the employer is obliged by statute to have insurance so that funds are available if he is found to be vicariously liable.[3] Where an employee has been negligent, if the employer is found vicariously liable, the employer can, in theory at least, recover the damages he has paid from the employee, since the employee's delictual conduct constitutes a breach by the employee of the contract of employment.[4] In practice, an employer – or his insurers – do not exercise this right to sue the employee for breach of contract.

(2) Delicts of an employee

The first issue is to determine whether the relationship of employer and employee exists between the person who committed the delict and the person alleged to be vicariously liable: whether the person who committed the delict is working under a contract of employment (*locatio operarum*) or is an independent contractor, working under a contract for services (*locatio operis faciendi*). The traditional test for distinguishing between a contract of employment and a contract for services is that of 'control':[5] an employer has the power to control not only what the employee should do but also *how* he should do it. If A has a cleaner who regularly cleans A's house,

---

1 See pp 219 ff below.
2 On joint and several liability, see p 146 above.
3 Employers' Liability (Compulsory Insurance) Act 1969. In Scotland, it has been held that failure to insure can result in the directors of a company being personally liable in a claim for damages for breach of statutory duty: *Quinn v McGinty* 1999 SLT (Sh Ct) 27. In England, it has been held by the Court of Appeal that no civil liability lies for breach of the Employers' Liability (Compulsory Insurance) Act 1969: see *Richardson v Pitt-Stanley* [1995] QB 123, [1995] 1 All ER 460, CA.
4 *Lister v Romford Ice and Cold Storage Co Ltd* [1957] AC 555, [1957] 1 All ER 125, HL.
5 *Yewans v Nokes* (1880) 6 QBD 530.

there is a contract of employment, since A can tell the cleaner not only what to do but the manner in which the work is to be done. On the other hand, if A wishes to have a suit dry cleaned, while he may tell the cleaners what to do, A does not have the power to tell them how to carry out the dry-cleaning process: here A is simply entering into a contract for the services of the dry cleaner and not a contract of employment.

The 'control' test remains a useful criterion where the work involved is relatively unskilled. But it is of less value where the alleged employer is a company or large organisation and the work involved is specialist and sophisticated. The courts have therefore had to develop other criteria. Where a person works as an integral part of an organisation, he is likely to be working under a contract of employment, particularly if there is some element of control.[1] Although the parties' expressed intention in their contract is an important factor, the 'label' they have used to describe their relationship is not decisive. As Lord Denning MR observed in *Massey v Crown Life Insurance Co*:[2]

'If the true relationship of the parties is that of master and servant under a contract of service [a contract of employment], the parties cannot alter the truth of that relationship by putting a different label upon it'.

On the other hand, if the relationship between the parties is ambiguous, the 'label' in the contract may be a crucial factor in determining the true relationship between them.[3] An important consideration is the economic reality of the situation. If, for example, the worker supplies his own equipment and materials and takes the 'economic risk' inherent in the enterprise, it is more likely that he is an independent contractor than an employee.[4] On the other hand, where the worker purchases equipment using money lent to him by the other party to the contract who has an option to purchase the equipment for a nominal sum at the end of the contract, then the court would be likely to hold that this is a contract of employment, although technically the worker owns the equipment. Other important factors include the payment of national insurance contributions, the pension position, the

1 *Stevenson, Jordan and Harrison Ltd v MacDonald and Evans* (1952) 69 RPC 10, [1952] 1 TLR 101, CA.
2 [1978] ICR 590 at 594, [1978] 2 All ER 576 at 579, CA.
3 *Massey v Crown Life Insurance Co* [1978] ICR 590 at 594, [1978] 2 All ER 576 at 579, CA.
4 See, for example, *Ready Mixed Concrete (South East) Ltd v Minister of Pensions and National Insurance* [1968] 2 QB 497, [1968] 1 All ER 433.

payment of Schedule D or Schedule E taxation, whether or not the worker is paid a fee or a sum on a regular basis and the arrangements for termination of the contract.

The courts can therefore consider a wide range of factors. This has long been recognised as the proper approach in Scots law.[1] It should be emphasised that in the vast majority of cases, it will be clear whether the contract between the parties is one of employment or for services. However, in hard cases, ie where the nature of the contract is ambiguous, the multiple tests approach gives the courts considerable discretion in determining whether or not a contract of employment exists. Where the issue is whether a worker is an employee for the purpose of the doctrine of vicarious liability, it is thought that the courts would be reluctant to find that a worker was not an employee if this would mean that the pursuer would not obtain reparation because the defender was without requisite funds or insurance.

Having established that a contract of employment exists between the parties, the employer will be vicariously liable for the delicts committed by the employee 'in the course of the employment'.[2] In other words, before an employer is vicariously liable, the employee's acts or omissions which constitute the delict must fall within the scope of his employment. In short, the delict must be a mode or method – albeit wrongful – of the kind of work the employee is engaged to do. The classic exposition of the doctrine in Scots law is to be found in the judgment of the Lord President (Clyde) in *Kirby v National Coal Board*:[3]

'But, in the decisions, four different types of situation have been envisaged as guides to the solution of this problem. In the first place, if the master actually authorised the particular act, he is clearly [vicariously] liable for it. Secondly, where the workman does some work which he is appointed to do, but does it in a way which his master has not authorised and would not have authorised had he known of it, the master is nevertheless still

---

1 See, for example, *Short v J & W Henderson Ltd* 1946 SC (HL) 24, 1946 SLT 230; *United Wholesale Grocers Ltd v Sher* 1993 SLT 284, OH.
2 An employer is not vicariously liable unless all the aspects of the employee's conduct which constitute the delict have occurred in the course of employment. Thus, if A and B commit a delict, the employer of A is only vicariously liable if the combined conduct of both A and B amounts to a delict in the course of A's employment: *Credit Lyonnais Bank Nederland NV (now known as Generale Bank Nederland NV) v Export Credits Guarantee Department* [1999] 1 All ER 929, HL. Thus, if A's conduct per se does not constitute a delict, A's employer is not vicariously liable if B's conduct would be outwith the scope of A's employment, if A had carried out B's acts or omissions.
3 1958 SC 514 at 532–533, 1959 SLT 7.

responsible, for the servant's act is still within the scope of his employment. On the other hand, in the third place, if the servant is employed only to do a particular work or a particular class of work, and he does something outside the scope of that work, the master is not responsible for any mischief the servant may do to a third party. Lastly, if the servant uses his master's time or his master's tools for his own purposes, the master is not responsible.'

Taking these four situations in turn:

(1) If an employer has expressly or impliedly authorised the delictual conduct, the employee is acting within the scope of the employment and the employer is vicariously liable for the delict. In *Neville v C & A Modes Ltd*[1] for example, the pursuer was suspected of shoplifting by employees of the defender. She was forcibly taken from the street back into the shop and there accused of theft. She argued that the defender was vicariously liable for defamation of her character. The Inner House held that the defender's employees had a duty under their contracts of employment to protect the defender's property and take action to prevent theft. The employees' action had therefore been authorised by the defender, ie was within the scope of their employment, albeit that it may have been defamatory in the circumstances of this case.[2]

(2) If the employee does work which he was authorised to do, but does it in a way which the employer has not authorised and would not have authorised, nevertheless the employer is vicariously liable because the employee's act is still within the scope of his employment. In other words, the delictual act or omission is a mode – albeit a wrongful mode – of carrying out the work the employee was authorised to do. An example will illustrate the point. A is employed by B as a van driver. A drives the van carelessly or over the speed limit. As a result of his negligent driving, A injures C. In an action for reparation, B is vicariously liable for A's negligent driving. The careless driving is a mode – albeit a wrongful mode – of carrying out the work A was authorised to do. B would still be vicariously liable even if he instructed A not to drive carelessly or over the speed limit.

In *Taylor v Glasgow District Council*,[3] a building control officer had been given actual authority to issue building warrants and

1 1945 SC 175, 1945 SLT 189.
2 On defamation, see Chapter 15 below.
3 1997 SC 183, 1997 SLT 537.

completion certificates. He issued false documents as part of a fraudulent scheme with a development company. The company sold the property to Taylor, who sustained economic loss. It was held that the defender could be vicariously liable for the fraudulent conduct of its employee because he had been given actual authority to issue the documents. The fact that the defender did not benefit from the fraud was irrelevant: the only question was whether the employee's conduct was an improper mode of doing what he was authorised to do.[1]

(3) If the employee is employed to do a particular work or particular class of work, and does something outside the scope of his work, then the employer is not vicariously liable, since the employee was not acting within the scope of his employment. For example, A is employed by B to pack goods at B's warehouse. A decides to deliver goods to a customer and drives B's van. If A injures C as a result of A's careless driving, prima facie B is not vicariously liable, because A was not employed as a driver and was therefore not authorised to drive B's van. A's driving of the van is outside the scope of his employment and B is therefore not vicariously liable.

It may be difficult to determine what is the scope of a worker's employment. Obviously the terms of the contract are important, but the courts are not prepared to accept that for the purpose of vicarious liability, the scope of employment is limited to the employee's express contractual duties. In the example above, if to B's knowledge, A had delivered goods to a customer in the van on previous occasions, driving the van could well fall within A's employment, even though A's job description in his contract is that of a packer. Moreover, given that the pursuer has *ex hypothesi* been injured or suffered harm, courts will be reluctant to allow an employer to escape vicarious liability by arguing that the employee's failure to follow the employer's detailed instructions resulted in the employee acting outside the scope of employment (no vicarious liability) as opposed to engaging in a wrongful mode of carrying out the work the employee was authorised to do (vicarious liability).

Thus, in *Rose v Plenty*,[2] a milkman was expressly instructed by his employer not to use boys to help him deliver milk or to give

---

1 Sexual misconduct on the part of a teacher has been held not to be an unauthorised mode of carrying out his teaching duties. Consequently, the local authority was not vicariously liable: see *T v North Yorkshire County Council* [1999] IRLR 98.
2 [1975] ICR 430, [1976] 1 All ER 97, CA.

boys lifts in his milk float. In breach of this order, he continued to use a 13-year-old boy to help him. The lad was injured as a result of the milkman's negligent driving of the float. The employers argued that they were not vicariously liable, because the employee was acting outside the scope of his employment. In other words, his particular work was delivering milk without the help of young boys and therefore he was acting outside the scope of his employment when he delivered milk with the help of a 13-year-old lad. However, the Court of Appeal held,[1] that the express prohibition did not change the scope of the milkman's employment. As Lord Denning MR explained:[2]

'In considering whether a prohibited act was within the course of the employment it depends very much on the purpose for which it is done. If it is done for his employer's business, it is usually done in the course of his employment, even though it is a prohibited act . . . But if it is done for some purpose other than his master's business, as, for instance, giving a lift to a hitchhiker, such an act, if prohibited, may not be in the course of his employment . . . In the present case it seems to me that the course of Mr Plenty's [the milkman's] employment was to distribute the milk, collect the money and to bring back the bottles to the van. He got, or allowed this young boy, Leslie Rose, to do part of that business which was the employer's business. It seems to me that although prohibited, it was conduct which was within the course of employment . . . I agree it is a nice point in these cases on which side of the line the case falls.'

In certain situations it will be a question of degree whether the employee's conduct is or is not within the scope of his employment. In *Williams v Hemphill (A & W) Ltd*,[3] members of the Boys' Brigade were at a camp at Benderlock. A company of Girl Guildry was also at the camp. The girls were to return to Dollar by train. A lorry driver was instructed by his employer to take the boys back to Glasgow. He was persuaded by some of the boys to return to Glasgow via Connell, Stirling and Dollar railway stations, so that the boys could catch a glimpse of the girls. The shortest route back to Glasgow was via Loch Lomond. There was an accident and one of the boys, who had not instigated the change of route, was injured. The employers would not have authorised the route the driver had taken. The question was whether by deviating from the authorised route, the driver was no longer acting within the scope of his employment, with the result that the employer would not have been vicariously liable. The House of Lords held that it was

1 Lord Denning MR and Scarman LJ; Lawton LJ dissented.
2 *Rose v Plenty* [1976] 1 All ER 97 at 100–101.
3 1966 SC (HL) 31, 1966 SLT 33.

ultimately a question of degree whether, as a result of the deviation, the employee was no longer engaged on the employer's business. In this case, the dominant purpose of the journey was to transport the boys to Glasgow and the driver was still engaged on that task when the accident occurred, in spite of not having taken the most direct route. As Lord Pearce explained:[1]

'In weighing up, therefore, the question of degree whether the admittedly substantial deviation of the vehicle with its passengers and baggage was such as to make the lorry's progress a frolic of the servant unconnected with or in substitution for the master's business, the presence of the passengers is a decisive factor against regarding it as a mere frolic of the servant. In the present case the defenders remained liable, in spite of the deviation, for their driver's negligence.'[2]

(4) If an employee uses his master's time or his master's equipment for the employee's own purpose, the employer is no longer vicariously liable because the employee is no longer acting within the scope of his employment. As Lord Pearce indicated, in these circumstances the employee is acting on a 'frolic' of his own. So, for example, if during the time he is supposed to be working, an employee goes shopping, the employer will not be vicariously liable for any delict the employee may commit, since shopping is clearly outside the scope of the employment. Similarly, if a van driver, without authorisation, uses his employer's van to help a friend move house, the employer is not vicariously liable if an accident occurs during the move, because that is outside the scope of the employment.

Difficulties may arise, however, if the employee's delictual act or omission occurs at the workplace. In *Kirby v National Coal Board*,[3] a miner during a temporary break went to a prohibited place in order to smoke. When he struck a match, there was an explosion and the pursuer was injured. The court held that by going to the prohibited area in order to smoke, he was no longer acting within the scope of his employment – mining – and consequently the defender was not vicariously liable. On the other hand, in *Century Insurance Co Ltd v Northern Ireland Road Transport Board*,[4] an explosion took place when an employee lit a cigarette while transferring petrol. The House of Lords held that this was an

---

1 1966 SC (HL) 31 at 46.
2 Lord Pearce did indicate, however, that there must be limits set by common sense: for example, if the deviation involved going to Glasgow via Inverness!
3 1958 SC 514, 1959 SLT 7.
4 [1942] AC 509, [1942] 1 All ER 491, HL.

unauthorised mode of doing his job which was to transfer petrol and that the employer therefore remained vicariously liable.

Where a person is injured at work as a result of horseplay by other employees, the employer may escape vicarious liability if the horseplay constitutes 'a frolic of their own'. In *Smith v Crossley Bros Ltd*,[1] an apprentice was injured by fellow employees during initiation rites.[2] It was held that the employer was not in breach of the general duty of care to provide competent fellow workers.[3] Nor was the defendant vicariously liable, because the actings constituted a frolic and were outside the scope of the workers' employment. On the other hand, in *Harrison v Michelin Tyre Co Ltd*,[4] the employer was held to be vicariously liable when an employee who was standing on a duckboard was injured as a result of a fellow employee jumping on the other end of the duckboard for a lark. The court took the view that a reasonable person would consider that, even though the act was unauthorised, it was nevertheless 'part and parcel' of the job and accordingly not outside the scope of employment.[5]

It is generally accepted that travel to and from work is outside the scope of employment and that the employer is not vicariously liable for an employee's delicts at that time. However, where the employer retains an element of control, vicarious liability may continue before or after work. Thus in *Bell v Blackwood, Morton & Sons Ltd*,[6] an employer was held to be vicariously liable when the pursuer was injured by a fellow employee when leaving work. The employers had attempted to prevent employees from rushing downstairs to catch their buses and had supervised the descent of the stairway from time to time. In these circumstances, the employees were still within the scope of their employment when on the stairway where the accident occurred. Where an employee works at two places, it has been held that he is within the scope of his employment when travelling between them.[7]

---

1 (1971) 95 So Jo 655, CA.
2 The unfortunate lad had a compressed-air pipe placed in close proximity to his rectum.
3 See pp 207 ff above.
4 [1985] 1 All ER 918, [1985] ICR 696.
5 An owner of a night club has been held to be vicariously liable for assaults carried out by 'bouncers' on a customer who had kicked in the door of the premises: the bouncers were not on a frolic of their own but had been attempting to preserve the integrity of the club, albeit in a *very* unauthorised way! See *Vasey v Surrey Free Inns plc* [1996] PIQR P373, CA.
6 1960 SC 11, 1959 SLT (Notes) 54, OH.
7 *Thomson v British Steel Corpn* 1977 SLT 26, OH.

In certain situations, an employee may be hired out to work under the instructions of another employer. For example A, a general contractor, may hire equipment from B to be operated by an employee of B, but under A's instruction. If the 'borrowed' employee is negligent and injures one of A's employees or a third party, who is vicariously liable, A or B? The general rule is that the employer with whom the borrowed employee has a contract of employment remains vicariously liable, even though the employee works under the general instructions of another. Thus, in our example, B remains vicariously liable. B will only escape vicarious liability if he has delegated to A, not only the power to control what B's employee does but also *how* the employee should do the job. The onus rests on B to establish that the full plethora of control has passed from B to A. This will be almost impossible to establish where B's employee operates sophisticated equipment.

This principle was settled by the House of Lords in the leading case of *Mersey Docks and Harbour Board v Coggins and Griffith (Liverpool) Ltd.*[1] The plaintiff hired a mobile crane to the defendant which was to be operated by an employee of the plaintiff. It was agreed in the contract of hire that the operator of the crane was to be treated as an employee of Coggins. The craneman injured a worker while operating the crane negligently. The question arose whether the plaintiff or the defendant should be vicariously liable. The House of Lords held that *in a question with the injured third party*, vicarious liability could not be determined by the contractual arrangements made between the plaintiff and defendant, to which the injured person had not been a party. Prima facie, the plaintiff was the employer and was vicariously liable unless it could be established that full control of the craneman had passed to Coggins. While Coggins could tell the craneman what to do, since he was a highly skilled worker, they could *not* tell him *how* to do his job. Accordingly, Mersey Docks had failed to discharge the onus which lay upon them to prove that their employee had been transferred *pro hac vice* to Coggins. Therefore, as far as the injured person was concerned, he could sue Mersey Docks as vicariously liable for the negligence of their employee, the craneman. But, because of the terms of their contract of hire with Coggins, Mersey Docks could recover the damages from Coggins since they had agreed to treat the crane man as their employee.[2]

---

1 [1947] AC 1, [1946] 2 All ER 345, HL.
2 This principle has been accepted as part of Scots law: see *Park v Tractor Shovels Ltd* 1980 SLT 94, OH.

(3) Vicarious liability for independent contractors

As a general rule, a person is not vicariously liable for the delicts of an independent contractor whom he hires to undertake a particular job, for example, a taxi driver, a plumber, a builder etc. If, for example, A, a general contractor, hires the services of B, an independent contractor, and through his negligence B causes injury to C, an employee of A, A is not vicariously liable for B's delicts. If C is injured by the negligence of an employee of B, B will, of course, be vicariously liable to C. However, A may be liable in delict to his employee, C, if A's act in hiring B is a breach of A's general duty to take reasonable care for the safety of his employees.[1] But this is a breach of A's personal duty of care towards his employees – it is not *vicarious* liability for B's delictual act. To succeed against A, C must show that A did not take reasonable care in hiring B's services, for example, if A knows that B is incompetent or unqualified. The duty is analogous with that of taking reasonable care to provide an employee with competent fellow workers. However, in *Marshall v William Sharp & Sons Ltd*,[2] the defender hired the services of a worker who was paid an hourly rate for work done. The defender had full control over the actings of the worker concerned. The pursuer, an employee of the defender, was injured as a result of the worker's negligence. The Inner House held that the defender was *not* in breach of his personal duty to the pursuer to provide a competent independent contractor to work with him. Nevertheless, the court found that the defender was vicariously liable, in spite of the fact that the person who had injured the pursuer was an independent contractor. It is submitted that this decision can be supported on the ground that the defender had the power to control not only what the independent contractor could do but how he should do it. This is not usually the case when a person hires an independent contractor, for example, a taxi driver or a plumber. Thus, unless the hirer has the full plethora of control over an independent contractor, he will not be vicariously liable for the delicts of an independent contractor in carrying out a job.

In building contracts, an employer is liable to third parties for loss sustained as a result of an independent contractor carrying out hazardous operations on the site:

Employer——Main Contractor——Sub-contractor——Sub-sub-contractor

---

1 On an employer's duty to take reasonable care, see pp 205 ff above.
2 1991 SCLR 104, 1991 SLT 114.

But the main contractor is *not* liable for the delicts of the sub or sub-sub-contractors; nor is the sub-contractor liable for the delicts of the sub-sub-contractor. Thus a main contractor cannot sue a sub-contractor for damage to property owned by the main contractor as a consequence of a sub-sub-contractor's negligence.[1]

(4) Principal and agent

A principal can be vicariously liable for the delicts of his agent. This will arise if (i) the acts of the agent were expressly authorised by the principal; or (ii) the principal ratified the agent's acts after they were done; or (iii) the delict is within the actual or ostensible authority of the agent. For vicarious liability to arise it is not enough that X permits Y to do a particular act, for example, drive X's car: instead, X must have delegated a task or duty to Y.[2] The principle is important in the context of employment where an employer prima facie escapes vicarious liability because the employee is working outside the scope of his employment: the employer may still be vicariously liable as principal if in the circumstances the employee is acting within his actual or ostensible authority as the employer's agent at the time of the delictual act.[3]

C. CONCLUSION

The discussion of vicarious liability is important because it illustrates how the common law developed an exception to the principle that a person is not obliged to make reparation unless he has caused injury or harm as a result of his own *culpa* or fault. As a result of industrialisation, it became apparent that those who were injured by the delicts of workers would, in practice, have little likelihood of obtaining compensation from the worker himself. Accordingly, the doctrine of vicarious liability arose to enable the pursuer to sue the employer, in addition to the employee, since the employer was more likely to have funds or be insured.

---

1 *MTM Construction Ltd v William Reid Engineering Ltd* 1998 SLT 778, 1997 SCLR 778, OH.
2 *Morgans v Launchbury* [1973] AC 127, [1972] 2 All ER 606, HL.
3 *Taylor v Glasgow District Council* 1997 SC 183, 1997 SLT 537.

CHAPTER 13

Delict and the family

It is now proposed to consider delictual liability in the context of family relationships. We will be concerned with delictual liability *between* members of the family and the rights of members of the family to seek reparation if a relative is injured or killed.

A. TITLE TO SUE

At common law, spouses could not sue each other in delict. Thus, if a woman was injured as a result of her husband's negligent driving, she could not obtain reparation. This rule was clearly anachronistic, especially as the loss would ultimately fall on her husband's insurance company. The position was changed by s 2(1) of the Law Reform (Husband and Wife) Act 1962, which provides that each of the spouses has 'the like rights' to bring proceedings against the other in respect of a delict 'as if they were not married'. Where the action is brought during the subsistence of the marriage, the court has a discretion to dismiss the proceedings if it appears that no substantial benefit would accrue to either party if the action continued.[1] The court's discretion is unlikely to be invoked, because the action will proceed if any benefit accrues to the pursuer, even though the couple, as a family unit, will be no better off. Since the discretion in s 2(2) is both anomalous and unnecessary, the Scottish Law Commission has proposed that it should be repealed.[2]

A spouse is not liable for the delicts of the other spouse unless liability is established on a basis other than marriage itself. So, for example, a wife could be vicariously liable for a delict committed by her husband if she were his employer and the delict arose in the course of his employment.

As a general rule, a child or young person under the age of 16

1 Law Reform (Husband and Wife) Act 1962, s 2(2).
2 Report on Family Law (Scot Law Com No 135) Rec 54.

has no active legal capacity.[1] However, a child under 16 can instruct a solicitor in connection with any civil matter, provided she has a general understanding of what it means to do so. A child of 12 or more is presumed to be of sufficient age and maturity to have such understanding, although a child under 12 may instruct a solicitor is she in fact has such an understanding.[2] If the child has the capacity to instruct a solicitor, she has capacity to pursue or defend a civil action.[3] Thus a child with sufficient capacity can pursue an action in delict. If the child does not have such capacity, the action must be brought by the child's legal representative, who will usually be the child's parents.[4]

The Age of Legal Capacity (Scotland) Act 1991 does not affect the delictual responsibility of children and young persons under the age of 16.[5] Thus a child under the age of 16 can, theoretically at least, be sued if the child has committed a delict. Parents are not vicariously liable for the delicts committed by their children. But where a child causes injury or damage as a result of a parent's negligence, the parent may be liable for a breach of a duty of care which the parent owed to the pursuer. For example, if a child runs in front of a car and the driver is injured trying to avoid the child, the mother may be liable in delict if she has not taken reasonable care to ensure that the child was not on the road.[6] Because the 1991 Act does not affect the age of delictual responsibility, a child who has been injured may have any damages awarded reduced on the ground of contributory negligence.[7] Thus, in *McKinnell v White*[8] a child of five was held to be 50 per cent contributorily negligent because he ran in front of a speeding motorist. The Lord Ordinary (Fraser) took the view that by the age of five, a child brought up in an urban environment should have been aware of

---

1 Age of Legal Capacity (Scotland) Act 1991, s 1(1)(a).
2 ALC(S)A 1991, s 2(4A).
3 ALC(S)A 1991, s 2(5A).
4 Children (Scotland) Act 1995, s 1(1)(d). If the parent is the defender, for example, if the child was injured as a result of her mother's careless driving, a curator ad litem will be appointed to represent the child.
5 Age of Legal Capacity (Scotland) Act 1991, s 1(3)(c).
6 *Hardie v Sneddon* 1917 SC 1, 1916 2 SLT 197.
7 On contributory negligence, see pp 143 ff above.
8 1971 SLT (Notes) 61, OH. See also *McCluskey v Wallace* 1998 SC 711 (four-year-old child, 20 per cent contributory negligence). There is no general rule to determine the degree of a child's contributory negligence; the danger to which the child is exposed and the child's capacity to appreciate that risk are important: *Galbraith's Curator ad litem v Stewart (No 2)* 1998 SLT 1305, OH (eight-year-old child, no contributory negligence).

the danger of road traffic. It has always been competent for a child to sue his or her parent in delict.[1]

Where a foetus sustains injury *in utero*, the unborn baby has no right to sue in delict unless and until it has been born alive. Only on birth does a child obtain legal personality. However, provided the defender owed a duty of care towards the foetus, if the baby is born alive, an action in delict can be brought on the child's behalf in respect of the injuries sustained *in utero*. This is sometimes said to be a consequence of the civil law principle *nasciturus pro iam nato habetur quotiens de eius agitur*, ie that in a matter affecting its interests, an unborn child *in utero* should be deemed to be born (the *nasciturus* doctrine).[2] It is submitted that there is no need to rely on the *nasciturus* doctrine to achieve this result. Given that the defender owes a *Donoghue v Stevenson* duty of care[3] to the foetus, based on reasonable foreseeability of injury *in utero*, then if there is a breach of the duty which causes injury to the foetus, a delict will be committed when the baby is born. It is at that stage, ie when the baby is born alive, that the delict is completed because, while the breach of duty took place during the pregnancy, *damage* for the purpose of delictual liability is not sustained by the child until the child is born.[4] It is only then that the damage arises as a result of the breach of the duty of care: *damnum injuria datum*.

Because it is competent for a child to sue a parent, a mother who injures her foetus during the pregnancy can, in theory at least, be sued by her child in delict, provided the child is born alive. A mother clearly owes a duty of care to the foetus. If during her pregnancy she fails to take reasonable care, for example if she abuses drugs or falls down the stair when drunk, then she can be liable in delict if her breach of duty of care results in damage to the child when born alive. It would therefore appear that a mother carries a potential litigant in her womb for nine months! Similarly, a father who injures his wife's foetus through, for example, negligent driving, may be liable in delict if the child is born alive suffering from harm as a result of the injuries sustained *in utero*.

In practice, it is likely that where a foetus is injured *in utero* the mother will also have sustained injury. If the defender owed her a

---

1 *Young v Rankin* 1934 SC 499, 1934 SLT 445.
2 *Cohen v Shaw* 1992 SCLR 182n, 1992 SLT 1022, OH.
3 See *Donoghue v Stevenson* 1932 SC (HL) 31, 1932 SLT 317.
4 *Hamilton v Fife Health Board* 1993 SC 369, 1993 SLT 624.

duty of care which has been broken, the mother may sue for the injuries she has suffered. Where the mother miscarries as a result of the defender's breach of duty, she may obtain damages for the loss of her baby. Of course, in these circumstances, the unborn child has no title to sue because the child has not been born alive.

B. INJURY TO A RELATIVE

In *Robertson v Turnbull*,[1] it was held that where a person was injured, the defender did not owe a threshold duty of care to the victim's spouse or relatives who had suffered economic loss as a result of the injuries sustained. So, for example, members of the injured person's family could not sue in delict for loss of support.[2] The victim can, of course, sue for loss of future earnings as derivative economic loss.[3] Moreover, at common law, a pursuer who was injured could not recover damages for the economic loss suffered by a relative as a result of the pursuer's injuries, for example, where a spouse had given up work in order to nurse her injured husband.[4]

The common law on this point has now been superseded by s 8 of the Administration of Justice Act 1982.[5] This provides that where a person has sustained personal injuries, the injured person can recover damages which amount to reasonable remuneration for necessary services rendered to the pursuer by a relative.[6] The services rendered by the relative must be physical services, such as nursing. Thus it has been held that s 8 of the 1982 Act did not

1 1982 SC (HL) 1, 1982 SLT 96.
2 This is an example of non-recoverability of secondary economic loss. Similarly, a child cannot sue for economic loss incurred as a result of serious injuries suffered by his mother (she was in a persistent vegetative state): *Buckley v Farrow* [1997] PIQR Q78, CA.
3 On loss of future earnings, see pp 274 ff below; on derivative economic loss, see pp 67 ff above.
4 *Edgar v Lord Advocate* 1965 SC 67, 1965 SLT 158.
5 As amended by the Law Reform (Miscellaneous Provisions) (Scotland) Act 1990, s 69.
6 Relative includes the injured person's spouse or divorced spouse, heterosexual cohabitee, any ascendant or descendant, any brother, sister, uncle or aunt or their issue and any person accepted by the injured party as a child of the family: illegitimacy is irrelevant: Administration of Justice Act 1982, s 13. BNA nursing and home help rates can be useful but are by no means conclusive of what reasonable remuneration should be in a particular case. See, for example, *Kennedy v Lees of Scotland* 1997 SLT 510 (use of agency rates rejected as unsuitable where victim had not received substantial nursing, but only short visits from relatives).

apply when a relative had donated bone marrow to the pursuer, who would otherwise have died.[1]

The pursuer, ie the injured person, then accounts to the relative for any damages recovered under this provision.[2] Originally, damages could only be awarded in respect of necessary services rendered by the relative up to the date of the action;[3] but it is now provided that damages will be awarded for reasonable remuneration of necessary services likely to be rendered by a relative to the injured person in the future.[4] Damages are not available under s 8 of the 1982 Act if the relative expressly agreed that no payment should be made in respect of the services rendered or to be rendered.[5] Where the injured person has died before the action is concluded, the deceased's executor may recover damages for necessary services rendered by a relative before the victim died.[6]

Where a person who was not in employment was injured, at common law he had no right to sue for loss of earnings, since *ex hypothesi* he was not earning. This was particularly unfair to wives who had given up their jobs to look after the home or children. Section 9(1) of the Administration of Justice Act 1982 gives an injured person who has been providing unpaid personal services to a relative,[7] the right to sue for damages if the pursuer is unable to continue to do so as a result of the injuries sustained. The personal services must be services which (a) were or might have been expected to have been rendered by the pursuer before the injuries; (b) were of a kind which when rendered by a person other than a relative would ordinarily have been obtainable on payment; and (c) the injured person but for the injuries in question might have been expected to render gratuitously to a relative.[8]

In *Ingham v John G Russell (Transport) Ltd*[9] the Inner House refused to restrict the concept of personal services to services

---

1 *Duffy v Lanarkshire Health Board* 1998 SCLR 1142, 1998 Rep LR 119, OH.
2 Administration of Justice Act 1982, s 8(2). But where the relative is the defender, it has been held that a claim under s 8 is incompetent: *Kozikowska v Kozikowski* 1996 SLT 386. It was thought contrary to public policy that the pursuer should remunerate the person she blamed for her injuries – *sed quaere?*
3 *Forsyth's Curator Bonis v Govan Shipbuilders* 1989 SCLR 78, 1989 SLT 91.
4 Administration of Justice Act 1982, s 8(3), added by s 69 of the Law Reform (Miscellaneous Provisions) (Scotland) Act 1990.
5 Administration of Justice Act 1982, s 8(1) and (3). See *Denheen v British Railways Board* 1988 SLT 320n, 1986 SLT 249, OH.
6 See, for example, *McManus' Executrix v Babcock Energy Ltd* 1999 SC 569.
7 For the definition of relative, see the Administration of Justice Act 1982, s 13, discussed at p 224, note 6 above.
8 Administration of Justice Act 1982, s 9(3).
9 1991 SC 201, 1991 SLT 739.

which were rendered to the person of the relative, such as nursing, as opposed to the relative's property, such as cleaning the relative's house. It was enough that the services had been rendered *in person* by the injured person and therefore included maintenance or DIY services rendered by the injured person to his spouse. It is therefore clear that an injured woman, for example, can recover damages if she is unable to provide unpaid housekeeping and child-rearing services for her spouse, cohabitee or children. Because the personal services must have been rendered gratuitously before s 9 applies, the Administration of Justice Act 1982 recognises the fact that work in the home is still prima facie unpaid, but that its economic value is such that justice demands that the injured person should receive compensation for the inability to continue to provide it, even though technically the pursuer has not suffered any patrimonial loss, ie loss of earnings.

Where the injured person has died, a relative may claim as a head of loss a reasonable sum in respect of the loss of gratuitous personal services rendered to the relative by the deceased.[1] Before he can do so, the pursuer must be a relative who has the right to claim damages for loss of support by the deceased under the Damages (Scotland) Act 1976. Accordingly, it is to the provisions of the 1976 Act that we shall now turn.

C. DEATH OF A RELATIVE

If a person dies as a result of another's delict, two potential claims arise. First, the deceased's own claim, which can transmit to the deceased's executor who can pursue the action for the benefit of the deceased's estate. Second, a dependent claim by the deceased's relatives.

---

1 Administration of Justice Act 1982, s 9(2); *Ingham v John G Russell (Transport) Ltd* 1991 SC 201, 1991 SLT 379. It can be difficult to quantify the value of such services, particularly when the deceased was simply 'a normal, average married man living in family who did the correspondingly normal, average things which a father and husband does around the house, the garden and the family car': *Beggs v Motherwell Bridge Fabricators Ltd* 1997 SCLR 1019, 1998 SLT 1215 at 1223 per the Lord Ordinary (Eassie). See also *Ferrelly v Yarrow Shipbuilders Ltd* 1994 SCLR 407, 1994 SLT 1349n, OH; *McManus' Executrix v Babcock Energy Ltd* 1999 SC 569.

(1) The deceased's claim

Where a person is killed outright as a result of the defender's delict, the deceased's executor cannot raise an action in delict in respect of the death.[1] In these circumstances, the only claims are those of the deceased's relatives. However, if a person is injured and subsequently dies as a result of the injuries, the deceased's right to sue in delict in respect of personal injuries transmits to the executor, who can sue on behalf of the deceased's estate. This complex area of the law is now regulated by the Damages (Scotland) Act 1976.[2]

Where a person dies on or after 16 July 1992, the rights which vested in the deceased immediately before his death to sue for damages in respect of personal injuries transmit to the executor.[3] As a result, the executor can raise an action or, if an action has been raised by the deceased before he died, continue the action on behalf of the deceased's estate.[4] The executor may sue in respect of patrimonial loss, for example, loss of earnings sustained by the deceased, but only up to the date of death.[5] In other words, patrimonial loss attributable to any period after the deceased's death, for example, loss of future earnings, is non-transmissible to the executor. This is necessary to prevent double compensation, given that the defender may have to meet claims for loss of support brought by the deceased's relatives.

The deceased's right to damages by way of solatium is also transmissible to the executor,[6] but again in assessing damages for solatium, the court is to have regard only to the period ending immediately before the deceased's death.[7] Solatium is damages for pain and suffering arising from the personal injuries. In assessing

---

1 Where death is caused by a fatal accident, the courts, in England at least, will not award the deceased's executor damages for the deceased's fear of impending death: *Hicks v Chief Constable of South Yorkshire Police* [1992] 2 All ER 65, HL. In Scotland, the deceased's immediate family may have such a claim: see p 231 below.

2 This Act has been amended by inter alia the Administration of Justice Act 1982, the Law Reform (Parent and Child) (Scotland) Act 1986, the Consumer Protection Act 1987; the Damages (Scotland) Act 1993 and the Protection from Harassment Act 1997; it now bears little resemblance to the original Act. References in this chapter are to the Damages (Scotland) Act 1976 as amended unless otherwise stated. For the text of the amended Act see the Appendix below.

3 Damages (Scotland) Act 1976, s 2(1).

4 D(S)A 1976, s 2A.

5 D(S)A 1976, s 2(2).

6 D(S)A 1976, s 2(1). See, for example, *McManus' Executrix v Babcock Energy Ltd* 1999 SC 569.

7 D(S)A 1976, s 2(3).

damages for solatium, the court is entitled to have regard to the extent to which the deceased suffered because he was aware that his expectation of life had been reduced as a result of the injuries.[1]

The effect of these provisions can be illustrated by the following example. A is seriously injured as a result of the negligent driving of B. A dies two years after the accident.[2] If A had begun an action against B, A's executor can continue the action provided it has not been concluded.[3] If A had not begun proceedings, A's executor can bring an action against B.[4] However, the executor's claims for patrimonial loss and solatium are restricted to losses incurred by the deceased at the date of death: any patrimonial loss referable to a period after the date of death cannot be recovered by the executor. If the action is successful,[5] the damages awarded become part of the deceased's estate. This means that they will be distributed to the deceased's legatees if there is a will or to a surviving spouse and the deceased's heirs according to the rules of intestate succession where the deceased died without a will. If A has relatives, they may have a claim against B if A's death *was* as a result of the personal injuries A has sustained. It is to the relative's dependent claim that we now turn.

(2) The dependent claims

Where a person dies in consequence of personal injuries sustained by him as a result of the defender's conduct, then if the defender would have been liable to pay damages to the deceased if he had lived, she is also liable to pay damages to a certain class of the deceased's relatives.[6] It will be seen that a relative's right to sue is *dependent* on the defender being liable to pay damages if an action had been brought by the deceased in respect of the personal injuries sustained. Accordingly, the relative's claim can be defeated

---

1 Damages (Scotland) Act 1976, s 9A(1). Damages can also be awarded in respect of patrimonial loss arising from the fact that the injured person's expectation of life has been reduced: s 9(1) and 9(2). Where the action is brought by the executor, however, only patrimonial loss arising before the date of death can be recovered: s 2(2).

2 It is irrelevant whether or not the death was a result of A's injuries.

3 Damages (Scotland) Act 1976, s 2A(1)(b). An action is not concluded while any appeal is competent or before any appeal taken has been disposed of: s 2A(2).

4 D(S)A 1976, s 2A(1)(a).

5 Any defences, for example, *volens*, which B could use in an action by A are good against an action brought by A's executor. Similarly, damages can be reduced as a result of A's contributory negligence.

6 D(S)A 1976, s 1(1).

if the deceased would not have succeeded against the defender, for example, if the defender did not owe a duty of care to the deceased or had not broken the duty, or the deceased was *volens*. The relative's damages can also be reduced on the grounds of the deceased's contributory negligence.[1]

Before a relative's claim is triggered, the deceased must have died 'in consequence of *personal injuries* sustained by *him*'.[2] The Scottish courts have experienced difficulties where a child dies shortly after birth as a result of injuries sustained while *in utero*. In *Hamilton v Fife Health Board*,[3] the Lord Ordinary (Prosser) held that parents of a child had no title to sue, on the ground that before s 1(1) of the Damages (Scotland) Act 1976 was applicable, the death had to have been as a result of personal injuries sustained when the deceased had legal personality. Accordingly, since their baby had died shortly after birth as a result of injuries suffered while *in utero*, s 1(1) of the 1976 Act was not triggered, because a foetus has no legal personality until born alive. This narrow construction of s 1(1) of the 1976 Act was, however, rejected by the Lord Ordinary (Lord Morton of Shuna) in *McWilliams v Lord Advocate*,[4] decided seven months later.

The conflict was resolved as a result of the decision of the Inner House in an appeal from Lord Prosser's decision in the *Hamilton* case.[5] There the court held that, although the injuries were sustained by the foetus while *in utero*, the delict was completed only when the baby was born alive and suffered damage as a result of the defender's breach of duty of care: *damnum injuria datum*. At that stage, ie when born alive, the child could have sued the defender for damages for personal injuries. Consequently, when the child died as a result of these injuries, the parents' dependent action in respect of the death arose, ie s 1(1) of the Damages (Scotland) Act 1976 was triggered.

It should be noted that if the baby is not born alive, the parents do not have a dependent claim under s 1(1) of the Damages (Scotland) Act 1976. The reason is that the defender is not under any obligation to pay damages to the child because the delict was never completed, since the child never had legal personality. In this situation, the mother may well have her own individual right of

---

1 See, for example, *Beggs v Motherwell Bridge Fabricators Ltd* 1998 SLT 1215, 1997 SCLR 1019, OH (deceased 20 per cent contributorily negligent).
2 Damages (Scotland) Act 1976, s 1(1) (italics added).
3 1992 SCLR 288, 1992 SLT 1026, OH.
4 1992 SCLR 954, 1992 SLT 1045, OH.
5 *Hamilton v Fife Health Board* 1993 SC 369, 1993 SCLR 408.

action, if the defender's acts which injured the foetus *in utero* amounted to a breach of the duty of care which was owed to the mother herself.

The nature of the dependent claim turns on whether the pursuer is a member of the deceased's immediate family or a wider class of relatives specified in the Damages (Scotland) Act 1976.

(a) The immediate family

The deceased's immediate family consists of the following relatives:[1]

(1) the deceased's spouse;
(2) the deceased's cohabitee, ie any person not being the spouse of the deceased who immediately before the death was living with the deceased as husband or wife: it will be noted that this is restricted to heterosexual cohabitation;
(3) the deceased's children: this includes step-children and children accepted by the deceased as children of the family. Relationships by affinity are covered, ie the deceased's daughter-in-law or son-in-law.[2] Illegitimacy is irrelevant. In *Cohen v Shaw*,[3] the Lord Ordinary (Cullen) held that a child *in utero* at the time of his father's death had title to sue as a child, provided the child was born alive, ie a posthumous child is included;
(4) the deceased's parents: it is irrelevant that the deceased was illegitimate. Relationships by affinity are covered and consequently the deceased's mother-in-law or father-in-law are included.[4]

Members of the deceased's immediate family may claim damages for the following:

(1) Damages for loss of the financial support they would have obtained if the deceased had not died as a result of the injuries. This covers both loss of support up until the date of death and loss of support in the future. These claims can be substantial. Where both spouses were earning, the normal practice is to add their incomes together and deduct a percentage to reflect maintenance

---

1 Damages (Scotland) Act 1976, s 10(2) and Sch 1.
2 *McAllister v Imperial Chemical Industries plc* 1997 SLT 351, 1996 Rep LR 136, OH.
3 1992 SCLR 182n, 1992 SLT 1022, OH. In this case, Lord Cullen relied on the *nasciturus* principle.
4 *Monteith v Cape Insulation Ltd* 1998 SC 903.

for the deceased. The net figure so arrived at *minus* the earnings of the surviving spouse forms the loss of dependency.[1] An appropriate multiplier is then obtained by reference to the Ogden tables.[2] Where a woman married her husband knowing that he was dying as a result of personal injuries, her action for loss of support was still relevant.[3] As the Lord Ordinary (Clyde) observed:[4] 'The proposition appeared to be that a widow could claim no loss if the death was one which could have been reasonably expected. I find no precedent or principle to justify such an approach and no warrant for it in the simple wording of the statute'.

No account is taken of a widow's remarriage prospects[5] or her entitlement to a widow's pension.[6] If the deceased had obtained a provisional award of damages before his death, in assessing the relative's loss of support the court takes into account such part of the provisional award as was intended to compensate the deceased for any period beyond the date when he died.[7]

(2) Such sum of damages, if any, as the court thinks just by way of compensation for all or any of the following:

(a) distress and anxiety endured by the relative in contemplation of the suffering of the deceased before he or she died;[8]
(b) the grief and sorrow of the relative caused by the deceased's death;

---

1 *Wotherspoon v Strathclyde Regional Council* 1992 SCLR 806, 1992 SLT 1090. Where there are no dependent children, the dependency lies between 50 and 60 per cent of the combined incomes: *Phillips v Grampian Health Board* 1991 SCLR 817, 1992 SLT 659. Where there are dependent children, the dependency lies around 70–75 per cent of the combined incomes. This percentage should be proportioned between the children and the surviving spouse: *Campbell v Gillespie* 1996 SLT 503, OH. Damages for a widow's loss of support after the deceased would have retired have been assessed as half the likely pension and an appropriate multiplier: *Beggs v Motherwell Bridge Fabricators Ltd* 1997 SCLR 1019, 1998 SLT 1215.
2 *McManus' Executrix v Babcock Energy Ltd* 1999 SC 569.
3 *Phillips v Grampian Health Board* 1991 SCLR 817, 1992 SLT 659, OH.
4 1992 SLT 659 at 660.
5 Law Reform (Miscellaneous Provisions) Act 1971, s 4.
6 Damages (Scotland) Act 1976, s 1(5). See *Campbell v Gillespie* 1996 SLT 503, OH.
7 D(S)A 1976, s 1(5A).
8 It has been questioned whether Parliament intended the court to carry out 'the difficult – and often distasteful – task of trying to assess the feelings of pain and apprehensions of mortality of someone so abruptly and severely injured as to be in the imminent and real danger of death within a period of minutes': *Beggs v Motherwell Bridge Fabricators Ltd* 1998 SLT 1215 at 1223–1224 per the Lord Ordinary (Eassie). The sum awarded was £250!

(c) the loss of such non-patrimonial benefit as the relative might be expected to derive from the deceased's society and guidance if the deceased had not died.

These heads of loss replace the former loss of society award and were introduced by the Damages (Scotland) Act 1993[1] which amended s 1 of the Damages (Scotland) Act 1976. In making such an award, the court is not obliged to ascribe any of the award to any of the heads of damage. It has been judicially recognised that the amendment was intended to clarify the previous law as it had been developed by the courts, not to change the basis of such an award.[2] Accordingly, awards under the pre-1993 law can still be looked at for guidance. It has also been accepted that the amounts awarded under the pre-1993 law had fallen out of step with the general level of awards of damages for personal injuries.[3] We can therefore anticipate larger sums being awarded, in particular where head (a) is present: for example, when a child has died after months of unsuccessful treatment, or a spouse has been burned alive in a road accident after rescuers have been unable to free him.

(3) Reasonable funeral expenses.

(b) Specified relatives

The specified relatives include the deceased's divorced spouse, but not former cohabitee, grandparents, grandchildren, brothers and sisters, uncles and aunts, nephews and nieces and cousins. Such relatives include the appropriate 'in-laws'. Specified relatives are entitled to claim only for loss of the deceased's support and reasonable funeral expenses. The fact that the deceased had no legal obligation to support the specified relative is irrelevant: reparation is made for the loss of *de facto* financial support both before the date of death and in the future.

The right of a relative of the deceased to a dependent claim under s 1 of the Damages (Scotland) Act 1976 can transmit to the executor of the relative if the relative dies before an award of damages is made.[4] Thus, for example, if A dies leaving his wife, B, B's right to sue as a member of A's immediate family transmits to

---

1 Damages (Scotland) Act 1993, s 1(1). The heads of loss apply in relation to deaths occurring after 18 April 1993.
2 *McManus' Executrix v Babcock Energy Ltd* 1999 SC 569.
3 *McManus' Executrix v Babcock Energy Ltd* 1999 SC 569.
4 Damages (Scotland) Act 1976, s 1A.

her executor if she dies before an award of damages has been made to her. This applies where B, ie the deceased's relative, dies on or after 16 July 1992. In determining the amount of damages payable to the relative's executor, the court can only have regard to the period ending immediately before the relative's death.[1] This proviso, while obviously important in respect of the relative's claim for loss of support, could also affect a claim under s 1(4) of the 1976 Act if the relative died shortly after the deceased person.

Both the deceased's immediate family and the specified relatives can also seek compensation for the loss of the deceased's gratuitous personal services to them, by virtue of s 9 of the Administration of Justice Act 1982.[2] Otherwise,[3] no person is entitled by reason of relationship to damages in respect of the death of another person, except by virtue of the provisions of the Damages (Scotland) Act 1976.[4]

---

1 Damages (Scotland) Act 1976, s 1A.
2 *Ingham v John G Russell (Transport) Ltd* 1991 SC 201, 1991 SCLR 596; *McManus' Executrix v Babcock Energy Ltd* 1999 SC 569.
3 An exception is also made for claims under s 1 of the International Transport Convention Act 1983.
4 Damages (Scotland) Act 1976, s 1(7).

CHAPTER 14

Delict and road traffic

A. INTRODUCTION

In modern society, motor vehicles which are driven carelessly are a major cause of accidents. Accidents involving vehicles are probably the area of the law of delict with which ordinary people are most likely to be involved. Where a person suffers personal injuries or damage to property as a result of a road accident, the general principles of delictual liability apply. Indeed, the paradigm of a duty of care based on reasonable foreseeability of harm,[1] is the duty of care which a driver owes to other road users. The pursuer must establish a breach of duty on the part of the defender, causation and damage as in any other action for reparation.[2] However, because of the frequency of such accidents, the common law has been supplemented by statutory provisions designed to ensure that victims of road accidents receive compensation. Moreover, the practices of insurance companies are of particular importance in this area. The 'peculiarities' of delictual liability for careless driving are discussed in this section.

B. THE STANDARD OF CARE

As stated above, before a driver is liable in delict the pursuer must establish that he was in breach of duty; in other words, that the defender did not reach the standard of care of the reasonable driver in his situation and was therefore negligent.[3] In road traffic cases, considerable assistance in establishing that the defender did not exercise reasonable care is provided by the Highway Code, an HMSO publication. The Road Traffic Act 1988 provides:[4]

1 On duty of care generally, see Chapter 3 above.
2 See Chapters 5 and 6 above.
3 On negligence, see pp 119 ff above.
4 Road Traffic Act 1988, s 38(7).

'A failure on the part of a person to observe the provisions of the Highway Code shall not in itself render that person liable to criminal proceedings of any kind but any such failure may in any proceedings (whether civil or criminal . . .) be relied upon by any party to the proceedings as tending to establish or negative any liability which is in question in those proceedings.'

Although a breach of the terms of the Highway Code will not per se establish negligence,[1] if the conduct averred is in fact in breach of the Code then this will be highly persuasive in establishing that the defender did not take reasonable care.[2]

Under the Road Traffic Act 1988, it is a criminal offence to cause death by dangerous driving;[3] to drive dangerously;[4] to drive without due care and attention;[5] and to cause death while driving without due care and attention when unfit to drive through drink or drugs.[6] Moreover, statutory regulations, designed to protect road users, provide offences where vehicles are (1) constructed in such a manner as to create a hazard[7] and (2) used in such a way as causes danger to other road users.[8] Although breach of these statutory provisions and regulations does not give rise to delictual liability for breach of statutory duty,[9] a conviction will be important evidence in establishing negligence on the part of the defender.

1 For example, merely because the defender was driving above the speed limit does not in itself establish that he was not taking reasonable care: speed is not per se the cause of an accident. See *Colborne v Wallace* 1993 GWD 17-1121 per the Sheriff Principal (Nicholson).

2 See, for example, *Robertson v J Sidney Smith* 1999 GWD 4-214. Although the Highway Code is within judicial knowledge, its provisions cannot be used in place of evidence: *Cavin v Kinnaird* 1993 SCLR 618, 1994 SLT 111.

3 Road Traffic Act 1988, s 1. For these purposes, dangerous driving means driving which falls below what would be expected of a competent and careful driver, when it would be obvious to a competent and careful driver that driving in that way would be dangerous. The 1988 Act was amended by the Road Traffic Act 1991.

4 Road Traffic Act 1988, s 2.

5 RTA 1988, s 3.

6 RTA 1988, s 3(A). It is enough to be above the prescribed limits for alcohol.

7 For example, it is an offence to drive a vehicle which exceeds the maximum length stipulated in the Road Vehicles (Construction and Use) Regulations 1986, SI 1986/1078.

8 For example, it is an offence to carry an object on a vehicle which overhangs that vehicle in excess of a distance prescribed in the regulations, without the leading edge being suitably marked.

9 On breach of statutory duty, see Chapter 11 above.

C. OBTAINING COMPENSATION

It is obvious that cars and other motor vehicles create considerable hazards to road users, whether they be pedestrians, cyclists or other drivers. To ensure that there is a fund available to provide compensation in the event of delictual liability as a result of a road accident, the owner of a vehicle is obliged to take out insurance. A motor vehicle must be insured in respect of 'third party liability', ie it must be insured in respect of delictual liability for a person other than the owner himself. This compulsory third party insurance covers liability for causing death, or personal injuries, or property damage to the victim. It is a criminal offence to drive a vehicle which does not have a valid third party liability policy of insurance[1] or to allow a vehicle to be driven without such insurance.[2]

Although it is only third party liability insurance which is compulsory, many drivers purchase additional insurance to cover their own losses which are incurred in an accident for which they are wholly or partly responsible. These losses include, for example, the cost of repair of the insured's own vehicle and the cost of hiring an alternative vehicle for a limited period while the insured's vehicle is being repaired. These are known as insured losses. Where a driver purchases additional insurance as well as third party liability insurance, this is known as a comprehensive policy of insurance. Comprehensive insurance does not usually cover death or personal injuries sustained by the driver as a result of his own negligence. It is common practice for the insurer to require the holder of a comprehensive policy to meet the first part of a claim made under that policy. This is typically between the first £50 and £300 of the claim. This sum of money is known as uninsured loss. Moreover, any loss not covered by the comprehensive policy, such as a claim in respect of death or personal injury of the driver, is an uninsured loss.

To summarise the position. If, as a result of negligent driving, A causes physical harm or damage to B, B can sue A in delict and his compensation will be covered by A's compulsory third party insurance. If B has a comprehensive insurance policy, he may elect to claim for his insured losses under the policy, but he is not obliged to do so; he must, of course, sue A for any uninsured losses. If the

1 Road Traffic Act 1988, s 143(a).
2 RTA 1988, s 143(b).

accident was not the result of A's negligence, B cannot sue A; but if B has a comprehensive policy of insurance, he can claim under the policy for insured losses, even if the accident was the result of B's negligence.

Where a person suffers damage as a result of another driver's negligence, if he elects to claim for insured losses under his comprehensive policy of insurance, then the principles of subrogation apply. This means that the insurer 'steps into the shoes' of the insured and is entitled to sue the negligent driver to recover the monies paid out under the comprehensive policy of insurance. In these circumstances, the action is raised in the name of the insured rather than in the name of the insurance company. The defender is cited personally, but again under principles of subrogation, the defender's compulsory third party insurance company will in effect take over the defence if the action has been intimated to them.

In practice, insurers may have inter-office agreements whereby actions do not have to be raised, even if delictual liability is disputed. The insurers accept that they will meet their own outlays under the appropriate insurance policies without attempting to recover these from each other in defended civil proceedings, in order to reduce their overall expenses. However, such agreements, often known as 'knock for knock' agreements, are becoming far less common because insurers are battling to minimise losses. Insurers who previously would have 'confirmed' a knock for knock agreement with the third party insurers are resorting to litigation to recover their outlays under their comprehensive insurance policy in full.

It should be emphasised that whether or not a comprehensive insurer confirms a 'knock for knock' agreement with a negligent driver's third party insurer, this does not affect the insured driver's right to sue the negligent driver personally in delict to recover his uninsured losses. If he is successful, he is entitled to look to the defender's compulsory third party insurer for any sums not recovered from the defender which are due under the decree, provided appropriate intimation of the action has been made to the insurance company.

An insurance company may be entitled under general principles of contract to refuse to indemnify the insured losses. This could arise, for example, if the insured was in material breach of the terms of the policy of insurance by not paying the premiums, or if the policy could be rescinded by the insurance company on the ground of misrepresentation. However, where a pursuer successfully obtains decree against a negligent driver and seeks to recover his compensation from the defender's compulsory third party insurer, under the Road Traffic Act 1988 the insurance company cannot refuse payment on the ground that under general principles of contract it is not bound to indemnify the insured defender, unless the insurance company takes steps to obtain a declarator from the court that it is entitled to avoid the policy.

Similarly, should a driver cancel a compulsory third party liability policy of insurance, the insurer remains liable for any losses suffered by a third party in a subsequent accident caused by the negligence of the driver, provided the contract has not been rescinded. The insurance company can then recover its outlays from the 'former' insured driver. In these circumstances, the insurer is known as a 'Road Traffic Act insurer'. However, the Road Traffic Act insurer will escape liability if the company does not retain an insurable interest in the vehicle. This would occur, for example, if the 'former' insured driver sold the car with the actual policy document in the glove compartment!

Motor Insurers Bureau

The legislation requiring owners of vehicles to have third party liability insurance was clearly designed to protect third parties. Such protection is not afforded where an individual flouts the law and drives a vehicle without appropriate insurance cover, although, of course, it is possible in these circumstances that the defender will have sufficient assets to meet a successful action for reparation.

In order to protect third parties in this situation, a body called the Motor Insurers Bureau (MIB) entered into an agreement with the Ministry of Transport on 17 June 1946 to provide from 1 July 1946 compensation for victims of road accidents where the injured parties were unable to obtain compensation due to the defender's lack of appropriate third party insurance. There have been various revised agreements since then, but the present text covering accidents on or after 31 December 1988 provides compensation for victims of those accidents in respect of both death and personal injuries, and property damage. The December 1988 Agreement followed an EEC Directive[1] on motor insurance

---

1 Second Council Directive 84/5, OJ L8 11.1.84 p 17. This Directive has been held not to be directly effective: *Evans v Motor Insurers Bureau* [1999] Lloyd's Rep IR 30.

requiring member states to extend third party insurance to include property damage.

Clause 2 of the agreement provides that the MIB will 'pay or satisfy or cause to be satisfied to or to the satisfaction of the person or persons in whose favour the judgment was given' any sum due under the decree or judgment which remains unsatisfied for a period of seven days from the time at which the decree or judgment should have been in force. The MIB's liability includes any element of interest or expenses included in the decree.

This obligation is, however, subject to certain conditions, the most important being that notification of the commencement of the proceedings must be given to the MIB before, or within seven days after, the commencement of the proceedings. The claimant must take all reasonable steps to obtain judgment or decree against all those liable for the personal injury, death or property damage, and against any principal where such a person is a servant or agent. Additionally, the MIB will have no liability where the claim is in respect of damage to a motor vehicle where the claimant knew or ought to have reasonably known that at the time of the use of the vehicle it was not properly insured in terms of the Road Traffic Act 1988.

Similarly, where the claim is in respect of personal injury, the MIB has no liability where the claimant was a passenger in or on a vehicle which he knew or should reasonably have known was not insured in terms of the Road Traffic Act 1988, although this exception applies only where the decree the MIB is being asked to satisfy is obtained against the owner or person using the vehicle in which the claimant was a passenger. The MIB has no liability if the accident does not take place on a road or highway to which the public has access.[1]

The MIB's liability in respect of property claims is limited by the fact that there is currently a £175 excess payable, ie the first £175 is not paid. The Bureau's maximum liability is £250,000. The MIB is only required to compensate for damage which is required to be insured against by law, ie under compulsory third party insurance.

Where an offending driver cannot be traced, this agreement is of no effect. However, a sister agreement, referred to as 'the MIB untraced drivers' agreement' then comes into play. Amongst other variations, it should be noted that this scheme differs from the

---

1 *Clarke v Kato* [1998] 4 All ER 417, [1998] 1 WLR 1697, HL (MIB not liable where accident took place in a car park).

foregoing by excluding claims for property damage. Moreover, it covers only claims for death or personal injuries as a result of accidents on or after May 1969.[1] There have been a number of revised agreements: the latest, the fourth agreement, operates in respect of accidents on or after 1 July 1996.

1 The Second Council Directive 84/5 does not cover the circumstances where the driver cannot be traced.

CHAPTER 15

Defamation and verbal injury

A. INTRODUCTION

The law has long recognised a person's interest in her honour and reputation. Accordingly, where A makes a false statement about B with the intention of harming B's honour or reputation, then B has a delictual action against A. In Roman law, there was a specific remedy, the *actio injuriarum*, which provided compensation (solatium) for insult (*contumelia*). In order to succeed, it had to be established that a false statement was made with the intention of insulting the victim. It followed, therefore, that the action lay even if the statement had only been made to the victim herself, ie where the statement had not been made to a third party. If the statement had been published to a third party and, as a result, the victim suffered economic (patrimonial) loss, in the later Roman Empire such loss could, in theory at least, be recovered under general principles of *culpa*: *damnum injuria datum*. Accordingly, where intention to insult could not be established, but the statement was made carelessly to a third party, the only damages that could be obtained were for patrimonial loss: but, if intention to insult could be established, solatium would also be available under the *actio injuriarum*.

Given the influence of Roman law, Scots law could have developed a simple set of principles:

(1) if A makes an untrue statement about B to B, with the intention of insulting B, then B can sue A for solatium even if the statement is not published to a third party, provided intention to insult can be proved;

(2) if A makes an untrue statement about B to C, then B could recover damages for patrimonial loss on the basis of *culpa* but only obtain solatium if intention to insult could also be established.

But since *culpa* covers both intentional and unintentional, but careless, conduct, the fact that the remedies were originally based on two separate, if related, principles, ie *culpa* and the *actio injuriarum*, was overlooked.[1] Moreover, the law in this area was influenced by the English law of libel and slander, with its emphasis on the defendant's malice. As a result, the Scots law of defamation and verbal injury is complex and contentious, and it is difficult to reconcile all the authorities.

The modern law appears to proceed on two major delicts: defamation and verbal injury. These will be considered in turn.

B. DEFAMATION

Defamation is the delict which is committed when a person makes an injurious and false imputation against the character or reputation of another person. The victim is usually a natural person but could be a trading company,[2] partnership or voluntary association. However, since legal persons such as companies have no feelings, they can only recover for patrimonial loss and not solatium. Because, by statute, it does not have corporate status, a trade union cannot sue.[3] A local authority also cannot sue,[4] but if individuals (for example, councillors) are defamed by attacks on a council, they can sue in their own right. Where a person has died, the executor can continue any action raised by the deceased before his death and recover both solatium and patrimonial loss. If no action has been raised by the deceased, the executor can raise an action but can only recover any patrimonial loss to the estate incurred before the death.[5] These rules are not affected by the Damages (Scotland) Act 1976.[6]

1 For discussion of the confusion, see T B Smith *A Short Commentary on the Law of Scotland* (1962, Greens) pp 724–732.
2 *Incorporation of Fleshers of Dumfries v Rankine* Dec 10 1816 FC. If the individual board members are also defamed, they can sue in their own right. If the defamation is actually of the individuals, the company cannot sue.
3 Trade Union and Labour Relations (Consolidation) Act 1992, s 10(1); *Electrical, Electronic, Telecommunication and Plumbing Union v Times Newspapers Ltd* [1980] QB 585, [1980] 1 All ER 1097.
4 *Derbyshire County Council v Times Newspapers Ltd* [1993] AC 534, [1993] 1 All ER 1011, HL. Similarly, the government cannot sue qua government; cf individual ministers. This principle has been extended to political parties: *Goldsmith v Bhoyrul* [1998] QB 459, [1997] 4 All ER 268, QBD.
5 Ie the executor cannot recover solatium. See generally *Neilson v Rodger* (1853) 16 D 325; *Auld v Shairp* (1874) 2 R 191; *Smith v Duncan Stewart & Co Ltd (No 2)* 1961 SC 91, 1961 SLT 67.
6 Damages (Scotland) Act 1976, s 2(4) as substituted by s 3 of the Damages (Scotland) Act 1993. On the 1976 Act generally, see pp 227 ff above.

For an action to be successful, it must be shown that the defender made a false statement which was defamatory of the pursuer, with the intention to harm the pursuer's character or reputation. However, and this is very important, if the pursuer proves that the statement concerned the pursuer (a question of fact) and is defamatory (a question of law), then the court presumes that the statement is false and was made with the intention to harm him. The onus thereafter lies on the *defender* to prove either that the statement was true (*veritas*) or that it was made without the intention to harm the pursuer. Moreover, the law will also presume that a person will be upset if defamed and it is therefore not necessary for the pursuer to prove loss in respect of insult (solatium); but if patrimonial loss is also claimed, such loss has to be established by the pursuer.

(1) The false statement

The pursuer must establish that the defender made a statement about the pursuer: this is a question of fact. The statement will usually take the form of words, written or spoken. Scots law does not make a distinction betweeen oral and written communication for the purpose of the law of defamation.[1] However, any form of communication can amount to a statement, so that it could consist of a television or radio broadcast, a picture, cartoon or effigy.[2] In Scots law, the statement does not have to be communicated to a third party: it is enough if it is communicated only to the victim himself.[3] In these circumstances, however, only damages for insult (solatium) can be awarded. Before damages for patrimonial loss can be awarded, the statement must have been published to third parties.[4] If a defamatory statement is repeated, every person who repeats the statement commits a separate delict. So, for example, if A makes a defamatory statement about B to a newspaper reporter, who repeats it to his editor, who publishes it in his newspaper, then the editor and the reporter, as well as A, are liable to B in delict.[5]

---

1 In English law such a distinction is made: oral communication constitutes slander; written communication constitutes libel.

2 In *Monson v Tussauds Ltd* [1894] 1 QB 671, CA, placing a waxworks effigy of the plaintiff (who had been acquitted of murder) in the Chamber of Horrors along with convicted murderers constituted a slanderous statement.

3 *Ramsay v Mackay* (1890) 18 R 130.

4 If the pursuer published the statement to a third party, he is personally barred from claiming patrimonial loss: *Will v Sneddon, Campbell and Munro* 1931 SC 164, 1931 SLT 125.

5 See, for example, *Carroll v British Broadcasting Corpn* 1997 SLT (Sh Ct) 23.

It should be emphasised that once the pursuer has established that a defamatory statement was made by the defender, the law *presumes* that the statement is false. The onus then lies on the defender to show that the facts in the statement were true (*veritas*). But before the pursuer has the benefit of this presumption, the statement must be defamatory. It is to that concept that we now turn.

(2) Defamatory nature of the statement

A defamatory statement is one which 'tends to lower [the pursuer] in the estimation of right thinking members of society generally'.[1] Although it is settled that some types of statement are clearly defamatory, the categories of defamation – like the categories of negligence[2] – are never closed. The question whether or not a statement is defamatory is one of law, to be decided by the court.[3] The test is objective, ie whether the reasonable person would decide that this type of statement was defamatory. The statement must be read in the context of the publication as a whole.[4]

The meaning of the material is that which an ordinary, reasonable, fair-minded reader would infer from the language, not what the author intended the statement to mean.[5] It is the general view of society as a whole which is important, not the views of the section of society in which the pursuer moves. However, as the mores of society change, what might once have been regarded as derogatory by right-thinking members of society in the past, may not be so regarded by them today. Thus, for example, in 1934 it was thought to be defamatory falsely to state that a woman had been the victim of rape.[6] That might not be regarded as defamatory

---

1 *Sim v Stretch* [1936] 2 All ER 1237, HL, at 1240 per Lord Atkin.
2 *Donoghue v Stevenson* 1932 SC (HL) 31 at 70 per Lord MacMillan; see p 62 above.
3 Accordingly, the defence can make a plea to the relevancy of the issue.
4 *Charleston v News Group Newspapers Ltd* [1995] 2 AC 65, [1995] 2 All ER 313, HL (defendant published pornographic photograph superimposing the plaintiffs' heads on the bodies: accompanying article explained that the plaintiffs had been victims of an illicit computer game. The meaning of the material had to be determined on the basis that the reasonable person would have read the article and not simply looked at the photograph and headlines). See also *Norman v Future Publishing Ltd* [1999] EMLR 325; *McCann v Scottish Media Newspapers Ltd* 1999 GWD 10-473.
5 *Charleston v News Group Newspapers Ltd* [1995] 2 AC 65, [1995] 2 All ER 313, HL; *McCann v Scottish Media Newspapers Ltd* 1999 GWD 10-473.
6 *Youssoupoff v Metro-Goldwyn-Mayer Pictures Ltd* (1934) 50 TLR 581, CA.

today, when victims of rape are treated with sympathy rather than shunned.

The following are examples of defamatory statements, but it must always be remembered that these are only examples and that other types of defamatory statements may arise.

(a) Imputations on moral character

It is defamatory to undermine a person's moral character. Thus it is defamatory to call a woman a prostitute or an adulteress or even to suggest that she lacks 'proper womanly delicacy'.[1] At one time it was clearly defamatory to state that a person was homosexual.[2] However, with the increasing tolerance of homosexuality, it has been observed judicially that an allegation of homosexuality should no longer be regarded as defamatory per se.[3] Nevertheless, allegations that a nun was dishonest, unchaste and a lesbian have been held to be capable of amounting to defamation.[4]

Defamatory statements are not restricted to imputations on sexual morality. Thus it is defamatory to call a person a hypocrite.[5] It appears no longer to be defamatory merely to call a person a liar or a 'stranger to the truth':[6] but to call a person a thief and a liar has been held to be defamatory.[7] To state that a woman whose child had died was a heartless and uncaring mother is defamatory.[8]

(b) Imputations of criminality

It is defamatory to accuse a person of a serious crime which ordinary people do not commit or condone, such as murder[9] or theft.[10] It would not perhaps be defamatory to accuse a person of careless driving (or tax evasion?). If the defender pleads *veritas*, he can rely

---

1 *Cuthbert v Linklater* 1935 SLT 94. But would this be regarded as defamatory today?
2 *AB v XY* 1917 SC 15, 1916 2 SLT 210; *Kerr v Kennedy* [1942] 1 KB 409, [1942] 1 All ER 412.
3 *Quilty v Windsor* 1999 SLT 346.
4 *Prophit v British Broadcasting Corpn* 1997 SLT 745, OH.
5 *Stein v Beaverbrook Newspapers Ltd* 1968 SC 272, 1968 SLT 401.
6 *Carroll v British Broadcasting Corpn* 1997 SLT (Sh Ct) 23. Cf *Watson v Duncan* (1890) 17 R 404.
7 *Gilbert v Yorston* 1996 SCLR 1122, 1997 SLT 879, OH.
8 *McCabe v News Group Newspapers Ltd* 1992 SLT 707, OH.
9 *Waddell v British Broadcasting Corpn* 1973 SLT 246.
10 *Sutherland v British Telecommunications plc* 1989 SLT 531.

on the fact that the pursuer committed such a crime even if the offence is 'spent' under the Rehabilitation of Offenders Act 1974.[1] Similarly, it is defamatory to say that a person should be in jail, since this implies that he is guilty of a crime.

(c) Imputations against competence or conduct

Statements which disparage a person's professional competence or conduct are defamatory, for example, to accuse a doctor of gross professional negligence[2] or a professor of his inability to teach[3] (or write textbooks on delict?). Allegations of conduct which is unprofessional in the circumstances are also defamatory, for example, to accuse a solicitor of conducting a case for his own – as opposed to his client's – interests,[4] or to allege that a prison warden had sexual relations with a prisoner.[5]

(d) Imputations of financial unsoundness

It is defamatory falsely to allege that a person is insolvent[6] or is unwilling[7] or unable to pay his debts.[8]

(e) Disparaging public character

Persons who enter public life are expected to be able to withstand a degree of criticism[9] – or even ridicule[10] – in respect of the way in which they carry out their public duties. However, although the test may be stricter, allegations of, for example, dishonesty in carrying out a public office would, it is thought, constitute defamation. Statements undermining a public figure's sexual morality, ie concerned with his private as opposed to public life, are, of course,

---

1 Rehabilitation of Offenders Act 1974, s 4.
2 *Simmers v Morton* (1900) 8 SLT 285, OH.
3 *Auld v Shairp* (1875) 2 R 940.
4 *McRostie v Ironside* (1849) 12 D 74.
5 *Winter v News Scotland Ltd* 1991 SLT 828.
6 *AB v CD* (1904) 7 F 72.
7 *Outram v Reid* (1852) 14 D 577.
8 *Mazure v Stubbs Ltd* 1919 SC (HL) 112, 1919 2 SLT 160.
9 *Mutch v Robertson* 1981 SLT 217.
10 *McLaughlan v Orr Pollock & Co* (1894) 22 R 38 at 42 per Lord McLaren; *Brooks v Lind* 1997 Rep LR 83, 1997 GWD 13-570 (pursuer was said to be part of council 'mafia', and a joint venture he was involved in was described as 'sheer lunacy and gross administration': held not to be defamatory).

defamatory. In England, it has been held to be potentially defamatory to call a famous actor 'hideously ugly': this could lead an ordinary person to infer that he was repulsive, and consequently lower him in the public's estimation and make him an object of ridicule.[1]

(f) Imputations on health

It is defamatory falsely to allege that a person is insane or has obnoxious physical defects or is suffering from certain illnesses, such as venereal disease or AIDS.

A statement or action may appear to be harmless, yet when taken in the context of the facts and circumstances in which it was made, a defamatory meaning may be inferred. For example, it is not prima facie defamatory to display a wax effigy of a person in a waxworks: but to put it in the Chamber of Horrors along with those of convicted murderers implies that the person concerned is also a murderer.[2] Similarly, to announce the birth of twins to a married couple in a newspaper appears innocuous, until it is appreciated that they married only a month before, thus implying pre-marital sexual intercourse.[3] In this situation, Scots law allows a pursuer to plead the facts and circumstances from which the defamatory meaning of the statement or act can be drawn. This is known as 'the doctrine of innuendo'.

The onus rests on the pursuer to state the meaning of the acts or statement in the light of the relevant facts and circumstances. Thus, in *Cuthbert v Linklater*[4] the pursuer argued that the defender, an author, had defamed her when a female character in his novel took a Union Jack from Edinburgh Castle and placed it in a men's public urinal. An ardent Scottish nationalist, the pursuer had in fact taken a Union Jack from Stirling Castle and had tossed it at a guard. Consequently, by innuendo, a reasonable reader would assume that the character in the novel was meant to be her and that she was capable of acting indelicately. The court accepted the argument.[5]

1 *Berkoff v Burchill* [1996] 4 All ER 1008, [1997] EMLR 139, CA.
2 *Monson v Tussauds Ltd* [1894] 1 QB 671, CA.
3 *Morrison v Ritchie & Co* (1902) 4 F 645.
4 1935 SLT 94.
5 See also *Wragg v DC Thomson & Co Ltd* 1909 2 SLT 315, where a newspaper published an article that a certain George Reeves had shot his wife twice and then killed himself. The paper omitted to mention that the incident took place in the USA. At the time it was published, George Reeves, a famous music hall artiste, was appearing in Glasgow. The court held that there was an innuendo that the incident referred to him.

The test on whether an innuendo can be inferred is that of the ordinary reasonable person,[1] ie whether a reasonable person would regard the words as offensive if placed in the same position as the pursuer. The question whether the statement or act *plus* the innuendo placed upon them by the reasonable person amount to defamation is a matter of law to be decided by the court. It is a question of fact whether the statement or act was taken as having a defamatory meaning by those to whom it was actually communicated.

(3) Intention to harm the pursuer

Once it has been established that a statement is defamatory, not only is it presumed to be false but it is also presumed that the statement was made with the intention of harming the particular pursuer (malice). A defender can rebut the presumption of falsehood by pleading *veritas*, ie that the statement was in fact true.[2] The question then arises whether or not the defender can rebut the presumption of malice by proving that he did not intend to harm the particular pursuer.

Authority suggests that the presumption of intention to harm cannot be rebutted. In *Hulton (E) & Co v Jones*,[3] a newspaper published an article about an apparently fictitious character, Artemus Jones. This article contained material which would have been defamatory if Artemus Jones was an actual person. However, there was a 'real' Artemus Jones who sued the newspaper. The defence was that since the newspaper did not know of the existence of the plaintiff, it could not have intended to defame him. The House of Lords rejected this defence.

Although *Hulton v Jones* was an English case, Scots law appears to be similar. In *Outram v Reid*,[4] a newspaper published a list of bankruptcies including 'John Reid, wine and spirit merchant, Glasgow'. There were two John Reids who were wine and spirit merchants in Glasgow, one of whom was indeed bankrupt, while the other was solvent. The latter successfully sued in defamation, even though the defender was not aware of his existence. Similarly, the unfortunate couple, the birth of whose twins was prematurely

1 *Duncan v Associated Scottish Newspapers Ltd* 1929 SC 14 at 21 per Lord Anderson.
2 On *veritas*, see pp 252–253 below.
3 [1910] AC 20.
4 (1852) 14 D 577.

announced, sued successfully in spite of the fact that the defender did not know of their existence nor had intended any harm.[1] And Mr Reeves was also able to sue, even though the story concerned another Mr Reeves who lived in America.[2]

Although the issue appears to be settled, it is the present writer's view that the solution adopted by the courts is unprincipled. Instead, the courts should have accepted that the defender did not have the intention to insult the pursuers in these cases and accordingly no damages should have been awarded for solatium. However, as is clear from the Scottish decisions, there was an element of fault on the part of the defenders in publishing the statements. In *Outram v Reid*,[3] for example, the defender omitted the address of the bankrupt Mr Reid, which had been published in the Official Gazette: if it had been published in the newspaper, the confusion would have been avoided. Again, in *Morrison v Ritchie & Co*,[4] the defender was criticised by the court for failing to check that the facts in the announcement were accurate.

Given that it is (at least) arguable that the defenders were at fault in these cases, the pursuers were entitled to damages for patrimonial loss on general principles of *culpa* but not solatium. They would also have had to establish patrimonial loss, which would have been difficult in *Morrison*. But until the issue is reconsidered by the Inner House, it must be accepted that the presumption of intention to insult is now irrebuttable and solatium, as well as patrimonial loss, can be recovered in these circumstances.

It is unlikely, however, that the matter will be litigated. Section 4 of the Defamation Act 1952 provides a statutory defence which could cover the situations discussed above. Where there has been an innocent publication,[5] the publisher can make an offer of amends. If the offer is accepted, that is the end of the matter. If it is not accepted, then there is a defence that the offer was made as soon as it was practicable to do so and that it has not been withdrawn. If, however, the statement published was not written by the

---

1 *Morrison v Ritchie & Co* (1902) 4 F 645.
2 *Wragg v DC Thomson & Co Ltd* 1909 2 SLT 315.
3 (1852) 14 D 577.
4 (1902) 4 F 645.
5 Ie which the publisher did not intend to refer to the pursuer expressly or by innuendo and in either case took reasonable care in relation to the publication: Defamation Act 1952, s 4(5). The reasonable care provision might not have been satisfied in the cases we have discussed.

publisher, the defence is only available if the words written by the original author were without malice.

Under the Defamation Act 1996,[1] an offer of amends can be made even if the statement was not innocent. The offer must contain a correction and apology which can then be published: it should also provide for compensation.[2] Once the offer is accepted, the aggrieved party can no longer sue for defamation but can enforce the offer by proceedings in court.[3] The court can award conpensation if this has not been agreed by the parties.[4]

If an offer of amends is made but not accepted by the aggrieved party, this is a defence in any subsequent action for defamation.[5] But this defence is not available if the defender knew or had reason to believe that the statement referred to the aggrieved party *and* was false and defamatory of the pursuer: however, it is presumed until the contrary is shown that the defender did not know and had no reason to believe that was so.[6]

At the time of writing, this procedure has not been brought into force: when it is, s 4 of the Defamation Act 1952 will be repealed.

(4) Defences

(a) Veritas

As we have seen, if a statement is defamatory, the law presumes that it is false. This presumption can be rebutted. The onus lies on the defender to prove that the statement was true.[7] If truth (*veritas*) is established, this is a complete defence. What is necessary to establish *veritas* will depend on the nature of the defamatory statement. To allege that someone is a murderer can be justified by proof of one act of murder; but to say someone is a thief implies that he is currently dishonest and *veritas* is not established simply by showing he was twice convicted of petty theft 23 years before.[8] A similar approach is taken in respect of immorality: to allege that a 50-year-old man is homosexual would not be justified by

---

1 Defamation Act 1996, ss 2–4.
2 DeA 1996, s 2(4).
3 DeA 1996, ss 3(2) and (3).
4 DeA 1996, s 3(5).
5 DeA 1996, s 4(2).
6 DeA 1996, s 4(3).
7 *Baigent v British Broadcasting Corpn* 1999 GWD 10-474.
8 *Fletcher v Wilsons* (1885) 12 R 683.

establishing that he engaged in homosexual acts with the captain of the First XV, when he was a schoolboy.[1]

If more than one fact is alleged, *veritas* will operate only if all the facts which are defamatory are proved true.[2] Conversely, if some non-defamatory facts are admitted to be false, then the defence will still succeed if the defamatory facts can, nevertheless, be shown to be true.[3] By s 5 of the Defamation Act 1952 it is provided that:

'in an action for defamation in respect of words containing two or more distinct charges against a pursuer, a defence of *veritas* shall not fail by reason only that the truth of every charge is not proved if the words not proved to be true do not materially injure the pursuer's reputation having regard to the truth of the remaining charges.'

If, however, the allegations are not separable but are part and parcel of a single defamatory allegation, the section does not apply.

(b) In rixa

Statements made *in rixa*, ie during a quarrel, an argument or a brawl, do not give rise to an action in defamation unless the pursuer can prove that they were made with intent to injure.[4] The defence is more likely to succeed if the defender has apologised. It is *not* a defence that the statement was made as a joke.[5]

(c) Vulgar abuse

If the words used amount to mere vulgar abuse, then no action in defamation lies. To call someone a 'bitch' or a 'dickhead' is not actionable, since it is not meant to be taken seriously.

---

1 Assuming, of course, that it is still defamatory to allege that a person is homosexual. On allegations of immorality, see *Brownlie v Thomson* (1859) 21 D 480 at 483 per Lord Murray.
2 *Fairbairn v Scottish National Party* 1979 SC 393, 1980 SLT 149.
3 *Sutherland v Stopes* [1925] AC 47, HL.
4 *Christie v Robertson* (1899) 1 F 1155; *Carroll v British Broadcasting Corpn* 1997 SLT (Sh Ct) 23.
5 *Prophit v British Broadcasting Corpn* 1997 SLT 745.

(d) Fair retort

If A makes a statement about B, B is entitled to the opportunity to reply. If B's retort is defamatory, it is not actionable unless A can prove that it was said with intent to injure.[1]

(e) Fair comment

Where a defamatory remark takes the form of an opinion, for example that a novel is badly written or an actor gave a bad performance, the defender can plead the defence of fair comment. In order to succeed, the defender must prove: (1) that the statement is a comment on fact or facts; (2) that the facts upon which the comment is made are true;[2] and (3) that the facts concern some matter of public interest. If this can be proved, the onus shifts to the pursuer to show that the comment was made with the intention of harming the pursuer. The comment must be honestly made and relevant to the facts upon which it was based. Thus, a theatre critic who criticises a play, must honestly hold the opinion that the play is bad[3] and must restrict his comments to the play rather than the playwright.[4]

(f) Privilege

A person who makes a defamatory statement may have the defence of privilege. In certain situations, public policy demands that a person should be free to speak without fear of litigation on the grounds of defamation. There are two forms of privilege: absolute privilege and qualified privilege.

(i) Absolute privilege. Where a statement is protected by absolute privilege, it cannot form the basis of an action for defamation or verbal injury.[5] It does not matter that the statement is

---

1 *Gray v Scottish Society for the Prevention of Cruelty to Animals* (1890) 17 R 1185; *Carroll v British Broadcasting Corpn* 1997 SLT (Sh Ct) 23.
2 Where the statement contains facts and opinion, the defence of fair comment is not lost if the facts upon which the opinion is based are true even if other facts are false: Defamation Act 1952, s 6.
3 *Turner v Metro-Goldwyn-Mayer Pictures Ltd* [1950] 1 All ER 449, [1950] WN 83, HL; *Telnikoff v Matusevitch* [1992] 2 AC 343, [1991] 4 All ER 817, HL.
4 *Merivale v Carson* (1887) 20 QBD 275, CA.
5 On verbal injury, see pp 259 ff below.

defamatory or was made with the intention to harm the victim (malice). The following situations are covered by absolute privilege:

(a) Statements made in the Westminster Parliament. Any statement made in the Westminster Parliament has the protection of absolute privilege. This includes statements made in parliamentary committees. The statement does not have to be relevant to the proceedings. It is not restricted to statements made by members of either House: it would include, for example, a statement made by a witness giving evidence to a Select Committee. It does not extend to statements made by members of Parliament outside the Houses. Where the conduct of a person in or in relation to proceedings in the Westminster Parliament is in issue in defamation proceedings, that person can waive, for the purpose of the defamation action, the privilege that prevents proceedings in Parliament from being impeached or questioned in court.[1] This is to enable an MP, for example, to rely on his own conduct in Parliament in order to pursue an action of defamation while, of course, retaining the defence of absolute privilege for statements he has made in Parliament!

(b) Statements made in judicial proceedings. A statement made by a judge in the course of judicial proceedings is protected by absolute privilege even if it was made maliciously.[2] However, the statement must be made while the judge is acting judicially, ie it must be relevant to the case which is subject to the proceedings.[3] Advocates or solicitors pleading the case also enjoy absolute privilege,[4] provided the statement is relevant to the case. Witnesses giving evidence have absolute privilege as long as the evidence is pertinent to the case.[5] Any findings of fact by a jury are subject to absolute privilege. But parties to a civil action do not enjoy absolute privilege – only qualified privilege.[6] Absolute privilege extends in like way to the participants in quasi-judicial proceedings or tribunals, for example, courts martial, public inquiries, arbitrations, children's hearings, industrial tribunals etc.

1 Defamation Act 1996, s 13.
2 *Haggart's Trustees v Lord President Hope* (1824) 2 Sh App 125, HL; *Primrose v Waterston* (1902) 4 F 783, 10 SLT 37.
3 *Watt v Thomson* (1870) 8 M (HL) 77.
4 *Rome v Watson* (1898) 25 R 733, 5 SLT 377. The privilege extends to written pleadings.
5 *Watson v McEwan* (1905) 7 F (HL) 109. This privilege extends to statements made in precognitions: *B v Burns* 1994 SLT 250.
6 See p 257 below.

(c) Reports authorised by the Westminster Parliament. Reports of proceedings and papers etc published by or under the authority of either House of Parliament attract absolute privilege.[1] Fair and accurate reports of proceedings before a court are absolutely privileged, provided they are published contemporaneously with the proceedings.[2]

(d) Any statement made in proceedings of the Scottish Parliament and any publication of any such statement authorised by the Scottish Parliament are absolutely privileged.[3]

(e) Miscellaneous. The Lord Advocate is absolutely privileged in respect of what he does in relation to prosecutions on indictment. This protection extends to procurators fiscal and Advocates Depute acting on the Lord Advocate's instructions. Ministers of the Crown are also protected, provided the statement is made in the proper exercise of their functions. Reports of the various ombudsmen are also absolutely privileged.

(ii) Qualified privilege. When a statement is protected by qualified privilege, the defender is assumed to have acted in good faith and an action of defamation or verbal injury[4] will not succeed unless the pursuer can show that the statement was made with the intention of harming the pursuer (ie with malice). Qualified privilege arises in the following circumstances:

(a) Duty or interest to speak. Where a person has a legal duty to speak, the statement is protected by qualified privilege. The protection extends to situations where there is a moral or social duty to speak, for example, to report a crime or inform a reporter to a children's hearing of child abuse. Complaints to the chief constable about the conduct of police officers attracts protection if an action of defamation is brought against the complainer by the officer who was the subject of the complaint.[5] Similarly, a letter to the deputy chief executive of the prison service about the unfitness of an employee to serve as an officer, has been held to attract

---

1 Parliamentary Papers Act 1840.
2 Defamation Act 1996, s 14. Courts include any court in the United Kingdom, the European Court of Justice, the European Court of Human Rights and United Nations' international criminal tribunals.
3 Scotland Act 1998, s 41.
4 On verbal injury, see pp 259 ff below.
5 *Fraser v Mirza* 1993 SC (HL) 27, 1993 SLT 527.

qualified privilege.[1] A person who gives a reference enjoys qualified privilege.[2] Whether a situation involves a duty to speak which attracts qualified privilege is a question of law to be determined by a court. So, for example, when an employer sent a letter to the Department of Health stating that the plaintiff should be placed on an index of persons unsuitable for work with children, qualified privilege did not attach to the employer's letter.[3] Defamatory statements made to the British Broadcasting Corporation are not protected by qualified privilege, since the BBC is no different from other media organisations.[4] Qualified privilege also arises where a person has an interest to speak, for example, replying to criticism.[5] In these situations, the person who receives the statement must have a reciprocal interest in the information. So, for example, a complaint about the conduct of a police officer is protected by qualified privilege if made to the relevant chief constable but not if made to a newspaper editor.

(b) Reports of proceedings in Parliament in the press or other media attract only qualified privilege. The position is the same in respect of reports of judicial and other quasi-judicial proceedings.[6]

(c) Parties to a civil action enjoy only qualified privilege in respect of statements made in civil proceedings. If, however, the pursuer can prove that the statement was made with the intention of harming the pursuer (ie maliciously) then an action for defamation or verbal injury may lie.[7] This delict is often called 'judicial slander'.

(d) Under the Defamation Act 1996,[8] the publication of certain types of reports is subject to qualified privilege.

1 *Quilty v Windsor* 1999 SLT 346. In *Pearson v Educational Institute of Scotland* 1997 SC 245, 1998 SLT 189, a report on the competency of the pursuer to be head of a college, which the union had sent on to a government department, was held to attract qualified privilege.
2 *Farquhar v Neish* (1890) 17 R 716. However, even if not made maliciously, the writer of the reference may be liable in negligence: *Spring v Guardian Assurance plc* [1995] 2 AC 296, [1994] 3 All ER 129, HL, discussed at p 87 above.
3 *S v Newham London Borough Council* [1998] 1 FLR 1061, [1998] 3 FCR 277, CA.
4 *Baigent v McCulloch* 1998 SLT 780, OH.
5 *Campbell v Cochrane* (1905) 8 F 205; *Carroll v British Broadcasting Corpn* 1997 SLT (Sh Ct) 23.
6 *Richardson v Wilson* (1879) 7 R 237, 17 SLR 122; *Cunningham v Scotsman Publications Ltd* 1987 SC 107, 1987 SCLR 314, OH.
7 *Williamson v Umphray and Robertson* (1890) 17 R 905, 27 SLR 742.
8 Defamation Act 1996, s 15 and Sch 1. Detailed treatment is outwith the scope of the present text.

(g) Responsibility of publication

By s 1 of the Defamation Act 1996, a person has a defence to an action of defamation if he can show that: (i) he was not the author, editor or publisher of the defamatory statement; (ii) he took reasonable care in relation to its publication; and (iii) he did not know and had no reason to believe that what he did caused or contributed to the publication of a defamatory statement. The defence is designed to protect persons concerned with printing, processing, producing, distributing or selling newspapers, books, films, CDs, software etc which contain the defamatory material.

As we have seen, where a statement is subject to qualified privilege, it can be the subject of an action of defamation or verbal injury[1] if the pursuer acted maliciously. In the present writer's view, this simply means that the defender intended to harm or insult the pursuer, although it has been contended that it is sufficient to show that the defender was not motivated by duty or interest. But if that were so, at least in the case of duty or interest to speak, qualified privilege would not attach in the first place. However, as the authorities stand,[2] malice can be established if it can be shown that the defender abused the privileged occasion – as well as proving that he intended to injure the pursuer. Nevertheless, proof of malice is difficult.[3] It may be inferred from extreme language, a previous personal vendetta between the parties or the fact that the defender did not believe that the statement was true.[4] It is not enough simply to establish that the statement was defamatory.[5]

(5) Damages

In an action for defamation and verbal injury,[6] the pursuer is entitled to solatium in respect of insult and hurt feelings sustained, and compensation for any patrimonial loss. Where the case is one of defamation, insult is presumed, but any patrimonial loss must be averred and proved. Although patrimonial loss, if it has been sustained, is relatively easy to assess, solatium is more difficult

---

1 See pp 259 ff below.
2 See especially *Fraser v Mirza* 1993 SC (HL) 27, 1993 SLT 527 at 531 per Lord Keith of Kinkel.
3 For an example of the difficulties, see *Fraser v Mirza* 1993 SC (HL) 27, 1993 SLT 527.
4 *Horrocks v Lowe* [1975] AC 135, [1974] 1 All ER 662, HL.
5 *Adam v Jackson* [1917] AC 309.
6 On verbal injury, see pp 259 ff below.

because it involves no little degree of speculation. In practice, solatium is usually a modest sum in Scots law.[1] Everyone is assumed to be of good character, so solatium is unlikely to be increased if the pursuer is particularly good. But the more eminent the pursuer, the greater the loss of reputation, and, consequently, more will be awarded by way of solatium. In general, the worse the allegation, the greater the sum that will be awarded; in particular, the sum may be increased if the defender has persisted in the defamatory allegations against the pursuer.[2] However, at the end of the day, solatium is intended to compensate loss:[3] a person who brings an action primarily to clear his name will only receive a nominal sum.[4]

An award of solatium can be mitigated as a result of a number of factors. First, if the pursuer's character or reputation is already tainted before the defamatory statement, evidence can be led by the defender to show that the pursuer did not therefore suffer as much as an ordinary person.[5] An immediate retraction of the statement and an apology will mitigate the loss.[6] This will also be the case if the pursuer provoked the defender into making the defamatory statement.[7] If the statement has been published by more than one person, the defender can mitigate the damages the pursuer should receive if the pursuer has already received damages in respect of the same words, or words to the same effect, from a third party.[8] So, for example, if A and B defame C using the same words, if C sues A, A can plead mitigation if C has already received damages from B.

C. VERBAL INJURY

Where a statement is made which is not defamatory,[9] the law will not presume that it is false, made with intent to injure, and caused

1 See, for example, *Gilbert v Yorston* 1996 SCLR 1122, 1997 SLT 879, OH (no evidence that any third party believed the defamatory material: no effect on pursuer's career. Pursuer was awarded £1,500 damages for solatium).
2 *Baigent v British Broadcasting Corpn* 1999 GWD 10-474 (awards of £60,000 and £50,000 were made against the BBC: the attack on the pursuers' personal integrity and professional ability was very vindictive).
3 *Stein v Beaverbrook Newspapers Ltd* 1968 SC 272, 1968 SLT 401.
4 *Gilbert v Yorston* 1996 SCLR 1122, 1997 SLT 879, OH.
5 *C v M* 1923 SC 1, 1922 SLT 634.
6 *Morrison v Ritchie & Co* (1902) 4 F 645.
7 *Paul v Jackson* (1884) 11 R 460.
8 Defamation Act 1952, s 12.
9 On the categories of defamatory statements, see pp 246 ff above.

insult to the victim. However, it does not follow that where the non-defamatory statement has undermined a person's character or reputation, that he is without a remedy. Scots law recognises that non-defamatory statements can amount to civil wrongs which are actionable in delict. These are known as verbal injuries.

The most common situation where an action will lie for verbal injury are cases where a non-defamatory statement is made which holds up the pursuer to public hatred, ridicule and contempt. In *Paterson v Welch*,[1] the defender stated that the pursuer had made the comment that if children from the poorer classes were allowed to attend Madras College, this would 'contaminate the genteel children' currently attending that school. To state that a person holds a controversial opinion is not defamatory, ie it does not lower him in the estimation of right-thinking persons. However, the court was prepared to allow the case to proceed as an action for verbal injury provided the pursuer could aver and prove that: (1) the statement was false; (2) the statement was intended to injure the pursuer; and (3) that injury had in fact been sustained by the pursuer.[2] Thus, unlike a case of defamation, where falsity, intention to injure and injury are presumed, in cases of verbal injury, the onus lies on the pursuer to prove these facts.

In *Steele v Scottish Daily Record and Sunday Mail Ltd*[3] the defender made a statement in its newspaper's legal advice and consumer rights page that the pursuer, a car dealer, had acted harshly in refusing to cancel a hire purchase agreement with a customer who had got into financial difficulties. 'Have a heart, that's my message to Motor Dealer, Mr Steele' ran the headline. The statement was not defamatory, since it merely suggested that the pursuer was a hard businessman. Nevertheless, the Inner House held that Steele would have an action if he could prove that the statement was false, that it was intended to harm him and had, in fact, caused him harm. The case failed on the basis that the article was not intended to hold Steele up to public hatred, ridicule and contempt, but had been written to persuade him to give his unfortunate customer a better deal. Therefore, before an action can lie for verbal injury on this ground, the effect of the statement, apart from being false, must have been intended to cause the pursuer to be despised or condemned by ordinary members of the public.[4]

---

1 (1893) 20 R 744.
2 *Paterson v Welch* (1893) 20 R 744 at 749 per the Lord President (Robertson).
3 1970 SLT 53.
4 *Steele v Scottish Daily Record and Sunday Mail Ltd* 1970 SLT 53. See also *Burns v Diamond* (1896) 23 R 507, (1896) 3 SLT 274.

An action for verbal injury will also lie if A makes a false statement about the state of B's property, for example, that B's house is falling down[1] (slander of property). Similarly, an action will lie if A falsely alleges that B does not own property which he wishes to sell[2] (slander of title) or if A falsely states that B's business is not run well[3] (slander of business). To succeed in these situations, B must prove that the statement was false, intended to harm B economically and actually caused B patrimonial loss.[4] Because there is no intention to injure the pursuer's character or reputation, solatium cannot be recovered;[5] in other words, only patrimonial loss can be recovered. Thus, in order to be actionable as a verbal injury, the statement must have been made to a third party.

Finally, an action for verbal injury may lie if A defames B with the intention of harming C. Because C has not been defamed, ie C's reputation has not been directly attacked, C cannot sue A in defamation. However, if C can prove that A's defamatory statement in respect of B was false, was intended to harm C and did harm C, then in principle, C should have an action for verbal injury against A.[6] So, for example, if a person defames a woman by calling her a prostitute, not only can she sue in defamation but her husband could have an action based on verbal injury if he could prove that the statement was false, that it was made to injure him and in fact did so. Unlike his wife's case of defamation, where these three requisites are presumed in her favour, in his action for verbal injury, the onus lies on the husband to establish these facts.

A defender in an action of verbal injury can rely on the same defences that are available in an action of defamation.[7]

D. *CONVICIUM*

It is an essential requirement of defamation and verbal injury that the statement is false. However, some writers argue that Scots law

---

1 *Argyllshire Weavers Ltd v A Macaulay (Tweeds) Ltd* 1965 SLT 21, OH.
2 *Philp v Morton* (1816) Hume 865.
3 *Craig v Inveresk Paper Merchant Ltd* 1970 SLT (Notes) 50, OH.
4 *Argyllshire Weavers Ltd v A Macaulay (Tweeds) Ltd* 1965 SLT 21, OH.
5 Unlike the public hatred, ridicule and contempt cases where, as in defamation, both solatium and patrimonial loss are recoverable. Unlike defamation, insult must be proved before solatium can be obtained.
6 *North of Scotland Banking Co v Duncan* (1857) 19 D 881 at 887 per Lord Deas. Cf *Broom v Ritchie & Co* (1905) 6 F 942, where the distinction between defamation and verbal injury was not clearly drawn.
7 Discussed at pp 252 ff above.

recognises another form of verbal injury, *convicium*, where *veritas* is no defence.[1] *Convicium* involves holding the pursuer up to public hatred, ridicule and contempt, and in so far as it ever had an independent existence in Scots law, it has now, it is submitted, been overtaken by the genus delict of verbal injury where the statement has to be false before it is actionable.[2]

In the present writer's view, it is too late for the courts to revive this delict, particularly since it could undermine freedom of speech, given that *veritas* is no defence. Instead, the legislature must give consideration to whether it is desirable to introduce a statutory remedy for unwarranted intrusions into an individual person's privacy.[3] The scope of the remedy – where *veritas* would be no defence – would be determined after balancing an individual's interest in privacy against the public interest in freedom of speech. This is clearly a task for the Scottish Parliament rather than the judiciary, who would have to develop principles which were, arguably, never part of Scots common law.[4]

1 See, in particular, Walker *Delict* (2nd edn, 1981) p 736.
2 See pp 259 ff above.
3 See *Infringement of Privacy* (Lord Chancellor's Dept, Scottish Office, July 1993).
4 This chapter is strongly influenced by Dr K McK Norrie's seminal article 'Hurts to Character, Honour and Reputation: a Reappraisal' 1984 JR 163.

Part IV

DAMAGES

Chapter 16. Damages 265

Introduction

The purpose of this last chapter is to give a short account of the law of damages. It begins with a discussion of the difficulties raised by the question of remoteness of damages. There follows an explanation of how damages are calculated. Finally, there is an outline of the rules on prescription and limitation which are relevant to delictual liability.

CHAPTER 16

Damages

A. REMOTENESS OF DAMAGES

It will be remembered that Scottish courts once took the view that delictual liability would not be imposed upon a defender if the pursuer's injury was too remote.[1] However, in the present writer's view, these cases should now be analysed as situations where the court was unwilling to impose a duty of care on the defender, ie the duty of care was being used as a threshold device to deny delictual liability. But even where there has been a breach of a duty of care and the defender is liable to make reparation to the pursuer in respect of the pursuer's personal injuries or damage to property, it does not follow that the defender must compensate the pursuer for every loss arising from the delict. Some losses are 'too remote'. Consider the following example:

A, as a result of his careless driving, knocks down a pedestrian, B. B will recover damages for pain and suffering (solatium)[2] and derivative economic loss. The latter will include loss of wages between the date of the accident and the date of the action; future loss of earnings from the date of the action, if B is unable to work or can work only at a lower-paid job;[3] the cost of medical treatment and nursing up to the date of the action and the cost of such care in the future. However, if as a result of the accident, B was unable to give instructions to his stockbroker to purchase shares which he had intended to buy, or if B was unable to post his football coupon, the profits B would have made on the shares or the dividend he would have won if the coupon had been posted are not recoverable, even though they arise from the fact that B was incapacitated as a result of the accident. These losses are too remote and cannot therefore be recovered.

---

1 See pp 126 ff above.
2 For the calculation of solatium, see pp 272 ff below.
3 For the calculation of loss of future earnings, see pp 274 ff below.

What criteria do the courts use to determine whether or not losses are too remote? The classic statement of the rule on remoteness of damages in Scots law was articulated by the Lord Ordinary (Kinloch) in *Allan v Barclay*:[1]

'The grand rule on the subject of damages is, that none can be claimed except such as naturally and directly arise out of the wrong done; and such, therefore, as may reasonably be supposed to have been in the contemplation of the wrongdoer.'

However, there is a potential contradiction inherent in this statement. While many losses which are reasonably foreseeable also directly arise from the wrong done, it is possible to envisage situations where a loss directly arises from the delict but is not reasonably foreseeable and vice versa, ie a loss which is reasonably foreseeable but does not arise directly from the delict.

This problem has been a matter of particular concern in England. In *Re Polemis and Furness, Withy & Co Ltd*,[2] the Court of Appeal held that the question whether particular damages are recoverable depends only on whether they were the direct consequence of the delictual act; provided some damage was reasonably foreseeable so that there was a breach of a duty of care, the defendant is liable to compensate for all the damage directly resulting from the breach of duty, even if those losses were unforeseeable.

In this case, stevedores carelessly allowed a plank to fall into the hold of a ship. The falling plank caused a spark which in its turn ignited petrol vapour in the hold. The vapour caused a fire which destroyed the vessel. The court held that while the fire was not a reasonably foreseeable consequence of allowing the plank to fall, some damage to the vessel was. In the light of these findings, the court was prepared to hold that since it was reasonably foreseeable that some form of damage would result from the negligent act, damages in respect of the fire, albeit not reasonably foreseeable, were nevertheless recoverable as a direct consequence of the foreseeable harm. Although this case is often cited as authority for the proposition that reasonable foreseeability plays no part in determining the extent of recoverable damages, such a conclusion may not be entirely justified. If it had been held that it was not foresee-

1 (1864) 2 M 873. The case was concerned with whether an employer could recover damages for the loss of his injured employee's services. In other words, it was concerned with the defender's liability rather than remoteness of damages. Today it would be analysed as an example of non-recoverability of secondary economic loss: see pp 100 ff above. However, the passage has always been regarded as an authoritative statement of remoteness of damages.
2 [1921] 3 KB 560, CA.

able that the plank would cause any damage at all, the court might well have held that the consequences of the fire were too remote.

However, it may appear illogical to insist that some damage to the pursuer must be foreseen as a reasonable and probable consequence of the defender's act or omission before there is a breach of a duty of care, ie delictual liability, yet allow the pursuer to recover losses directly arising from that breach which were not reasonably foreseeable. In *Overseas Tankship (UK) Ltd v Morts Dock and Engineering Co, The Wagon Mound,*[1] the Privy Council declined to follow *Re Polemis.*[2] In this case, a ship was being bunkered when some oil being loaded on board spilt into the harbour as a result of the carelessness of the appellant's employees. Morts' employees were welding nearby when the spillage happened. Some molten metal from their operations fell onto some debris which caught fire; this in turn set the oil alight, causing substantial fire damage to the wharf owned by Morts.

It was found as a fact that it was not reasonably foreseeable that the oil could have been ignited in such a way. Although it was reasonably foreseeable that the oil spillage would cause some harm to the respondent's dock, ie by fouling the dock, nevertheless the court held that the appellants were not liable for the damage caused by the unforeseeable fire. If *Re Polemis*[2] had been applied, it is arguable that the appellants would have been liable for the damage caused by the fire, because some damage, ie the fouling of the dock, was foreseeable and the fire could be regarded as a *direct* result of the breach of duty[3] – albeit that the fire was unforeseeable. However, since damage by fire was not reasonably foreseeable as a probable consequence of the spillage, it is submitted that in this case there was no breach of duty of care, ie there was no delictual liability and therefore it is not a remoteness of damages case at all.[4]

The Scottish courts have not given authoritative guidance on the matter; instead, reliance is simply placed on Lord Kinloch's 'grand rule'. In *Kelvin Shipping Co, The Baron Vernon v Canadian Pacific Railway Co, The Metagama,*[5] Viscount Haldane LC opined[6] that when

1 [1961] AC 388, [1961] 1 All ER 404, PC.
2 *Re Polemis and Furniss, Withy & Co Ltd* [1921] 3 KB 560, CA.
3 Although in this case it is equally arguable that the fire was *indirectly* caused as a result of the molten metal falling on the oil.
4 Cf *Hughes v Lord Advocate* 1963 SC (HL) 31, 1963 SLT 150, where injury by fire was reasonably foreseeable: only the extent of the injuries was not. For full discussion, see pp 116 ff above.
5 1928 SC (HL) 21, 1928 SLT 117.
6 1928 SC (HL) 21 at 25.

'a collision takes place by the fault of the defendant's ship, the damage is recoverable, in an action for damages if it is the natural and reasonable result of the negligent act, and it will assume that character if it can be shown to be such a consequence as in the ordinary course of things would flow from the situation which the offending ship created.'[1]

Although there are obiter dicta that *Re Polemis*[2] does not reflect the law of Scotland,[3] in *Campbell v F and F Moffat (Transport) Ltd*[4] the Lord Ordinary (Lord Cameron of Lochbroom) held that the test was not whether the loss was reasonably foreseeable but whether it arose naturally and directly out of the wrong. In that case, the pursuer was injured in a road accident and, as a result, his employment was terminated in 1989. Two years later, his former employer closed the mill where the pursuer had worked and gave the employees then working at that date *ex gratia* redundancy payments. In his action for damages, the pursuer sought compensation for the loss of the redundancy payment he would have received if his employment had not been terminated two years earlier as a result of the accident. Lord Cameron took the view that this loss was not so utterly speculative that it could not amount to a natural and direct consequence of the accident.

It is submitted that in Scots law it is too simplistic to see the question of remoteness of damages in terms of reasonable foreseeability on the one hand and direct consequences on the other. The courts use a combination of both tests in assessing whether the loss is a natural consequence of the delictual act. It is only if the loss is utterly speculative[5] that the loss will be too remote and not recoverable in an award of damages.

What is clear, however, is that in a case of personal injuries, the defender takes her victim as she finds him. If, for example, A, as a result of her carelessness, burns B, if B has a predisposition to cancer which is triggered by the burn, with the result that B dies, A is liable for B's death even if that was not reasonably foreseeable as a consequence of the burn. In this situation, reasonable foreseeability of death is treated as irrelevant or, alternatively, the defender is deemed to have reasonably foreseen that the pursuer

---

1 However, this case was clearly concerned with the existence of liability rather than remoteness of damages.
2 *Re Polemis and Furniss, Withy & Co Ltd* [1921] 3 KB 560, CA.
3 See, for example, *Cowan v National Coal Board* 1958 SLT (Notes) 19, OH, per the Lord Ordinary (Cameron).
4 1992 SCLR 551, 1992 SLT 962, OH.
5 As it is submitted is the case in the examples of the loss of profits on the shares and the loss of a football pools' dividend: see p 265 above.

could have been an ill, as opposed to healthy, person.[1] Moreover, as we have seen, where the pursuer is a primary victim, the defender is liable for causing mental or psychiatric illness, even though such illness was not reasonably foreseeable: a case of an eggshell personality rather than an eggshell skull![2]

We have been considering the question of remoteness of damages in the context of delictual liability for unintentional, but careless, conduct. Where the intentional delicts are concerned, the defender is liable to make reparation for all losses suffered by the pursuer which directly arise from the delict – whether or not these losses are reasonably foreseeable. The intention to injure the pursuer, which is an essential requisite of these delicts, disposes of any question of remoteness of damages.[3]

B. CALCULATION OF DAMAGES

(1) Introduction

The purpose of an award of damages is to compensate the pursuer for those losses which arose as a result of the delict. It is intended, so far as money can, to place the pursuer in the financial position he would have been in if the delict had not occurred.[4] Where the claim is in respect of damage to property, damages are relatively simple to assess, ie the cost of repair or replacement of the property.[5] In wrongful birth actions, damages include the anticipated costs of bringing up a child.[6] Greater difficulties arise in calculating damages in pure economic loss and personal injury cases and these deserve fuller treatment.

---

1 *McKillen v Barclay Curle & Co Ltd* 1967 SLT 41. This is known as 'the eggshell-skull rule'.

2 *Page v Smith* [1996] AC 155, [1995] 2 All ER 736, HL: discussed at p 71 above.

3 See, for example, *Smith New Court Securities Ltd v Scrimgeour Vickers (Asset Management) Ltd* [1997] AC 254, [1996] 4 All ER 769, HL: discussed at pp 53–54 above.

4 See, for example, *O'Brien's Curator Bonis v British Steel plc* 1991 SC 315, 1991 SCLR 831, 1991 SLT 477 at 480 per the Lord President (Hope).

5 The pursuer still incurs a reparable loss, even though he could have pursued a contractual claim against a third party to repair the property: *Ford Motor Co Ltd v HLM Design Ltd* 1997 SLT 837, OH.

6 *McClelland v Greater Glasgow Health Board* 1999 SC 305.

(2) Pure economic loss claims

In some situations when delictual liability for pure economic loss has been recognised, it is relatively simple to calculate the loss. For example, in the case of a disappointed legatee, the loss is the value of the lost legacy.[1] Where a surveyor has been negligent and failed to discover defects, the loss to the purchaser is either the cost of repair or the diminution in the value of the property.[2] But difficulties have arisen in quantifying loss, when the pursuer has been induced to enter into a transaction as a result of the defender's misrepresentation.

(a) Fraudulent misrepresentation

It is well settled that when A has entered into a transaction as a result of B's fraudulent misrepresentation, B is liable for all A's losses arising directly from the transaction, even though some of them might not be reasonably foreseeable.[3] This would include losses which A incurs as a result of a general fall in the market value of the assets involved in the transaction.

(b) Negligent misrepresentation

What is the position if A has entered into a transaction as a result of B's negligent misrepresentation? When the misrepresentation takes the form of *advice*, ie B advises A to enter into a particular transaction, then B is liable for all the losses incurred by A as a consequence of entering into the transaction, provided such losses are reasonably foreseeable.[4] Again, this could include losses which A incurs as a result of a general fall in the market value of the assets involved in the transaction.

However, when the misrepresentation takes the form of B providing *information* which A uses to decide whether or not to enter a particular transaction, the House of Lords[5] has imposed a cap on B's potential liability. In other words, B is only liable for that part of A's loss which was a reasonably foreseeable consequence of the information being wrong. Consider the following examples:

---

1 *White v Jones* [1995] 2 AC 207, [1995] 1 All ER 691, HL.
2 *Patel v Hooper & Jackson* [1999] 1 All ER 992, CA.
3 *Smith New Court Securities Ltd v Scrimgeour Vickers (Asset Management) Ltd* [1997] AC 254, [1996] 4 All ER 769, HL.
4 *Bristol and West Building Society v Rollo Steven and Bond* 1998 SLT 9, OH.
5 *South Australia Asset Management Corpn v York Montague Ltd* [1997] AC 191, [1996] 3 All ER 365, HL.

(i) B *advises* A to lend £10 million to C, using C's property as security. C defaults. Owing to a general fall in the market value of property, C's property is now worth only £5 million. A can recover from B all foreseeable losses arising from his entering into the transaction with C, ie £10 million – £5 million = £5 million.

(ii) B tells A that C's property is worth £15 million. In fact, it is worth only £12 million. A decides to lend C £10 million, using C's property as security. C defaults. Owing to a general fall in the market value of property, C's property is now worth only £5 million. A's loss is £10 million – £5 million = £5 million. However, B is only liable to the extent that his information was wrong, ie the difference between the negligent valuation and the actual value at the time the information was given: £15 million – £12 million = £3 million.

There are difficulties in defending the judicial reasoning for applying a cap in negligent information cases.[1] Nevertheless, it appears to be settled law. Moreover, where the pursuer has been contributorily negligent in entering into the transaction (which is often the case), the House of Lords has held that the deduction should be made from the pursuer's total loss, not the loss recoverable after the cap has been fixed.[2] So if, in example (ii), A was 20 per cent contributorily negligent, A's damages would be £5 million – £1 million = £4 million: and A would still recover £3 million from B.

It should also be remembered that in cases of fraudulent as well as negligent misrepresentation, the pursuer must take reasonable steps to mitigate his loss.[3]

(3) Personal injury claims

Where a party suffers personal injuries as a result of the delictual conduct of the defender, he is entitled to obtain reparation in respect of the physical injury and for any derivative economic loss which he has sustained as a result. Again, 'the objective' is, so far as money can, to compensate the injured party for the consequences of the wrongful act.[4] The pursuer can claim in respect of

---

1 See eg Thomson 'Damages for Misrepresentation' 1997 SLT (News) 301.
2 *Platform Home Loans Ltd v Oyston Shipways Ltd* [1999] 1 All ER 833, HL.
3 *Standard Chartered Bank v Pakistan National Shipping Corpn* [1995] 2 Lloyd's Rep 365.
4 *Admiralty Comrs v SS Susquehanna (Owners)* [1926] AC 655, HL.

loss, injury and damage suffered. It is now the practice to divide the claim into various heads of damages. Although it is sensible and convenient to do so, it is always important to remember that these are not several discrete claims but a *single* claim which can be regarded as falling into several parts for the purposes of quantification.[1] Compensation for the pain and suffering as a result of physical injury is known as 'solatium'; compensation in respect of derivative economic loss is known as 'patrimonial loss'.

(a) Solatium

It is, of course, clear that no money sum can in effect compensate for physical injury. In *Wright v British Railways Board*[2] Lord Diplock said of the English equivalent of solatium that

'such loss is not susceptible of *measurement* in money. Any figure at which the assessor of damages arrives cannot be other than artificial and, if the aim is that justice meted out to all litigants should be even handed instead of depending on idiosyncrasies of the assessor, whether jury or judge, the figure must be "basically a conventional figure derived from an experience of awards in comparable cases".'[3]

In *McMillan v McDowall* the judge opined that 'While the assessment of solatium is not a precise science and has frequently been called a jury question, the view of [a Lord Ordinary] in a similar case must be treated with respect'.[4]

The court therefore approaches the question of solatium on the basis of comparing one case with another and making a determination taking into account the severity and nature of the injuries sustained by the pursuer. The court assesses solatium as at the date of the proof and does not attempt to assess solatium as it would have been at the date of the injury itself.

In making an award for solatium the court takes into account not only the extent of the injury but also the pursuer's awareness of pain.[5] No award can be made under this head therefore if, as a result of his injuries, the pursuer has been rendered permanently unconscious. Such awards are made not only in respect of physical injury. A person who, for example, suffers from an identifiable

---

1 *Irving v Hiddleston* 1998 SCLR 350, 1998 SLT 912, OH.
2 [1983] 2 AC 733, [1983] 2 All ER 698, HL.
3 [1983] 2 All ER 698 at 699 (Lord Diplock's emphasis). It is submitted that the position is the same in Scots law.
4 *McMillan v McDowall* 1993 SLT 311, OH, at 312 per T G Coutts QC.
5 *Lim Poh Choo v Camden and Islington Area Health Authority* [1980] AC 174, [1979] 2 All ER 910, HL.

psychological condition can be awarded damages where the condition arises as a consequence of a delict.[1] In *Maclean v Lothian and Borders Fire Brigade*,[2] an award of solatium took into account the pursuer's loss of congenial employment.

In making its assessment of solatium, the court takes into account not only the pain and suffering which has been experienced by the pursuer but also the pain and suffering which he is likely to experience in the future. A global award is made. The award also takes into account the pursuer's loss of amenity. Everything which reduces the pursuer's enjoyment of life, which has been sustained as a result of the accident, will be reflected in a claim for solatium. It has been held in England that the important element in such a claim is the fact of deprivation of amenity and not whether the injured person is aware of such deprivation.[3] Also included in an award of solatium is the pain and suffering occasioned when the pursuer is, was, or at any time will be, likely to become aware that his expectancy of life has been shortened by his injuries.[4]

(b) Patrimonial loss

Having assessed damages in respect of solatium the court must then turn to the question of patrimonial loss. The court first of all assesses damages in respect of past loss, that is loss incurred between the date of the accident and the date of the proof. It then attempts to assess the pursuer's future loss.

(i) Damages for patrimonial loss to the date of proof. If the pursuer has been out of work since the date of his accident, he will be entitled to be compensated for his loss of wages. In addition, the pursuer will frequently have a claim for expenses. The general rule is that reasonable expenses are recoverable. Consequently, reasonable medical expenses can be recovered even if it is shown at a later

---

1 *Clark v Scottish Power plc* 1994 SCLR 202, 1994 SLT 924; *Lawson v Scotdem Ltd* 1999 GWD 8-393. Distress has, on occasion, been the subject of an award of solatium even in the absence of physical injury or mental illness: *Fraser v D M Hall & Son* 1997 SLT 808, OH (*sed quaere*).
2 1998 SCLR 1004, OH.
3 *Lim Poh Choo v Camden and Islington Area Health Authority* [1980] AC 174, [1979] 2 All ER 910, HL. Of course, if the person has been rendered unconscious, he will not obtain compensation for pain and suffering.
4 Damages (Scotland) Act 1976, s 9A as added by s 5 of the Damages (Scotland) Act 1993. However, the deceased's fear of impending death in a fatal accident is not included in any award of solatium: *Hicks v Chief Constable of South Yorkshire Police* [1992] 2 All ER 65, HL.

stage that they are unnecessary.[1] Expenses need not be confined to medical or nursing services. By s 8 of the Administration of Justice Act 1982,[2] when a person has sustained personal injuries or has died in consequence of personal injuries sustained, the defender is liable to pay damages in respect of necessary services which have been, or will be, rendered to the injured person by a relative in consequence of the injuries in question. Section 9 of the Administration of Justice Act 1982[3] also imposes an obligation upon the wrongdoer to pay to the injured person a reasonable sum by way of damages when he is unable, as a result of the accident, to render gratuitous personal services to his family.

In calculating loss of earnings, the pursuer's income tax must be taken into account and his liability to pay national insurance contributions.[4] Accordingly, in so far as past patrimonial loss is concerned, the wages which form the basis of the calculation are the pursuer's net earnings.

(ii) Damages for future patrimonial loss. This head of claim is by far the most important in assessing damages in respect of personal injury. The first stage is to assess damages in respect of future loss of earnings. This is done by taking the loss of the pursuer's net earnings at the date of proof and calculating that on an annual basis. The courts do not attempt to speculate on future rates of taxes and national insurance contributions, but base their calculation on the rates current at the date of proof.[5] No allowance is made for possible increases in the pursuer's earnings if he had not been injured. The figure produced is known as the 'multiplicand'.

The second stage is to find a 'multiplier'. The Ogden tables provide actuarial calculations of lump sums which are required to provide incomes for different persons at different ages. In *Wells v Wells*,[6] the House of Lords laid down that the rate of return on the

1 *Clippens Oil Co Ltd v Edinburgh and District Water Trustees* 1907 SC (HL) 9, 15 SLT 92; *Rubins v Walker* 1946 SC 215.
2 Discussed at pp 224 ff above.
3 Discussed at pp 225 ff above.
4 *British Transport Commission v Gourlay* [1956] AC 185, [1955] 3 All ER 796, HL; *Cooper v Firth Brown* [1963] 2 All ER 31, [1963] 1 WLR 148.
5 *British Transport Commission v Gourlay* above.
6 [1998] 3 All ER 481, [1998] 3 WLR 329, HL. The House of Lords felt empowered to lay down a three per cent return, because the pursuer would be assumed to invest the damages in index-linked government stock rather than in equities, which might give a higher return but which, of course, are a less safe investment. Under s 1 of the Damages Act 1996, the Lord Chancellor and the Secretary of State for Scotland have the power to prescribe the rate of return. Their power has not yet been exercised.

investment of the damages should be three per cent, and that the Ogden tables should be used as the *starting-point* for finding the appropriate multiplier. The traditional Scottish approach was to use the Ogden tables as a check on the multiplier, which was found by less scientific methods. Nevertheless, the guidelines laid down by the House of Lords in *Wells*[1] have been followed by the Scottish courts.[2] After taking the appropriate multiplier for the tables, there will usually be a deduction to take into account contingencies relating to the pursuer other than death, for example, early retirement or redundancy.

The third stage is for the court to multiply the multiplicand by the multiplier to give a lump sum. So, for example, if the multiplicand is £20,000 and the multiplier is 10, then the total sum awarded is £200,000. The court can also take into account lost wages which the pursuer would have earned if his life expectancy had not been reduced as a result of the accident.[3] The pursuer is expected to live off the income and capital, the theory being that the lump sum will have been consumed by the date the pursuer dies!

Where a pursuer is severely injured, damages can be awarded for the cost of her maintenance, nursing and medical care in the future. Again, the multiplicand/multiplier method is adopted. The court assesses the cost of maintenance and care on an annual basis and then applies a multiplier based on the Ogden tables.[4] It should be noted that in a personal injuries' case, the multiplier is applied at the date of proof: if, however, the pursuer died of his injuries between the date of the accident and the proof, the multiplier is applied at the date of death.[5]

Loss of pension rights can also be taken into account in assessing future patrimonial loss[6] as can the pursuer's general loss of value in the labour market. In *Hill v Wilson*,[7] damages were awarded for impairment to earning capacity, as opposed to loss of future wages. It is particularly difficult to assess damages when the injured

---

1 *Wells v Wells* [1998] 3 All ER 481, [1998] 3 WLR 329, HL.
2 *McNulty v Marshalls Food Group Ltd* 1999 SC 195; *McManus' Executrix v Babcock Energy Ltd* 1999 SC 569.
3 Damages (Scotland) Act 1976, s 9(1) and (2).
4 For the courts' approach before *Wells v Wells* [1998] 3 All ER 481, [1998] 3 WLR 329, HL, see *O'Brien's Curator Bonis v British Steel plc* 1991 SC 315, 1991 SCLR 831, 1991 SLT 477.
5 On death from personal injuries, see pp 226 ff above.
6 *Mitchell v Glenrothes Development Corpn* 1991 SLT 284, OH (conventional multiplicand/multiplier method used).
7 1998 SC 81, 1998 SLT 69, OH.

person is a child. In such a case, 'it has never been suggested that damages should be assessed on such a basis, namely on a basis which provides not only reasonable compensation but in effect a guarantee of future financial security'.[1] In some cases, the court will abandon the multiplicand/multiplier method of calculating future patrimonial loss. This would happen where, for example, the pursuer has been able to continue working albeit on light work at a reduced wage, or there is evidence that the pursuer will be able to resume employment in the very near future, even though the job may be lower-paid than previously.[2]

In the last few years, many personal injury cases have been tried by jury. Juries tend to award higher damages than judges, particularly in relation to solatium. Although a court can order a new trial if the sum awarded is excessive, it will not do so unless the damages awarded are beyond what a reasonable jury would award and there is serious injustice: the fact that a judge would have awarded considerably less is not sufficient.[3]

(4) Interest

Having assessed the quantity of damages, the court is obliged to consider the question of interest. Interest is payable under the Interest on Damages (Scotland) Act 1958, as amended by the Interest on Damages (Scotland) Act 1971.

Although solatium is awarded as a lump sum, it is important for the purpose of awards of interest to distinguish past and future solatium. Past solatium is a sum awarded for the pursuer's pain and suffering until the date of proof. But if the pursuer is experiencing pain and suffering and loss of amenities at the date of the proof, the court will estimate damages to compensate the pursuer for the fact that these may continue in the future. So, for example, a court might award a total sum of £10,000 by way of solatium, made up of £6,000 for past solatium and £4,000 for future solatium. Interest on past solatium is paid at the average court rate for the period between the date of the accident and when the 'pain' diminished: this could, of course, have occurred before the date of the proof. Interest on future solatium is paid at one half of the

---

1 *O'Connor v Mathews* 1996 SLT 408, OH, at 412 per the Lord Ordinary (Marnoch).
2 *Stevenson v British Coal Corpn* 1989 SLT 136.
3 *Girvan v Inverness Farmers Dairy (No 2)* 1998 SC (HL) 1, 1998 SCLR 72, 1998 SLT 21.

average court rate for the period from the date of the proof until the date when the court estimates that the 'pain' will have diminished. This therefore requires an apportionment to be made between past and future solatium.[1]

Subject to the court's discretion, interest on patrimonial loss runs from the date of the accident.[2] Again, although a global sum is awarded, damages are divided between past and future loss. In the case of past losses, interest is awarded at one half of the average court rate from the date of the accident to the date of proof. There is no interest payable on awards in respect of future patrimonial loss.[3] The rules applicable to interest in respect of personal injuries operate without prejudice to the general rule which awards interest at the court rate from the date of decree until the date of payment by the defender.

(5) Deductions from awards

Deductions may have to be made from an award of damages for patrimonial loss. Section 10 of the Administration of Justice Act 1982 prohibits the taking into account for the purposes of reduction of damages any benefit the pursuer received in respect of: (a) any contractual pension or benefit[4]; (b) any pension or retirement benefit to which s 2(1) of the Law Reform (Personal Injuries) Act 1948 applied; (c) any benefit payable from public funds in respect of any period after the date of the award of damages which is designed to secure to the injured person or any relative of his a minimum level of subsistence; (d) any statutory redundancy payment;[5] (e) any payment made to the injured person or to any relative of his by the injured person's employer following upon the injuries in question where the recipient is under an obligation to reimburse the employer in the event of damages being recovered in respect of his injuries; and (f) any payment of a benevolent character made to the injured person or to any relative by any person

---

1 *Keicher v National Coal Board* 1988 SLT 318; *Preston v Grampian Health Board* 1988 SLT 435.
2 *Macrae v Reed & Mallik Ltd* 1961 SC 68, 1961 SLT 96.
3 *Hill v Wilson* 1998 s SLT 69.
4 *Lewicki v Brown & Root Wimpey Highland Fabricators Ltd* 1996 SC 200, 1996 SCLR 680, 1996 SLT 1283 (payment under employer's long-term disability scheme held to be a contractual benefit and not deducted: cf if it had been treated as earnings or remuneration from employment).
5 Reversing *Wilson v National Coal Board* 1981 SC (HL) 9, 1981 SLT 67. An *ex gratia* non-statutory payment falls to be deducted: *Duncan v Glacier Metal Co Ltd* 1988 SCLR 320, 1988 SLT 479, OH.

following upon the injuries in question. The section directs, however, that any remuneration or earnings from employment, any unemployment benefit payable from public funds payable prior to the date of the award of damages, or any payment of a benevolent character made by the person responsible for the accident to the injured person, shall be taken into account. Any savings to the pursuer as a result of being maintained in hospital is deducted.[1]

Prior to the introduction of the Social Security Act 1989, in assessing damages for patrimonial loss, a deduction was made of only one half of the value of certain specified benefits, ie sickness, invalidity or disablement benefit, which the pursuer had received during a period of five years from the date of the accident; but in *Hodgson v Trapp*[2] the House of Lords held that the full value of other benefits, such as attendance and mobility allowances, was to be deducted. However, the Social Security Act 1989 made major changes and the law was consolidated in the Social Security Administration Act 1992, Part IV (ss 81–104): Part IV has now been restated, with amendments, in the Social Security (Recovery of Benefits) Act 1997.

When damages are awarded, heads of loss are relevant for the purpose of the Social Secuirty (Recovery of Benefits) Act 1997:

(1) compensation for earnings lost during 'the relevant period';
(2) compensation for the cost of care incurred over the relevant period; and
(3) compensation for loss of mobility during the relevant period.

The following benefits paid over the relevant period are deducted as follows:

From head (1): disability working allowance, disablement pension, incapacity benefit, income support, invalidity pension and allowance, jobseeker's allowance, reduced earnings allowance, severe disablement allowance, sickness benefit, statutory sick pay, unemployability supplement and unemployment benefit;

From head (2): attendance allowance, the care component of disability living allowance and any disablement pension increase;

---

1 Administration of Justice Act 1982, s 11.
2 [1989] AC 807, [1988] 3 All ER 870, HL.

From head (3): mobility allowance and the mobility component of disability living allowance.[1]

'The relevant period' is five years from the date of the accident or five years from first claiming benefit as a consequence of a disease. Thus, benefits paid over that five-year period are recoverable from the relevant head of loss. Payments which are paid thereafter are not recoverable. When damages are paid *before* the end of five years, the relevant period ends at the date of payment; therefore, benefits paid after that date but before the five-year period ends are not recoverable.[2] The person paying damages, the compensator, deducts the amount of recoverable benefits from the pursuer's compensation[3] which he then pays to the Secretary of State.[4]

A major effect of the legislation is to abolish the provision that only one half of the specified benefits should be taken into account in assessing damages. Under the Social Security (Recovery of Benefits) Act 1997, all the specified benefits received by the pursuer during the relevant period are fully to be taken into account. Benefits received after the relevant period are not affected and are not to be taken into account. The position is therefore that both pursuers and defenders are worse off under the new legislation.

As far as the pursuer is concerned, he is worse off by not keeping half the value of any sickness, invalidity or disablement benefit received during the relevant period. He is, however, better off in that after the relevant period, those benefits which would have previously been deducted in full when assessing damages under the rule in *Hodgson v Trapp*,[5] for example, attendance and mobility allowances, are no longer taken into account. Most importantly, damages awarded for solatium are no longer subject to deduction of recoverable benefits. The defender is worse off in that (i) he now pays the specified benefits in full during the relevant period, whereas before he paid only half their value to the pursuer as damages, and (ii) he can no longer take the advantage of the rule in *Hodgson v Trapp*,[5] ie that the full value of other benefits paid to the pursuer would be deducted when assessing the damages.

---

1 Social Security (Recovery of Benefits) Act 1997, Sch 2.
2 Social Security (Recovery of Benefits) Act 1997, s 3. See *Mitchell v Laing* 1998 SC 342, 1998 SCLR 266, 1998 SLT 203. This case provides an excellent example of literal construction of a statute by the Lord President (Rodger).
3 Social Security (Recovery of Benefits) Act 1997, s 6. The compensator obtains a certificate specifying the amount of recoverable benefits paid to the pursuer.
4 Social Security (Recovery of Benefits) Act 1997, s 7.
5 [1989] AC 807, [1988] 3 All ER 870, HL.

When the compensation is less than a prescribed sum, it will be
treated as a small payment, and no deduction in respect of benefits
paid during the relevant period will be made.[1]

C. PROVISIONAL AND INTERIM DAMAGES

The normal rule in actions of damages for personal injuries is that
the damages are assessed once and for all at the date of proof. As a
consequence, pursuers used to delay bringing proceedings for a
considerable period until they could ascertain the full extent of
their loss. Pursuers often suffered hardship during the period
between the accident and the date of proof. The situation was
particularly unfair if the pursuer's physical condition was likely to
deteriorate as a result of the injuries at some time in the future after
the date of the proof. In *Stevenson v Pontifex and Wood*[2] the Lord
President (Inglis) observed:[3]

'I hold the true rule of practice based on sound principle to be, that
though the delict . . . be of such a nature that it will necessarily be followed
by injurious consequences in the future, or though it may for this reason
be impossible to ascertain with precise accuracy at the date of the action
. . . the amount of loss which will result, yet the whole damage must be
recovered in one action.'[4]

A pursuer's position in these circumstances has, to some extent,
been alleviated by s 12 of the Administration of Justice Act 1982,
which provides that the court is entitled to make an award of provisional damages in respect of personal injuries. Such an award can
be made when it is proved, or admitted, that there is a risk that at
some definite or indefinite time in the future, the pursuer will, as a
result of the act or omission of the defender, which gave rise to the
cause of the action, develop some serious disease or some serious
deterioration in his physical or mental condition.[5] Provisional
damages can only be awarded where the defender was, at the time
of the accident giving rise to the cause of action, either a public
authority or an insured person.[6] The purpose of this provision is

1 Social Security (Recovery of Benefits) Act 1997, Sch 1.
2 (1887) 15 R 125.
3 (1887) 15 R 125 at 129.
4 See also *Dunlop v McGowans* 1979 SC 22, 1979 SLT 34 at 39 per the Lord
   Justice-Clerk (Wheatley).
5 Administration of Justice Act 1982, s 12(1)(a).
6 AJA 1982, s 12(1)(b).

therefore to give the pursuer an opportunity to claim damages in circumstances where his position is likely to worsen but where he cannot assess the full extent of his loss because the condition will take some time to deteriorate.

Before an award of provisional damages can be made, the pursuer must establish that there is a risk[1] that at some time in the future he will develop some serious disease or some serious deterioration in his physical or mental condition. Although assessment of the risk may be difficult,[2] it is clear that the risk must be more than *de minimis*.[3] There must be evidence that there is the possibility of a *serious* deterioration in the pursuer's condition.[4] If, for example, the pursuer's health or disability will incrementally become worse, there are no grounds for an award of provisional damages, because there is no 'clear cut and severable threshold' when the pursuer could apply for damages in the future on the basis that a serious deterioration had in fact taken place.[5] Although the deterioration must be as a consequence of the delictual act or omission of the defender that led to the pursuer's personal injuries in the first place, nevertheless in deciding whether or not the deterioration is serious, account must be taken of the effect of such deterioration upon the pursuer's physical abilities in the context of his ordinary life: '[s]eriousness cannot be assessed in a vacuum'.[6] Damages can only be deferred in respect of the serious deterioration in the pursuer's condition.[7]

---

1 Cf the approach of the Lord Ordinary (Dervaird) who suggested (obiter) that if there was no risk but a certainty that there would be a deterioration, this would *not* be a suitable case for provisional damages: *Prentice v William Thyne Ltd* 1989 SLT 336n, OH, at 337.

2 *Potter v McCulloch* 1987 SLT 308, OH, at 310 per the Lord Ordinary (Weir).

3 *White v Inveresk Paper Co Ltd* 1987 SC 143, 1988 SLT 2, OH, at 6 per the Lord Ordinary (Murray).

4 *White v Inveresk Paper Co Ltd* 1987 SC 143, 1988 SLT 2, OH, at 5 per the Lord Ordinary (Murray). See also *Potter v McCulloch* 1987 SLT 308, OH, at 310 per the Lord Ordinary (Weir); *Meek v Burton's Gold Medal Biscuits Ltd* 1989 SLT 338n, OH, at 339 per the Lord Ordinary (Prosser). In *Bonar v Trafalgar House Offshore Fabrication Ltd* 1996 SLT 548, OH, the Lord Ordinary (Gill) held that the court must determine what the apprehended deterioration is: contingent liability cannot be imposed on a defender unless the nature and extent of that liability is clear.

5 See also *Prentice v William Thyne Ltd* 1989 SLT 336n, OH ('clear and sensible threshold'); *Robertson v British Bakeries Ltd* 1991 SLT 434 ('recognisable threshold').

6 *Robertson v British Bakeries Ltd* 1991 SCLR 450n, 1991 SLT 434, OH, at 439 per the Lord Ordinary (Osborne).

7 *Meek v Burton's Gold Medal Biscuits Ltd* 1989 SLT 338n, OH.

Even if the pursuer satisfies the statutory criteria, the court is not obliged to defer the award of damages. The interests of the defender in not being called upon to pay further damages at some indefinite time in the future must also be considered.[1] Accordingly, an application for provisional damages is unlikely to be successful, unless the medical evidence establishes that the deterioration is likely to take place in, say, a period of not more than ten years. Moreover, the court has the discretion to stipulate a time limit after which the pursuer is unable to claim further damages for a deterioration in his condition.[2] In *McColl v Barns*,[3] for example, where it was established that there was a risk that post-traumatic epilepsy might occur within seven years of the date of the accident, the pursuer was allowed to apply within that period for a further award of damages if the risk should in fact materialise. In the course of his judgment, the Lord Ordinary (Morison) said:[4]

'In my opinion this is a most appropriate case for such an order to be made. An assessment made to reflect the possibility of the condition occurring would be unrealistic and impracticable. If no assessment were made and the risk were to materialise, the pursuer would be unjustly deprived of compensation for a serious injury which would be a result of the accident. Since the additional risk becomes negligible after a period of seven years from the date of the accident I shall restrict the order . . . to that period. . .'

The court is also entitled to award interim damages. Interim damages are to be distinguished from provisional damages in so far as they do not depend upon a pursuer suffering from a continuing disability, the eventual seriousness of which cannot be ascertained. Interim payments can be made in the Court of Session in terms of Rule of Court 89A(1) and will be awarded if the court is satisfied that the defender or defenders have admitted liability or that if the action proceeded to proof the pursuer would succeed in a question of liability without any substantial finding of contributory negligence on his part.[5] The court must be satisfied that it is 'practically certain' that the pursuer will succeed on the question of liability, and that any finding of contributory negligence will not be so large as to have a material effect on the assessment of the amount the

---

1 *Paterson v Costain Mining Ltd* 1988 SCLR 71, 1988 SLT 413, OH.
2 Administration of Justice Act 1982, s 12(2).
3 1992 SCLR 907, 1992 SLT 1188, OH; see also *Lappin v Britannia Airways Ltd* 1989 SLT 181n, OH (five years).
4 *McColl v Barns* 1992 SLT 1188 at 1190.
5 See, for example, *Hutcheson v Ascosmit Co* 1992 SLT 1115.

pursuer is likely to recover as damages.[1] An interim award is taken into account in making the final award and will not be made against the defender unless that defender is either a person who is insured in respect of the pursuer's claim or is a public authority or 'is a person whose means and resources are such as to enable him to make interim payment'.[2]

D. PRESCRIPTION AND LIMITATION

A pursuer may lose her right to obtain reparation if she does not begin proceedings against the defender within certain prescribed periods. By s 6 of the Prescription and Limitation (Scotland) Act 1973[3] the obligation to make reparation for a delictual act[4] is extinguished after five years. The five-year prescriptive period runs from the date on which the delict is complete, ie when the pursuer suffers *damnum*.

'The right to raise such an action accrues when *injuria* concurs with *damnum*. Some interval of time may elapse between the two . . . and . . . in such circumstances time is to run from the date when *damnum* results, not from the earlier date of *injuria*.'[5]

This could cause injustice in cases where the damage suffered is latent and the pursuer does not discover that, for example, his house is unstable as a result of defective foundations until five or more years after the damage was in fact sustained. In such situations, time begins to run only when the pursuer first became, or could with reasonable diligence have become aware of the damage.[6]

---

1 *Cowie v Atlantic Drilling Co Ltd* 1995 SC 288, 1995 SCLR 335, 1995 SLT 1151; *Cleland v Campbell* 1998 SLT 642, OH.
2 Rule of Court of Session 89A(1).
3 In this section references are to the Prescription and Limitation (Scotland) Act 1973, as amended, unless otherwise stated.
4 Prescription and Limitation (Scotland) Act 1973, Sch 1, para (1)(d).
5 *Dunlop v McGowans* 1980 SC (HL) 73, 1980 SLT 129 at 132–133 per Lord Keith of Kinkel; see also *Renfrew Golf Club v Ravenstone Securities Ltd* 1984 SLT 170, OH; *Strathclyde Regional Council v Border Engineering Contractors Ltd* 1997 SCLR 100, 1998 SLT 175, OH; *Osborne & Hunter Ltd v Hardie Caldwell* 1999 SLT 153.
6 Prescription and Limitation (Scotland) Act 1973, s 11(3). However, the long-stop 20 years' prescription begins to run from the date the damage occurred: s 7. In theory, therefore, a claim for reparation for latent damage could prescribe after 20 years without the five-year prescriptive period being triggered.

There are, however, important exceptions to the general rule. First, liability for defective products under Part I of the Consumer Protection Act 1987 is extinguished after 10 years.[1] Liability for defamation prescribes after 20 years.[2] Importantly, delictual liability in respect of personal injuries or death no longer prescribes.[3] However, a claim for damages for personal injuries, death or defamation must be brought within a period of three years. This is known as a limitation period. If the action is not commenced within the three-year period, the pursuer cannot enforce his rights unless the defender waives his right to defend the action on the ground that the limitation period has expired.

In the case of personal injuries or property damage as a result of a defective product, the action is not competent if it is brought after a period of three years from the date when the pursuer knew that it was reasonably practicable for him to be aware that there was a defect in the product, that the injury or damage was caused by the product, that the injury or damage was sufficiently serious to bring an action for reparation and that the defender was liable under s 2 of the Consumer Protection Act 1987.[4] A similar limitation period applies to actions brought in relation to death caused by a defective product.[5] In respect of defamation actions, it is simply stated that the three-year limitation period runs from the date when the right of action accrued.[6]

An action for damages for personal injuries must commence within three years from the date on which the injuries were sustained.[7] However, the three-year period does not begin to run from the date when the injuries were sustained unless it was reasonably practicable for the pursuer to be aware of all the following facts: that the injuries were sufficiently serious to bring an action of damages;[8] that the injuries were caused by an act or omission; and that the defender was responsible for the act or omission.[9] So, for

1 Prescription and Limitation (Scotland) Act 1973, s 22A, Sch 1, para 2(ggg). In this case the 10 years run from the date the product is first put on the market, not the date when the *damnum* occurs.
2 Prescription and Limitation (Scotland) Act 1973, s 7(1) and Sch 1, para 2(gg).
3 PL(S)A 1973, ss 6(2), 7(2) and Sch 1, para 2(g).
4 PL(S)A 1973, s 22B.
5 PL(S)A 1973, s 22C.
6 PL(S)A 1973, s 18A(1).
7 PL(S)A 1973, s 17(1) and (2). If the act or omission which caused the injuries was continuing, the three-year period runs from the date when the injuries were sustained or the date when the act or omission ceased, whichever is later.
8 *Blake v Lothian Health Board* 1993 SLT 1248, OH.
9 *Kirk Care Housing Association Ltd v Crerar and Partners* 1996 SLT 150, OH.

example, where a pursuer sustained personal injury as a result of the defender's delictual conduct, but the pursuer did not know that he was injured, as in the case of an insidious disease, the three-year period only begins to run when it was reasonably practicable for him to realise that the illness was attributable to the defender's acts or omissions, ie when he knows he is ill. Similarly, the three-year period will only begin when the pursuer knows that the defender is responsible for the delictual conduct; if this knowledge arises after the date when the injuries were sustained, the three-year period only begins to run from the later date. A similar limitation period applies to actions for damages brought in relation to death which has resulted from personal injuries.[1] In all these limitation periods, time does not run against a pursuer who is or was under legal disability by reason of non-age or unsoundness of mind.[2]

However, in the case of the limitation periods in respect of actions for damages in respect of personal injuries or death from personal injuries *and* actions for defamation or verbal injury, the court has a discretion to allow the action to proceed outwith the three-year period if 'it seems equitable to do so'.[3] All the circumstances of the case are taken into consideration, including the length of time in bringing the action, whether the pursuer was responsible for the delay, whether there is an action available against the pursuer's solicitor if the solicitor was responsible for the delay, the inconvenience to the defender etc.[4] The issue is entirely a matter for the discretion of the presiding judge. In practice, the power is used sparingly in claims for personal injuries or death from personal injuries as a result of the knowledge provisions which have to be satisfied before the three-year limitation period begins to run.

1 Prescription and Limitation (Scotland) Act 1973, s 18.
2 PL(S)A 1973, ss 17(3), 18(3), 18A(2), 22B(4), 22C(3). No causal connection is required between the period of non-age and the delay: *Paton v Loffland Bros North Sea* 1994 SLT 784.
3 Prescription and Limitation (Scotland) Act 1973, s 19A.
4 For examples, see *McCullough v Norwest Socea Ltd* 1981 SLT 201, OH; *Carson v Howard Doris Ltd* 1981 SC 278, 1981 SLT 273; *Donald v Rutherford* 1983 SLT 253, 1984 SLT 70; *Whyte v Walker* 1983 SLT 441, OH; *Clark v McLean* 1994 SCLR 564, 1995 SLT 235.

Appendix

Damages (Scotland) Act 1976

(c 13)

ARRANGEMENT OF SECTIONS

1 Rights of relatives of a deceased person
1A Transmissibility to executor of rights of deceased relative
2 Rights transmitted to executor in respect of deceased person's injuries
2A Enforcement by executor of rights transmitted to him
              *   *   *
4 Executor's claim not to be excluded by relatives' claim: and vice versa
5 Provisions for avoidance of multiplicity of actions
6 Limitation of total amount of liability
7 Amendment of references in other Acts
8 Abolition of right to assythment
9 Damages due to injured person for patrimonial loss caused by personal injuries whereby expectation of life is diminished
9A Solatium for loss of expectation of life
10 Interpretation
              *   *   *
12 Citation, application to Crown, commencement and extent

Schedule 1 – Definition of 'relative'
              *   *   *

1. Rights of relatives of a deceased person

(1) Where a person dies in consequence of personal injuries sustained by him as a result of an act or omission of another person, being an act or omission giving rise to liability to pay

damages to the injured person or his executor, then, subject to the following provisions of this Act, the person liable to pay those damages (in this section referred to as 'the responsible person') shall also be liable to pay damages in accordance with this section to any relative of the deceased, being a relative within the meaning of Schedule 1 to this Act.

(2) No liability shall arise under this section if the liability to the deceased or his executor in respect of the act or omission has been excluded or discharged (whether by antecedent agreement or otherwise) by the deceased before his death, or is excluded by virtue of any enactment.

(3) The damages which the responsible person shall be liable to pay to a relative of a deceased under this section shall (subject to the provisions of this Act) be such as will compensate the relative for any loss of support suffered by him since the date of the deceased's death or likely to be suffered by him as a result of the act or omission in question, together with any reasonable expense incurred by him in connection with the deceased's funeral.

(4) If the relative is a member of the deceased's immediate family (within the meaning of section 10(2) of this Act) there shall be awarded, without prejudice to any claim under subsection (3) above, such sum of damages, if any, as the court thinks just by way of compensation for the loss of [all or any of the following—
   (a) distress and anxiety endured by the relative in contemplation of the suffering of the deceased before his death;
   (b) grief and sorrow of the relative caused by the deceased's death;
   (c) the loss of such non-patrimonial benefit as the relative might have been expected to derive from the deceased's society and guidance if the deceased had not died,
and the court in making an award under this subsection shall not be required to ascribe specifically any part of the award to any of paragraphs (a), (b) and (c) above.]

(5) [Subject to subsection (5A) below] in assessing for the purposes of this section the amount of any loss of support suffered by a relative of a deceased no account shall be taken of—
   (a) any patrimonial gain or advantage which has accrued or will or may accrue to the relative from the deceased or from any other person by way of succession or settlement;
   (b) any insurance money, benefit, pension or gratuity which has been, or will be or may be, paid as a result of the deceased's death;

and in this subsection—
'benefit' means benefit under the Social Security Act 1975 or the
Social Security (Northern Ireland) Act 1975, and any payment
by a friendly society or trade union for the relief or maintenance
of a member's dependants;
'insurance money' includes a return of premiums; and
'pension' includes a return of contributions and any payment of a
lump sum in respect of a person's employment.

[(5A) Where a deceased has been awarded a provisional award
of damages under section 12(2) of the Administration of Justice
Act 1982, the making of that award does not prevent liability from
arising under this section but in assessing for the purposes of this
section the amount of any loss of support suffered by a relative of
the deceased the court shall take into account such part of the
provisional award relating to future patrimonial loss as was
intended to compensate the deceased for a period beyond the date
on which he died.]

(6) In order to establish loss of support for the purposes of this
section it shall not be essential for a claimant to show that the
deceased was, or might have become, subject to a duty in law to
provide or contribute to the support of the claimant; but if any
such fact is established it may be taken into account in determining
whether, and if so to what extent, the deceased, if he had not died,
would have been likely to provide or contribute to such support.

(7) Except as provided in this section [or in Part II of the
Administration of Justice Act 1982] [or under section 1 of the
International Transport Conventions Act 1983] no person shall be
entitled by reason of relationship to damages (including damages
by way of solatium) in respect of the death of another person.

NOTES to s 1
Sub-s (3): See the Administration of Justice Act 1982, s 9(2).
Sub-s (4): Words substituted by the Damages (Scotland) Act 1993, s 1(1).
Sub-s (5): Words added by the Damages (Scotland) Act 1993, s 1(2).
Sub-s (5A): Sub-s added by the Damages (Scotland) Act 1993, s 1(3).
Sub-s (7): Words added by the Administration of Justice Act 1982, s 14(1); and by
the International Transport Conventions Act 1983, Sch 1, para 4(a).

**[1A. Transmissibility to executor of rights of deceased
relative**

Any right to damages under any provision of section 1 of this
Act which is vested in the relative concerned immediately before

his death shall be transmitted to the relative's executor; but, in determining the amount of damages payable to an executor by virtue of this section, the court shall have regard only to the period ending immediately before the relative's death.]

NOTES to s 1A
Section added by the Damages (Scotland) Act 1993, s 2.

[2. Rights transmitted to executor in respect of deceased person's injuries

(1) Subject to the following provisions of this section, there shall be transmitted to the executor of a deceased person the like rights to damages in respect of personal injuries (including a right to damages by way of solatium) sustained by the deceased as were vested in him immediately before his death.

(2) There shall not be transmitted to the executor under this section a right to damages by way of compensation for patrimonial loss attributable to any period after the deceased's death.

(3) In determining the amount of damages by way of solatium payable to an executor by virtue of this section, the court shall have regard only to the period ending immediately before the deceased's death.

(4) In so far as a right to damages vested in the deceased comprised a right to damages (other than for patrimonial loss) in respect of injury resulting from defamation or any other verbal injury or other injury to reputation sustained by the deceased, that right shall be transmitted to the deceased's executor only if an action to enforce that right had been brought by the deceased before his death and had not been concluded by then within the meaning of section 2A(2) of this Act.]

NOTES to s 2
Section substituted by the Damages (Scotland) Act 1993, s 3.

[2A. Enforcement by executor of rights transmitted to him

(1) For the purpose of enforcing any right transmitted to an executor under section 1A or 2 of this Act the executor shall be entitled—
    (a) to bring an action; or

(b) if an action for that purpose had been brought by the deceased but had not been concluded before his death, to be sisted as pursuer in that action.

(2) For the purpose of subsection (1) above, an action shall not be taken to be concluded while any appeal is competent or before any appeal taken has been disposed of.]

NOTES to s 2A
Section added by the Damages (Scotland) Act 1993, s 4.

3. ...

NOTES to s 3
Section repealed by the Damages (Scotland) Act 1993, s 7(3).

4. Executor's claim not to be excluded by relatives' claim: and vice versa

A claim by the executor of a deceased person for damages under section 2 of this Act is not excluded by the making of a claim by a relative of the deceased for damages under section 1 of this Act; [or by a deceased relative's executor under section 1A of this Act; nor is a claim by a relative of a deceased person or by a deceased relative's executor for damages under the said section 1 or (as the case may be) the said section 1A] excluded by the making of a claim by the deceased's executor for damages under the said section 2. . . .

NOTES to s 4
Words added by the Damages (Scotland) Act 1993, s 7(2), Sch, para 1.
Words repealed by the Administration of Justice Act 1982, s 14(2)(a).

5. ...

NOTES to s 5
Section repealed by the Administration of Justice Act 1982, Sch 9, Pt 1.

6. Limitation of total amount of liability

(1) Where in any action to which [this section] applies, so far as directed against any defender, it is shown that by antecedent agreement, compromise or otherwise, the liability arising in relation to

that defender from the personal injuries in question had, before the deceased's death, been limited to damages of a specified or ascertainable amount, or where that liability is so limited by virtue of any enactment nothing in this Act shall make the defender liable to pay damages exceeding that amount; and accordingly where in such an action there are two or more pursuers any damages to which they would respectively be entitled under this Act apart from the said limitation shall, if necessary, be reduced *pro rata*.

(2) Where two or more such actions are conjoined, the conjoined actions shall be treated for the purposes of this section as if they were a single action.

[(3) This section applies to any action in which, following the death of any person from personal injuries, damages are claimed—
  (a) by the executor of the deceased, in respect of the injuries from which the deceased died;
  (b) in respect of the death of the deceased, by any relative of his [or, if the relative has died, by the relative's executor].]

NOTES to s 6
Sub-s (1): Words substituted by the Administration of Justice Act 1982, s 14(2)(b)(i).
Sub-s (3): Sub-s added by the Administration of Justice Act 1982, s 14(2)(b)(ii).
Sub-s (3)(b): Words added by the Damages (Scotland) Act 1993, s 7(2), Sch, para 3.

---

7. Amendment of references in other Acts

In any Act passed before this Act, unless the context otherwise requires, any reference to solatium in respect of the death of any person (however expressed) shall be construed as a reference to a loss of society award within the meaning of section 1 of this Act; and any reference to a dependant of a deceased person, in relation to an action claiming damages in respect of the deceased person's death, shall be construed as including a reference to a relative of the deceased person within the meaning of this Act.

8. Abolition of right to assythment

After the commencement of this Act no person shall in any circumstances have a right to assythment, and accordingly any action claiming that remedy shall (to the extent that it does so) be incompetent.

9. Damages due to injured person for patrimonial loss caused by personal injuries whereby expectation of life is diminished

(1) This section applies to any action for damages in respect of personal injuries sustained by the pursuer where his expected date of death is earlier than it would have been if he had not sustained the injuries.

(2) In assessing, in any action to which this section applies, the amount of any patrimonial loss in respect of the period after the date of decree—
  (a) it shall be assumed that the pursuer will live until the date when he would have been expected to die if he had not sustained the injuries (hereinafter referred to as the 'notional date of death');
  (b) the court may have regard to any amount, whether or not it is an amount related to earnings by the pursuer's own labour or other gainful activity, which in its opinion the pursuer, if he had not sustained the injuries in question, would have received in the period up to his notional date of death by way of benefits in money or money's worth, being benefits derived from sources other than the pursuer's own estate;
  (c) the court shall have regard to any diminution of any such amount as aforesaid by virtue of expenses which in the opinion of the court the pursuer, if he had not sustained the injuries in question, would reasonably have incurred in the said period by way of living expenses.

[9A. Solatium for loss of expectation of life

(1) In assessing, in an action for damages in respect of personal injuries, the amount of damages by way of solatium, the court shall, if—
  (a) the injured person's expectation of life has been reduced by the injuries; and
  (b) the injured person is, was at any time or is likely to become, aware of that reduction,
have regard to the extent that, in consequence of that awareness, he has suffered or is likely to suffer.

(2) Subject to subsection (1) above, no damages by way of solatium shall be recoverable in respect of loss of expectation of life.

(3) The court in making an award of damages by way of solatium shall not be required to ascribe specifically any part of the award to loss of expectation of life.]

NOTES to s 9A
Section added by the Damages (Scotland) Act 1993, s 5.

10. Interpretation

(1) In this Act, unless the context otherwise requires—

. . .

'personal injuries' includes any disease or any impairment of a person's physical or mental condition [and injury resulting from defamation or any other verbal injury or other injury to reputation] [, or injury resulting from harassment actionable under section 8 of the Protection from Harassment Act 1997];
'relative', in relation to a deceased person, has the meaning assigned to it by Schedule 1 to this Act.

(2) References in this Act to a member of a deceased person's immediate family are references to any relative of his who falls within subparagraph (a), [(aa),] (b) or (c) of paragraph 1 of Schedule 1 to this Act.

(3) References in this Act to any other Act are references to that Act as amended, extended or applied by any other enactment, including this Act.

NOTES to s 10
Sub-s (1): Words repealed by the Damages (Scotland) Act 1993, s 7(3). Words added by the Damages (Scotland) Act 1993, s 7(2), Sch, para 3; and by the Protection from Harassment Act 1997, s 8(8).
Sub-s (2): Word added by the Administration of Justice Act 1982, s 14(4).

11. . . .

NOTES to s 11
Section repealed by the Damages (Scotland) Act 1993, s 7(3).

12. Citation, application to Crown, commencement and extent

(1) This Act may be cited as the Damages (Scotland) Act 1976.

(2) This Act binds the Crown.

(3) . . .

(4) . . .

(5) This Act extends to Scotland only.

NOTES to s 12
Sub-ss (3), (4): Sub-ss repealed by the Damages (Scotland) Act 1993, s 7(3).

SCHEDULES

SCHEDULE 1

DEFINITION OF 'RELATIVE'

1. In this Act 'relative' in relation to a deceased person includes—
    (a) any person who immediately before the deceased's death was the spouse of the deceased;
    [(aa) any person, not being the spouse of the deceased, who was, immediately before the deceased's death, living with the deceased as husband or wife;]
    (b) any person who was a parent or child of the deceased;
    (c) any person not falling within paragraph (b) above who was accepted by the deceased as a child of his family;
    (d) any person who was an ascendant or descendant (other than a parent or child) of the deceased;
    (e) any person who was, or was the issue of, a brother, sister, uncle or aunt of the deceased; and
    (f) any person who, having been a spouse of the deceased, had ceased to be so by virtue of a divorce;
but does not include any other person.

2. In deducing any relationship for the purposes of the foregoing paragraph—
    (a) any relationship by affinity shall be treated as a relationship by consanguinity; any relationship of the half blood shall be treated as a relationship of the whole blood; and the step-child of any person shall be treated as his child; and
    [(b) section 1(1) of the Law Reform (Parent and Child) (Scotland) Act 1986 shall apply; and any reference (however expressed) in this Act to a relative shall be construed accordingly.]

NOTES to Sch 1
Para 1(aa): Sub-para added by the Administration of Justice Act 1982, s 14(4).
Para 2(b): Sub-para substituted by the Law Reform (Parent and Child) (Scotland)
   Act 1986, Sch 1, para 15.

SCHEDULE 2

*   *   *

NOTES to Sch 2
Schedule repealed by the Damages (Scotland) Act 1993, s 7(3).

Index

A coelo usque ad centrum, 20
Actio de effusis vel dejectis, 181
Actio de positis vel suspensis, 181
Actio injuriarum, 243
Advocates
  immunity, 155
  professional negligence, 155
Aemulatio vicini, 21–22, 181
Age of legal capacity, 12, 221–222
Agency
  vicarious liability, 220
Agricultural produce, 161
Aircraft
  occupiers' liability, 188
  trespass, 20
Algae, 173
Animals
  common law liability, 169, 170,
    171
  dangerous animals, 170
    wild animals, 172
  domitae naturae, 170
  employers' liability, 169
  ferae naturae, 170
  keepers, meaning, 171
  meaning, 171–174
  occupiers' liability, 169
  statutory regulation, 170–176
  strict liability, 170–176
    defences, 174–176
    liable parties, 171
  trespass, 175, 176
  volenti non fit injuria, 174
Assault, 12–15
  children, chastisement, 15
  consent, 12, 15
  defences, 14
  self-defence, 14

Assault – *contd*
  sports, 14
Assignation
  consumer contracts, 96
  delictual rights, 107
Assythment, 3–4
  abolition, 292
Auditors, 81

Bacteria, 173
Bankers, 88
Bills of lading, 103
Bookmakers, 196
Boycotts, 47
Braer disaster, 102
Breach of arrestment, 3
Breach of duty of care, 111–128
  criteria, 111–127
  foreseeability, *see*
    FORESEEABILITY
  standard of care, *see* STANDARD
    OF CARE
  voluntary acts or omissions,
    111
Breach of statutory duties
  delictual liability, 96–97,
    193–198
  criteria, 194
  presumptions, 194–195
  protected classes, 195, 197
  volenti non fit injuria, 198
  health and safety at work, 209
  lack of insurance, 146
  standard of care, 198
  strict liability, 6–7, 198
Building
  contracts, vicarious liability,
    219–220

Building – *contd*
  defective buildings, 95–100
  regulations, breach, 96–97
Burst pipes, 182, 185
Business
  course of business, 162
  slander of business, 261
  wrongful interference, 40–42

Causation, 60, 76, 129–140
  causa causans, 135–139
    foreseeability, 136–138
    order of events, 138–139
  causa sine qua non, 129–135
    'but for' test, 129–131
    several causes, 132–135
  contributory negligence, *see*
    CONTRIBUTORY NEGLIGENCE
  product liability, 164
Children
  actions against parents, 223
  chastisement, 15
  damages for death of parents,
    230
  death from injuries *in utero,* 229
  delictual liability, 222
  in care, 197, 200–201
  legal capacity, 221–222
  unborn children—
    duty of care to, 76, 223
    title to sue, 223
Circumvention, 3
Closed shops, 43, 46
Coal mining, 125
Cohabitees
  damages for death, 230
Competition, 35
Complex structures
  defective buildings, 98
  product liability, 157, 159, 160,
    166
Computer hacking, 32
Confidential information, 30–33
Conspiracy, 45–50
Consumer protection, *see*
    PRODUCT LIABILITY
Contract
  breach, inducement, 36–39, 45

Contract – *contd*
  defective performance, delictual
    liability, 88–94
  fraudulent misrepresentations,
    51
  of employment, and services
    agreements, 210–212
  or delictual remedies, 60, 85, 95
  wrongful interference with
    performance, 39–40, 89
  Junior Books, 92, 104
Contractors
  vicarious liability, 219
Contributory negligence, 122,
    143–145
  animals, 176
  causa causans, 137
  damages, 145
  drunkenness, 69
  employers' liability, 209
  joint liability, 146
  product liability, 166
  socii criminis, 145
Contumelia, 12, 243
Convicium, 261–262
Corporal punishment, 15
Cranes, 20
Cricket balls, 120
Criminal injuries compensation,
    15
Criminal law
  and delict, 3–5
Culpa, 119–126
  basis of delict, 57
  careless conduct, 57
  defamation, 243
  meaning, 1, 5, 11
  nuisance, 184–186

Damage to property
  leased property, 106
  quantification of damages, 269
Damages
  contributory negligence, 145
  Damages (Scotland) Act 1976,
    287–296
  Damages (Scotland) Act 1993,
    232

Damages – *contd*
  death of relatives, 227–233
  defamation, 258–259
  interim damages, 282–283
  joint liability, 139
  nuisance, 184–186
  provisional damages, 280–282,
    289
  quantification, *see*
    QUANTIFICATION OF DAMAGES
  remoteness, 127, 265–269
  road traffic, 237–241
  socii criminis, 145
Damnum absque injuria, 2,
  62 (n 1)
Damnum fatale, 177
Damnum injuria datum
  meaning, 1, 5
  requirement, 128
  unborn children, 223
Dangerous animals, 170
  wild animals, 172
Dangerous driving, 236
Death
  damages, 227–233
Defamation, 243–259
  changing social attitudes, 246
  damages, 258–259
  defences—
    fair comment, 254
    fair retorts, 254
    in rixa, 253
    privilege, 254–257
    responsibility for publication,
      258
    veritas, 247, 252–253
    vulgar abuse, 253
  imputations—
    conduct, 248
    criminality, 247
    financial unsoundness, 248
    health, 249
    incompetence, 248
    moral character, 247
    public character, 248
  limitation of actions, 284
  meaning, 244
  offers of amends, 251, 252

Defamation – *contd*
  prescription, 284
  requirements, 245
    defamatory statements,
      246–250
    false statements, 245
    intention to harm, 250–252
    vicarious liability, 213
Defective buildings, 95–100
  breach of regulations, 96–98
  complex structure doctrine, 98
Defective products
  meaning, 163–164
    expected use, 163
    get ups, 163
    instructions, 163
    purpose, 163
  product liability, *see* PRODUCT
    LIABILITY
  reasonable expectations, 163,
    164
  standards of safety, 164
Deforcement, 3
Delict
  and breach of contract, 60
  and criminal law, 3–5
  meaning, 1
  or contractual remedies, 85, 95
Desuetude
  assythment, 4
Detention
  lawful detention, 18
  wrongful detention, 17
Disclaimers, 84
Discretionary powers
  extension of limitation period,
    285
  public authorities, 198–199
Dogs, 169, 172, 174
  guard dogs, 175
  occupiers' liability, 189
Donoghue v Stevenson, 58–67
Drink driving, 236
**Driving without due care and
  attention**, 236
Drugs
  pregnant mothers, 223
  side effects, 166

Drunkenness
contributory negligence, 69
pregnant mothers, 223
Dust, 133–134
Duty of care, 57–67
breach, 111–128, *see also*
STANDARD OF CARE
concept, 11
Donoghue v Stevenson, 58–67
neighbourhood principle, 58–67
solicitors, 152–156
threshold device, 76
economic loss, 78–107
to foetuses, 76
tripartite test, 64–67
variation with social changes,
62

Economic delicts, 35–50
conspiracy, 45–50
inducement to breach of contract,
36–39
intimidation, 42–45
wrongful interference—
with business, 40–42
with performance of contracts,
39–40
Economic loss, 78–107
beneficiaries of wills, 153
breach of statutory duty, 97
careless misrepresentation,
79–85
defective buildings, 95–100
defective performance of
contracts, 88–94
Junior Books principles, 89–94
derivative economic loss, 61,
101, *see also* PATRIMONIAL
LOSS
meaning, 78
relatives, 224
foreseeability, 64
fraud, 51
general duty of care, 85–88
requirements, 87
Henderson v Merrett, 85–88
judicial reluctance to allow
reparation, 25, 61, 64

Economic loss – *contd*
policy considerations, 196
product liability, 95
professional liability, 149
quantification of damages,
270–271
secondary economic loss,
100–107
proximity, 103
transferred losses, 105
unwanted pregnancies, 77
whether reparable, 2
Ejection, 3, 21
Electricity supply, 101
Emergency medical treatment, 12
Employers' liability, 63, 205–209
animals, 169
contributory negligence, 209
defective equipment, 206–207
safe system of working, 205, 207
safe working environment, 208
standard of care—
reasonableness, 206
to particular employees, 121,
207
volenti non fit injuria, 209
Employment
course of employment, 212–218
delictual remedies, 195
occupiers' liability, 209
secondary economic loss, 101
vicarious liability, *see* VICARIOUS
LIABILITY
Enticement, 16
Entrapment, 16
EU law
health and safety at work, 209
motor insurance, 239
**European Court of Human
Rights**
corporal punishment, 15
Executors
transmission of claims—
defamation, 244
personal injuries, 227, 232,
289–291
enforcement, 290
Extortion, 3

Family, *see* RELATIVES
Fault, *see* CULPA
Fire services, 201–202
Foetuses, *see* UNBORN CHILDREN
Foreseeability, 63, 66, 70,
111–119
causa causans, 136–138
extent of injuries, 116
identity of wronged persons,
115
pure economic loss, 64
reasonableness, 113–115
property owners, 178
remoteness of injury, 126–127
third party interventions, 118
Forgery, 3
Fraud, 51–54
damages, 53–54
entrapment, 16
mens rea, 52–53
passing off, 29
vicarious liability, 213–214
Fraudulent misrepresentation,
42, 49, 51, 85
quantification of damages, 270
Fumes, 182
Funeral expenses, 232
Fungi, 173

Game, 161
Gifts, 96
Goodwill, 27

Harassment, 19
Health and safety at work, 70,
209
Hedley Byrne principles, 79–81
Hillsborough disaster, 74
Hire purchase, 24–26
Homosexuality, 247
Human rights
inhuman and degrading
punishment, 15

Importers
product liability, 161, 165
Income tax
loss of earnings, 274

Inducement to breach of
contract, 36–39
Industrial actions, 35–36, 50
Industrial espionage, 32
Information
confidential information,
30–33
whether property, 30
Injuria, 2
Innuendoes, 249
Institutional writers, 3, 6
Insurance, 65
lack of statutory insurance, 146
misrepresentations, 238
Motor Insurers Bureau,
239–241
power cuts, 102
road traffic, 237–241
knock for knock agreements,
238
subrogation, 238
vicarious liability, 210
Intentional delicts, 11–33
relating to persons, 12–19
relating to property, 20–33
Interdicts
nuisance, 183, 186
trespass, 20
Interest
quantification of damages, 276
Interim damages, 282–283
Intimidation, 42–45
Intrusion, 3, 21

Joint liability, 146
apportionment of damages, 139,
146
joint and several liability, 146
producers of product
components, 161–162
product liability, 60
Judicial proceedings
absolute privilege, 255
qualified privilege, 257
Judicial review, 195
Junior Books principles, 89–94
Jury trials
quantification of damages, 276

Landlords
  repair obligations, occupiers'
    liability, 191
Latent defects, 60, 97
  prescription, 283
Lawburrows, 5
Legal capacity
  age, 12, 221–222
  medical treatment, 12
Legal profession, 152–156
Legatees
  solicitors' duty of care, 153–155
Letters of slains, 4
Lex Aquilia, 6
Liberty
  infringement, 17–19
Limitation of actions
  defamation, 284
  limitation period—
    commencement, 284–285
    extension, 285
    personal injuries, 284
    product liability, 284
Lloyd's names, 86
Local authorities
  breach of statutory duties,
    96–97
  defamation, 244

Magistrates
  wrongful imprisonment, 18
Malice, 22
  defamation, 258
Medical expenses, 273
Medical negligence
  causation, 130, 131
  duty of care, 69
  standard of care, 150, 151
  state of scientific knowledge,
    115
Medical treatment
  consent, 12–14
Mens rea
  fraud, 52–53
Mental health detention, 18
Mentally disabled persons
  termination of pregnancies, 77
Miscarriage of justice, 18

Misrepresentation
  contractual relationship, 80, 81
  disclaimers, 84
  economic loss, 79–85
  fraudulent misrepresentation, 42,
    49, 51, 85
  damages, 270
  Hedley Byrne principles, 79–81
  insurance, 238
  negligence, 52, 53
  quantification of damages, 270
  remoteness, 81, 83
Molestation, 3
Motor cars
  occupiers' liability, 188
Motor Insurers Bureau, 239–241
Moveable property
  intentional delicts, 22–33
  wrongful interference, 23–25

National insurance
    contributions
  loss of earnings, 274
National security, 33
Negligence, 62, 119–126, *see also*
    STANDARD OF CARE
  product liability, burden of proof,
    157
  professional negligence, *see*
    PROFESSIONAL NEGLIGENCE
Neighbourhood principle, *see*
    PROXIMITY
Neighbouring property
  aemulatio vicini, 21–22, 181
  common law liability, 178–180
  nuisance, 182–186
Nemo dat quod non habet, 24
Nervous shock, 70–76
  foreseeability, 74
  primary victims, 71
  secondary victims, 72, 116, 127
    love and affection test, 74
    requirements, 75
Noise, 182, 183
Nominated sub-contractors, 91
Non-harassment orders, 19
Novus actus interveniens, 135,
    136, 138

Nuisance, 182–186
  culpa, 184–186
  damages, 184–186
  interdicts, 183, 186
  title to sue, 186

Occupiers' liability, 63, 70,
    177–192
  animals, 169
  common law, 177–180, 187
    adjacent property, 178
    non-natural use of land, 178
  control of land, 187
  employers, 209
  intentional delicts, 20–22
  landlords' repair obligations,
    191
  premises, meaning, 188
  statutory regulation, 187–192
  trespass, 175, 187
  volenti non fit injuria, 191
Offshore installations, 23
  occupiers' liability, 188
Omissions, 69, 111

Packaging, 161
Parents
  damages for death of children,
    230
  delictual liability for children,
    223
  duty of care, 69
Parliamentary privilege, 255
  Scottish Parliament, 256
Passing off, 23, 27–30
  meaning, 28
Patrimonial loss
  defamation, 251, 258
  personal injuries—
    diminished expectation of life,
      293
    future loss, 274–276
    quantification of damages,
      273–276
  transmission to executors, 227,
    228
Pension rights, 275
Performers' rights, 195

Personal injuries
  conjoined actions, 292
  damages—
    deceased's claims, 227
    dependent claims, 228–233
    limitation, 291
    transmission to executors, 227,
      290
  limitation of actions, 284
  meaning, 294
  quantification of damages,
    271–276
  unborn children, 229
Piper Alpha, 75
Planning
  breach of statutory duties, 196
Pneumoconiosis, 123, 132
Police
  complaints, 256
  duty of care, 108, 200, 201, 203
Policy considerations, 63, 66, 67
  bookmaking, 196
  denial of duty of care, 76, 108
  determination of reasonableness,
    115
  economic loss, 196
  justiciability, 199
  socii criminis, damages, 145
  solicitors' duty of care, 153
Pregnant women
  delictual liability, 223
  unwanted pregnancies, 77
Premises
  meaning, 188
Prescription
  prescriptive period, 283
    commencement, 128, 283
Presumptions
  defamation, 245, 246
    intention to harm, 250
  remedies, breach of statutory
    duties, 194–195
Privacy
  protection, 2, 262
Privilege
  absolute privilege, 254–256
  defamation, 254–257
  qualified privilege, 256

Privity of contract, 154
Product liability, 63, 157–167
  agricultural produce, 161
  burden of proof, 157
  causation, 164
  course of business, 162
  defective products, *see* DEFECTIVE
      PRODUCTS
  defences, 164–167
    complex products, 166
    contributory negligence, 166
    EC regulations, 165
    state of knowledge, 165
  Donoghue v Stevenson, 59–61
  economic loss, 95, 158
  importers, 161
  limitation of actions, 284
  limitations, 60
  own branders, 161, 165
  packagers, 161
  prescription, 284
  products, meaning, 160
  safety, 163
  statutory regulation, 158–167
  strict liability, 158–167
    exceptions, 159
    liable parties, 161–162
  suppliers, 162
Professional negligence, 149–156
  advice, 80
  advocates, 155
  economic loss, 149
  solicitors, 152–155
  surveyors, 82, 84, 87
Property, *see also* MOVEABLE
      PROPERTY; OCCUPIERS' LIABILITY
  intentional delicts, 20–33
Protozoa, 173
Provisional damages, 280–282,
      289
Provocation, 14
Proximity, 58–67
  Donoghue v Stevenson, 58–67
  fair, just and reasonable criterion,
      64–67
  foreseeability, 63, 66
  Junior Books, 91
  nervous shock, 74

Proximity – *contd*
  secondary economic loss, 103
Public authorities
  breach of statutory duties,
      198–204
  exercise of discretionary powers,
      198–203
Public interest
  breach of confidentiality, 33
  competition, 35
  defence for nuisance, 183
Public law, 198–204

Quantification of damages,
      269–280
  deductions, 277–280
  economic loss, 270–271
    mitigation of loss, 271
  legal negligence, 155
  personal injuries, 271–276
    interest, 276
    jury trials, 276
    patrimonial loss, 273–276
    solatium, 272–273

Railways
  occupiers' liability, 190
  volenti non fit injuria, 141
Rape, 15, 246
Reasonableness
  disclaimers, 84
  employers' liability, 206
  foreseeability, 113–115
  occupiers' liability, 188, 189–190
  product safety, 163
  standard of care, 119–126
Redundancy payments, 277
References, 87
  privilege, 257
Relatives
  death, 226–233
    deceased's claims, 227–228
    dependent claims, 228–233,
        288–289
    rights, 287–289
  immediate family, 230, 288, 294
  injuries to, 224–226
  meaning, 224, 294, 295

Relatives – *contd*
necessary services, 224
transmission of claims to
executors, 232, 289
unpaid personal services, 225
Remoteness of damages, 127,
265–269
criteria, 266
reasonable foreseeability, 266
'thin skull' principle, 268–269
Remoteness of injury, 126–127
Reparation
meaning, 1
Restitution, 1
Road traffic, 235–241
duty of care, 70
insurance, 237–241
nervous shock, 71–74
standard of care, 235–236
Roman law, 6, 181
actio injuriarum, 243

Safety
product liability, 163, 164
Scientific knowledge defence
medical negligence, 115
product liability, 165
Seat belts, 144
Secondary victims
foreseeability, 116
nervous shock, 72, 116, 127
love and affection test, 74
requirements, 75
Seduction, 15–16
Self-defence, 14
Service agreements
and contracts of employment,
210–212
Shipping, 65
Ships, 23
occupiers' liability, 188
Siblings
title to sue, 4
Slander of business, 261
Slander of property, 261
Slander of title, 261
Slipping, 124, 125
occupiers' liability, 188

Smells, 182
Social security benefits
deductions from awards of
damages, 277–280, 288–
289
Social workers
duty of care, 197, 200
Socii criminis
damages, 145
Solatium, 2
death of relatives, 288, 292
defamation, 251, 258
meaning, 227
personal injuries—
loss of expectation of life, 273,
293
quantification, 272–273
transmission to executors, 227
unlawful sexual intercourse,
16
Solicitors
duty of care, 152
legatees, 153–155
instructions by children, 222
professional negligence,
quantification of damages,
155
Sports
assault, 14
volenti non fit injuria, 142
Spouses
damages—
death of spouses, 230
divorced spouses, 232
delictual liability for each other,
221
title to sue, against each other,
221
Spuilzie, 3, 5, 24, 25
Squatters, 21
Standard of care, 119–126
medical practitioners, 150–152
precautions—
cost, 123
practicality, 123
probability of injuries, 120
reasonableness, 119
road traffic, 235–236

Standard of care – *contd*
seriousness of potential injuries, 121, 207
usual practice, 125
medical practice, 150
utility of activities, 122
State of the art defence, 115, 165
Statutory duty, *see* BREACH OF STATUTORY DUTIES
Sterilisation, 77, 138
Strict liability, 198
animals, 170–176
health and safety at work, 208
meaning, 6
product liability, *see* PRODUCT LIABILITY
Subrogation, 238
Suppliers
product liability, 162
Surveyors' negligence, 82, 87
disclaimers, 84
quantification of damages, 269

Thefts
defective products, 165
duty to prevent, neighbours, 179–180
Title to sue
breach of statutory duties, 48
conspiracy, 50
nuisance, 186
secondary economic loss, 101, 102, 105
leased property, 106–107
siblings, 4
spouses, against each other, 221
unborn children, 223
Trade names, 27
Trade secrets, 30
Trade unions
conspiracy, 46
contracts—
inducement to breach, 35
wrongful interference with performance, 39
defamation of, 244

Trade unions – *contd*
immunity, 50
intimidation, 43
Trespass
delictual liability for animals, 175, 176
heritable property, 20–21
moveable property, 22–23
occupiers' liability, 175, 187

Unborn children, 76
duty of care to, 76, 223
legal personality, 229
personal injuries, 229
title to sue, 223
Unfair contract terms, 86
disclaimers, 84
Unjust enrichment, 1, 24, 25

Verbal injury, 259–261
Vicarious liability, 113, 142, 209–220
agency, 220
building contracts, 219–220
employment relationship—
course of employment, 212–218
employees and self-employed, 210–212
instructions from other employers, 218
fraud, 213–214
independent contractors, 219
insurance, 210
state agencies, 204
Violent profits, 5
ejection, 21
Viruses, 173
Vitium reale, 23
Volenti non fit injuria, 141–143
animals, 174
breach of statutory duties, 198
employers' liability, 209
occupiers' liability, 191
rescuers, 142

Water
aemulatio vicini, 21

Wills
  beneficiaries, solicitors' duty of
    care, 153
Wrongful detention, 17
Wrongful imprisonment, 18

Wrongful interference
  with business, 40–42
  with moveable property, 23–25
Wrongful life, 76
  quantification of damages, 269